Alison Alexander was born in Hobart, where she studied history at the University of Tasmania. Her Ph.D topic was 'The Public Role of Women in Tasmania, 1803–1914'. She has written commissioned histories of institutions, ranging from cities to a football club, occasionally lectures at university, and has written three biographies, of writers Mary Grant Bruce and Marie Bjelke Petersen, and of the wives and mistresses of early Tasmanian governors. Alison and her husband, a psychology lecturer, have three children.

A Wealth of Women was commissioned by the Commonwealth Office of the Status of Women in the Department of the Prime Minister and Cabinet and funded by the National Council for the Centenary of Federation

A Wealth of Women

*Australian women's lives from
1788 to the present*

Alison Alexander

with
Prue Torney-Parlicki

DUFFY AND SNELLGROVE
SYDNEY

Published by Duffy & Snellgrove in 2001
PO Box 177 Potts Point NSW 1335 Australia
info@duffyandsnellgrove.com.au

This edition published in 2002

Distributed by Pan Macmillan

© Alison Alexander 2001 (except Chapters 5 and 10)
© Prue Torney-Parlicki 2001 (Chapters 5 and 10)

Cover design by Alex Snellgrove

Cover images (clockwise from left):
1) Reproduced with permission of Photodisc
2) Baby Evangeline Gabriel in the bath, 1907
Courtesy of the State Library of South Australia
3) Ladies Reel Team, 1919
By permission of the National Library of Australia
4) Lily Stirling (1892) (detail), by Tom Roberts 1856 - 1931
Purchased through The Art Foundation of Victoria
with the assistance of the
Chase Manhattan Overseas Coporation, Fellow, 1981
National Gallery of Victoria, Melbourne

Typeset by Cooper Graphics
Printed by Griffin Press

ISBN 1 876631 45 7

visit our website: www.duffyandsnellgrove.com.au

Contents

Preface	vii
Early Days	1
The Australian Woman	25
Snapshot: Food	66
Building a Nation	69
The First World War	113
Snapshot: Health	126
Beginning the Struggle	129
The 1920s	145
Snapshot: Fashion	178
Hard Times	181
The Boom Years	215
Snapshot: Education	256
The Women's Movement	259
The Struggle Continues	275
Snapshot: Inventions	294
Today	297
Acknowledgments	323
Notes	329
Picture Credits	343
Index	345

preface

What has life been like for Australian women? What opportunities have they had? What hardships have they faced? What contribution have they made to Australia? What are their stories?

This book was written to answer questions like these. It opens with convict women, dumped in an alien land, with only their wits and skills to help them survive. Then pioneer women, traditional heroines, working with their menfolk to carve out a livelihood in a harsh land; and the Aboriginal women they dispossessed, struggling to keep their traditional culture in the face of physical hardship and racial oppression. The British ideal of womanhood – staying at home while men ran the country – was never totally accepted in Australia, where conditions meant women had to work hard both inside and outside the home. At the end of the nineteenth century, opportunities expanded for white women, in education, careers and public life, at the same time as the birthrate fell from seven children per white mother to 'only' four.

In the 1920s advances in science, like electric light, began to introduce an easier domestic life, but authoritative experts tended to make life more difficult. Today's mothers would be daunted by Dr Truby King's advice to pregnant women: no sex, alcohol, tea, coffee, cakes or biscuits, but a daily cold shower and a three-mile walk with a cheerful, kindly companion.

A recurring theme for many women was hardship, especially during the Depression and the two world wars, when they had to keep the family, and sometimes the family business, going while the men were away. Better times arrived in the 1950s, boom years when more and more women could enjoy technological advances – washing machines, refrigerators, cars, television, easy-care fabrics like rayon, and from the 1960s easier contraception with the Pill. The arrival of millions of migrants transformed life, with new ideas and traditions. Indigenous women benefited less and many still lived in appalling conditions, suffering from the effects of racism and poverty. In 1967, a referendum removed discriminatory clauses from the Constitution, but racism remained entrenched in some sections of white Australian society.

Great changes began in the 1970s, when demands for women's equality gathered strength. This was made easier by law, and many women could take advantage of new opportunities, though others were prevented by poverty or lingering social discrimination. At the start of the twenty-first century, some women are so well known that newspapers can refer to them by their first names only – Cathy, Natasha, Kylie. Let us hope that women's equality continues to advance in practice until all Australians, male and female, of whatever background, can share equally in our country's opportunities.

An example of the women described in this book is Gertrude Teague, brave and determined, who shows that the stereotypical Australian woman did exist. Born in 1885, she grew up in St Kilda where she went to school. 'Many times I had the dunce's cap on, nothing to boast of I know there has to be some duds in the world', she wrote philosophically. Her parents did not get on, her father drank, and the family moved to Broken Hill, where Gertrude started dressmaking. She did not like sewing or sitting quietly, so became a servant. There 'I saw the best boy in the world and he saw the best girl so he said and we threw in our lot together'. George Teague was a miner, but suffered from silicosis, and married life was a struggle as he had to give up one job after another. They lived in huts made of bags, eating corned beef, rabbits and bread, and five children were born. Despite the hardship, Gertrude adored her husband and made the best of things: 'I was

Preface

as happy as the little birds that were building all around our camp'.

At one stage a station owner took pity on them and gave George a job boundary riding. 'It was like out of hell into heaven ... we thought I was a lady we had one stone room to cook eat and sitting room all in one and we had a large tent under a brush shed for a bedroom for four of us.' Then George saw crows eating his freshly stretched rabbit skins, tried to shoot them, and shot his own foot. 'Well just think [how] I felt dear readers, our nearest neighbours 18 miles away and the horse in the paddock and I just started to think about another increase in the family.' She caught the horse, put a mattress in the dray, managed to get George in and drove him and the children to the neighbours. George went to hospital in Adelaide, and Gertrude returned home, doing his work as well as her own.

When George came back, his silicosis was worse, and to provide slightly easier work they opened a shop in Olary, west of Broken Hill. 'I battled along as best I could my hart breaking at the thought of my partener who I knew must leave me for ever soon, and how I had to smile through it all when I went in to serve a coustomer [but] it is wonderful what we can do if our hart and sole is in our undertaking', wrote Gertrude. She was again pregnant, for 'it does not matter how ill a man is these things will happen'. The baby died and Gertrude quickly became pregnant again, though George was now bedridden. He died in 1912, three months before the last baby was born. Gertrude battled on, eventually marrying again, and in 1929 she and her second husband took over the Waukaringa hotel, just as the Depression was starting. Through all the problems of her life Gertrude kept her sense of humour, and her memoirs are wryly entertaining. She died aged eighty-five.

Gertrude's story was provided by her granddaughter, in response to the history search which provided much of the material for this book. The four hundred replies show common threads running through the lives of Australian women. The most obvious is hard work – at home, with children, in employment, in voluntary work. Few Australian women lay about on sofas; almost all had to work, either hard, very hard or extremely hard. But they coped, another common thread. Stories show women as pragmatic, independent, cheerful, generous and strong. Some other 'womanly' qualities are seldom mentioned; no women are shown as dainty, beautiful or clinging, and not many as clever or career-minded. (Most replies, for a history book, dealt with women who lived before about 1960.)

This is obviously how many people want to see their ancestors. This book cannot study all the millions of women who have lived in Australia, but only those whose lives are recorded, the stories people have chosen to remember. There must have been women who were impractical, selfish or whingeing, but people do not talk about them. To a certain extent this is a selected characterisation of Australian women.

But it is only a selection from what did happen, and there have been forces which encouraged certain character developments. A small, scattered population in a country liable to drought, floods and fire meant those who succeeded were the capable ones. Especially in times of trouble, people relied on each other, so if not natural it was at least sensible to help others, since you might need help yourself. Generosity was particularly expected of women, supposed to have kind, nurturing natures. And most people who came to Australia arrived poor – they were the ones who could not succeed at home – and had to make their way in the world. This encouraged independence and courage, doing what you could without complaining, since grizzling helped no one. The tough life of rural Australia is often held to have forged the male character, but it had just as much effect on women. Sophistication, sweetness, dependence, even the traditionally admired beauty, were not much help in difficult conditions. As Aboriginal women had already done, the newcomers had to adapt to the land, and certain characteristics did emerge.

Technological developments over the last fifty years have made life less challenging physically, but the ideal of the national character was already formed, and so our women are presented as being – and many really were – brave, generous, cheerful and resourceful. In the twenty-first century, these traits are still

Preface

valued, as shown by the answers to the question: Who is an Australian woman you admire, and why? The answers mentioned a mixture of attributes. Cathy Freeman, for her courage in reaching the top despite adversity, as well as her skill in running. Natasha Stott-Despoja, for her integrity and strength, and her intelligence. Dawn Fraser, for her courage, independence, warmth and generosity. Sara Henderson, for her gumption, and her work for breast cancer. Kylie Minogue for her looks, Joan Sutherland for her voice, Roma Mitchell for her fight for justice. A mix of traditional traits, and others more valued in recent years, show how ideas have developed. When we think of the women we know, our families and friends, we can see how they too demonstrate these attributes, and how they fit into this enthralling story – the lives of millions of Australian women.

chapter one

Early Days

Betty King claimed to be the first white woman to set foot in Australia. She arrived in Sydney in 1788 with the First Fleet, and when she died seventy years later, a respectable settler, she was well known for this feat. Since she was the last surviving First Fleeter, no one could dispute it. The claim was not correct, however, and Betty had not always been so respectable. In 1787, recently married, illiterate, and aged nineteen, she was sentenced to transportation for seven years for stealing a silk handkerchief. She was sent to Australia, and never saw her husband again. Throughout the trip, she was in trouble. She was one of a group of women nicknamed the Fighting Five, and was disciplined for having sex with sailors, which was strictly forbidden. She spent long periods in irons, sometimes handcuffed to another woman. Perhaps Betty was the first female convict to step ashore – probably pushing her way to the front – but the marines' wives had landed several days earlier.

Betty was sent to the settlement at Norfolk Island, where she was again in trouble, receiving twenty-five lashes for being absent without leave. For some years she lived with a male convict, and they grew grain and ran pigs on their small farm. Then she bought land from Samuel King, a constable. Eight years later the settlement was closed and the inhabitants were moved to Van Diemen's

Land (Tasmania), and there Betty married Samuel. They were granted land in a picturesque valley near Hobart, where they grew wheat, barley and potatoes and pastured sheep, employed a convict themselves and were nicely established. Betty mostly remained out of trouble, though she was once admonished for being drunk and disorderly – at sixty-two. She died seven years after Samuel, aged almost ninety, and her grave still stands in a disused Methodist churchyard in a peaceful valley. Pine trees and silver wattle grow around it, symbolising the mixed British–Australian heritage.

Working class, young, illiterate and transported for robbery, Betty was typical of the 24,000 convict women transported to Australia between 1788 and 1856, as part of the British settlement. Though their lives varied, most followed a similar pattern. After committing petty theft in Britain, they were arrested and convicted, usually for seven years. They were torn from everyone they knew, and suffered a long – about seven months – and arduous voyage to Australia, where they were sent to the two convict colonies of New South Wales and Tasmania. They were often at risk of rape or assault. On arrival, they were assigned to settlers as domestic servants, which masters often saw as including sexual services, but at least the women were maintained by someone else. Once they were released they were on their own, in a society where men held all power and predominated numeri-

The keeper of the Jug

Early settlers liked claiming to be first at something, and Ann Collins claimed she was the first white baby born in Australian waters, off Sydney Heads in 1791. Eliza Paterson, wife of an officer and also on the ship, gave the family a china jug to commemorate the event.

After Ann's death, the jug was passed down through the female line of her family. Early in the twentieth century it was broken, but it was skilfully repaired, and at present Enid Sherwood, one of Ann's great-great-granddaughters, has the honour of being Keeper of the Jug.

Early Days

cally – at first there were six men to every woman. Very few women returned to Britain. In the Australian convict colonies, somehow they had to find a way to support themselves. How did they do it?

The main way was in providing what men valued – housekeeping and sexual services, either as a mistress or a wife, in the way women had supported themselves for centuries. Scarcity gave women some bargaining power, at least the ability to change partners if one failed, though the dominance of men, and attitudes of the times, meant women could not gain much public power. Some established businesses such as a shop, a dairy or a farm, and others helped their menfolk run family enterprises.

Maria Lord is an example of a woman who did all these activities. She was transported for theft, and after a rough trip in which most of the women were sick, arrived in Sydney in 1804, aged twenty-four. She was assigned to a settler as a servant, and like many servants, she was soon pregnant. With other unemployed and pregnant convicts she was sent to the Female Factory at Parramatta, where in April 1805 Lieutenant Edward Lord appeared, looking for a female companion.

Edward, an arrogant, confident man, was an army officer in the almost entirely male expedition which established Hobart in 1804. The story goes that at the Factory he ordered all the women to parade before him, and selected Maria – rather surprisingly, as she was seven months pregnant. 'She was at once let out, and he took possession of her, as truly a slave to do his behests, or suffer for neglect or refusal', wrote a contemporary. This was another common fate for a female convict: living with a man in order to support herself and any children. The colony offered few better methods.

Maria's daughter Caroline was born in June and was somehow passed off as Edward's child, and all three went to Hobart. Maria, who was literate and turned out to be a shrewd businesswoman, brought goods with her and opened one of the first shops in the town. Stories of her acumen abound. When news arrived that floods had destroyed maize crops in New South Wales, she raised her price for maize from a penny a pint to half a guinea,

126 pennies. A man whose wife was having a baby and longed for a cup of tea bought Maria's last pound, for the outrageous price of six guineas – and even today, $12.60 is expensive for 450 grams of tea. Maria made most of her profits from dealing in spirits, however. When one cargo of rum arrived, she and three other merchants cornered the market, buying all they could and selling it at up to quadruple the price.

While Maria was earning money, Edward was smuggling liquor, acquiring land grants and 'fooling away' their money gambling and in 'other base propensities'. So he was not much help, and neither were successive pregnancies, but overall the Lords were doing well. They were accepted in what passed for high society, and Maria was a good friend of the chaplain, drinking tea with him and making him jelly from his raspberries. Edward was in Sydney in 1808 during the Rum Rebellion, when officers successfully rebelled against Governor Bligh; with an eye to the winning side, he joined the rebels and obtained another land grant and a pardon for Maria. Back in Hobart he married her – an unusual move, as officers did not usually marry convict mistresses. Maria was in Sydney herself in 1810, so missed the only chance an ex-convict had to preside as governor's lady, when Edward was, briefly, acting governor. She continued her business activities in Sydney in her own style, grazing cattle on crown land and asking permission afterwards.

Edward visited England, but Maria and the children stayed in Sydney. This was hardly surprising, for Edward's uncle was a baronet, and an ex-convict wife and children born before the wedding would have been hard to explain. When he came back they returned to Hobart, built the best house in town and a large country home, and enjoyed an active social life, giving balls and dinners. More children were born, eight altogether, with only one dying, a good record for the times. Pregnancies did not bother Maria, and when she opened a shop in the northern settlement at Launceston she made the long, rough trip when she was four months pregnant. She did not enjoy her children's company for long, however, as from the age of about six all except Caroline were sent to England for their education. Edward made several

Early Days

trips too, trying to export cattle and wool without a great deal of success.

While he was away Maria ran their businesses much more competently. She still dealt in rum, but also sold meat to the government and passenger tickets to Sydney, administered deceased estates, dealt with debtors and bought expensive imported merino rams. Her letter books show her to be an astute businesswoman, quick to demand recompense for any imperfections in goods ordered, quite able to write a stiff letter to the governor over his shortcomings, but sometimes let down by Edward's incompetence, such as when he forgot to send out accounts. The Lords owned 35,000 acres of land, 6,000 cattle and 7,000 sheep, and had seventy-five employees, mostly convicts. Largely through Maria's efforts, Edward was said to be the richest man in the colony. When church pews were allocated in order of rank, Maria Lord, former convict and mistress, was in pew number one.

So all was progressing favourably, but in 1823, during one of her husband's absences, Maria sent her three-year-old daughter off to boarding school and started an affair with a young emigrant, eighteen years her junior. This can be followed through the chaplain's diary. For months he recorded joint dinners, fruit picking expeditions and country trips; then suddenly it all stopped, an agent arrived from London to run the Lords' enterprises, the powers granted to Maria were withdrawn, she retired to the country, and finally Edward, 'vindictive and implacable', returned. He had only one aim, to take Maria's lover to court. All records are lost of this dramatic case, in which on one day a Lord servant was in the box from 9.00 am till 2.30 the next morning – over seventeen hours – with only an hour off for refreshment.

Edward won the case and left immediately for England, taking the youngest child, so Maria was left with Caroline and little else, for everything legally belonged to her husband. Undaunted, she opened a new shop, which became known as the best in Hobart. She was reconciled to Edward, for in 1827 he returned and stayed with her, though he also fathered another son by a convict servant. Generally he lived in England, where he had five more offspring by his children's governess. Without Maria's assistance he did not prosper, and had to sell his properties.

Maria never saw four of her children again, but the two eldest boys came out to Tasmania. One died young, drowned while swimming in the river; the other was devoted to his mother, and bought a fine country house for her retirement. A businesswoman to the last, she rented out part of it. Edward died in 1859 and left Maria an annuity, but she did not receive it as she had died two months earlier, aged seventy-nine.

Many other convict women were also enterprising, as they had to be in a new country where they depended on their own efforts. My own ancestor Jane Hadden left behind in Scotland a husband and six children when she was transported for assault with violence. In Australia, once she was free, she set up a laundry, but found a more lucrative career in 'forming an intimacy' with a wealthy, elderly landowner. His even older wife was found dead, having fallen or been pushed into the fire, and a month later Jane married him, though her first husband was still alive. Like many another convict she has plentiful descendants, and in the 1980s a large family reunion consisted of thoroughly respectable and well-behaved Australians.

Maria and Jane tried to fit into society, though their methods were sometimes questionable, but some women were more rebellious. Jemmy the Rover was Irish, convicted of theft, sent to Hobart, and as usual was assigned to a settler as a servant. Repeatedly charged with being drunk and disorderly, using obscene language or absconding, she had a reputation as a fighter and a drinker. She absconded and lived in the bush for a year, dressing as a man and working as a timber splitter, but was recaptured. She escaped from the Female Factory by removing her cell bars with a sharpened spoon and scaling the wall, using a strip of blanket and a pile of tubs. There were more recaptures and escapes, but she was eventually granted a pardon, and five years later died in hospital in poor circumstances.

What did these women contribute to Australia? They were resourceful and cheerful, often without much regard for authority, but mostly able to maintain themselves in a tough

Early Days

A child convict

Mary Wade was born in London in 1777, and her father died shortly after her birth. As a girl she earned money by begging and street sweeping, and when she was eleven she was convicted of theft. She was transported on the Lady Juliana, notorious as being little more than 'a floating brothel', and arrived in Sydney with little education or training, and no family support – a very unpromising start.

Nevertheless, Mary succeeded in making a life for herself. She was sent to Norfolk Island, where she lived with a male convict and bore him at least five children. When his sentence expired they returned to Sydney, where Mary was assigned to him as a servant, as was often done. He went away sealing in about 1806, and Mary moved in with Jonathan Brooker, another ex-convict who was working as a farm labourer. More children were born, and the parents were married in 1817, probably when they had saved up the relatively large sum for the licence and fee. They received a land grant at Illawarra, but were burnt out by a bushfire in 1823. Jonathan died fairly soon afterwards, but Mary lived to eighty-two. Her death certificate recorded that seven children survived her and fourteen predeceased her, a total of twenty-one births. Some probably died at birth or shortly after, which would explain why their births were not recorded.

environment. Some made commercial contributions, like Maria's shop and Jane's laundry. Others helped run family enterprises, particularly farms but also shops, hotels or other businesses, as was usual in Britain at the time. Their main achievement, however, was founding families and homes, and women were largely responsible for turning giant prisons into communities – rough and ready communities perhaps, but the foundation of modern Australia. At the time and later, the authorities – middle-class men – criticised them as drunken, irresponsible whores, but they lived in much the same way as they had done in Britain, doing whatever was necessary to support themselves and their children. As might be expected, being mainly taken up with their own

A woman who married well

Mary Smallshaw was a Welsh silk throwster, which meant she twisted strands of silk together to form thread. At the age of twenty-four she was convicted of theft. There is a reference to a child; if she had one, she had to leave it behind. She was described as a neat and pretty little woman, fond of reading poetry.

Mary arrived in Sydney in 1818 and was at once sent to Tasmania, where the governor had requested convict women as 'wives for overseers and most decent prisoners'. Mary did better than this, for a year later she married the clerk of the magistrate's court, a most respectable position. He died a few months later, and soon Mary was living with the magistrate himself, Captain Andrew Barclay. He was sixty-three, and she was twenty-seven. A daughter was born in 1820, and next year her parents were married. Andrew was described as 'a hard-swearing old sea dog fond of preparing, and presumably drinking, his own wine who had only married Mary to legitimise the child'; but whatever the reason, whatever Andrew was like, whatever the difference in ages, Mary had achieved a great coup for a convict woman in marrying so well. Andrew was wealthy with large estates in the country, they lived comfortably, the daughter married well herself and three grandchildren were born. Mary died in 1839 aged forty-five, and her eighty-year-old husband followed her seven months later.

survival they had little interest in the original inhabitants, Aboriginal women, and the lives of the two groups were almost completely different.

Most women were working class, living in areas like the Rocks in Sydney, where life was surprisingly comfortable, considering that the town was new and the people not wealthy. A visitor described newly unfolded cloths on dining tables and shining dinner utensils, and archaeological digs have produced fine china and glassware, good quality clothes and shoes, and comfortable furniture. There were less prosperous aspects, however: dirt,

Early Days

disease and a high infant mortality rate.

Women chatted in the streets, or dropped into each other's houses to eat, drink, sing, buy or sell. They played a reasonably equal role, whether in the family business, a party or a brawl, for life had its violent side and there were reports of people throwing china, shouting, and hitting each other. Most women lived in families, married or as de facto wives. There was no great advantage in marriage, for living together unmarried was not as unacceptable as it became later, and single women kept control of their property and children, and could change partners more easily if a man proved inadequate. People often formed either marriages or more elastic partnerships for practical reasons. Was the woman able to help in the business? Was the man a good provider? They used words like 'comfort' to describe relationships, but there is evidence of deeper affection. A man cried openly at the inquest into his wife's death, and a woman in the Female Factory wrote her husband a note saying 'I am almost out of my mind at not seeing you', and twice jumped over the wall to visit him. A man was called out at night to help a neighbour and thought of staying to comfort him, but remembered that his wife was waiting up for him, so went home.

Heterosexual sex with different partners was seen as normal. Sex could be short, a business transaction more than an erotic adventure: one man described in court how he retired with a woman to a rented room, and stayed there for about five minutes. Rare detail appeared in the trial of James Larra, a respected merchant. He and his wife Phoebe were an affectionate couple until Phoebe became ill with dropsy (oedema), and told a friend that she thought this was because James used a candle in intercourse. James admitted that since his wife was enthusiastic and he felt himself an old man, incapable of satisfying her, he resorted to the candle. Phoebe died in agony from dropsy, and rumour led to James' arrest and trial. He was acquitted, but his reputation suffered.

Babies were born at home, with help from a doctor, midwife or neighbour. There was little contraception except withdrawal or abstinence, neither ideal, so women had large families. Babies were breastfed, the only way for a baby to thrive. With small houses and little schooling available, children were very much part of family life. They helped with the family enterprise as soon as they could, serving in the shop, herding animals, and helping round the house. Physical punishment was accepted as normal. There were plenty of illegitimate children, which was not a great disadvantage, either to them or their mothers. When relationships failed, people lived alone or found new partners, but marriages were probably ended more often by death – the average lifespan was still under fifty in 1850.

There were few middle-class women in the colonies, and they too often had irregular married lives. Government House should have been respectable if anywhere was, but of seven governors in Hobart between 1803 and 1820, three openly had mistresses

A convict on Melville Island

Most female convicts were sent to New South Wales or Tasmania, but in 1824 the British established a small colony at tropical Melville Island in the north, among the Tiwi people. The hundred white inhabitants were mostly men, but there were a few female convicts and wives.

Jane Richardson was transported to Sydney in 1816, and after receiving her ticket of leave, married another convict in 1824. Her husband John was overseer of the government gardens, and was appointed gardener on Melville Island. Jane and their baby son Matthew went with him. They impressed the Colonial Secretary, Jane as 'most respectable' and Matthew as 'very promising'.

At Melville Island, John set about establishing gardens and Jane bore another child, but she was worried about her and her children's health and safety, for the Tiwi were resisting invasion and malaria was rife. She was granted permission to return to Sydney, but John was caught selling sly grog and the permission was revoked, a hard punishment for Jane. They finally returned when the settlement was abandoned in 1829, but in Sydney Jane died after giving birth to her third child.

(usually convicts), and of those who were married, one was corrupt and grasping, one was a drunkard, and one was Edward Lord, with his ex-convict wife Maria. The fourth brought his wife, but she left him for an army officer, who fought a duel with the governor and lost, after which she went to live with the judge advocate. But the most astonishing vignette from these years was recorded by the chaplain, who described a convivial drinking party which consisted of himself, the governor, his daughter by one mistress, his present mistress and her husband.

Most women had little time for activity outside the home, though a few branched out. Anna King, married to the governor, started an orphanage where she even accepted or rejected marriage proposals for the girls. She was a great support to her husband, describing herself as his partner in his labour and anxieties; he called her his 'under-secretary'. However, some males had a higher opinion of women. A clergyman's son added to a letter, 'N.B. I have put Mrs before Mr because I think that ladies generally have command in this country'.

By the 1820s the original small convict settlements centred on Sydney and Hobart were spreading out. The population was growing, with not only convicts but ex-convicts and their children, and free settlers. Many lived by farming, so the original settlements expanded as people looked for land. Then came the challenging task of setting up a home and farm, with little equipment or outside help.

Often the pioneers were single men, but there were also couples or families, and several contemporary observers noted that men accompanied by women coped better than men on their own. Not only did women provide a more comfortable and civilised home, but they helped with the hard work of running a farm. The following stories show women who adapted well and badly, who failed and succeeded when faced with the difficulties all pioneers experienced.

In New South Wales, colonists were at first hemmed in by the barrier of the Blue Mountains. These were crossed in 1813, and the government built a basic, steep road and set up a convict establishment at Bathurst on the far side of the mountains. In 1822 the first respectable white family crossed the Blue Mountains. They were Elizabeth and Thomas Hawkins, their eight children aged from one to twelve, and Elizabeth's seventy-year-old mother. Tough times in England led them to emigrate to Sydney, where Thomas, an ex-purser in the British navy, was put in charge of government stores at Bathurst.

It took a while to organise their 'cavalcade', as Elizabeth called it, of horses, bullocks, dogs, carts and drays, thirty-four cattle and nine male convicts. They packed a table and twelve chairs, cooking utensils, bedding, food, clothes and a few tools. Then, on the Saturday before Easter, they set out on their 'tremendous journey', as Elizabeth told her sister in a long and vivid letter.

The first part was easy, over a good, flat road to the edge of civilisation at Parramatta, where they picked up a female convict servant at the Factory. A local landowner asked Elizabeth, Thomas and three others to a sumptuous dinner: mock turtle soup, boiled fowl, a round of beef, three kinds of fish, curried duck, goose and wildfowl, madeira, burgundy and ale – all for seven people.

Farewelled by the landowner and a friendly Aboriginal group, they started off the next day. After only a quarter of a mile, one of the drays bogged and they spent hours extricating it, so they only covered a mile and a half before having to camp for the night. It was a beautiful evening, and after the youngest children were in bed Elizabeth took Thomas' arm and surveyed the scene. The men cooking round a fire in the moonlight looked more like a party of bandits than anything else, and on the other side of the camp were their older children, trying to see who could make the best fire, 'as happy as it was possible for young hearts to be. Then I seemed to pause', wrote Elizabeth. 'It was a moment I shall never forget. For the first time for many a long month I seemed capable of enjoying and feeling the present moment without a dread for the future ... the dawn of independence was opening on us.' Thomas played a tune on a flute and their daughter Eliza danced, 'in a place where perhaps no one of her age had ever trod before'.

They woke to find that some of the animals had strayed, so

Early Days

The first white female in Perth

At the age of two, Charlotte Davis became the first white female to set foot in the colony of Western Australia. Thomas Davis of Hampshire was employed as government blacksmith, and in 1829 he and his family sailed to Perth with Governor Stirling. The ship struck a sandbank, so to lighten the load, heavy stores and some of the less socially desirable emigrants – artisans and their families, who had little clout when it came to complaining – were landed temporarily on Carnac Island.

The island was small, barren and waterless, though this last problem was solved by five days of incessant rain and gales. The group, soaked to the skin, were left to fend for themselves, with no shelter or beds. Their only food was salt beef and biscuits from the ship, and they had one knife and one mug between them. But they rose to the occasion, and the officer in charge of the stores reported good health and discipline. Finally they were taken to the mainland, a sailor carried Charlotte ashore and she made the first white female footprint.

The Davis family set up house in the new settlement of Perth. The first years were difficult, with shortages of food and labour, but the Davises, employed by the government, coped relatively well. At eighteen, Charlotte married the licensee of the Royal Oak inn at Toodyay, and they had four children. She proved an excellent hotel manager, and they built up a very good trade. Charlotte was also the local midwife. She died aged fifty-eight, and her descendants later erected a memorial to the pioneering Davis family.

while the men rounded them up, the family went on to the next stopping place, a house inhabited by soldiers who cared for government cattle. It was the worst night Elizabeth ever spent. A disreputable woman provided a small, dirty room which contained nothing but a sofa with a bark seat. Here they waited, desolate and miserable, until the carts arrived at nine o'clock. Then they could put down mattresses for the children, who slept restlessly, for the room was cold and crawling with bugs. Outside all was noise and confusion: the woman had stolen some of their spirits and she and some men were tipsy, other men were swearing and arguing, and a flock of sheep kept up a continual patter with their feet. Thomas, who had worked all day without food, kept guard over their possessions all night.

The family were relieved to leave the next day, and Elizabeth described how she, her mother and the girls walked ahead, gathering bunches of wildflowers. Then came another ascent, which brought its usual problems. During the whole trip they were plagued by straying stock, bullocks which refused to pull the carts and lay down, and accidents – a shaft breaking, or a dray becoming bogged. At the end of each day's exhausting travel, Elizabeth and her mother prepared food and beds for the children, who were also tired and often cross. Sometimes they put up their tent, and at other times stayed in huts, which were unlike anything in England. To make them, tree trunks were stuck in the ground,

Jessie Crozier

Jessie and John Crozier left Scotland for Australia as assisted emigrants in 1838. John was the overseer of properties around Bungendore in New South Wales, and Jessie bore him four children. In 1846 they branched out on their own, with a small flock of sheep and a bullock dray, and Jessie gave birth to their fifth child under the dray, helped by Aboriginal women. After two years' nomadic life, building up their flock, they leased land at the junction of the Murray and Darling rivers in Victoria. Their first house was a typical pioneer dwelling, a slab hut with walls of gum slabs and the roof thatched with river reeds. It stands today in the Meringur Pioneer Park, believed to be the oldest such building in Victoria.

Both John and Jessie worked extremely hard on their property. For twenty-two years Jessie was almost continually pregnant or breastfeeding her family of eleven children; she also ran the house, tended the vegetable garden, organised the children's education, gave medical help including delivering babies to local people, and was helpful to Aboriginal people, earning the title of

Early Days

and bark was tied on for the walls and roof. One hut had a shelf of bark as a bed, but sleep was impossible because of bugs and fleas. The family's provisions consisted of salted beef and half a pig, flour for damper, tea, sugar and butter. They only had two meals each day, breakfast and dinner, though Elizabeth, an experienced mother, took some food with her during the day 'to keep us from starving'.

The worst section of the trip was the dreaded 'Big Hill', the western descent from the mountains. Even the memory was so appalling, wrote Elizabeth, that she could not describe it and offered Thomas the pen, but he refused, so she had to go on. From the top the descent looked so fearfully steep that they had to stop 'to recover resolution'. Elizabeth assisted this by giving out food and wine. Then the men began cutting down trees to tie behind the carts to act as brakes, such an alarming precaution that Elizabeth, her mother and the children decided to go on foot.

> *'Ministering Angel of the Darling'. A vigorous, forthright person, Jessie administered strict justice with a birch broom. She had no time for false modesty, such as a woman fainting at the sight of blood or of a scantily-clad Aboriginal man.*
>
> *John and Jessie prospered, and in 1867 bought Oaklands, an estate near Adelaide, with a large homestead surrounded by vineyards and grazing land. John was elected to the Legislative Council, but Jessie never really settled to life in Adelaide. When John asked her if she would like to watch him give his maiden speech she answered, 'Noo, John, I would dee o' vera shame', which became a family saying. She was inclined to disapprove of John's social activities, and walked through one of his garden parties carrying a bucket of swill to feed the pigs. Jessie was much more interested in helping the needy, especially women and children abandoned by men who went off to the goldfields. She continued her interest in Aboriginal people, making a paddock available for them to camp, as they were not welcome in the city. Her great-granddaughter's name Keera, which means 'billabong', is a legacy from Jessie.*

'How we got down I cannot tell', but despite pains in their legs and 'violent trembling all over', and having to carry the younger children, they managed to reach the bottom in safety.

There they waited. It was hot, but Elizabeth gave out sugar candy, and they drank from a spring. The hours dragged on: 'never before was such a party of females without any protection for so many hours at the foot of the mountains'. As sunset approached, Elizabeth and her mother became even more worried, and alarmed at the 'horrid noise' of laughing jackasses (kookaburras), but finally the rest of the party arrived. It was 11.00 pm before they had dinner and could go to sleep.

Shortly afterwards they halted for a day by a river, where Elizabeth and her mother gave the children all a good wash and change of clothes, so instead of being a day of rest it was one of great fatigue, she wrote. 'Completely sick and tired of the journey', they pressed on: there was another dangerous river, another steep hill, a swamp and heavy rain, but finally they came to the plains of Bathurst, and their house was pointed out. 'What a welcome sight!' Their journey of 140 miles (219 kilometres) – which now takes a couple of hours – had lasted eighteen days.

Not only did Elizabeth and Thomas cope well with this trip, but so did Elizabeth's elderly mother. The other woman, the convict, was hardly mentioned. In Bathurst their situation was excellent, with a house, vegetable garden and three cows: Eliza and Mary asked their mother to tell the relations back home that they had churned the family's first butter. Elizabeth thrilled her English readers with her account of snakes so venomous that no one bitten survived, though she admitted that she had only seen one. Seclusion from the world could be a drawback, but it did not bother Elizabeth: 'I think there can be no doubt but we shall do well'. They did. Thomas was given a large land grant on which they built a good house, three more children were born, and they joined the prosperous landed gentry. Thomas died aged fifty-six, and Elizabeth lived to be ninety-two.

Less successful were the Whatley family in the new colony of Western Australia, a planned settlement to which the wealthy were encouraged to emigrate from Britain by the promise of land

Early Days

grants, and labourers by assistance with their passage. Anne and John Whatley, with their two small daughters, were among the first to arrive in 1829. Their wealth entitled them to a land grant of 8,000 acres, and by April 1830 they were settled in their wattle and daub cottage, which looked very pretty, thought Anne, especially when John put her Parisian ink drawings on the walls. She was proud of her hens and vegetable garden, and sent the governor some turnips.

Unfortunately, the Whatleys were accident-prone. First their house was flooded, then a curtain above the baby's cradle caught

An adventurous life in the Far North

In 1870 Margaret Fulford's husband was appointed manager of a station in the Gulf Country of far north Queensland, so they left their home in Grafton, New South Wales with their seven-week-old daughter. Margaret rode the first hundred miles (160 kilometres) side-saddle holding the baby in an improvised sling, 'a long tedious and tiring journey'. She caught a bad cold from camping on damp ground, and was so ill that she stayed behind with her mother for six months while her husband went to the station. In February 1871 she started out again, and reached Townsville by riding, with the baby in the saddle in front of her, then by coach and ship.

Her husband met her, and they proceeded by horse and cart through rough, steep country, where he caught fever and Margaret had to take charge. Fortunately he had recovered by the time they reached the Burdekin River, which was flooded, and they only just managed to cross, in great danger of being washed downstream. At the station Margaret was confronted with a four-roomed slab hut, a bed made of saplings, many ants, and a bark kitchen with a camp oven – but the trip had been such a nightmare that she welcomed it, and did not leave it for another nine years. In the way expected of women she made it more comfortable, lining the walls with old calico tents which she papered with pictures cut out of magazines, and making furniture of packing cases.

fire, and John was only just in time to save the child. Soon after that John drowned, trying to take a cow across a river in too small a boat. Anne was left a twenty-three-year-old widow with two children, and pregnant with the third. She returned to England, and it must have been the last straw when they stopped at Launceston on the way, and gossips claimed she was not Mrs Whatley but Mrs Griffiths, who the year before had left her husband and run away with a ship's captain.

South Australia was set up on much the same lines as Western Australia, and among the assisted labourers to emigrate were a newly married Irish couple, Annie and Matthew Caldwell. They arrived in Adelaide in 1841 with little more than the clothes they stood up in, wrote their daughter Martha in her memoirs. They worked for wages until they had enough to lease a small farm at Gumeracha, north-east of Adelaide, but they lacked water, and Irish farming methods did not transplant well to Australia. Life was a 'hard daily round of work and family ... felling trees, grubbing out stumps, building fences of brush or logs and sinking tanks for water – working, waiting, living by grit, zeal and enterprise'. Worse was to come. Matthew died in 1856, leaving Annie pregnant and with seven children to support. Fortunately she had courage, foresight and determination, and she was to need them. Everyone had to help, and the family scraped a living by selling eggs, butter and farm produce. The children attended the local school, a four-mile walk away – Annie was determined to do the best she could for them. But seasons were dry and despite their hard work, 'things were not too prosperous'.

Stories were being circulated about land available cheaply in New South Wales, and in 1864 Annie called a family conference, and they decided to move there. Annie sold everything except five horses, some cattle, Lassie the dog and a tilted wagon, similar to covered wagons in America – a tilt was a canvas cover stretched round a wooden frame. The family carried matches, water and food: fresh and salted meat, tinned fish and jam, potatoes, flour, sugar, and suet for dumplings on Sundays, when there was no travel and the girls did the washing. They always managed to keep clean, said Martha. Before they left, a neighbour who made wine

Early Days

gave Annie some grape-stones which she used to make yeast, so she could bake 'lovely bread' in the camp oven. She also made a johnny cake from flour, cream of tartar and baking soda, which she would fry in a pan, then toss. She tried to teach the children how to toss the 'johnny', but none of them could manage it. Their meals were varied by the boys, who caught fish or shot wild duck or turkey. They let Martha have a turn, and she became quite a good shot.

Annie had her medicinal supplies of castor oil, medicinal salts and senna, a laxative used as a general remedy. 'How we youngsters hated the lot of them!' But they looked forward to evenings, when by the light of a candle Annie read aloud, popular romances or the latest novel by Dickens. One night the reading was disturbed by the terrifying thunder of cattle hooves, as a bellowing mob stampeded from a camp a mile away. The horses bolted, though they were hobbled, and it took the boys two days to bring them back. On the trail Annie or the older boys drove, and everyone else walked to lighten the load, the girls going ahead to remove obstacles such as overhanging branches. Sometimes they were visited by Aboriginal parties; Annie gave them tobacco, and they provided information about roads and creeks ahead.

The family travelled through Bendigo and continued to Albury, in New South Wales at last. The 560-mile (900-km) trek had taken them eight weeks. Annie sent the boys off to find good land, which they did near Holbrook. Under the *Selection Act*, settlers could select land and buy it cheaply, paying back the price over time. The Caldwells selected a block in John's name, even though Annie was paying for it and John was under twenty-one. Annie calculated that in twenty-eight years it would be paid off.

In two days they reached their selection. There they built a slab hut, with timber uprights and rafters, and bark for walls and roof, tied on with greenhide thongs. There was no stringy bark and they had to use box bark, which was harder to strip; but everyone helped and, wrote Martha, 'even if the place was not very stylish, we thought it wonderful after being housed in a dusty waggon riddled with roaches for so long'. Next came a shed and stockyard. 'How hard we all did work! Mother seemed able to turn her hand

Pioneer cookery

Convicts and other white women continued to cook much as they had done in Britain, using any ingredients available, including local produce. Other ingredients in these recipes are basic – flour, bacon, eggs, salt, pepper. Kangaroos were a staple of early settlement, and this recipe shows how the meat could be preserved.

Kangaroo steamer

Take the most tender part of the kangaroo, being careful to remove all the sinews. Chop it very fine, about the same quantity of smoked bacon (fat); season it finely. Let it steam or stew for two hours; then pack or press tight in open-mouthed glass bottles; the bung must be sealed down, and the outside of the bottles washed well with white of egg, beaten; preserved in this way it will keep good for twelve months or more.

When the kangaroo was freshly killed, women could make this delicacy:

Slippery Bob

Take kangaroo brains and mix with flour and water and make into a batter. Well season with pepper and salt. Pour a tablespoon at a time into an iron pot containing emu fat and take out when done.

Another method of keeping meat was salting or 'curing' it.

To cure meat, bush-style

If available, mix and heat up 2 cups common salt, 1 oz saltpetre, 2 oz bay salt, 2¼ cups brown sugar and ¾ cup vinegar. If not available, use plenty of common salt by itself. Cut the meat into joints, and make a few cuts in the thicker parts of large pieces. Rub the salt or salt mixture well into the meat, over every surface, and leave it on a bed of gum leaves, covered from the flies by day, and spread out in the open air at night. After 2–3 weeks it can be hung to dry.

to any sort of man's work after her ten years as sole manageress.'

Although the boys were growing up, Annie was in charge and kept all family members up to their work. They hurriedly cleared land to get in a crop of wheat, and everyone helped to fence it.

Early Days

They bought twelve cows with calves, and Martha rode round them, bareback, as they grazed. Milk was now plentiful, and they made butter and cheese. To make butter, women beat cream by hand 'to the turn', in a wooden churn with a plunger, which sounds rather like a potato masher. For cheese, Annie and the girls made rennet from the stomach of a calf which had not been allowed to eat grass, and was killed at six weeks. The rennet was used to curdle milk, and the whey was pressed out of the curd. This was 'well rubbed up', salt and a little colouring were added, then it was wrapped in cheesecloth and put in a vat, where it was pressed for three weeks. Annie thought a cheese needed six months to develop a good flavour, but the demand was so strong in Albury that it never reached this age. Martha wrote that 'we all felt very happy in our new home'. Annie would sing as she 'flew round' doing her many tasks in the day, and at night she was always sewing and mending and darning. 'She never complained.' She died aged sixty-nine, surrounded by her family.

A different type of pioneer was Mary McConnel, another of the newly married wives who arrived in Australia as emigrants, this time in Brisbane in 1849. Coming from an elite social background, Mary was shocked to find she had to use cups without handles, and that visitors did not use calling cards, but wrote on the door with chalk if they found people not at home. Her husband David built a large house on his country estate and they moved there with their children. Mary was a kind mistress to their labourers, helping the ill and holding church services. Wealth could not prevent all problems, however: one baby died while teething, and Mary became ill with a gangrenous leg, and only drastic treatment with 'liquid caustic' saved her.

Mary and David had, for the time, a sympathetic view of Aboriginal people, 'not by any means so low down in the scale of the human race, as they are generally supposed to be', said Mary. One woman, 'Long Kitty', liked to have charge of Mary's baby son, which Mary allowed after she made Kitty bathe in the river. 'She would look proudly over the country and say, stretching out her arms, "All this 'yarmen' (land) belonging to me." It did seem hard to have it all taken from them, but it had to be', wrote Mary. She provided a school for the Aboriginal children, where girls learned to read and sew, and sing verses and hymns.

Many women undertook such philanthropic activities, but Mary took hers into the public realm. She was particularly interested in children's health, at a time when small children were not admitted to hospitals, and decided that Brisbane needed a children's hospital. She organised fundraising and brought qualified staff from England herself. The Royal Brisbane Children's Hospital opened in 1878, and Mary remained deeply involved with it until her death.

By this time, Australia's central north had been settled, and in 1869 the first boatload of women and children arrived in the new town of Darwin to join their menfolk. Eliza Tuckwell and her offspring were among them. Some of the women made money by taking in single men's washing, wrote Eliza, and others shocked her by drinking as much as the men. 'I could mention their names but it would not do.' Eliza had a shaky marital relationship, once advertising in the local paper that she would not pay her husband's debts, and when he died suddenly, she worked as a nurse and midwife and opened a boarding-house to support her six children. A staunch Methodist, she was often seen on her verandah in the late afternoon, sitting on her rocking chair and humming hymns. In the 1897 cyclone which wrecked Darwin her house was flattened, but with help from the disaster fund she rebuilt her house, and lived on until 1921.

The women described above are only a few of the pioneer women in nineteenth-century Australia. All had to cope with new experiences, from cups without handles to major domestic tasks which they had never dreamed of doing. There has been something of a cult of the pioneer in Australia and most are remembered in a celebratory way, so the stories above are probably too rosy; many women found harsh circumstances overwhelming and there were cases of suicide and murder, but there were many cheerful stories as well. What was not so cheerful was that the land the pioneers used was taken from its original owners. Though individuals sometimes helped Aboriginal people, generally whites ignored them – as in Elizabeth Hawkins' comment that her daughter was dancing where no one of her age had ever danced before – or thought, like Mary McConnel, that since Aborigines did not cultivate their land they did not deserve it.

chapter two

The Australian Woman

The first forty or so years of white settlement were fairly rough and ready, with morals shockingly lax by later standards, and women able to use their capabilities in a variety of ways. A turning-point came in about 1830, when new ideas about women's place were growing, separating them from the world of men. The ideal Victorian woman stayed at home, the linchpin of the family, engrossed in the 'natural' womanly interests of caring for husband and children. She should be pure: no more extra-marital sex, drinking and fighting, as in the bad old days. She was dependant on her menfolk, and Victorians liked the image of the man as the pillar and the woman the clinging vine around it. Men's sphere was public life, earning money and running the country, and women's sphere was private life in the home, keeping the household functioning.

Probably no one woman fitted the ideal exactly, in Australia even less than in Britain, but it was the middle-class view of what all women should be, rich and poor, rural and urban, black and white, and many women tried to live up to it. Most carried it out in externals at least: in this period, 95 per cent of women married, and 93 per cent of marriages produced children. So 88 per cent of all women bore children, and spent decades bearing and rearing them, as well as running the house and other womanly activities.

Their role also included raising the tone of society. Caroline

Chisholm, famous for assisting immigrants, pointed out to the British government that the teachers, churches and books it planned to introduce would never achieve much in improving Australian society without 'God's police' – 'wives and little children – good and virtuous women'. Woman, according to writer Miles Franklin, 'brought culture to the primordial fastnesses'.

What was a woman's life like in Australia in the Victorian heyday, the 1830s to the 1870s? Let us take a hypothetical Australian girl called Sarah, a popular name of the period, and follow her through her life, as illustrated by episodes from women's diaries and letters. Middle-class views will predominate, because most women who wrote diaries and letters were middle class, and because this class took up the ideal with the most enthusiasm – they were cushioned by money from many of the more disagreeable aspects. Almost all white women, however, had some similar experiences.

Sarah was likely to be born legitimate – the new moral code frowned heavily on illegitimate births – and one of a large

Amelia's five husbands

Multiple marriages are not unknown today, but they were also common in the nineteenth century, when marriage was the most usual way for a woman to provide for herself, especially in the emergency of being left alone by death, with no income. In 1849 Amelia White married Thomas Williams and had two children, but Thomas died while Amelia was pregnant with the second baby. This was a precarious position for a woman, and Amelia married William Grills, a farmer near Armidale. They had three children, but William died from tuberculosis. So Amelia married Charles Millington, who died in 1869. Amelia was now forty-three. Shortly afterwards she married a Mr Palmer, who presumably died too as in 1872 she married Benjamin Chuter. This was the longest of her marriages, but Benjamin died in 1883 and left Amelia for the fifth time a widow, an intimidating figure in her rustling black silks and taffetas.

The Australian Woman

family. She probably had a reasonably happy childhood. Twenty-year-old Christiana Brooks wrote a fond description of her family in country New South Wales. Her father was a 'nice looking old gentleman', and her mother 'just what you would fancy the good mother of a family who is adored by her children and who is never so happy as when they are all with her'. She had five sisters. Mary, aged twenty-three, was stout but lively and good-tempered, Jane sensible and agreeable, and Honoria very tall, fond of dancing and of being admired by fine young men. Charlotte at seventeen was at an awkward age, not good-tempered but at least affectionate; Maria at thirteen was as wild as a young colt, but she too had an affectionate heart. Their only brother Henry was 'good-hearted'.

Despite Charlotte, this family sounds almost too good to be true, and indeed it was. Years earlier the nice-looking old gentleman had been in charge of convict transports, and at one stage had been shipwrecked with a female convict. The illegitimate offspring of this union was brought up by his wife with her children, but is rarely mentioned. In Australia, even the most outwardly respectable family could have a murky past.

Girls like Sarah enjoyed playing, sometimes with dolls, mostly outside. Annie Crozier would tuck her dress into her bloomers so she could keep up with other children and climb trees, young Mary McConnel and her brothers fought battles using long sticks as spears, tried to catch shrimps and eels in the creek, chased lizards and played with frogs. Even a bishop's daughters jumped and laughed, dirtied their pinafores making a mud house, and played 'Here we go round the mulberry bush' so enthusiastically that their mother took refuge in her room. She was not the only one. When rain meant her children were confined inside, Mary Mowle wrote in her diary that she was 'almost driven to distraction … the incessant uproar & confusion is terrible, & it taxes my utmost fortitude & good temper to bear with them'. Other mothers were proud of high spirits: 'our children are as wild as kangaroos and mischievous as monkeys', wrote Christiana Brooks of her own youngsters.

'The Australian girl', as she was called, amazed outsiders. Tall,

Hard conditions in northern Queensland

At the age of fourteen, Margaret Fitzgerald married Joseph Eccles, a horse teamster. Joseph transported goods from the north Queensland coast to various inland goldfields, and their first five children were born on one of these. Life was notoriously hard there, and after three babies had died, the family moved to the coast, where Margaret bore two more children.

In 1879 there was a tin rush to Herberton, and Joseph and Margaret went to manage a hotel half-way to the mines, at what was to become Mareeba. In October 1881 Margaret, still only twenty-seven, gave birth to their eighth child. She was not well but went back to work to run the hotel and care for her family. Her condition worsened, and though the Port Douglas doctor rode through the night to reach her, she died. A frangipani tree she had grown in her garden marked her grave until the 1990s.

attractive, independent, energetic, she was to them too vigorous, without interest in intellectual pursuits or English manners – she often went to dances without a chaperone! 'You meet with very few quiet patient girls here', an English governess wrote sadly. Perhaps mothers were too busy for strict discipline, or agreed with Sarah Wentworth, mother of ten, that it was no use constantly trying to force children against their will. 'I am quite sure pushing too much is not the way to make others do all you wish.'

Despite this happy life, girls could be aware that they were valued less than boys. An extreme example was a seven-year-old whose brother died. She stood in the corner of the room where his coffin lay, as mourners filed in to pay their respects. 'What a pity it was the boy!' she heard one say. 'The girl could have so easily been spared.'

As she grew older, Sarah was increasingly confined by education and housework. As the century progressed, more children were educated, in government or private schools, or by governesses or mothers at home. Standards of education were generally not high: teachers were mostly untrained, private schools tended to come and go, mothers had little spare time. They often thought that girls especially did not need rigorous education, and Mary Gilmore's memoirs show how patchy schooling could be. Born in 1865 in the New South Wales countryside, at four she learnt the alphabet from her father (and at six taught it to her younger brothers), then joined neighbouring children for lessons with their tutor, attended the local school, and at eight went to Mr Pentland's Academy in Wagga Wagga and learnt Greek. The school was destroyed by floods, so she moved to the state school, and at twelve started her teaching career as a pupil-teacher. This erratic education somehow produced one of Australia's most notable writers.

Rather than any career needing academic training, the main career for Sarah was expected to be, and indeed was, marriage. It was by far the most successful way in which a woman could gain a living and a place in the community. There were more men than women in Australia during the whole nineteenth century, which meant that almost all women could find a husband.

Sarah's mother prepared her for marriage at home, teaching her to cook, sew, clean and wash, as well as more artistic accomplishments. Ex-convict Sarah Lawson was shaky on spelling and grammar, but encouraged her daughters' music, writing: 'I have bought Rebecca a piano she plais very well Hannah and Sophia is learning'. Music and art raised the tone of the home, had practical uses for entertainment and decoration, and showed that a girl was accomplished, which was presumed to attract husbands.

So Sarah can keep house, play a waltz on the piano and embroider a pretty tablecloth, and she attracts an eligible young man. Josephine Bussell met Henry Prinsep at an 'At Home', and they went riding and sailing, though always as part of groups. He admired her skill at riding and her piano playing – so it did work. A month after they met, they fell behind the others when out riding, and Henry declared his love for her; and though Josephine said it was too early to speak of such things, she gave him cause to hope. One evening, shortly afterwards, he held her hand even though an aunt was watching. It was just as well that they were formally engaged soon afterwards, and they married in the local church eighteen months later.

Even more romantic was the story of Mrs Spencer of Perth. 'It was very wrong of me', she began, but ... Her mother died, her father was at sea, and she was in the charge of a governess. One day when she was seventeen she had been at the races, but was separated from her carriage and caught in a heavy shower of rain. A young man came to the rescue and sheltered her under his umbrella. 'That is how my acquaintance with my future husband began.' They decided to elope, so she met him early one morning and they drove away. Her father was furious – she did not reveal why the young man was not suitable – but forgave her when a son was born, and she never regretted her choice.

Not everyone had such a romantic marriage. Eliza Louden was the daughter of a Melbourne merchant. Her parents did not approve of her young man, and forbade her to see him. A middle-aged farmer thought she would make a suitable wife and asked for her hand. Though she barely knew him, she agreed, so he drove his dray to Melbourne, married her in the Richmond Wesleyan church, and after a modest wedding breakfast, took her home on the four-day dray trip.

As a girl in Western Australia, Louisa Clifton thought marriage was an unhappy state for a woman, but as the years rolled on she decided she needed a 'prop and support, a kindred heart', and married George Eliot. There was much custard making and table planning, she wrote, and on the wedding morning she was shivering with nervousness. Her attendants, 'the dear girls', dressed her in her white merino wedding gown, a white satin bonnet and elegant veil, white satin shoes and a white crepe shawl from 'dear George'. The marriage took place in the drawing room, and after an excellent breakfast Louisa changed into a green cloth habit and cap. Amid cheers she and George set off on a long, cold ride during which they had to shelter under trees from rain and tempestuous wind. They arrived at his home in the dark, but the housekeeper had a blazing fire and they were thankful to have finished their 'comparatively not unpleasant journey' – so perhaps he was a kindred heart. At any rate, they had seven children.

Once the wedding was over Sarah had to settle down to

The Australian Woman

> ### Mental illness disrupts family life
> Mary Ann Scott's husband William was a miner on the Victorian goldfields. After the birth of her seventh child, she suffered from 'puerperal mania' – postnatal depression? puerperal fever? – and was admitted to the Ararat Lunatic Asylum in 1879, aged thirty-two. She died shortly afterwards, of 'disease of the brain', leaving William 'in very poor circumstances having to provide for a family of young children'. He himself died in a mining accident two years later. Three of the children were admitted to the Ballarat orphanage, while the youngest was cared for by his grandmother and her third husband, who was cruel to him, according to stories passed down to descendants.

married life with all its pleasures, responsibilities and pitfalls. A Western Australian diarist wrote in 1859 that a Mr and Mrs Brockman had arrived on their way to Perth, '*rather* soon for a bride to appear in public'. Brides were unlikely to have been well prepared for the sexual side of marriage, and the wedding night must have been a surprise if not shock for many. Perhaps that was why Louisa was nervous. Other brides did not come inexperienced to their wedding nights, and about a fifth bore a child within nine months of marriage. But even if they knew little beforehand, brides soon learnt, and weddings brought results. More than four-fifths produced a baby within two years, the average number of children was seven, and there were some huge families of up to twenty.

In childbirth women were sometimes attended by doctors, who were often experienced, but had little training and could not do a great deal to help. Ether, chloroform and forceps were available, but they were new and not often used. More women turned to midwives, who were cheaper, and mostly kindly and competent, though there are a few stories of ignorant midwives – one, for example, had not heard of the afterbirth.

In isolated areas women sometimes had to give birth with no expert help. The Gilberts of South Australia were travelling overland with cattle, completing twelve-mile stages each day and occasionally running out of flour. One Thursday morning they woke to find the bullocks gone, but they traced them and drove them ten miles through the rain to camp by a creek; then 'to night was Confind Son Thursday 25 of May at the Crick', wrote Mrs Gilbert. Presumably her husband helped her, for there was no one else. They stayed in camp for three days, but then went on. Similarly, a nineteen-year-old woman had her first baby in a hut in the bush, cut off from help by floods and with only her husband to help.

The infant mortality rate (deaths of infants under a year old) was high, averaging 122 per one-thousand live births or over one baby in ten – and there were stillbirths as well. It was a rare family which did not lose at least one child. Childbirth was also a danger for women, the third greatest cause of death for those of childbearing age. Women's attitudes ranged from stoicism to fear of death as the birth approached, the 'dreaded ordeal' as Mary Mowle wrote. And even if women did not die, with childbirth so common, family members could be unsympathetic. One husband commented that they might as well go to England as his wife could have her baby on ship just as well as on land, and a daughter wrote rather heartlessly after her mother miscarried: 'To-day has been a trying time for us in many ways, besides the grief of having Mamma ill, for, of course we have had everything to do, and think about, and, tonight, we are very weary'.

But most babies and mothers lived, so let us assume that Sarah had her child safely. She almost certainly breastfed the baby, so was almost continually either pregnant or breastfeeding from twenty, the average age when women married, till thirty-seven, the average age when childbearing stopped. Breastfeeding gave some protection against conception, which with the pattern of bearing a baby every two years or so, suggests that most couples did not use contraception. There was little available in any case. Annie Baxter Dawbin, childless herself though not for want of trying, advised a poor neighbour not to have any more children. The neighbour replied, 'But how it is possible for married persons to avoid it?' Men echoed this question. In 1827 Governor Arthur described his family of seven, finishing with Fanny, the youngest, 'and so I trust she will remain', and thirty years later in Adelaide, Joseph Elliott wrote home that the baby linen was put away, he hoped for a long time. Trust and hope were not enough, and there were four more Arthur children and six more young Elliotts. The main methods of contraception were abstinence, obviously not an option for these men, or withdrawal, which was not reliable.

There are plenty of examples of both good and bad marriages, but the idea of a companionate marriage – where the couple were partners instead of master and handmaid – was growing, and one English visitor wrote that wives in Australia were treated with 'twenty times the respect' they were shown in England. Many

A centenarian of the nineteenth century

Mary Ann Foote and her husband worked on a sheep station with their ten children, but disaster dogged them. Soon after they arrived, their goods were burnt in a fire, a flood washed away their belongings, two sons died when a dray overturned, and their twelve-year-old daughter was burnt to death – she had been lighting a fire to cook her father's dinner when a spark set fire to her clothes.

Mary Ann's husband was one of a party who discovered the Barossa goldfields in 1868, for which he received a government reward, but soon afterwards he died of typhoid. Five years later Mary Ann senior married a blacksmith, giving her age as fifty-four, but her new husband died too, and she married for a third time, at seventy. This husband used to beat her, but she outlived him as well.

In 1913 Mary Ann turned a hundred, and from then on was invited to the annual Proclamation Day ceremonies, commemorating the founding of Adelaide, where she lunched with the governor. She retained all her faculties, and a journalist admired her brisk walk, firm handshake and indomitable spirit – she insisted on helping her daughter with the housework. Mary Ann finally died aged 107, able to the last, as a reporter wrote, to 'chat in the most interesting manner'.

women wrote appreciatively of their husbands. Ann Hordern of Sydney wrote that her husband 'is very kind to me and the children and he does all in his power to comfort us and make us happy'. In 1830 Sophy Dumaresq gave an ecstatic picture of marriage. At five o'clock in the morning she was dragged '*neck & heels*' out of bed; 'of course I need not name the perpetrator of so *tyrannical* an act, none but a man & a husband cd be guilty of such *cruelty*'. Before her marriage she had to ask someone else to talk to Henry about the delicate subject of water-closets, but now stories which had made her blush she thought very good fun, and it was all Henry's fault. Sophy did not like Sydney, its climate, the gloomy country, the depraved lower orders of people, but she was '*very very* happy', as nothing could exceed Henry's 'care, tenderness, cheerfulness & unremitting solicitude towards me in Every way'.

Not every woman was so blessed. Mary Mowle and her husband Stewart had plenty of arguments when they were poor and struggling. Once Mary had to put the children to bed early as she had no wood, candles, tea, meat or flour so could not feed them, and she was furious when Stewart arrived home having spent some of their scanty money on a counterpane and a lamp at a sale. She recorded this in her diary, then blacked out the next five lines. But when Stewart obtained a well-paid job, arguments ceased and he became 'dear Stewart'.

However happily married, whatever their social class, women were busy. The ideal Victorian lady left physical work to the servants, but in Australia servants were often either unsatisfactory or difficult to obtain. In 1859, in regions where families had comparable incomes, well over half English families had servants, but only 12 per cent in Australia. Even when they had servants, mistresses were often unenthusiastic about them. 'You have no idea what a plague the servants are here', wrote Rachel Henning from her brother's station near Bathurst. 'If a few married ladies meet, it is quite ridiculous to hear the chorus of lamentation that they strike up. One has had a new American stove knocked to pieces; another every scrap of crockery broken; another her gowns pawned; another, bills run up in her name at every shop in the town.' Then, if you did find a good servant, her skills were also sought after by a husband. Several mistresses wrote that they might as well advertise as matrimonial agencies, so often did their servants leave to marry.

Despite all these problems, those who could afford them saw servants as vital. Jane Williams of Bothwell wrote, 'While we were out, the woman servants broke into a spirit box, got tipsey, & we are at present without a servant – Mama *ironing clothes* all day!' Those without servants, either temporarily or permanently had, like Jane's Mama, to do the work themselves, 'not very pleasant I can assure you', as one girl wrote.

To begin with, there was cooking. The poor and itinerant cooked over an open fire, with a basic diet of tea, damper and meat. Cooking was easier in a camp or Dutch oven, a large iron pot on legs with a lid. It was set in a bed of coals and more coals

Sad death in childbirth

Sarah Nicolson was a teacher, and in 1878 married a Swiss, Charles Amiet. They had a store in Inverleigh, Victoria, and had seven children, of whom two died in infancy. Sarah ran the store when Charles went to seek his fortune in Western Australia, and when he returned he selected isolated land in Gippsland, leaving her to sell the store and move the family. She gave birth to her eighth child during the move.

After her ninth child was born, she was told not to have more as she would die, so when she was expecting her tenth child she made arrangements for her children's care. When the birth was imminent, she took her three-year-old son and walked three miles to a neighbour. The terrain was rough, the track steep, and when Sarah stopped to rest, she would sing 'Nearer My God To Thee', have a cry, then move on. The child was born at the neighbour's, and Sarah died six days later. In 2000, her descendant Bethe van Boven and her cousins visited the farm site and sang 'Nearer My God To Thee' in Sarah's memory – 'not a dry eye on the tractor', wrote Bethe.

were piled round and over it. Enclosed fuel stoves arrived in the 1850s, but few could afford them, and there was still the chore of keeping the fire going.

There was not a wide variety of food. Flour, sugar, dried fruit, potatoes, oil, eggs, butter and meat were the major items bought – Australians ate vast amounts of meat, well over twice what Britons ate. Most people continued the diet of their British forebears, bread, meat, potatoes and other vegetables, boiled puddings to fill up the cracks, as well as fruit, cakes and biscuits.

Preparing food with simple equipment was time-consuming – it took fifteen or twenty minutes to beat eggs with a fork to make a cake. There were a few attempts to make cooking easier. 'Having just gobbled up two Custards I must note what you say about Custard Compound, what will they invent next?' wrote Maria Windeyer in 1844. In 1851 she told her son, 'One of the cakes I thought you might perhaps like to take to Mr Shelley, since it is made of some of those nice eggs he so admired, we call it a sponge cake'.

Caroline Chisholm described a colonial dinner for twelve in 1850: a large hindquarter of roast pork, a piece of beef cooked in a pot, and potatoes, peas and other greens. Father carved, and the eldest daughter poured cups of tea. To follow there was a peach pie, an orange tart and custards, made by the husband. Her description was published in England to encourage emigrants; it does not seem likely that many husbands really did make custards in 1850 when the kitchen was mostly seen as a female preserve, but it was a novel way to advertise Australia, the land where husbands helped with the cooking.

Water was obtained from creeks, rivers or lakes, and in towns it was delivered to households, though there was worry about its purity. Keeping food fresh was a problem, especially in country areas remote from shops. Meat was kept in a safe, which hung outside. Water on the top seeped down through the hessian sides, and the breeze evaporated it and kept the meat coolish, but it did not last more than a couple of days. When an animal was killed, some meat was eaten fresh but the rest was salted, another job for the housewife. The fat was used to make soap, candles or creams

The Australian Woman

> ## A divorce case of 1870
>
> *After seventeen years of marriage and ten children, Emma Clark filed for divorce. She testified that her husband hit her, jumped on her with boots on, dragged her round the room by her hair, emptied the chamber pot over her, and sexually abused her. He led his horse into the room where she was recovering from childbirth, tied the bridle to her body, and beat the horse to make it pull her out of bed. He tied her to a dray to which was harnessed his untamed horse, and enjoyed watching her agonies for three-quarters of an hour. He threatened that if she went against him, he would quit the colony, and leave her in a lunatic asylum and the children in an orphanage.*
>
> *When Emma finally filed for divorce, she was dying, and dropped the case on condition that her solicitor was paid. One might ask why she did not leave her husband earlier, but like many women she was vulnerable, with no money, no capacity for earning, no one to help her or stand up for her, and above all, the children to consider.*

for the face and hands, eaten as dripping on bread or used as suet instead of butter in cooking.

By the end of the period recipes were being published in a few books and newspapers, and show that new ideas were developing. In 1870 the *Australian Town and Country Journal* included a complicated recipe for 'A Hen's Nest for a Children's Party'. You made a small hole in eggs, emptied them and filled them with blancmange (extremely difficult!), which set, or at least you hoped it would. You pared lemon rind thinly, boiled it, cut it in thin strips to resemble straw, and preserved them with sugar. You filled a small deep dish with jelly, arranged the straw on top, peeled the eggs and sat them in the nest. Very pretty – and very exhausting.

As well as cooking, providing food meant a great deal of work, often done by women. Some who lived in towns did less, but even there, people grew fruit and vegetables, and kept hens and often a cow. Cows had to be milked twice a day, milk put aside for the cream to rise, and butter made. Hens had to be fed, eggs gathered, and surplus eggs preserved in salt or sawdust, against the times when hens did not lay. Yeast was made from potatoes or hops. Surplus fruit and vegetables were made into jam or pickles.

Many of these processes needed skill and experience. Mary Mowle 'tried to churn a little cream in a quart but after working hard for a full hour found that the only thing I had succeeded in doing was to cut all my fingers with the edge of the spoon'. At fifteen Mary Kennedy could make butter as well as her mother, prepare and cook a turkey, and knead and bake bread. This meant knowing the right heat in the brick oven to cook it without burning and manipulating the wooden 'peel' to remove it, 'and let no novice think that they can do it, it is also an art'. She could wash, starch and iron, and make great boxes of candles, with the fat just the right heat to enable them to 'draw'.

Then there was the endless housework, dusting furniture, sweeping and scrubbing floors, cleaning, washing dishes, all with little more equipment that a duster, mop, broom and bucket. Washing clothes meant heating water, scrubbing the clothes, rinsing them in more water, wringing them out and drying them. A whole day had to be set aside for this. Then came starching and ironing, with heavy flat irons, heated by the fire. They cooled quickly and had to be changed often, and ironing was a real chore. But before it could be washed and ironed, clothing had to be made, and this was often done at home by hand, until treadle machines appeared in the 1860s. Machines made sewing much easier, but were expensive, and until families could afford one, women sewed endlessly by hand.

Even by the 1850s, women did not wear many different types of clothes, to judge by a list of clothes emigrants were advised to bring. Dresses, cotton and flannel petticoats, chemises, corsets, stockings, nightgowns and caps, pocket handkerchiefs, neck handkerchiefs, bonnets, cloak and shawl, boots and shoes were the total. No knickers, no separate blouses (a nuisance for washing), and nothing really warm for winter, unless you wore everything at once.

Edith Cowan is usually remembered as the first Australian woman elected to parliament, but she had other interests as well, and in 1928 she gave a talk to the Western Australian Historical Society about Early Fashions. In 1830, she said, dresses had tight bodices, sleeves full at the top and tight at the wrist, and moderately full skirts, stiffened by petticoats and adorned with deep flounces. Then came pagoda sleeves, tight at the top and hanging at the wrists with lace under-sleeves. They looked nice, but were troublesome as it was hard to keep them out of teacups and gravy bowls. Portraits show that for adult women at least, necklines were almost horizontal and quite low, but Edith did not mention this.

Crinolines were fashionable in the 1850s, made by covering four narrow 'steels' with tape and running them horizontally into a calico petticoat. Dresses could use twenty yards of material. This must have made housework difficult, and Edith disapproved; the crinoline disappeared in about 1868, and 'we may be sure no woman desires its revival'. The 1870s saw narrow skirts with bustles at the back, and trains 'with which we assisted the municipality to clean the streets'. Wide skirts could be good for games, as young Iley Hoddinott found. The children would hide under their grandmother's skirts, and their mother would dutifully ask her if she had seen them. 'No dear, I think they went outside', would be the answer. 'Of course it happened so often they all knew, but it was fun.' The huge skirts must have also made dresses expensive, but photographs show that even poor women could make a fashionable display when dressed in their best. Probably many clothes were handed down among families.

Small waists were fashionable and women wore corsets, called stays. In 1838 Ann Hordern advertised that she had received a consignment of ten thousand stays for her Sydney shop, as well as 'a quantity of large sized French stays'. This was no accident. When she started her shop in 1825, she asked her mother to send out large stays 'as women's [sizes] run large'. Perhaps, with abundant food and a healthy climate, Australian women were not so much fat as generally large – by now they were taller than their English counterparts.

As well as being responsible for the family wardrobe, women dealt with health. Medical knowledge was limited, doctors were few and expensive, and hospitals were mainly for the destitute, so women provided remedies. These varied from soothing drinks like camomile tea, and home-made 'medicines' like poultices, to commercial medicines like castor oil. Mary Jane Hunter in Tasmania wrote several cures in her recipe book. For a sore throat, simmer a slice of bacon in vinegar then wrap it in muslin and apply to the throat. Pineapple juice never fails to cure diphtheria. Foreign bodies in the throat can be removed by forcibly blowing in the ear. Cobwebs stop bleeding. A Queensland girl described how when chopping wood her father nearly cut off his big toe. Her mother tried everything to stop the bleeding, even putting

Women's lib in the 1870s

Mary Ann Merchant chose emigration to Australia over becoming a governess in England. 'The worst decision I ever made', she used to tell her son. 'Where are the gas lights and footpaths?' She married a farmer, had ten children of whom four died young, and helped with everything, including the ploughing. One day her husband complained that she was not ploughing in a straight line. 'She left the paddock never to return and would only look after the house and children (her women's lib in 1870)', wrote her descendant Barbara Brown-Parker. 'Grandpa admired his mother for her stand, for as the eldest son he did what he was told.'

There are other stories of women defying their husbands. In Western Australia, Mary Ann Church broke her husband's leg, and he told police he was in bodily fear of her. Ellen Ryan married at sixteen, and six years later, in 1873, she and her husband went to the gold rushes in the Northern Territory. Ellen realised where the real wealth lay, and a few weeks later took out the licence of the local hotel. She was the first to run anything more than a gin shanty, and was extremely successful, eventually building a fine hotel in Darwin and breeding racehorses. This was all without William, for in 1877 she left him, owing to his threats, cruelty and drunkenness. She paid him £50 to go away, which, reported the local paper, he did gladly.

the foot in a bowl of flour (!) but eventually set the children to gather cobwebs and applied them, which did the trick. Mary Mowle used her doctor-father's remedy for flu, soaking the feet in hot water and taking 'a glass of hot stuff'. Not every woman liked being an angel of mercy, and Mary 'abominated' nursing sick children.

Mary Gilmore recalled how plants were used as remedies: bottle-brush soaked in water made a syrup for sore throats, wattle-bark was made into a lotion for burns, eucalyptus vapour helped chills and pains. Opium was sold by hawkers, Chinese and white. Addicts among 'decent people' were rare, said Mary, but they did include some station owners. 'Ordinary people' took opium in its more respectable form of laudanum, as a sedative, like aspirin later.

With childcare, cooking, housework, sewing and nursing, one might wonder if Sarah had time for anything else, and some women of the time wondered this too. 'The same old story, get up, dress the children, feed the poultry, breakfast, go to work, put Kate to sleep, hear Florence her lesson, dine, read, feed chickens, work till sunset, feed chickens, stroll about till dusk, put Kate to bed, have tea, undress the others – play for an hour (my chief solace) work till eleven, go to bed & rise next morning to recommence the same routine', wrote Mary Mowle ('play' referred to the piano, and 'work' to needlework, 'everlasting & must-be-done needlework'). The next section is blacked over but includes 'what a life to lead what a waste of existence? what will it lead to ...'.

Even Mary had some recreation, in reading and playing the piano, which were enjoyed by many women. Observers were astounded at the number of even poor homes which had a piano. Other pleasures were walking and riding, and from the early days Australian women loved swimming. Entertainment generally had to be organised by the participants, and people enjoyed communal occasions like picnics and dances, which ranged from informal family affairs to much grander occasions. Mrs Manning in Sydney described an evening party for about twenty-five people. At the start people did puzzles or told fortunes and tea was handed round, then the table was moved to a corner and someone played a tune for dancing. Mrs Manning did not allow much loitering between dances, though sometimes they had a song, and generally a table of men played cards in a corner. At about 11.00 pm, refreshments appeared, sandwiches of whatever they happened to have, cakes and sliced oranges. There were no knives, forks or plates and people ate or not as they liked. To drink there was 'very inexpensive wine' and water.

Christmas was the main family celebration. Mary Mowle's Christmas consisted of presents, prayers, roast beef and plum pudding, then a stroll on the beach, 'quiet happiness'. Young Mary McConnel described Christmas in her Queensland home. Although the temperature was over 100°F (about 40°C) all the British customs were observed. The hall was decorated with glossy-leaved branches and good wishes written on linen, and a church service was held. Dinner consisted of roast turkey and champagne, plum pudding and mince pies, with the shutters closed to keep out the blinding light. Only bunches of grapes and watermelons 'recalled us to our torrid surroundings'. In the evening there was a Christmas tree with gifts, spangles and candles, and someone dressed up as Father Christmas.

Australian customs took over on Boxing Day, with horse races and a picnic. Women and girls wore their new gowns, neighbours splashed through the creek, tents were put up, there were kegs of ginger ale and laundry baskets of ripe fruit, and competition in the races was keen. The day ended with a dance in the schoolhouse, and as children slept, 'the throbbing of the accordion and the sound of time-beating feet on the floor were soon part of their dreams'.

All this recreation sounds reasonably egalitarian, but nineteenth-century Australia did have its social distinctions, 'as marked as the division between night and day', said Mary Gilmore. In England social distinctions were based on birth, background and money; in Australia money and respectable behaviour were the requirements, which meant that people could raise themselves by their own efforts. So descendants of convicts could rejoin society, if they earned enough and behaved respectably, and never said anything about their past.

One family could have a mixture of social levels. Margaret Scarlett's father was the stationmaster at Redfern in Sydney. He forbade her to marry his friend, wealthy Chinese merchant Quong Tart, so she waited until she was twenty-one then married him. Her father erased her name from the family and forbade anyone to speak to her or he would cut them off without a shilling, though her sister Isabella gave him a shilling and went to see her. Isabella herself married Colonel Croker, officer and gentleman, whose family looked down on the Scarletts. However, when Isabella's son Jack married Gwen Bucknell, Gwen's landowning family looked down on the landless Crokers; but Gwen's mother had been a Brooks, wealthier landowners, who looked down on the Bucknells. So there was a chain of five families, all looking down on each other. To top it all off, the Brooks at the top of the pile were descended from a convict, which they did not know.

When a woman like Isabella Croker moved up the social scale, she had to learn quickly how she was expected to behave, and etiquette books emerged. *Australian Etiquette* explained the rather daunting behaviour expected of the 'true lady'. She was an expert on the niceties of introducing people to each other, knowing when to leave calling cards and so on. In the street she was 'wrapped in a mantle of proper reserve, so impenetrable that insult and coarse familiarity shrink from her, while she, at the same time, carries with her a congenial atmosphere which attracts all, and puts all at their ease'. There are no instructions as to how she manages the simultaneous mixture of reserve and friendliness; probably such books described the ideal rather than what people actually did.

Elsie Devlin, living on a country station in New South Wales, received clearer instructions. By the time she was six, she was determined to be 'a lady with a capital "L"', and she and her sister used to play 'ladies', wearing their mother's old dresses, bonnets and gloves. Once she was about to go out with her father and he noticed she had not put on her gloves. 'No lady ever performs part of her toilet in public', he admonished her. 'Am I a lady?' she asked. Her father answered that he hoped she would be one day.

Priorities in a fire

Fire was always a danger in wooden houses, and Bessie Bussell of Western Australia described how her family coped when this disaster struck. One evening she was reading a letter with her brothers Ally and Len, 'when Emma came in very calmly and said "The house is on fire, Mr. Len." ... I said "Ally, I shall go and save the Encyclopaedias". So she carried out the books, Ally and Len pulled out furniture, Emma saved kitchen articles, a second servant Phoebe was 'beyond compare', and all in all 'we have saved wonderfully, but lost immensely'. Bessie herself lost all but a couple of dresses and a pair of stays – but she saved the Encyclopaedias.

'A true lady always treats others as she would like to be treated, is polite to others, even if they are rude to her and always be ready to be helpful to others less fortunate than herself.' In later life Elsie mused, 'I wonder did I ever achieve my ambition to be a Lady – with a capital L. I have very grave doubts about it at times'.

Being a Lady was important to the upper social echelons, but how important was it to the majority of Australian women? Many do not mention it, but the tone of women's writings implies that for most, being a lady was not the central concern. Women had fewer servants, they had to do more work themselves, they did not have the time to bother so much with social niceties, and Elsie's lighthearted, almost facetious, approach to being a Lady seems reasonably typical of the attitude of many.

Probably more from kindness than ladylike requirements, many women did help the unfortunate. Most did so privately, assisting family, neighbours and sometimes employees, but there were a few women's societies, helping hospitals or orphanages. Often this was from a religious motive, for by the Victorian period the churches had grown more influential. Many women had genuine religious convictions, of course, but even for doubters, church was attractive. Often religious observation was the only uplifting area in a hard-working existence. When a woman had spent the week labouring from dawn until dusk, what a relief it must have been to dress everyone in good clothes and go to church, where she acted in accordance with religious beliefs, heard encouraging sentiments and pleasant music, won general approval for correct behaviour, and sat down for an hour. Afterwards there were friends to be met and clothes to inspect. Inner refreshment came not only from religion but from books and poetry, and from the landscape, 'the quiet dreamy charm of the mountains', of trees and flowers. Mary Gilmore loved to watch poplar leaves falling, chain lightning in a storm, the white trunks of newly stripped gum trees.

There were other outlets for women's talents. Girls often learnt to draw and some went on to become excellent artists, and combined this with scientific interest. Margaret Forrest was best known as a Western Australian premier's devoted wife, but she was also a fine illustrator of wild flowers and enjoyed extended painting excursions with her friend Ellis Rowan. Ellis was particularly intrepid, hauling herself up a cliff face by rope to find unusual flowers.

Art and music were part of the general civilising effect of women, often noted and praised. Jane Grant married a pastoralist in the remote north-west of Australia in 1875, and moved to the station. A woman visitor wrote, 'You seem to have jumped from barbarism to civilization since Mrs Grant's advent. What a marvellous influence we charming women have. What would become of you poor miserable men without us?'

Women could also demonstrate courage and fortitude at a time when communities were rough and police forces still being formed. Margaret and Sandy Morrison lived at Yan Yean, Victoria, in the 1850s. Sandy liked a drink or two, and would take the dray to the nearby 'Rose, Shamrock and Thistle', leaving Margaret to tend the farm and their nine children. One day, Ned Kelly and his bushranging gang rode through, and Margaret later found that one of the horses was missing, a strawberry roan. Months later the Kelly gang rode through again, so Margaret confronted them, accusing Ned of stealing her roan and demanding to examine his horses. Ned gave in, and Margaret examined the horses and recovered her roan.

A feature of stories of women's lives is the great strength many showed, sometimes physical, more often mental. Jane Yates' husband Benjamin was transported to Australia in 1824, and after several years, Jane and three children were allowed to join him. They arrived to find that Benjamin had a second conviction, and was working in a chain gang. Over the next three years Jane, illiterate and with no status in the colony, sent the governor five petitions pleading for Benjamin to be assigned to her, and was finally rewarded. At the other end of society's spectrum, Christiana Brooks' mother had a great interest in politics, and wrote her views so firmly ('I quite agree with the Chief Justice ...'; or of the Bank of New South Wales, 'its Directors must learn prudence and limit discounts ...') that it has been suggested her diary was really written by a man, on no other evidence.

In the nineteenth century, the number of Australian women was constantly being added to by emigrants, most from Britain. 'We are both very well pleased with Sydney, and think we shall get on here very well', wrote twenty-year-old Jeannie Young. The house she and her husband Edward lived in was unlike those in England. It was plain, with seven rooms and a large yard, where Edward chopped wood and gardened. 'Indeed he makes quite a general servant of himself, and is quite a help to me. In the evening he reads aloud while I sew or knit.' They both 'felt better than at home'; the weather was splendid, and they enjoyed sails on the harbour and rides to the coast. Costs were the same, and altogether Jeannie had no complaints.

After bearing and raising children, keeping the house, enjoying some recreation, charitable work and spiritual stimulation, what then happens to Sarah? Though many lived to a ripe old age, often helping daughters to care for their families, the average woman died younger, and in the 1850s life expectancy for white Australians was 46. By the time of the 1881 census, again for whites only, life expectancy for women was 52, and for men 49.

Reading books and newspapers of the period, one might think that the Victorian ideal provided Australian women with happy, fulfilling lives, staying at home, absorbed in their family, with few aspirations to earn money or enter public life. In many cases it did, but later research makes it clear that for many women, life was anything but ideal. Sometimes women had to earn, or family life was destroyed by disease or death, or a marriage was inadequate. Legally, women had almost no power: they could not vote, their husbands owned their property, and it was expected that a man represent them. Many women had happy family relationships and their fathers and husbands looked after them satisfactorily, but if things went wrong, they could be in a difficult position.

A major cause of problems was unsatisfactory marriage. The husband could fail to earn a living through low wages, unemployment or being in jail; he could be alcoholic or violent; he could desert the family or die; or husband and wife could be incompatible. This happened in many families, from poor to wealthy. Divorce was impossible until the 1850s, but even then it was difficult. A man could sue for divorce on the grounds of adultery alone; a woman had to have grounds of adultery as well as incest, sodomy, bigamy, rape, desertion or cruelty. Divorce and judicial separation were also expensive and unacceptable socially, so only a handful of couples took the plunge.

The official attitude was shown when a woman petitioned for a judicial separation because her husband ill-treated her – beating her and chasing her from the house with a hatchet. The judge dismissed her petition, saying that a wife should ensure her safety by obedience to her husband; she was supposed to be subject to him, and it was her duty to put up with his failings. So if women were hit by their husbands, it was their own fault. No wonder that when a woman complained of her husband beating her, an Anglican clergyman's wife advised her to fill her mouth with water to stop herself provoking him with spiteful answers. The woman replied that the Catholic nuns had already recommended this.

One woman who struggled to live married life as society expected was Matilda Wallace. In 1859, aged twenty-one, she emigrated from Somerset to join her brother and sister in Adelaide. On leaving home, she wrote in her memoirs, she had made up her mind to make the best of everything, and she had to start this on her first day in Australia. After landing she was given a puzzling drink of 'shandy-gaff' (probably beer and lemonade), then walked through ankle-deep sand and travelled by railway, coach and horse-back to her sister's house, to be greeted with a 'coo-ey' by her brother-in-law – all very novel.

Two years later Matilda married Abraham Wallace, an Irish emigrant who lived at Mount Gambier. Tragedy struck when their first baby died. Abraham, always restless, did not want to stay in the area, so they set out for Queensland with a wagon and horses, sleeping in the wagon at night. By this time Matilda was pregnant again. The sand in the Mallee came up to the horses' knees, and a shepherd told Abraham he should not have brought his wife to such an area. When they reached Mount Murchison Matilda fell ill from drinking bad water, so Abraham decided to stay and open a shop. He sent for goods, but the plan petered out and he went off to try to sell the goods at surrounding stations.

Matilda, left alone, was terrified when a group of Aborigines camped nearby, as she had been told that they ate white people. They turned out to be friendly, giving her eggs and saying they would not have left a lubra by herself. Matilda nearly burnt the house down trying to smoke out mosquitoes, then, when

Women in the wine trade

Mary and Christopher Penfold arrived in Adelaide in 1844, where Christopher practised as a doctor. They planted a vineyard round their home and made fortified wines for patients, and as Christopher's health declined, Mary and her servant Ellen Timbrell developed the wine-growing business. Christopher died, and with Mary as proprietor and blender, Penfold Wines grew to be the largest wine business in Australia.

Similarly, in 1853 Buxton and Mary Laurie established the Southcote vineyards near Port Elliot. After Buxton died in 1876, Mary continued wine-growing, as well as raising eight children, running cattle and keeping an orchard. She was South Australia's first registered woman vigneron and wine maker.

Abraham returned after a month away, 'I was very ill indeed for three weeks, having a little son and losing him'.

They reached Queensland, after dramas with floods and thirst and hunger – at one stage they were down to one tin of sardines – but could not take stock across the border, so returned to Mount Murchison. They spent the next decade moving round inland New South Wales and South Australia (it is difficult to tell from Matilda's memoirs exactly where), never in the same place for longer than six months. Abraham, wrote Matilda, 'was of such a roving disposition and such an explorer by nature, that he used to go away for weeks at a time', looking for land to settle, buying sheep and occasionally taking sheep or wool to market, then, when the land turned out to be unsuitable because it lacked water or belonged to someone else, looking for new land. They were dogged by problems such as lack of water or food, immense heat, floods and unreliable assistants. Though Matilda was too loyal to say so, Abraham was clearly not a good organiser.

Matilda had little say in what was happening and was often left by herself to cope as best she could. She decided early on that she did not want to be alone, but this had no effect on Abraham, though for a while she did have a ten-year-old nephew for company. Once in the ten years, she started to cry when Abraham announced that he was leaving again, at which, she wrote, he seemed quite hurt, saying it was poor comfort to think of his wife being so sentimental.

In her matter-of-fact way, Matilda told story after story of her activities. When Abraham was away she often had to look after the thousands of sheep, drenching them, finding water, scaring off wild dogs or overseeing lambing – which she did successfully, with the help of the best of her assistants, 'an old lubra'. Although Aborigines were friendly and never harmed her, she remained afraid of them, and they often camped near her. Another alarming event happened when she woke one morning to see a policeman pointing a revolver at her, having mistaken her for a criminal.

Even when Abraham was there, things were not always easy. At one shearing time, both Abraham and the hired man hurt themselves, so Matilda had to finish the job, 'which I may here tell you was a great success', she wrote proudly. On another occasion there was a rat invasion, and once Matilda spent two days taking burrs from Abraham's feet.

Matilda never seemed to think of leaving Abraham and returning to her family, but supported him throughout. She showed most sorrow when two babies, born in the outback, died very young. When her fifth baby was due she went to Menindee, the first time in seven years she saw 'civilization'. The inhabitants of the town had heard about her life and expected to see a big, rough woman, she wrote, so were surprised to find her small and delicate. Her baby daughter lived, though after three weeks Matilda had to take her back to camp, where the infant became ill. Abraham promptly took sheep to Adelaide, and Matilda found her baby a great comfort. 'I often prayed fervently to the Lord to spare my darling to me.'

On Abraham's return he wanted Matilda to accompany him on their next move, but with the baby so young and herself in delicate health she was unwilling. 'Was she going to give in now?' asked Abraham, and he promised (as one can imagine he had promised all through these years) that if she would keep going for six months, they would have a settled home. 'I made up my mind to try once more and do my best', wrote Matilda.

Finally, in 1872, they did find a permanent home, setting up Sturt's Meadows station in the Barrier Ranges, about eighty kilometres north of Broken Hill. Abraham also established Elsey cattle station in the Northern Territory, later the setting for Jeannie Gunn's book *We of the Never-Never*. In 1884 he appointed managers and the family retired to a new house at Reynella, but only a few months later Abraham was found bleeding to death, having cut his throat. 'Oh, Abe, why did you do it?' cried Matilda, and he replied, 'I am tired of the world and the world is tired of me'. His obituary described Abraham as 'this splendid pastoral pathfinder', but from his treatment of his wife, one might well describe him in less glowing terms.

At least Matilda did not have to suffer violence or abuse, as many women did, though this was an unsavoury aspect of life which people hushed up at the time. In the 1850s Isabella Marshall ran away from an arranged marriage in Ireland to Adelaide, where she married a shoe-maker. Her husband turned out to be a ne'er-do-well, 'a waster and gambler', who eventually disappeared, leaving Isabella with seven children. She kept them by dressmaking, and in 1876 married Ernst Promnitz. This was a disaster. She bore triplets, who died; a daughter was kicked by a horse and admitted to a mental institution; and Ernst was a paedophile, who abused the youngest daughter and made sexual approaches to the grandchildren.

The family moved to a farm on the Mallee, where Isabella described her life as near to slavery. She arranged for the youngest daughter to live with her son and his wife, but the son, seeing himself as head of the family, forbade her to leave Ernst. Eventually they returned to Adelaide and, not surprisingly, Isabella 'took to the sherry'. Family tradition has it that she was a 'hard woman' – again, perhaps not surprisingly, with the difficulties she had faced in life.

Some women did leave unhappy marriages. Ann Crebbin told her children that when their ship was wrecked on the voyage to Australia, her husband John was first into the lifeboat, concerned only for his own safety. This obviously rankled. They stayed together for a while, trying then abandoning farming, and moving to Melbourne where three children were born, but in 1865

Australia's first woman minister

The Unitarians were a small Protestant group with independent congregations, and the Melbourne church was having difficulty finding a minister. Martha Turner was visiting her brother, who sometimes preached there, and she occasionally took his place. In 1873 she was elected minister, and bravely preached on the text, 'Let your women keep silent in Church', emphasising individual responsibility. She married, but continued as minister until 1883. An intellectual woman who liked 'quiet loafing', Martha Turner inspired Catherine Helen Spence, who became a lay preacher at the Adelaide Unitarian church.

they parted company. Ann went to live with William Wilson, and after John went back to Britain, she married William, stating that she was a spinster. This marriage appeared happier; at any rate, they had six children and remained together. Leaving your husband for another man was not socially acceptable, however, and it was a brave woman who took this step.

Another way in which life could be disrupted was by children's deaths, and there are many sad examples. Elizabeth and John McCallum and their eleven children had a sheep farm on the Eyre Peninsula, and Elizabeth was so used to childbirth that one morning when a visitor said he heard crying, she answered, as she cooked the breakfast, 'Yes, we had a bonny wee boy born in the night'. In 1872 their eldest son, at school in the nearby town of Port Lincoln, caught diphtheria. His parents went to nurse him, but he died. They returned home, burning their clothes to avoid carrying infection, but the other children caught the disease.

Hiding the Convict Stain

Families went to great lengths to hide descent from convicts, which if known and talked about was a social disgrace, but which could be hidden successfully. Sarah Bunker, the daughter of First Fleet convicts, married a convict who drowned, married another convict, and altogether had fifteen children. When her daughter Hannah married, Sarah's second husband made the new son-in-law promise to keep the convict origins secret – and the son-in-law himself is thought to have had a similar background.

As far as descendants can untangle the story, Hannah married William Henry Lewis, who died, and his brother William Charles took over the family. Hannah had ten children and proved, said her descendant Ric Richardson, 'exceedingly successful in hiding the truth'. Her grandchildren were told forcefully that there were no convicts in their family, whereas they were descended from three convicts in Hannah's family and probably three in the Lewis family. Research revealed the truth only in the late twentieth century, as has happened with many families.

The Australian Woman

Family tradition has it that an Aboriginal girl ran all the way to Port Lincoln to fetch the doctor, but by the time he arrived two more children had died. He ordered the rest of the family to go to Port Lincoln; tradition continues that for part of the way Elizabeth carried her dying girls in her arms, and could never stand up straight again.

In all, eight of her children died, the family Bible recording the deaths of John (16), Annie (18), Janet (12), Mary (10), Duncan (8), Thomas (6), Robert (4) and Elizabeth (2), all within eight weeks. Margaret (20), James (15) and John senior fell ill but recovered, and Elizabeth and the baby escaped the disease. Overall, over fifty people died in the district.

Another heart-rending episode happened on a Queensland station, the home of Jane Bardsley and her family. The station was being painted, and one of the painters gave three-year-old Jim Bardsley a paintbrush and a tin of water to play with. He became ill, blue round the mouth, and a doctor diagnosed lead poisoning from the paintbrush, and said there was no hope. Jane and her husband put Jim to bed between them. 'Mummie, cover me over I can see snakes everywhere, they are all over Daddy too', he wept. In the morning he was jet black around his mouth, but still tried to smile. Jane saw death creeping over his face, and his last words were 'Kiss me Daddy, quick'. 'I can write no more, my eyes are filled with tears', Jane ended.

A major problem for women was sexual abuse by men. In a pioneer society where many men could not find a female partner and many were of dubious character, sexual abuse was a strong possibility. Women suffered socially if they were suspected of having sex outside marriage – at the Castlemaine goldfield one girl took strychnine rather than face gossip about the married man in a nearby tent having 'taken liberties' with her – and even more if they became pregnant. Yet women, physically weaker than men, could often do little against male persuasion, promises of marriage or physical compulsion. Female servants were particularly vulnerable if the master of the house thought sex was part of their duties.

The problems of bearing illegitimate children are shown by the life of Isabella Williams. In 1853, aged fourteen, she became a servant for James and Rose Joy of Derrimut near Melbourne, both former convicts and now small farmers. Five years later Isabella and Rose appeared in court, as witnesses in one of James' many court cases against his neighbours, usually over straying stock. The local newspaper described Isabella as young, about nineteen. When cross-examined, wrote the reporter, she was bold and defiant. She did not know how old she was. She could read a little, but not write. She had not heard from her father for five years, and her mother was not mentioned. As the Joys' servant she earned £10 a year. She had three children. Their father was her business. Yes, she slept in the same room as James and Rose Joy, though not in the same bed. Mrs Joy did not object to her being there. The opposing lawyer said he scarcely knew what to call the two ladies concerned. Since he had to make some distinction between them – whether Mr Joy did or not – he would call them Mrs Joy No 1 and Mrs Joy No 2. When James Joy was questioned, the lawyer tried in vain to 'browbeat anything like shame' into him as he was 'evidently shame-proof', and joked about the children and his convict past.

The Joys' situation was clearly well known in the neighbourhood: Isabella, the servant girl, bore children regularly to her employer, with Rose Joy acting as midwife. The three adults continued to live and work together apparently happily, and twelve children were born and grew up on the farm. The neighbours could joke about the situation, but Isabella's situation was in fact precarious. She had no family, and there was no one to help her if she needed it; she was paid very little; she had no qualifications for other work, and it would be difficult for her to leave; and she had little alternative but to go along with James and Rose whether she wanted to or not. Once the children were born she was even more closely tied to the Joys. Despite all these disadvantages, she managed to stand up for herself against the ridicule of the lawyer, though he was older, educated, qualified, middle class and male, and she managed to establish a reasonably comfortable life for herself.

Of course, she might have been happy in the situation, and

> **A mother copes with disease**
>
> The diary of Emma Thomson, in outback Western Australia, shows how difficult it could be for a mother to deal with family illness. In October 1860, baby Guy had a nasty cold and two-year-old May had chicken pox and a cough, which became whooping cough. In November she was still sick, and Emma gave her a warm bath then a mustard poultice on her chest. 'Poor little pet very ill all night.' In December several neighbouring children died from measles and May was again ill. Everyone's health seemed better in 1861, when Emma had her third baby, but in January 1862 Guy was 'very poorly with his chest' for a fortnight. Remedies were first laudanum and castor oil, then the bath and poultice treatment.

from available evidence the Joys treated her quite well. Ten years later she was established on her own farm nearby, presumably with their help, and rate books described her as 'Isabella Williams, farmer'. When she was only thirty-nine she caught a heavy cold, which turned to pneumonia, and she died.

If a woman became pregnant and did not want or could not keep the baby, she could procure an abortion. Some doctors and midwives performed them, and various abortifacients were available, though abortion could end in the woman's death. Some women resorted to infanticide. In 1874 a baby's body was discovered in a Sydney public garden, wrapped in calico. A note pinned to it said that the baby's mother and father were Protestants, attending St Andrew's Cathedral. To avoid 'the shame that hangs over every woman who stoops to folly' the mother was going to the North Shore to dive into eternity. She left it to God and her seducer's conscience to punish him. It is hard to know how many such cases existed, for they were hushed up if possible, as were abortions and illegitimate children.

Even if a woman was well treated by her menfolk, another reason for her life being far from ideal was the amount of sheer hard work often necessary to make a living. This was the case for farmers and especially selectors, who could choose land to set up a farm and pay it off in easy stages. Even selectors who were successful in the end faced difficulties starting out, as shown in Dorothy Maguire's family. The Maguires, Irish farmers, were devastated when three children died within a fortnight. They emigrated to New South Wales and spent seven happy years working for 'the kindest and finest employers', Father as overseer at a cattle station, Mother running the dairy and the children helping with odd jobs and going to school. The family wanted to be independent, however, and as soon as the Selection Act was passed, they selected fifty acres in Kangaroo Valley. The land was fertile and well watered, but heavily timbered and isolated, with the nearest shop in Wollongong, two days' ride over the mountains.

The family consisted of the parents and the children, Edward (15), Catherine (13), Dorothy (10) and three younger ones. Their father made a hut of slabs with a bark roof and earth floor, then, wrote Dorothy, 'we settled down to a life of hard struggle and toil'. With primitive tools they cleared the land, 'very hard work'. They had no clock, and had to guess the time by tree shadows, and 'the hourly laugh of the Jackass, called the Settlers' Clock'.

Once the land was cleared, they planted, hoed, reaped, stacked, threshed and ground their wheat, and made damper. When they bought the 'luxury' of a camp oven, they could make bread, with yeast from their own hops. They tried growing arrowroot, but there was no market for it and they fed it to the calves. They kept cows, grew fruit and vegetables and were never idle, but 'we never complained', though there was plenty they could have complained about. Crops failed, and there were droughts, bush fires, caterpillars, grasshoppers, floods, snakes 'etc', wrote Dorothy. It was her job to keep birds off crops, which meant 'running up and down all day to frighten them'. They obtained honey and wax from wild bees, and made their own candles. The girls bleached young cabbage tree leaves and made hats, which they sold to stockmen at ten shillings each.

The Aborigines were numerous but did no harm, and the family gave them food whenever they asked. Dorothy enjoyed watching the men climb trees to catch possums. Other activities which she lists as amusements were meeting packs of dingoes, branding calves and breaking in young bullocks to yokes made by Edward. Once the bullocks were broken in, they carried heavy loads; before then, the family did this. 'I was mostly the pack horse.'

Edward, handy with tools, built a larger house, and Dorothy helped her father fell trees and crosscut them, then make fences, 'very heavy work for a frail girl'. The family selected more land, eventually 500 acres. 'Father and I put up the boundary fence all round.' She also churned butter and helped in the paddocks, and after the day's chores were done, did the sewing, cleaning and housework at night, by candlelight. She obviously resented the never-ending work, but 'there was no use saying No, I do not ever remember giving my Father or Mother a back answer'.

Finally the hard work paid off. They had a large farm, fifty cows and extensive crops, and 'from now on we became prosperous'. As more selectors arrived, a township grew up and people agitated for a school then a church. Community activities began, and the girls sewed and cooked for tea parties, bazaars and

A Collingwood foundling

Annie Gold was a foundling, discovered abandoned in a front yard in Gold Street, Collingwood, on a cold June morning. Another baby girl found that day died of exposure, but Annie, wrapped in an old coat, survived. She was cared for by the state: called after the street where she was found, sent to live with a series of four foster families, then at thirteen sent to work as a servant. At twenty-nine she married, and had seven children. Despite this unpromising start in life, Annie was a cheerful home-maker, who delighted in welcoming her own children and sang her way through her chores. She had a devoted husband, an abiding sense of humour, a loving attitude, and considered her life rich and fulfilling, although she and her husband were not wealthy and lived in a modest home. Sadly, Annie died quite young, of uterine cancer.

concerts. Father bought horses for his daughters, who broke them into side-saddle. Dorothy's memoirs end when a bridge over the Shoalhaven River was opened. They all had a day off, a bullock was roasted whole, speeches were made, and everyone tried to be first to ride across. Dorothy was proud to be the second girl to cross the Shoalhaven Bridge on horseback. All that hard work did her no harm: she married, had seven children and died aged ninety-one.

Another group of women who went outside the domestic limits prescribed for females were those in paid employment. Many women worked outside the home, to support themselves, supplement the family income, or assist in a family enterprise such as a farm or shop, sometimes taking this over when a husband died. By 1881, over a quarter of the total workforce were women, and a quarter of Australian women were in full-time employment. Many more worked part-time, and it is difficult to find a woman who did no work apart from housework at some stage in her life. I thought I had found one in Sarah Leake, sister of a grazier, who could write in her diary that she gave orders to the cook and spent the rest of the day reading; but even she acted as her nieces' governess.

By far the most common work, employing 60 per cent of those full-timers in 1881, was domestic service. Many working-class girls went into service at fourteen or so, and worked until they married. They gained experience in housework and some pay, and the middle-class gained servants. Conditions were generally poor – long hours, low pay, monotonous work, and worst of all a menial position – so Australian girls did not like becoming servants, but often it was the only job available.

There were few professional jobs open to women. Many were interested in the arts, painting, writing, playing music or acting, often with great skill and dedication. There were few opportunities to earn a living in this way, however. Teaching was the most common profession for those who had to support themselves or their families, and as primary school systems expanded in the 1870s, demand increased. In 1877 the scattered community near

Morwell in Victoria was given a school and Zenna Rintoull, a seventeen-year-old farmer's daughter, became the teacher. The school was the usual slab hut with a thatched roof and earth floor, and in winter rain poured in between the slabs, leaving the floor awash. Zenna walked along planks through the puddles. Thirty children aged from five to twelve were enrolled, but the average attendance was only sixteen, and this dropped sharply to seven after a snake was found in the classroom. Zenna continued to teach successfully, and two years later married the local blacksmith, but kept on teaching until only a few weeks before the birth of her first child. She continued to act as relieving teacher, though she had young children.

Women could also open schools of their own, which generally meant setting up a table and chairs in one room of the house and advertising for pupils – there were no regulations. Because most such schools were of low standard and tended to come and go, they did not provide a secure living. These teachers were almost all untrained, and teaching, like most women's jobs, involved women using the skills they had learnt at home in the wider community – running hotels and boarding houses, cooking, sewing, childcare, prostitution. A typical job where women used their family skills was that of the midwife. Susanna Massey had a hard life even before she was widowed. Her husband William, feckless at the best of times, was transported to Tasmania for theft, and she was left in England with six children to care for. After two years she was allowed to join him, but it must have been a sad trip: a daughter died of cholera, conditions were cramped, food was poor, and the journey took four months. In Tasmania they joined William at the farm where he worked and Susanna bore four more children, but then William died.

Susanna, in her forties, was left to care for eight children. She worked as a servant and farm labourer for William's employer, and as a midwife for the community, assisting everyone from the employer's wife downwards. She also taught her daughter Mary Ann her nursing skills. A year later she married again, and a few months later bore another child. The family moved to Colac in Victoria, where both Susanna and Mary Ann worked as midwives.

Mary Ann's daughter Louisa continued the family tradition. When she was fifteen she married Charles Merrin, a convict exile, whose engaging personality made people forgive a few further minor transgressions of the law, like non-payment of bills. Louisa

Irish orphans in Australia

The Irish potato famine of the 1840s left many children orphaned, and the British Government sent many girls in particular as emigrants to Australia, to become servants and wives in a country short of both. Once landed, these girls had to try to establish themselves, and the following stories show what could happen to them.

Sixteen-year-old Sarah Arbuckle found a job soon after landing in Melbourne, and within a year married Joseph Richardson, a hard-working, astute ex-convict, who bought and sold land, making a good profit. The family had a farm on Phillip Island, where they grew chicory and had a chicory kiln – chicory was used in making coffee essence. Sarah and Joseph had twelve children, of whom eleven survived to adulthood. Joseph died in 1892 and Sarah ran his estate very competently, charging farmers to use the chicory kiln, employing men to do digging and fencing, making and selling butter, lending money to her sons. She and Joseph kept a deep secret of their origins, convict and poor Irish, which was only discovered by their descendants in the 1990s.

Bridget Kenny was also sixteen when she arrived in Sydney. She travelled to Yass where she had a cousin and started to work as a servant, but her mistress had a violent temper and in a few months Bridget moved to a second job. Three years later she married Hugh Keon, a farm hand. They had a son, then before their daughter was born, Hugh was jailed. Bridget left with the children, and worked as a housekeeper. Sadly her son drowned, aged eight. Within a few years Hugh died, and Bridget married a German migrant and miner. They lived in a makeshift residence on the Young goldfields and Bridget gave birth to a son, then to twins, but died a week after the birth, along with one twin. She was only thirty-five.

bore him thirteen children, then like her grandmother was widowed, and had to earn a living. She too became a midwife for the local community. Between them, the three generations of women worked as midwives for fifty years. However, when Louisa died in her seventies, the local paper identified her only as the widow of Charles Merrin, with no mention of her own contribution to the community, an example of the lack of importance given to women's work.

Hardly any women lived away from their families – the few single women were expected to stay at home and help – but one exception was Catholic nuns, who came from Britain to spread God's word and provide education and health care. This was very much part of the Victorian ideal, women bringing moral uplift and civilisation. In 1846 the Sisters of Mercy under Mother Ursula Frayne arrived in Perth, to train Aborigines and European children. They arrived on a Friday and found the church dusty and shabby, with an old counter for the altar. By Sunday it was dusted and swept, with the floorboards nailed down, a calico ceiling, and a temporary altar decorated with calico and gold paper. The Sisters began a school attended even by the Protestant minister's children, and also visited the sick, but their only vehicle was a cart drawn by oxen, which stopped as they were used to at certain hotels. Nothing the driver did would budge them, to the Sisters' mortification.

Mother Ursula's independence and lack of docility irked the local Catholic authorities, and she went to Melbourne, where she ran a convent school for young ladies, a ragged school for poor children, an orphanage and a refuge for immigrant girls. Shrewd, witty, strong and very successful, Mother Ursula made a noteworthy contribution to Australian society.

The best known woman's name of this period belongs to another woman who made a noteworthy contribution, Maria Smith. She and her husband Thomas were orchardists in Sydney, and Maria sold fruit in the markets, where she was well known as Granny Smith. She was interested in growing apples, and developed a new variety. One day she brought home a gin case which contained the rotting remains of French crab apples. She tipped the mess in the creek, a seedling grew from it, and the family were impressed by the flavour of its apples. Maria planted seedlings taken from this tree, experimented with grafts, and gave cuttings to neighbouring orchardists. The apple's value for eating and cooking made it popular, eventually one of the most sought-after varieties in the world, but Maria did not live to see it, for she died in 1870. 'Smith's seedling' was first documented in 1890, and soon became the Granny Smith, a 'sport' or fixed mutation, described as a cross between the French crab and the Rome Beauty. To the irritation of Maria's descendants, several other places in Australia

Boring cooking

In the Australian classic Seven Little Australians, *Pip complained bitterly when his dinner was boiled mutton and rice pudding again. This food must have been extremely dull, not only to eat, but to cook – but for busy housewives, it was at least easy and quick, while rice pudding was a reasonably cheap way of filling up the family.*

Boiled mutton
Put a leg of mutton in boiling water, adding a little salt. Boil fast for five minutes, then simmer gently, 20 minutes per pound and 20 minutes over. Carrots and turnips may be added. Serve hot with mashed potatoes.

Rice pudding
1 oz rice   1 teaspoon butter
1 dessertspoon sugar   1½ gills water
½ pint milk
Wash the rice three times. Put rice in pie-dish, add water, cook in slow oven until the rice absorbs all the water. Add milk, sugar and butter and mix well. Bake in a very slow oven for 1½ hours.

Making household items at home
Homemade soap
Dissolve 1 lb caustic soda in 3 pints of water. Melt 6 lbs fat, tallow or lard. Let it cool, and add the caustic solution, stirring for two minutes. Pour into a mould lined with moistened cloth,

and even other countries claim the Granny Smith apple, but it undoubtedly came from Sydney, developed by the authentic Granny Smith.

How can we sum up the experiences of white women in the mid-nineteenth century? They had some things in common. They were expected, and usually hoped themselves, to marry. Most found that pregnancy, rearing children and keeping house dominated their lives. Though they undertook a variety of activities inside and outside the home, these were usually as part of a

and stand in a warm place for 24 hours. Remove and cut into blocks, and allow to harden for a month.

A certain cure for boils
Cut up finely a whole root of garlic and cover with a flask of rum. Let it stand a day or so, then take a wineglass every morning, first thing. As it is extremely unpalatable, have a cup of tea all ready to drink.

Mrs Salmon's Walnut Ketchup
Take 100 large walnuts, pound them in a stone mortar with 1/4 lb shallots, 1/2 lb salt, 1 pint good vinegar and 1/2 pint strong beer. Let it stand a week, stirring it two or three times a day. Strain through a flannel bag. Put 1/4 lb anchovies in, boil and skim. Strain again and add some cloves, whole nutmeg, grated black pepper finely crushed. Give the spice a boil and when cool bottle and cork it well.

And a dessert from the days when malnutrition was more of a problem than its opposite:

Custard fritters
Beat the yolks of 8 eggs with a spoonful of flour, half a nutmeg, a little salt and a glass of brandy. Add a pint of cream, sweeten, and bake in a dish. When cold cut into squares. Dip them in a batter made of 1/2 pint of cream, 1/4 pint of milk, 4 eggs, a little flour and grated ginger. Fry in good lard or dripping, then strew them over with grated sugar.

family, and society saw their role as remaining there. They had no right to vote, their husbands owned their property, and few played a part, or were even individually acknowledged, in public life.

This way of life kept almost all women extremely busy, with few who, like Florence Nightingale in England, had little to do and wondered how to fill their lives. Most women had only too much to do; they might not always enjoy it, but with fewer servants, fewer constraining traditions and far more pioneering activity than in Britain, they were certainly fully occupied. Their contribution to the development of their communities was appreciated, at least to a certain extent. This gave them a valued position, which meant that when ideas started to change in the 1880s and many women wanted to move outside the home, Australian women were able to do this more easily than in more traditional societies like Britain.

Snapshot

FOOD

1788	whites arrive eating British food, and continue in this way
1840s	Caroline Chisholm advertises Australia as the place where families eat meat three times a day
1840s	canning of food starts, with meat canned in Sydney (1845) and Newcastle (1847)
1868	Granny Smith develops her apple in Sydney
1870	Arnotts biscuits appear
1880s	tinned foods become widespread, such as meat, fish, vegetables, condensed milk (1882)
1898	Hannah Maclurcan publishes her popular *Mrs. Maclurcan's Cookery Book*
1899	Rosella Preserving and Manufacturing Co. makes its first tomato sauce
1902	the recipe for lamingtons is published
1907	first commercial ice-cream available, at Frederick Peters' factory in Sydney

Snapshot

1923	commercially prepared foods increase: Vegemite and Violet Crumble bars appear
1925	Aeroplane Jelly is first made, in Sydney. The song appears in 1938, sung by five-year-old Joy King
1935	Bert Sachse invents the pavlova, at the Esplanade Hotel in Perth
1939	the first sliced bread appears
1942	wartime rationing begins: first tea, then sugar, and later butter and meat
1951	Chiko Roll created, in Bendigo
1950s	Australian diet includes foreign dishes and moves away from British traditional foods
1960s	frozen food becomes popular
1970s	Asian food becomes popular
1990s	convenience foods widely used, and more people eat regularly at restaurants and from takeaways

chapter three

Building a Nation

The nineteenth century saw great technological changes – such as factories, railways, steamships, electricity – and rapid development in western societies. Ideas also grew that citizens of these countries should be treated more equally and given chances to fulfil their potential, which would also make them more useful to the state. The Australian colonies, with small populations and huge areas to develop, as well as egalitarian traditions from convict and gold rush days, were among the leaders.

Major change came in education, for this was one of the main ways in which people could be helped to make the most of their lives. In the 1870s, primary education became compulsory, for girls and boys alike. This meant huge expansion in government systems, though not everyone was convinced that education was of pre-eminent importance. Christina Houlahan's neighbour at Upper Orara in rural New South Wales was a widow with eight children, and if they did not arrive home straight after school she would fire a gun in the air. The teacher soon got the message – the children were not to be kept in. Their mother needed their help.

There were also private primary schools, some set up by Catholic teaching orders. Like state schools, these had strict discipline, and Kate MacAllan loved to tell her granddaughter Cate how she defied the nuns. A 'taunting miss' sat in front of her, and one day Kate dipped her plait in the inkwell. The nun brought

Kate to the front of the class for punishment, but instead of accepting it in the proper subdued fashion, she landed a punch on the nun's nose. 'I can see it all', wrote Cate. 'The clatter of wooden rosary beads hitting the floor, followed by the graceless thud of the nun – her protective veil tossed asunder, exposing a shaven head – the look of stunned shock on the faces of the students and the glow of satisfaction on Kate's young face.' Her punishment was to tour each classroom for a month and recite the alphabet backwards, something she could still do with verve in old age.

Secondary education for girls had been almost non-existent, but this too increased enormously. In 1879 South Australia set up the Advanced School for Girls, and other states followed. In her novel *Teens*, Louise Mack gives a picture of Sydney Girls' High in

A Sydney childhood

Alice McKee grew up in Sydney, and recalled 'wonderful childhood days where our only cares were torn clothes, or being late home for meals'. Next to the family home was an orange orchard, where the children would eat oranges until the juice 'literally ran from our ears'. They fished and cooled their feet in a nearby creek, or climbed trees after birds' nests.

Fires could be dangerous when women wore long skirts. One morning when Alice's mother was away, her older sister Clarrie was cooking porridge when her skirt caught alight. She threw herself on the floor and rolled about, trying to smother the flames. Alice woke their father, who flung bedclothes around Clarrie and put out the flames. Fortunately she was not badly burnt.

The children loved Empire Day, May 24. They would build a bonfire and save their money for crackers, and on the day itself they wore red, white and blue ribbons to school and sang patriotic songs, especially 'Advance Australia Fair'. At dusk, bonfires were lit and crackers were let off: Catherine wheels, double bungers, basket bombs. 'Truly unforgettable ... how we all enjoyed it, young and old alike.'

the 1890s. Lennie is thirteen when she passes the entry exam, and finds school a 'great, strange world' after lessons at home with her governess. Her class of forty-seven girls loves their teacher, who is strict but fair; they play tennis and informal chasing games, and start a school newspaper. Lennie is sometimes naughty but generally does well, until she fails the matriculation exam. She nurses her mother and teaches her sisters, and her friends become a teacher, an artist, a nurse (which Louise clearly sees as praiseworthy) and a society debutante (superficial).

Many similar private schools were set up, often by churches. They provided academic education as well as training in how to become a young lady (their major attraction over state schools), and often took boarders, so country girls could gain secondary education. Many of these schools were competent, modern establishments. Minnie Clarke, who had started her own education under a needy spinster who did not like children or teaching and was more interested in clean shoes than learning, helped her sister run the Girls' High School in Hobart. In 1911 she wrote in the school magazine: 'Sometimes I look round with a feeling like envy and think: Ah, if I had had the same chance! Your school with its manifold organisations and varied interests, your gymnasium and games, your teaching with its modern methods and constant appeal to the interests and intelligence of the scholars'. Reality was not always so elevated. The present author's grandmother went to a Sydney girls' school, but when her mother visited her, she looked over the wall and caught sight of the man next door having a bath. She immediately moved her daughter to another school. Many of the new schools failed for one reason or another or provided sub-standard education, but others succeeded, and the overall result was a great improvement in the amount and quality of education available for girls.

Some girls made huge efforts to obtain an education. Barbara Mann lived on a Tasmanian farm. She went to the local school and passed the qualifying exam (there was fierce competition) for the new high school in Launceston. Each day she and her sister rode their bicycles five miles to the railway station, took the train, and then walked a mile to school, where they missed the first lesson. When they arrived home wet and cold on winter nights, their supportive mother had a hot bath, dry clothes and dinner waiting. Despite being a 'train girl', Barbara was dux of Launceston High, and gained a scholarship to the university.

By 1881 women could attend Australia's three universities in Melbourne, Sydney and Adelaide, and later universities accepted them without question. Most women took either arts or science, general degrees which the majority used as qualifications for teaching, but some gained qualifications in medicine and a very few in law. This was part of another important change for women. There were more employment opportunities available, making a huge difference to many women's lives.

Professional careers developed, a major area being nursing. Earlier, nurses had been treated like servants, who brought patients the necessities of life; there was little idea that nursing involved any skill. Most sick people were nursed at home by their families, the few hospitals being for the poor, with dreadful conditions. In the 1860s Florence Nightingale revolutionised nursing in England, insisting on thorough training and hygiene. The New South Wales government asked her to send nurses to reform the Sydney hospital, and in 1868 Lucy Osburn and five trained sisters arrived. Born in 1835 into a wealthy family, Lucy Osburn was well educated, and became a nurse against her family's wishes – when she started training, her father turned her portrait to the wall. Brave, determined and energetic, she was rather autocratic but a good organiser. She was thirty-two when she arrived in Sydney, where she and her sisters were welcomed at the quay by cheering crowds.

They were not so warmly welcomed at the hospital. It was run by men, with a board, committee, superintendent and eight surgeons – an unwieldy and incompetent administration. The nurses were horrified at the conditions. The hospital was dirty, smelly, badly drained and riddled with vermin and rats. There was no running water. Patients with bedsores lay unwashed for days on mattresses rotten from urine, sometimes with cockroaches in their bandages. The untrained nurses were ragged, dirty and lazy. Some smuggled alcohol to patients, or had sex with them. They were treated appallingly themselves, sworn at and ordered round like menials by officials and patients alike. 'It will take me a long time to get this place into anything like order', Lucy Osburn wrote home. She was right.

A week after she arrived, her nurses were in the spotlight. Queen Victoria's son Alfred was visiting Sydney, with a great deal of pomp and publicity. At a picnic, he was shot in the back by an Irish nationalist, but two of Lucy's nurses cared for him assiduously and he made a complete recovery. They were idolised in the press, valuable public recognition for the value of trained, skilled nursing.

Meanwhile, Lucy was putting her ideas into practice in the hospital. She looked on nursing as a holy mission, the highest employment, to which nurses should be devoted. She was certainly devoted herself. By working from five in the morning until late in the evening, she made a start, dismissing the worst nurses and starting to train new ones. She organised a uniform to set

Caring for children

Orphaned children received care from women like Katherine Clutterbuck, better known as Sister Kate, an Anglican nun who arrived in Perth in 1901. She and other sisters brought out a party of orphans from London and established a home, which grew in numbers as unwanted babies were brought to her. More space was needed, and she bought land and established the first cottage-type children's home in a cowshed which, she said, 'would have been disdained by any self-respecting English cow'. This developed into a large concern, with Sister Kate becoming 'Mum' to over eight hundred children and 'Gran' to their children. Strong but gentle and loving, she aimed to provide a home atmosphere where children could feel loved and wanted. After she retired in 1933, she started a home for Aboriginal children. The homes ran into problems after her death, but Sister Kate herself was praised, and when she was awarded the OBE her old boys and girls sent her a telegram expressing their gratitude and affection.

them apart and tried to ensure that they were treated like professionals, not menials. Overall, Lucy introduced cleanliness and hygiene, order and skilled nursing, but it was an uphill battle.

The superintendent and doctors disliked change, which showed up their own incompetent system, and detested having a woman in charge. 'I can see clearly that if we have a matron, she should not have too much authority. She is a woman', wrote one doctor. They obstructed Lucy whenever they could, not providing servants to clean wards, refusing to do anything about the vermin, locking Lucy out when she left the hospital to visit friends, speaking rudely to her and the nurses, refusing to tell her when they were going to operate, trying to stop her having authority over the servants – an endless series of difficulties, great and small. Lucy's English sisters were little more support. Doctors had prophesied that having female nurses working with male staff and patients would lead to trouble, and this happened, with three of the five sisters having love affairs. Several nurses wanted to take Lucy's place (she earned three times their salary) and conspired against her. Fortunately, the government stood behind her, as did various powerful friends, and the Australian girls she was training proved excellent nurses.

Lucy's enemies tried another tack, turning a routine clear-out of old books into ritual Bible-burning. A sub-committee spent six weeks investigating the affair and finally cleared Lucy, but the business made her position in the hospital very difficult. Nevertheless, she continued to fight on.

The government, realising her situation, organised a royal commission which would either prove her wrong or vindicate her. Charges made against her could not be substantiated, evidence showing that, despite the administration's 'utter neglect of vital matters', Lucy's work had led to 'vast improvement'. Her salary was raised, she was given entire charge of nursing and staff, and slowly she managed to improve the hospital. When she left in 1884, she had firmly established the Nightingale system, whereby girls with some education were thoroughly trained and took their skills to hospitals throughout Australia. Often they met similar problems to Lucy's, but in the end the Nightingale system won

Building a Nation

> ### Certified insane
>
> *Catherine and William Jackson married in 1887, and lived at Bowna, New South Wales, where William was a labourer. They had eleven children, but in 1909 the two youngest girls died of whooping cough. Probably exhausted from nursing them and extremely upset, two months later Catherine was certified insane, as she was restless, sleepless, worried that her surviving children would be burnt (it was December, with many bushfires) and sometimes answered questions irrationally. Family members, who did not think she was insane, tried to have her released – 'she seems to be very anxious to get home to the children when ever I go out to see her', wrote her cousin – but William 'was having too much fun without her, lots of lady friends etc'. In the asylum Catherine made beautiful lace which she sold, and in 1919 she caught influenza and died.*

everywhere. Not only was the standard of nursing much higher, but a professional career was available for women; and with education compulsory, many girls had the qualifications to enter training. This was often hard with long hours and low pay, but it was available and many girls took it up – there were far more applicants than could be trained.

The change from the old system is shown by the responsibilities trained nurses were given. At the New Norfolk Cottage Hospital in 1889 the doctor went on holiday, leaving Minnie Shoobridge, the matron, 'with a man who had just come in with half his foot cut off in the most dreadful way, a woman just going to be confined & 3 or 4 other cases'. Probably Minnie loved it, as most nurses seemed to. Anne Stafford Bird in Rockhampton described problems with snakes, frogs ('nothing uncovered was safe from them'), cockroaches, 'extra-large silverfish', 'brazen little ants', locusts, mosquitoes, exhausting work, long hours and an extremely strict matron. Nevertheless, 'we all loved our work, and were happy'.

Nurses spread even to the most remote areas, and in 1894 two arrived on the goldfields in Western Australia. Some tents had been erected for a hospital and Clara Saunders, a waitress at the hotel, had been helping out, but she was glad when experts arrived. The nurses told her that it was hard work, as they had very little equipment or water, and men were often brought in from the outback so grimed with dust that it was hard to get them clean, while some seemed not to have had a change of clothes for months. The two nurses – 'very fine women', 'angels of mercy', as Clara called them – cared for seventeen patients in these conditions.

At the same time, other careers developed into professions with training, notably teaching. Young teachers had previously been trained on the job, often haphazardly; now teaching colleges provided years of training. When teachers were qualified, the expansion of education meant there were many jobs for women, though conditions varied. Pay was good in state schools, but could be very low in private schools, which often struggled to make ends meet and relied on attracting teachers by their higher social status. In 1900 the Melbourne *Argus* exposed 'sweating' (working for very low pay) for female teachers in private schools. A university graduate applied for six jobs. At a time when the lowest-paid government teacher earned £120 a year, she was offered from £13 to £20 a year, or to work for no pay at all and receive lessons in 'accomplishments'. These were appalling conditions, but some women accepted them, and felt they could do little about them. There were more applicants than jobs, and it was seen as 'unladylike', that damning word, for female teachers to insist on their right to a living wage.

Universities provided specific qualifications for a few professions, mainly medicine. Australia's first woman doctor was Constance Stone. Born in 1856, the daughter of a builder, she studied medicine in America and Canada, as women could not do this in Australia. In 1890 she returned to Melbourne and she set up a practice with her sister Clara, one of the first women allowed to study medicine in Australia. Like most early female doctors, Constance worked mainly with women and children. She inspired the establishment of the Queen Victoria Memorial Hospital, staffed by women for women. Victorian women responded

Building a Nation

enthusiastically to an appeal to donate a shilling each for the hospital, which was opened in 1899. Constance also formed the Victorian Medical Women's Society, assisted a number of charities and worked for women's suffrage, but died of tuberculosis in 1902, aged only forty-six.

A very few women worked in other professional jobs, as lawyers, veterinarians, dentists, masseuses (physiotherapists) and journalists. The first woman librarian at the state library of New South Wales was Nita Kibble, who, when she sat for the library test in 1899, deliberately used her initials instead of her full name. She achieved the highest score of the candidates and was appointed, as it was assumed that she was a man.

Some women became scientists through working with men. Dorothy Izett, married with eleven children, supported her family by running a stationery business. In 1901, aged fifty-seven, she left her husband and found a job as secretary to Dr Alan Carroll, founder of societies concerned with anthropology and children's health. Dorothy, a strong character, sub-edited the Anthropological Society's journal, and after Dr Carroll's death, continued his work by running the child health association and a dispensary to provide medicines for almost thirty years. She wrote five books dealing with health topics, the best known being *Health and Longevity*, first published in 1916.

Some women succeeded in the arts. Nineteen-year-old Dorothea Mackellar became famous for Australia's best-loved poem, *My Country*, and Ethel Turner for her novel *Seven Little Australians*, while some singers became famous not only in Australia but overseas, notably Nellie Melba. A few women had unusual jobs. Madame Illa in Adelaide advertised phrenology (predicting character and intelligence by the bumps on the head), palm reading, tips for races and 'letters answered'. In 1890 Queensland's governor was driven to the Mackay School of Arts by a female licensed cab driver. Dora Coghlan trained as a teacher, but when her husband lost money gambling, she learned shorthand at Sydney Technical College and became a law reporter. Deciding this would not make her fortune, she joined the New South Wales public service, the first woman to be appointed to the clerical division, and had a long and successful career.

Major new areas of women's employment were in offices, shops and factories. These jobs needed less training than professional jobs, and many women preferred them to the main alternative, domestic service, although all frequently meant long hours for low pay with poor conditions. Factories especially, often had inadequate lighting and ventilation, crowded, dirty workrooms, insanitary facilities and dangerous machines, and meagre pay. Women working in South Melbourne factories in the 1880s seldom earned more than 25 shillings a week, but the cost of rent, fuel and food for a widow and three young children was 26 shillings by 1890.

Even worse were conditions for outworkers who took work home. For women who had to mind small children, this was often the only way they could earn, and contractors took advantage of it to pay extremely low rates. This was the worst example of 'sweating'. Elizabeth Rogers of Adelaide supported herself, her sick husband and her four children by taking in sewing from a 'sweater'. By working from 7.30 am until midnight, she could earn 14 shillings a week. 'There are dozens round me who have to do the same', she told an inquirer.

Men also endured poor conditions (though higher pay) in factories, shops and offices, and formed trade unions which gained spectacular improvements. The unions were not interested in women, and even hostile, seeing them as competitors. Some unions worked with employers to see that women remained subordinate, for example keeping them out of better-paid jobs. Women, conditioned to be more docile, mostly did little about this, and it was notoriously difficult to interest them in joining a union.

Another problem was pay. Earlier in the nineteenth century women were sometimes paid the same as men, but increasingly men were regarded as the breadwinners, and women as supplementing the family income, which meant that they did not need a man's wage. Many women – widows, deserted wives, women with sick husbands, single independent women – worked to support either themselves or family members, but this was ignored,

Building a Nation

as was any idea of work having equal value whoever did it. By the early twentieth century women's wages were set at 54 per cent of men's. Only a few women protested, and a very few took industrial action. In the 1900s, as factories expanded in Melbourne in particular, the demand for female labour grew, and there was more union activity by women. Matchworkers, mostly women, formed a union in 1910, and the next year shoulderers in Bryant and May's factory went on strike. Shoulderers were paid by the crate for putting an inner cardboard ring in matchboxes, and said their earnings averaged 17 shillings a week, which factory records show was true. Management said they averaged 20 shillings a week, the amount a female factory inspector said a girl needed to keep herself decently. The shoulderers asked for

Never without a cooked galah

In the 1890s Christina Gordon and her husband Duncan went to the Western Australian goldfields, where Christina was 'as good a miner as any man, handling pick and cradle with the best of them'. Their next job was erecting 58 km of dingo-proof fence, after which with their two sons they went to the Tanami mining fields, where they made a small fortune. It was very isolated and housekeeping was difficult, but no matter where they went, said Christina with pride, she baked fresh bread every day, and was never without a crate of hens for eggs, 'or a side of bacon to sweeten a kangaroo's tail or a cooked galah'. On one particularly tough trip they were without water for seven days, only surviving because a camel calved and produced milk.

They moved up to a bough hut – 'a more comfortable place to live in you couldn't find' – where they were 'as happy as the day was long'. But lack of water forced them to leave, and Christina took over the well-known Victoria Hotel in Darwin. She was noted for her hospitality, becoming one of the best-known businesswomen in the town. She maintained high standards, shocking Darwin's inhabitants by insisting that no one smoke in the dining room, and that diners without jackets remove themselves to the second dining room.

a rise, management refused, and thirty-six girls went on strike. They were efficiently organised and had fierce determination, with a female leader taking charge of picket lines and addressing union meetings. Her name is unknown.

After a week, management offered half the extra amount sought, but the strikers refused. Soon 150 matchworkers were idle, and the strikers gave in and accepted management's offer, which increased their average earnings to 20 shillings. So the strike was moderately successful, though Labor leaders took little interest in it.

Although there were many new jobs for women, traditional ones remained, and domestic service was still the largest employer in 1911. Some servants were happy, but others complained in the new Labor press. A master took a servant to court for eating butter on her bread; an eighteen-year-old girl had to do all the work for a family of four in an eleven-room house, and milk the cows, for £13 a year; servants worked up to sixteen hours a day in hot, stuffy rooms, and were given inferior food and accommodation – one had to sleep in the woodshed. They wore humiliating uniforms, and mistresses changed their names if they thought fit. One servant, returning from her afternoon off, had to knock on the front door to tell her employer she was there, then go to the

Australia's largest family?

The Stephan family arrived in Queensland from Germany in 1877, the Labudda family the following year. Both settled in the Boonah area, and Johanna Labudda married Carl Stephan. They lived in Templin where they farmed a selection and built a slab hut, which was enlarged as children arrived, until eventually it had fifteen rooms. They were needed, for Johanna and Carl had what their descendant Terri Foley believes to be Australia's largest family, twenty-two children, all of whom lived to adulthood. Johanna's last baby was born when she was fifty and her eldest child thirty-four. She was the local midwife and nurse and, when her children left home, she turned part of the house into a hospital.

Building a Nation

> **Two bootee stories**
>
> *Two different stories with a common theme – the importance of what might seem small items, bootees. One pair enabled a family to keep going, the other demonstrates thrift, a much-praised virtue of the period.*
>
> *Emma Frey arrived in Australia from Switzerland, and married a Swiss engineer. They lived in Gawler with their three children, but in the depression of the 1890s Emma's husband lost his job. He tried to make a living by selling saucepans from door to door, but few people had the money to buy them. At one stage they had no money at all. Emma knew her sister would help if she could contact her, but had no money for the stamp. She rummaged through her possessions and found some wool, enough to knit a pair of baby bootees. She sold them for a penny, bought a stamp and sent a letter to her sister, who did help.*
>
> *Ada Fletcher lived with her family in Mackay. One day, she recalled, one of her baby sister's pretty pink crocheted bootees went missing. A day or so later a large snake was killed in the fowl house, and her father opened its stomach, since he was interested in these things. Inside was the missing bootee. It was washed thoroughly, and worn again.*

back door to actually enter the house. Marriage, the main escape, could be hard to organise if employers prohibited male visitors. And servants were still liable to sexual assault by men in the family. 'Nothing but slavery', concluded one servant in 1907.

Women also continued to set up their own enterprises within their families. One of the most successful was Polly Payne, who was born in 1854, and at eighteen married her cousin George. They arrived in Alexandra (north of Melbourne) penniless, and built a bark hut on the banks of the Goulburn River. Polly had nineteen children, but soon left their care to her eldest daughter ('believe me she had a short childhood', as a descendant wrote). Polly opened a mixed store and did a roaring trade, then built a row of shops: butcher, baker, bootmaker, haberdashery, a dressmaking establishment which sold its wares in the dress shop, tearooms where weary shoppers could catch their breath. Once a long-time customer mentioned that he had not seen Polly for a few days. She took him behind the counter, where the latest baby was lying in a strong cardboard box. A hard taskmaster, she always demanded perfection, but never turned away mothers of young children, always trusting them to pay when they could. It was her boast that they never let her down.

Overall, the changes from 1880 onwards were a turning point in women's education and employment. Women all received some education, and could use this to obtain training for a career, or a job in new areas like shops, offices and factories. They could support themselves, so did not have to marry to ensure their future, and 17 per cent remained single from the 1890s. Women could live independently of men, a huge change from the Victorian era. But there was a limit to women's opportunities. Nursing could develop because it was a traditional female occupation, but where men and women worked together a woman could never be senior to a man, and there were limits on women's promotion, encouraged by male-dominated trade unions. Women could enter new areas, but entrenched male interests made sure they remained at the lower levels.

Many women did not mind this. Most aimed to marry, and looked on employment as a useful occupation between school and marriage, earning money for the future. This meant they were not particularly worried about promotion, and there were not enough wanting more from a job to achieve much change.

And those opportunities which existed could not always be grasped. Mildred Hood, aged seventeen, lived on a small farm near Hobart. She wanted to become a doctor, 'to rescue the perishing and care for the dying', rather than have 'husband and children to be bothered with'. No one sympathised. Her parents thought she should stay at home, helping them, so Mildred taught herself subjects ranging from arithmetic to Greek and medicine, though 'I find it very hard being my own TUTOR'. Her diary ended in 1911, but a note adds that she did not achieve her ambition and 'never escaped until the day of her death from the thraldom of her family'.

Society seemed able to cope with women receiving more education and employment opportunities, but another proposed change was less well accepted. Philosophers had long argued that all citizens should take part in governing their country, and in the nineteenth century these ideas became popular. At first 'citizens' meant men, and when the Australian colonies were given self-government from the 1850s, only men elected parliaments.

At about this time a few women in Britain and America started to argue that women should be treated as equal citizens, but Australian women were slower to take up the cause. There were fewer women, they were busy, and the community seems to have appreciated their part in building up the new country, so they do not appear discontented – few Australian women complained about woman's lot in the middle of the century. It was only in the 1880s that demand for women's rights grew. Two groups of women were involved.

Since 1788, Australian society had been strongly masculine, with so many more men than women. This was especially so on the frontier and the goldfields, where drinking, gambling, violence and masculine mateship came to be seen as typically Australian. Women were not part of this mateship, and sometimes suffered from it, in particular from men who spent too much of their wages on beer instead of food and rent, and were

'I dread the place at supper time ...'

'Dear Ellen I would wish to write often but I cannot', wrote Ann Hickey to her daughter, from Hill End, NSW in the 1880s. 'I work very hard now as I go out four days of the week and I get ten shillings for them to wash and scrub.' Unfortunately, this job would end soon. She hoped Ellen would be home for Christmas and thanked her for sending £1, which she used to buy Johnny and Morry some boots. 'If you only heard the music when the four childer is crying altogether it would drive you mad I often pitty your father and for me I dread the place at supper time ... Dear Ellen I will now say good buoy for this time and I hope you will write soon.'

violent towards their families.

This was also the case in America, and there, in 1873, the Woman's Christian Temperance Union was born. It grew rapidly, and soon realised that fighting alcohol was not enough. To improve society, women had to fight against all its defects, and to gain influence, they had to have the vote. In the 1880s the Union spread its message further, and a missionary established ten branches in Australia, including one in Adelaide in 1885. Its members' main work was visiting public houses on Saturday evenings to preach against drink. Not surprisingly, women accustomed to thinking of themselves as wives and mothers at home found this daunting, and the branch dwindled to twelve active members.

Two women reinvigorated enthusiasm. Another American missionary revived the Adelaide branch and formed twenty-three more in South Australia, with a total membership of 1,112 women. They elected a state president, Elizabeth Nicholls, who was born in Adelaide in 1850, taught Sunday School in the Methodist church, and at twenty married the superintendent, Mr A. Nicholls. She always had 'an earnest desire to live a life which should benefit those around her', and this was not lessened by 'the cares of home', which included five children. Elizabeth had great gifts: she was earnest and determined, wise and dignified, shrewd and practical, a good lucid speaker with a touch of humour, and always cheerful. She joined the Union in 1886, and became not only state but national president. 'Agitate, Educate, Organize' was her slogan.

Under her leadership, women fought for many reforms, from temperance, the vote, equal moral standards for men and women and upholding women's dignity generally, to more specific changes such as using unfermented wine in communion, closing bars on Sundays, and appointing women as factory inspectors. It might be surprising that women found the courage to advocate these changes, but the Union's history explained that through faith in God they 'experienced a development of power, which enabled them to do what had hitherto seemed to them impossible'. Leaders encouraged them by showing that the Union's work

A convict couple in Sydney, 1793

Women and children taking their turns at the hard work as a party makes its way through the Australian countryside, in this case on the way to the diggings

The squatter's first home, 1840s, by Alexander Lang

*Can Mother be telling the children the age-old Australian dictum that they are not to go in the water until an hour after their lunch?
Family picnic at Balmoral, Sydney, 1881*

*A major aim behind all those piano lessons –
gaining masculine admiration*

Mary Morton Allport's vignette of a mother and her children

A woman mourns for her dead child, about 1870

> HERE
> lieth the mortal remains
> of Sarah Lane
> died 3rd Nov.r. 1844.
> aged 8 years.
> This little inoffensive child
> To Sunday school had trod
> But sad to tell was burnt to death
> Within the house of God

A gravestone in the Hamilton cemetery, Tasmania. Apparently Sunday School had finished and Sarah was waiting in the church vestibule for her parents, and stood too close to the fire.

Another danger: snakes.
'Christmas on the diggings, or the unwelcome visitor who came uninvited'.

was part of women's accepted role, a 'battle for home protection'. They praised members' 'patient, sweet womanliness and gentle bravery' – 'to every true woman the dearest spot on earth is Home Sweet Home' – even while encouraging women to act outside that home. 'None has the right to be a modest violet.'

These inspiring exhortations succeeded, and many women joined the Union, which became Australia's first national women's organisation. Most members were from the middle-classes – temperance rarely gripped the wealthy or the poor – and the Union gained its strongest support from non-conformist churches. It did not succeed in establishing temperance, but it gained other victories. It showed that women were capable of speaking in public, running meetings and an organisation, and it gave individuals the opportunity to do these things. By this it succeeded in elevating women's dignity and influence. It also had success with many of its other demands, such as regulations limiting hotels, and the vote.

By the 1880s, some other women were advocating women's suffrage. They did not come to this through the Union's path of wanting to reform society generally, but of wanting to improve women's position. Many had not achieved happiness by the usual

Federene

When Ellen and John Kirby's first child was born on Federation Day, January 1, 1901, they were so full of national pride and fervour that they named her Federene. They ran a soft drink factory in Bowen, where Federene grew up. A typical eldest daughter of the times, she helped raise her five brothers and sisters. She never married, but nursed her mother and father until their deaths. 'Thankfully for us the eldest daughter role has changed considerably', wrote her great-niece Denise McLean. 'Not that I mean to trivialise her life. She was just one of the millions of ordinary, decent, unheralded Australian people whose very solid though unspectacular achievements are the backbone of our families and societies.'

method of marriage. Henrietta Dugdale claimed to be the first Australian to argue publicly for women's rights, in a letter in the Melbourne *Argus* in 1869. She had arrived from England in the previous decade, and after her first husband drowned, married a friend of his, William Dugdale. They ran a dairy with their three sons, and Henrietta, an attractive, energetic woman, loved swimming, horseriding and music.

By 1870 the marriage had failed. William kept the boys (men always had custody of children) and Henrietta moved to Melbourne, where she made public her belief in the equality of the sexes and supported reforms to help women and children, such as fairer divorce laws, rehabilitation of prostitutes, castration of rapists and birth control – 'every form of disreputable opinion' as one critic wrote. Witty, emotional and rather melodramatic, she had radical ideas. She opposed the monarchy and Christianity, believing them patriarchal and oppressive, and described herself as a 'deist', a believer in 'true ethics'. She was in favour of 'rational dress' for women, refusing to wear a corset ('vile instrument of torture') and making herself a divided skirt. She also cut her hair short, an unheard-of action, and was a vegetarian, growing and cooking most of her food.

In 1883 Henrietta published a booklet, describing a Utopia where women take their rightful place as men's equals and marriage is a partnership. The greatest obstacle to human advancement, she wrote, was 'the most irrational, fiercest and most powerful of our world's monsters – the only devil – MALE IGNORANCE'. In 1884 she helped form the Victorian Women's Suffrage Society and was its first president. After William's death she again remarried, aged seventy-seven. By contemporary standards Henrietta was eccentric, but she was also a courageous pioneer who stirred other women to action.

Suffrage societies grew in most cities, along with branches of the Temperance Union. They were not as different as they might appear, for many women like Henrietta approved of temperance, and the Union worked for many women's rights, especially married women's control of their property and custody of their children, raising the age of consent to sexual intercourse (generally from twelve to sixteen) and the vote. Usually the two groups worked together well.

In South Australia members of the two groups formed the South Australian Suffrage League. There was strong opposition, with 'contempt and abuse poured on the "faddists" who supported the suffrage' by those who thought women should stay in the home. Undaunted, the League pressed on, arguing that it was only fair that everyone should have a say in making laws which affected them; it was absurd that 'mother influence' had no legal recognition; that the Bible advocated equal power for women ('Honour thy father and thy mother'); and that enlightened men agreed with them and vicious ones did not, probably because they were involved in the liquor traffic. Members distributed pamphlets, held meetings and lobbied. In 1893 they presented parliament with a huge petition of eleven thousand signatures, and the next year South Australian women won the vote, among the first in the world. Some Aboriginal women voted in the next election, among a group of a hundred voters at the mission at Point McLeay.

After women voted for the first time, Elizabeth Nicholls commented on the results, in her humorous way. She had not heard of any domestic quarrels or neglected children, and dinner was cooked on election day much the same as usual. There were no disorderly scenes at polling booths, women did not grow nervous, and results were more in favour of morality and temperance than in any previous election.

The South Australian experience was repeated in other colonies, starting in 1899 with Western Australia, and women gained the federal vote in 1901. Here the main influence was Maybanke Wolstenholme-Anderson from Sydney. After her husband, a drunkard, had deserted her, Maybanke opened a school to support her children, and, when laws were changed in 1892, obtained a divorce. Known as 'the most intellectual woman in Australia' and a good public speaker, she was an ardent supporter of women's rights but preferred to work behind the scenes. 'We shall win more by being soft', she wrote, 'so I am going to be wise as a serpent and harmless as a dove.' She succeeded. At the 1897

A marriage of ineptitude and passion

In 1890 Alice Wickham arrived in Maryborough from Britain with her husband and her daughter Anna, whose account of her childhood describes an unhappy marriage and a series of failures. When her father (never named) attempted to build a stable, Alice raged at him, 'seeing in his failure the ineptitude which a vigorous, passionate woman so loathes in her man', wrote Anna. Father made a meagre living running a music shop, while Alice, bored with housework, found a job teaching away from home at Hughenden. She fell in love with a salesman – Anna saw them kissing – but disapproved of the school system and resigned, and they rejoined Father in Brisbane.

Alice now set herself up as Madam Reprah, psychic and character-reader. Father strongly disapproved, wanting his wife to stay home, but Alice did well financially and branched out into giving public lectures. Father disapproved even more, shocking Anna when he struck Alice in one of their frequent quarrels. Finally Alice did stop her psychic work and became an insurance agent, but business was slack and she tried to commit suicide by drinking two bottles of Chlorodyne, a patent medicine containing opium. Anna became engaged at sixteen, mainly, it seems, to get away from her parents.

Federal Convention, she put forward a petition asking that no one with the vote should lose it through federation, which was difficult to argue against. Since women had the vote in South Australia, women's suffrage became part of the federation platform. When federation was achieved in 1901, all white Australian women won the vote. Since it was absurd that women could vote in federal but not state elections, New South Wales, Tasmania and Queensland and finally, in 1908, Victoria followed. Australian women received recognition relatively quickly, and women congratulated themselves that there was 'no need for Australian women to fight in an unwomanly way for justice'.

The campaign for the suffrage, and other reforms such as fairer divorce laws, and married women retaining ownership of their property and custody of their children (all granted by the 1890s) were only part of what the press called 'The Woman Movement' – women emerging from the home to take part in public life. Only a small percentage of women joined the Woman's Christian Temperance Union, even fewer what we might call radical feminist societies. The newspapers were also talking about the many more women involved in other activities outside the home.

Before the 1880s there had been only a few women's societies, mostly for wealthy women's charitable activities. Now all sorts of women formed dozens of societies for all sorts of reasons. Women's charities helped everyone in need – unemployed men, female factory workers, old women, the blind, prisoners, animals, consumptives, an endless list. The Anti-Plumage League tried to persuade women not to wear birds' feathers in their hats. St John Ambulance taught first aid. The National Council of Women, with delegates from many clubs, was formed to speak for all women. There were other national groups, such as the Church of England Mothers' Union, which had thousands of members throughout Australia. Such societies were established with almost no opposition, for even the most conservative man could hardly criticise women working for such worthy causes. Yet all involved women leaving home and joining groups run by women for women, and all demonstrated that women could act independently with success.

Flora Harris of Brisbane is a good example. Her mother was the first president of the Woman's Christian Temperance Union in Queensland, and Flora became responsible for its younger members. She often spoke at women's groups, supporting causes like women's suffrage, and she was also a good musician and church organist. She married, brought up three children, travelled widely and loved entertaining, which might have been enough for many women, but she also continued with her philanthropic activity. She had a gift for establishing and running charities, such as the Travellers' Aid which met women train travellers at their destination, the Children's Playground Association, the Bush Children's Health Scheme, a Bush Club for isolated women, and the committee which built a women's

An unhappy childhood

Eva Andrew was born in 1892 to Bennet and Sophia Andrew, in South Australia. Bennet wanted sons, but after two boys, the next six babies were girls, who, he often said, were useless. Bennet was a jack of all trades and master of none, Eva wrote, and her mother's work was endless. She 'just scrambled through and that was all'. Bennet became ill and was given port wine to build him up, and acquired a taste for it. Meanwhile, Sophia went out washing and cleaning, and the girls attended school on the rare occasions when they had boots to wear.

The family joined the Salvation Army, and 'they were that armified that Mum dressed [the girls] in Salvation Army bonnets for school, and oh, what fun the girls at school had!' But their father continued to drink, 'the ruination of everything and everybody'. He would beat Sophia, once so much that she lost the power of speech for three months. 'I often used to wonder why Mum still lived with him. But ... she was a mother and it was us that she suffered all this for'. Eventually he did move out.

Eva's sister Ciss was very pretty, with a waist only the span of two hands. A sister would put a knee against her back and pull the cords of her corset hard, 'though the life just about squeezed out of Ciss'. She had a chest like a pouter pigeon, no sign of a stomach, 'but – her seat!! It was tremendous!!' Ciss became pregnant, and Sophia turned her out, so she lived with Bennet. At seventeen Eva married, and at thirty-four, when dying with nephritis, she wrote her memoirs so that her three children would know her story.

college at the university of Queensland.

Not only charitable groups flourished. There were literary and musical clubs, intellectual or social clubs, societies for those interested in science, photography, foreign languages or philosophy. During the Boer War, patriotic clubs raised money for comforts for the troops. Women also joined men's societies, such as the Field Naturalists. Friendly Societies for men had begun in the 1840s, to provide social activities and health insurance. Now there were women's societies, like the teetotal Rechabites and the Rebekah Lodges of the Oddfellows. There were also clubs for girls, and the Florence Nightingale Girl Aids were established in Victoria in 1909 and renamed Girl Guides two years later. Australian girls liked camping and hiking and the movement expanded, despite criticism from those who considered such activity most unladylike. Even small, isolated towns had their clubs, such as the Zeehan Ladies' Shakespeare Society on the isolated west coast of Tasmania.

Particularly popular with Australian women were sporting clubs. Before the 1880s women had played hardly any organised sport, but when clubs appeared, women took them up enthusiastically. There were team sports, like tennis, cricket, hockey, basketball ('exceedingly pretty') and rowing. Women also played golf, croquet, ping-pong and started rifle-shooting in clubs. Bicycles became popular, not just as sport but as a way of transport, and a female journalist commented that women were keener to be emancipated by the bicycle than the vote. Horse

Margaret Bignell helps to establish a profession for women

After her husband, a pharmacist, died in 1897, Margaret Bignell obtained registration as Victoria's first registered woman pharmacist. She was officially untrained, but presumably she had learnt by helping her husband. She carried on the business he had established, employing only women.

Training in pharmacy was available at the Melbourne College of Pharmacy, with the first woman qualifying in 1899. Six years later Margaret inspired the formation of the Victorian Women Pharmacists' Association to promote women's interests, especially salaries. This was because the Sale Hospital was offering to employ a woman at only £50 a year (with board), which the Association thought disgraceful. The salary was raised to £75. Having ensured that women could practice pharmacy equally with men, in 1913 the Association disbanded, as its objectives had been met.

riding continued popular, with an innovation in the 1890s which 'shook the heavens': women started riding astride! They found this far more practical, comfortable and safer than riding side-saddle, but at first trousers were unthinkable and women wore divided skirts. Some did wear trousers when bushwalking, however, and in 1897 a girl published an account of how she and another girl wore trousers when, with some male relations, they climbed Adamson's Peak in a four-day hike. Skirts, she said, were 'completely out of the question for a mountain climb'.

The first mention of women playing lawn bowls in Victoria was in 1881, when women were admitted to the Stawell men's club. In Melbourne, two ladies' bowling clubs were formed in 1899, and by 1907 there were six. That year, some forward-thinking women formed the first ladies' bowling association in the world. Women from the six clubs began inter-club competition, wearing their tight-waisted, high-necked frocks which swept the greens, and broad-brimmed hats secured with scarves tied under the chin. In 1907 the Fitzroy Club won the pennant competition, and Miss Cooper of the Melbourne Cricket Club Bowling Club became Champion of Champions. 'A sporting triumph', as the Victorian Ladies' Bowling Association writes.

On the whole the community accepted this. Instead of criticism of ladies for undertaking activities like bowls, in the press at least the meaning of 'lady' widened to include all respectable women, such as those in trade unions. 'Womanly' was now the highest praise for females: the restrictions of the lady were becoming less important than the more natural qualities of the woman, particularly warmth and compassion. And 'unwomanly' was the ultimate criticism, far worse than 'unladylike'. Although there was some diehard grumbling and obstruction, women's new activities seemed acceptable to most people. Newspapers made the odd facetious comment, but on the whole approved of the New Woman, who played hockey, lectured, rode a bicycle and was 'prepared to do anything'.

Epitomising the New Woman was the swimmer Fanny Durack. Her parents ran a pub in a tough area of Sydney, and Fanny, born in 1889, was the third of their six children. A tomboy and a daredevil, on a family holiday in Newcastle she ignored warnings about the surf and was knocked down by a large wave. A large St Bernard dog rescued her, but her horrified father insisted she learn to swim, so she was taken to Sydney's only organised bathing establishment for women, Mrs Page's baths at Coogee. Her parents could only afford the entry fee, not lessons, so Fanny taught herself dog-paddle by watching other girls. Once she could swim, her parents let her go to the Domain Baths at Woolloomooloo, where part of the harbour was roped off against sharks and women were allowed to swim in a corner. This time Fanny taught herself breast-stroke by watching men swim. Her strong arms and powerful shoulders were ideal for swimming.

There were problems when it came to competition. Feminist Rose Scott was president of the Ladies' Swimming Association and, though a keen advocate of women having the vote, she disapproved strongly of mixed bathing: women could only swim in public places in the 'ladies' hour' when men were absent. Moreover, they wore heavy, voluminous neck-to-knee woollen outfits, which slowed them down. Most girls did not aim to swim fast and

Annette Bear

Annette Bear's father established the Chateau Tahbilk vineyard, and she received a modern education in England, where she trained in social work and met leaders of the women's movement. In 1890, in her late twenties, Annette returned to Melbourne. An excellent organiser, much liked by all, she became a leading light in the Australian women's movement. Among other achievements, she campaigned for the age of consent to be raised from twelve to sixteen and for the appointment of women as factory inspectors, organised fundraising for the new Queen Victoria Women's Hospital, and united various women's groups in the fight for the vote. In 1894 she married William Crawford, and as Annette Bear-Crawford was one of the first to use both maiden and married names. Four years later she was a delegate to the Women's International Conference in England, but died of pneumonia in London.

were happy to play around in the shallows. However, as in other spheres, horizons were widening for women, and Fanny had more opportunities for swimming when the Sydney Council opened a bathing area with separate places for men and women.

Fanny's potential was recognised by two male champions, who taught her a new stroke, the trudgen, a mixture of overarm and breast-stroke. In 1902 the first New South Wales Ladies' Championships were held (no men were allowed to watch), and included a race for girls. Fanny entered, but at the start of her heat she swallowed a mouthful of water and could not continue. It was two years before she felt confident enough to go in another race, but this time she came second to Australia's leading female swimmer. This was the start of many victories, though for a while she was eclipsed by Wilhelmina (Mina) Wylie, whose father took over Mrs Page's Baths. In 1911 Mina defeated Fanny, and later that year both switched to a new stroke, the Australian crawl, in which Fanny defeated Mina. They trained against men, the only competition strong enough. Rose Scott was appalled, and denounced women who swam publicly with males. So did Sydney's Catholic Archbishop, who said that mixed bathing was 'destructive of that modesty which is one of the pillars of Australian society'. Fanny ignored them. She helped male lifesavers work on a reel line at Coogee Beach, and when warned that such behaviour would bring trouble, said, 'I did go out on the line. I see no harm in it. I'll do it again if I want to'.

By this time the Olympic Games had been revived, though the International Olympic Committee refused to allow women to compete. Women attracted crowds, however, and local organisers wanted them, so in 1900 women played golf and tennis, in 1904 archery, and in 1908 skating, tennis and gymnastics. But there was no swimming, and Australia's first female champion, Annette Kellermann, never competed in the Olympics. Instead she gave demonstration swims in England and performed a vaudeville aquatic act, and in 1907 was arrested on a Boston beach for wearing a daring skirtless one-piece bathing suit. The case made headlines, which a film producer saw, and Annette became the first Australian star of American movies. In a competition with ten thousand contestants she was judged the perfect woman – 'from the neck down', she joked.

The 1912 Olympic managers in Stockholm managed to include women's swimming, with two races, a relay and an individual 100 metres (the Olympics used metric measurements). The best female swimmers in Australia were now Fanny and Mina, but they had a struggle to make the Games. The Ladies' Swimming Association forbade women to enter competitions when men were present, but all five swimming clubs under its control voted that Fanny and Mina should be nominated for the Olympic team. Rose Scott resigned. Then the Australian Olympic organisers said there was not enough money for their fares. A family friend set up a fund which raised enough money to send Fanny and help Mina; Mina's family paid the rest; and Fanny's sister paid her own fare, so that the girls had a chaperone.

In Stockholm, Fanny and Mina wore long myrtle-green dresses for the opening ceremony, and green caps and costumes for swimming, with a green cloak to wrap round themselves when out of the pool, for decency. Fanny won her heat of the 100 metres in the world record time of 1 minute 19.8 seconds, and she and Mina swam in the final. The pool had no individual lanes, recalled Mina, so the race was 'like swimming in the harbour'. Fanny led from the start, even when she ran into the side of the pool, and in her 'beautiful Australian crawl' won by four metres, in 1 minute 22.2 seconds. Mina came from behind in the last twenty metres to win the silver medal. The girls were so thrilled that they asked if they could swim two legs each in the relay, but officials refused. Australians went wild with excitement at the news that local women had won the world's first gold and silver swimming medals, and Fanny became the nation's heroine.

Fanny and Mina toured Europe and America giving exhibitions, and there was so much interest that more women's swimming races were scheduled for the next Games. When war broke out, however, the Games were cancelled. In Australia Fanny broke twelve world records, over distances ranging from 100 yards (1 minute 6 seconds) to one mile (about 1500 metres: 26 minutes 8 seconds). Once the war was over she hoped to continue competing overseas, but she had problems with both Australian and American officials, then developed appendicitis just before the 1920 Games and had to withdraw. She married and ran a pub with her husband, coached children in swimming, and died in 1956.

All the women who served as examples of the Woman Movement, and most of those who showed the influence of education and better employment opportunities, came from cities. Education, more employment, the vote, societies and sport all affected some women at the time, and prepared the way for substantial change in the future, but another factor did more to change many women's lives immediately, in both town and country. This was a dramatic fall in the birthrate.

Until the 1870s almost all Australian women married, and almost all marriages produced an average of seven children. This meant that from the ages of twenty to forty or so, most women were extremely busy with pregnancies, breastfeeding and childcare, not to mention housework and helping in the family business. Even if they wanted to do anything else, they had little

A well-known philanthropist

Janet, Lady Clarke, was a major Melbourne philanthropist. Born Janet Snodgrass at Doogalook in 1851 and self-educated, she became governess to William Clarke's children and married him. He inherited vast wealth and was later knighted, and Janet handled her transition in lifestyle most capably, becoming a leader of Victorian society for thirty years and entertaining lavishly. She specialised in serving as the active president of numerous appeals, such as the Women's Hospital and the District Nursing Society. In the 1890s depression, she organised soup kitchens for the unemployed. She headed the University Funds Appeal and gave the huge sum of £6,000 to Janet Clarke Hall, a college for women students. She also led intellectual societies such as the Alliance Française. Janet Clarke died in 1909, survived by six children and three step-children.

time for it. But in the 1880s the birthrate started to fall, to four children per mother by 1911, just over half what it had been. This had a huge effect on women's lives: fewer exhausting pregnancies, less chance of death, less childcare, less housework and fewer mouths to feed, so more time for other activities like paid or voluntary work, or recreation.

Why did it happen? The birthrate fell not only in Australia, but all over the western world. Though evidence is limited, it was probably part of the other changes of the time – compulsory education, more training for careers, a rising standard of living and more opportunities generally. This meant more alternatives to marriage, and a rising number of women remained single and did not bear children. Education for women generally does result in a fall in the birthrate. It also meant children could not help at home, while new laws prevented them being employed. Before the 1870s, large families were an economic asset. Children did not cost much to bring up; they were useful in family enterprises, then started earning. Now, however, they had to go to school instead of earning or helping, while rising living standards and training for jobs meant they cost more to bring up. More opportunities meant that some parents preferred to have fewer children and give them a better start in life.

The birthrate did not fall because contraception was much easier. Some contraceptives were available and more had been developed, and in Melbourne Brettena Smyth, who continued to run her husband's shop after he died to support her children, widened her stock to include them. She advertised 'best female French, English, German and American contraceptives, French preventives (male), enemas and syringes', and thought the new cervical caps were by far the best; they had 'never been known to fail where instructions are carried out'. Other methods all had some drawback. Withdrawal was 'extremely hurtful to the man' and led to impotence. Sponges, condoms, strenuous coughing and douching were unreliable (and condoms, made of thick rubber, must have been unexciting to use). Taking arsenic and other drugs in small doses daily, with the aim of lessening male vigour, led to ill-health. Holding the scrotum to prevent ejaculation could lead to sterility and impotence. Cocoa butter pessaries and injecting oil into the vagina before intercourse were useless. The cervical caps were expensive, however, and only a few women had access to Brettena's shop. Presumably many relied on the other methods, none particularly dependable and some painful or otherwise uninspiring. One woman described how she made cocoa butter and quinine pessaries at home. They were always messy to use, she said, and especially unpleasant when the butter went rancid.

A contraceptive method which appears to have been more widely used than modern women might imagine was abstinence. It was taken for granted that women endured rather than enjoyed sex, and many feminists saw the aim of sex as either conceiving children or providing male pleasure, which they put far down their list of necessities. Some thought marriage was slavery and should be abolished, others condoned marriage only when men controlled themselves. Abstinence was the only way women could triumph over men's coarser nature, said Vida Goldstein (single), while temperance leader Bessie Lee (married) said marriage had been degraded to 'the most unholy gratification of men's worst desires ... A man and a woman before marriage are expected to be pure; let them remain so after marriage, living together in the holiest, best of all unions.' Louisa Lawson (divorced) called the bedroom a Chamber of Horrors where frail women 'are expected to endure nightly this horrid ordeal', and Miles Franklin (single) was even harsher: marriage was 'rabbit work'.

There is not a great deal of evidence, but it appears that some couples did consider abstinence. When Bessie Lee was widowed, she married again quite quickly. In 1900, forty-year-old Marion Haynes wrote her lawyer husband a chatty letter ending, 'We are both pretty old and it is time to give up bedmates. I am off to have a little supper, so goodnight, love, kiss for yourself'. Apparently her husband did not agree with her suggestion, for she died in childbirth two years later.

Whatever the method of contraception, fewer children were born, and one fascinating explanation hinges on current events. Victorian prudery meant that couples were reluctant to discuss contraception, and because most methods needed co-operation, many couples did not practise them. However, in 1877 several people were tried in Britain for publishing a pamphlet which described contraception, and in 1888 a similar trial took place in Sydney. Newspapers covered these trials in detail and the subject entered the public domain, so married couples could discuss contraception more easily, besides being able to buy the pamphlet. Whatever the reason, by the 1890s probably a quarter of all couples were practising birth control.

> ### Women must be pure: the Dean Case
>
> *Though the press often supported the New Woman and her activities, change was neither total nor immediate. George Dean was a Sydney ferry master, a handsome hero who saved the lives of several female passengers. In 1895 his nineteen-year-old wife Mary bore a daughter, but soon afterwards her food and drink started to taste strange. Samples were sent to a chemist for analysis, and strychnine and arsenic were found. George was arrested. This was the sort of case the Victorian press loved, and it was widely reported throughout the British Empire. The jury was unanimous: George was found guilty and sentenced to hang.*
>
> *The press saw the handsome hero as innocent, and public outcry resulted in a royal commission. George's motives and actions were not probed, but Mary and her mother's entire lives were microscopically examined. Her parents' convict past was unearthed, and she and her mother were called whores and witches, bringing down a good man. It was Mary's past which was on trial, not George's actions. She was criticised for smiling, crying, frowning, looking the judge in the face or looking down – whatever she did was wrong, and she was called 'the most hated woman in Sydney'. Then it emerged that George had told his solicitor he was guilty. He was jailed and Mary vanished, to marry a grazier four years later. Her fate, says her biographer Donna Lee Brien, was bound up with the social change of the times, and the changing role of women; but change had not gone far enough for her to receive fair treatment.*

Only a fifth of these, 5 per cent of the total, used contraceptives. The main method was withdrawal, followed by abstinence, douching, then abortions. These were illegal, but were performed by doctors, midwives, friends or the women themselves. Doctors could dilate the cervix, other people could introduce foreign bodies, and women could 'pass an instrument into their own wombs' or take abortifacients, advertised as curing 'female irregularities'. They ranged from herbal remedies such as tansy and ergot of rye, to more dangerous mixtures which included lead or mercury. They were often strong purgatives and many did not work, though ergot, for example, was effective. Since abortions were mostly done in secret it is impossible to establish figures, but it appears that they were numerous. Women sometimes died or were left invalids, but the percentage of deaths was small enough not to be a deterrent.

Much of the evidence about abortion appeared in 1904 when New South Wales held the world's first royal commission into the birthrate. Australian governments were alarmed at the news that fewer white babies were being born. They thought the white population was small enough already, compared with the hordes to the north, the so-called Yellow Peril. Immigration from Asia was stopped, but governments also encouraged white mothers to bear more children, and the royal commission tried to find out the reasons for the birthrate's fall. Its all-male members blamed women's selfishness and love of luxury and social pleasures.

Early women drivers

Soon after cars appeared in Australia, women started driving. In 1911 Ivy Cole was the first woman in Victoria to obtain her licence, driving a policeman round the block in her father's De Dion Bouton. The authorities had not planned for women drivers, and when the policeman issued the licence, he had to strike out every 'his' and write 'her'. Two years later Mrs Hypatia Monk-Adams of Turramurra was the first woman to compete in a motor reliability trial, between Melbourne and Sydney.

Building a Nation

> **Northern Territory women**
>
> *Though the Northern Territory was far distant from the rest of Australia, its few women – the ratio of men to women was 100:8 – embraced new ideas and were often independent, in a variety of ways. A teacher, Catherine Pett, took only a fortnight off when she had a baby. Women owned and trained horses, and ran them in races. Eliza Ryland assaulted a man for using indecent language to her. After considerable discussion, women were allowed to join the Debating and Literary Association, where some presented papers. In 1892 in a Catholic ceremony, a couple were married without the usual mention of 'obey', but in terms of mutual honour and love.*
>
> *As the Territory was part of South Australia, women received the vote in 1894, and most eligible women enrolled. Three were so enthusiastic about their new status that on their wedding certificates, under 'occupation', they wrote 'citizen'.*

Not surprisingly, women tended to think poorly of this conclusion, one writing to the *Bulletin* that it was all very well for men to condemn women for selfishness, but they were not considering 'the agonies of child-bearing, with its precedent horrors ... [and] resultant limitations'. Governments ignored this. Instead they tried to limit the availability of contraceptives and information about birth control, and stop deaths of white babies. Ante-natal care began, with the world's first ante-natal clinic established in Adelaide in 1910. From 1912 the government gave all new mothers a maternity allowance of £5, to pay for qualified help in childbirth. Authorities also tried to regulate people who cared for babies.

With many illegitimate babies born, particularly to servants, an industry had grown up whereby women, called 'baby farmers', earned a living by caring for them. Others were cared for in orphanages. These babies often died – one orphanage had an 83 per cent death rate. There were many reasons. There was a high infant mortality rate at the best of times, especially from 'summer diarrhoea'. Artificially fed babies were in particular danger, for baby food was of poor standard and often given unhygienically. Baby farmers were often poor and could not charge much, and there must have been a temptation to skimp on the babies' food. Sometimes women received a lump sum for the baby, which made temptation even stronger. And little happened to them when babies did die, as police and the community seemed to accept the situation (what else could you do with these babies?).

In 1903 a baby died in Brisbane Hospital from malnutrition. At the inquest, Alice S— stated she was a widow with six children, caring for five babies for a very small income. A boy had died in April. In May she took charge of nine-day-old Eva, whose mother, a servant, visited Eva once. Alice fed Eva on condensed milk and water, and when she had diarrhoea, cured it with castor oil, and brandy in water. In October Eva came out in a rash and Alice took her to hospital, where she died. Despite this, and the evidence of malnutrition, Alice was allowed to continue looking after babies. Governments did try to regulate baby farmers, but nothing was done to help single women care for illegitimate children.

There were, however, other efforts to help women care for babies and children. Motherhood was glorified as women's highest calling. Midwives and hospitals were registered; some kindergartens and playgrounds were set up for children; and general improvements in water supplies, sewerage, slum clearance and milk supplies led to less disease. This was responsible for the second great demographic change of the period – a dramatic fall in the infant mortality rate.

During the nineteenth century the white Australian infant mortality rate (deaths of infants under one year old, per thousand infants) had been high. The average varied from a peak of 139 in 1875, to a low of 100 in 1900, but there was no marked decline, and the figure in 1903 was the same as in 1870 when records started, 111. There were some horrific figures in individual colonies – 181 in South Australia in 1875, 212 in the Northern Territory in 1904, which meant that more than one baby in five died. Generally, however, at this date the decline started, with a

Building a Nation

national average of 82 in 1904. This fell to 69 in 1911.

As we have already seen, having fewer children made women's lives far less difficult, and having fewer babies dying, with its associated anguish, must also have improved women's lives considerably. Governments were of course pleased with the drop in infant deaths, but they were not so pleased with the birthrate, which continued to fall (though more gradually): women knew when they were well off.

What impact did all these changes have on women's lives? Many new ideas such as more professional employment for women took some time to have a real impact, and though more women stayed single, the vast majority still saw marriage and motherhood as their natural role. For some housework was easier, with electric lighting, gas stoves and carpet sweepers, but these were expensive, and most women continued to keep house in much the same way as their mothers. The following biographies of women show that change was slow to come and for most, life was hard. Some impact of the changes can be seen, but what can

'Pluck and fortitude' in a scientist

Ethel White's husband Samuel was an ornithologist, and the couple travelled widely throughout Australia collecting specimens. Their longest journey of ten weeks by camel with Aboriginal guides took place in 1913. It covered 3,000 kilometres, said to be a world record for a woman.

Newspaper reporters interviewed Ethel about this trip, as an example of 'Woman, the Explorer'. 'If women want to go exploring, they must be prepared to rough it', she told them; she had enjoyed the best parts, and 'quietly endured' the others. She took only a change of clothing and no accessories, and one small dish was her bath, laundry and kitchen. Her camel was 'not exactly a rocking chair', and very smelly. But 'I never lost heart, thank goodness'. Her tasks had been packing specimens, cooking, writing Samuel's diary at his dictation, and making herself generally useful. 'We had no room for drones.' The reporters left, having 'realised conclusively what true greatness means'.

A Wealth of Women

also be seen, very clearly, is that few women were given over to selfishness, luxury and social pleasures. They were mostly hard-working, uncomplaining, devoted to their families, coping with life as well as they could, often with a touch of humour, making the most of opportunities as their convict forebears had done.

A contrast to talk of professions and the vote – but also a contrast to the grim picture of women ground down by a hard life, like Henry Lawson's fictional drover's wife – is the story of a real life drover's wife, Margaret Golding, described by her daughter Thele as the ideal mother. Born in Queensland in 1891, at seventeen Margaret married a drover, and they had eleven children. Even after childbirth, life had to go on, and once Margaret got herself out of bed shortly after the baby was born to cook tea, as her husband was due home from a droving trip. The family had a hard life. As they moved round, they lived in tents or huts, with unlined walls, dirt floors, canvas beds, boxes for chairs and wardrobes, and a hammock made of hessian bags for the baby. Margaret made all the family's clothes, sewing late into the night on her machine, singing hymns as she worked.

Washing involved a great deal of labour. Water was carted from creeks in kerosene tins, and Margaret washed clothes in a copper heated over an open fire. She ironed with flat irons

Margaret Golding's Puftaloons

All the family talk about the Puftaloons Mum used to make. We still make them – not as well as Mum used to in her camp oven or over an open fire. This is the recipe:

2 cups self-raising flour
Pinch of salt
   Just add enough water to make a dough, to scone consistency. Do not use milk.
   Place on floured board, do not knead. Cut into small rounds, place in hot oil and cook until golden brown. Delicious with butter or golden syrup or plum jam.

Thele Norris, Margaret's daughter

heated on the stove, and had to be careful not to smudge whites with black specks of ash. Many clothes were starched, using commercial starch if she had any, if not a mixture of flour and water.

When the family was on the move, Margaret drove a five-horse van across rivers, through rough terrain, up and down steep slopes. Once the van looked as if it would roll into a river bed far below, and was only saved by a tree in the way. On droving trips, Margaret went ahead of the mob to set up camp. She would find wood, set up the beds and cook tea in a camp oven – damper, corned meat with cabbage, puftaloons, and as a treat 'doughboys' and golden syrup. Sometimes she would catch an eel and cook it over the fire – 'delicious', recalled Thele. If Margaret could get cream, she put it in a golden syrup tin and walked round shaking it until it turned to butter, but sometimes the family was down to bread and dripping.

Margaret had remedies for all illnesses: a drop of kerosene on sugar for sore throats, sulphur and treacle if the blood was 'out of order', a poultice of sugar and soap for boils, wearing a red flannel to ward off colds, Condy's Crystals to stop infection, castor oil to stay regular. 'Mum was the best nurse and would sit by our beds late at night. I suppose she prayed a lot', wrote Thele. However, even Margaret's devotion could not save one of her little sons when he drank caustic soda. Another child died at birth. When Margaret herself needed help, Dad had to provide it, and when an inch-long splinter from a stump ran into Margaret's leg, he cut it out with a razor. 'We were frightened for Mum and were not allowed to look, but Mum didn't utter a word.'

Margaret was not a scholar, but always encouraged her children with their homework, sitting near them in the evening as they worked by the light of a kerosene lamp or a candle. 'She couldn't help, but would sit with us to give us moral support when the task just seemed beyond us.' But she had learnt much from life, and taught her children how to survive if they were lost in the bush, and how to pray. They would walk six miles to go to church.

Despite all the hardships and poverty, said Thele, Margaret never complained. 'If she was surrounded by her family, well that was enough for her.' Many brothers and sisters meant lots of fun for the children, and happiness came from having a mother 'who was always there for us, to catch us when we fell and to teach us to love one another. She was hardworking, brave, devoted. She lived her life for her family and we loved her, this wonderful woman – our mother, the best mum in the world'.

Settled life on farms could be as hard as an itinerant life. In the 1890s, Mary Pennefather's mother went from the east to the Western Australian goldfields, where she worked as a cook in a hotel, and married Ernest Pennefather, a miner. Mary was their second child, born in 1907. Ernest did well, and though he knew nothing about agriculture, bought a farm near Kellerberrin. Years of frustration and hardship lay ahead, wrote Mary.

Ernest cleared land and started to farm, and his wife worked hard to support him. 'She kept things running smoothly on the home front and without her unselfish devotion to us all, dad could never have managed', wrote Mary. She and her brother Harry helped too, caring for the hens, gathering wood and bringing in the cows. The only toy Mary ever had was a doll, the children never tasted sweets, but she and Harry were 'perfectly happy' playing in the bush. But 'I have no happy memories of my school days'. She was not scholastically inclined, and the teacher delighted in humiliating her, making her wear a dunce's cap and destroying her confidence.

From 1912 rainfall was poor and life, always hard, became even harder. The family lived on tinned meat and potatoes, which gave Mary's mother migraines and Ernest dreadful sores, known as 'barcoo rot', caused by a lack of vitamins. The children remained healthy – probably the parents gave them the best food. Fortunately, in 1916 the government decided to help farmers, and the family obtained a windmill. This made a huge difference. With adequate water they could increase stock, grow vegetables, keep pigs and bees. Mary's mother could even make the occasional plate of toffee.

Once a month the family held a church service in their home. People came from far and near. They sat on the verandah on planks laid between kerosene tins and covered with rugs, mother played hymns on the piano, and afterwards there was afternoon

Building a Nation

> ### The Grand Old Woman of Queensland Labour
>
> *Born in England in 1839, Emma Miller migrated with her family to Brisbane, where she became prominent in the labour movement. Widowed three times, she worked as a seamstress to maintain her family. She helped form a women's trade union in 1890, though the depression of the 1890s meant it did not flourish, and she pushed for equal pay and votes for women and the formation of a workers' political party, stressing that the labour movement was as important for women as for men. At the age of sixty-seven she went on an organising tour of western Queensland.*
>
> *During a general strike in 1912, workers held a protest march, in which seventy-three-year-old Emma led a women's contingent. Incensed when police charged them with batons, she reputedly dug her hat pin into the Police Commissioner's horse, which threw him. Her courage and spirit endeared her to labour followers, who called her Mother Miller, the Grand Old Woman of Queensland Labour. At her death in 1917, the flag at Brisbane Trades Hall flew at half mast, and tributes arrived from throughout Australia.*

tea, for which ladies brought a plate.

Farming could be easier, though it always involved hard work. Sarah Thornbury, from Pawleena, Tasmania, taught in the local school before marrying a farmer. 'All good farmers and their wives were joint partners', wrote her daughter. As well as the usual chores Sarah unyoked bullocks, delivered lambs, drove sheep, and combed possum and kangaroo skins for the furrier. She made cherry wine and turned pigs into bacon, ham, sausages, brawn and black puddings – you ate 'the whole pig except the squeal'. She made pies from parrots shot in the orchard, roasted swan, curried or baked rabbits, and made kangaroo and wallaby soup, patties and stew.

Sarah sewed beautifully. She made her three children beautiful christening gowns with tucks, feather stitching and lace insertion

A tough old biddy

'All my female ancestors seem to have been very strong women with minds of their own', wrote Aileen Sullivan. From the 1880s her great-grandmother, Mary Ann Dempsey, and husband William ran the Boundary Hotel in Burwood, Victoria. Patrons were mainly timber splitters and itinerant workers, pretty rough customers, and Mary Ann kept firm order. After William died, with the help of a daughter Mary Ann continued to run the pub with an iron hand, until she died in 1917, aged ninety-seven. Family tradition has it that she had the people terrorised for miles around: 'a tough old biddy', said Aileen.

(a strip of fine embossed calico, inserted into garments). After darning her husband's socks and patching his trousers, for relaxation Sarah crocheted, did drawn-thread work and tatted. She made her own clothes: silk drawers with long legs, buttoned at the waist and slit from the waist to the crutch at the back; camisoles with tucks and insertions; petticoats with cotton lace round the hem, tied at the waist with tape; long dresses also finely trimmed.

Under all this, women wore the only garment they could not make at home, corsets – 'agony', as Jane Bardsley wrote to a friend. 'I am not at all slim ... the fat has to go to some other part of the body when I get my waist to number nineteen [48 cm?]. My fat seems to shoot up to my neck, I can easily rest my chin on it. I think it is much better to be round the neck than the stomach, don't you think so?'

Other women had less respectable preoccupations than Sarah and Jane. The Timmins girls, Mary, Emily and Laura, lived in the Western Plains of New South Wales. Wonderful horsewomen, they were said never to open a gate but jumped over, and when hard-pressed, cleared fences to take a short cut. Their parents, of convict stock, were respected and hard-working, but their daughters joined their brother Jack in the bush sport of 'cattle duffing' (removing neighbours' animals). One day the three girls were chased through the bush by the police, and escaped by taking a short cut home. The police knew who they were, but when they rode up to the homestead a short time later they were greeted by three attractive, innocent-looking girls in frilly blouses who offered them tea and hot scones.

In 1885 a large mob of cattle disappeared from a neighbouring station. The police cornered the thieves – Jack, Mary and a friend, William Lawler. Astounded at the girl's presence, they let her ride beside them back to town. She escaped, but Jack and William were sent to gaol. Understandably, Mary's parents were upset when she eloped with William.

Meanwhile, Emily fell hopelessly in love with Henry Readford, otherwise known as Captain Starlight the bushranger, who had been plying his trade in the district. He was tall and dashing, but married. Emily became pregnant, which was generally disastrous for single women at this period, but at one stage was helpful to

Madame Brussels of Melbourne

Caroline Hodgson was born in Germany in 1851, and at twenty married Studholm Hodgson in a fashionable London church. They emigrated to Melbourne where Studholm joined the police, but they separated in 1874. Caroline next appeared as Madame Brussels, running the most sumptuous brothel in Melbourne. It was in Lonsdale Street, situated conveniently close to Parliament House. Caroline had an interest in eight other brothels, her main rivals being Scotch Maude and Annie Wilson. Her furniture was supplied by Buckley and Nunn, her capital came from an overdraft with the Bank of London, and she associated with Sir Samuel Gillott, solicitor and Minister for Labour, who lent her money. Social reformers called her 'the wickedest woman in Melbourne', but with her well-placed contacts she was safe from interference.

Following her husband's death, Caroline 'lived a colourful life' and married a pimp and procurer seventeen years her junior. He deserted her on their honeymoon, and Caroline divorced him. She lived with an adopted daughter until her death from diabetes in 1908, and was buried in the St Kilda cemetery beside Studholm.

her and Starlight. When they were caught red-handed with a mob of herefords, Starlight claimed he was her brother. Because of her condition, the jury were sympathetic and they were released. Starlight rode off into the sunset, and Emily's parents forgave her on the condition that she keep secret the name of the father of her child. The baby, Peter, was reared by her brother and his wife with their own fifteen children, and later Emily married and reared a fine family herself. (The Duchess of York's sister Jane married into this family. Her first husband, Alex Makim, is Peter's great-grandson.)

White Australian women were largely British, but migrants continued to arrive from continental Europe, with Germans the largest national group. Selma Stanitzki's grandparents came from German-speaking Poland to a farm in South Australia, where Selma was born in 1878. When she was eighteen, her father and brothers pioneered land on the Murray River, and she kept house for them. There she was courted by Alfred Henschke, who rode his bicycle 160 km to see her. They married in 1907, and ten months later Selma bore the first of twelve children. She was forty-six when the last was born, and told her daughter Irma she would not have had so many had she known how to avoid it. The family lived on the now world-famous Henschke vineyard in the Barossa Ranges.

Selma was a wonderful mother, recalled Irma, making every child feel special. She had immense strength of character, was conscientious and caring, and always dignified, despite the work of such a large family. Her Christian faith gave her spiritual strength. Her husband was gentle in times of stress, and there was a great bond between them. They spoke German in the home, and the children answered in English. Their food reflected their background, and included noodle soup, German wurst (sausage), streusel kuchen, and on Sundays, as a treat for children, a small glass of father's white wine.

It is difficult to generalise on the situation of women when individuals led such different lives, but the press certainly thought that by 1914, women had more opportunities. What they had called the 'age of transition' became 'the age of woman' – 'these

Building a Nation

> ### Selma Stanitzki's Noodle Soup
> *Mother made her noodle soup simply by simmering a fowl, covered with water, an onion, maybe some herbs from the garden, a little nutmeg or mace, salt and black peppercorns. When it was tender, she removed the fowl and browned it in butter and bacon to be served as the main course. Into the stock she put diced carrot, turnip and parsnip and home-made noodles. And most important, lots of chopped parsley added just before serving. My father loved it and would eat two or three servings.*
> Irma Dallwitz, Selma's daughter

advanced days, when women are absolutely refusing to be dictated to by "mere man"'. 'There is our share of work awaiting us', ran a letter from a woman, published in a conservative newspaper. 'I want women to realise what it is to be really independent in thought and action.'

During the late nineteenth century women came to Australia from other cultures than European. They usually immigrated with their menfolk, though in much smaller numbers.

Asian women came mainly from China and Japan. Chinese men arrived from mid century, attracted by gold. Most were single or left their wives at home, but a few Chinese women arrived. Die Hoe, born in Canton, arrived in Western Australia in 1895. She married Ah Woo, who had emigrated twenty years earlier, and they ran a shop in Broome. She was similar to the stereotype of a Chinese woman, married and respectable, whereas the stereotypical Japanese woman was a prostitute. Japanese men started arriving in the 1880s to work in the pearling industry, and a small number of women was brought from Japan either as servants or to provide sexual services for Japanese and European men, returning to Japan in their old age. They were quiet and self-effacing, though their lives tended to be hazardous, liable to violence and robbery. In 1893 the Japanese government organised a report on the forty or so women: they were mostly in their twenties, bought in Japan from poor families by a procurer who sold them in Hong Kong. There they gained experience then were sent to Australia, where they could earn four times as much. Some moved on to run brothels or other businesses with considerable success.

Indentured labourers from Melanesian islands, known as Kanakas, came to Queensland from 1864 to work in the sugar industry in particular. Theoretically they came voluntarily for a period limited by contract, but there are suggestions that force was sometimes used. The Islanders too were mainly men, but some married women were recruited, with a few marriages hastily organised so women could escape from arranged marriages or run away with other men to Australia. Some met further difficult situations here. In 1880 a husband and wife were sent to properties three miles apart. The authorities suggested the wife choose one of the 'boys' there, but she ran back to her husband, who 'clasped his faithful wife to his manly bosom'. A group who came to reclaim her were beaten off.

Women worked in the sugar fields, or sometimes as servants. In both cases, work was hard, and it was difficult to continue the traditions of their homelands. They were often the victims of rape or other violence, sometimes from Melanesian men. Many women were converted to Christianity, especially by Florence Young's Plymouth Brethren mission in Bundaberg, and as Christians they had a more equal role than they had traditionally.

With the White Australia policy in full force and racism widespread, however, all these women, and their menfolk, were treated as inferior by white Australians, and from 1901 non-European immigration was entirely prohibited and no further women arrived. Some returned home, but others established families in Australia, and a small number of women of non-European descent continued to add variety to Australian womanhood.

chapter four

The First World War

In March 1914, Mary Jane Miller arrived in Fremantle from England. Back home she had briefly entered a convent, but seeing posters advertising the wonderful life in Australia, Mary Jane decided to emigrate. In Fremantle it was 106°F [40°C]; she had £5 in the world, she knew no one in Australia and decided she would not stay. But since she could not return immediately, she found a job as housekeeper with 'some nice people'. Their kitchen was antiquated, but they provided what Mary Jane asked for – a gas stove, lino on the floor – '& soon I had the place looking quite homey'. The butcher stared at the changes when he came to collect the order. Mary Jane said, 'Butcher, I must have better meat'. 'How long have you been out?' he asked, but did as she asked.

The next Saturday he asked her to the football. 'I had never been to any sports [but] I thought he is very nice & a Catholic too', she wrote. So they went to the football, had tea in a cafe and went to the trots; then he took her to meet his family, where she had the alarming experience of being chased by a race horse goanna. Mary Jane decided she liked Australia, 'the wide open Spaces & the glorious Freedom of life & to think that one could go out without a hat & being all dressed up'.

So later in 1914 they married, but then something happened which changed Mary Jane's life, and that of many women. Seventeen-year-old Lillian Paton recalled how she heard the news. She

A Wealth of Women

was helping her mother in their shop-cum-post-office-cum-tearooms in Towrang one Monday morning in August. The newspaper arrived in the train from Sydney, and she spread it out on the counter. The headlines stated that Britain was at war with Germany, so Australia was at war too.

The First World War had a considerable impact on women. Many were affected immediately, as husbands, fathers or sons went off to fight, and women had to keep the family going at home until the men returned. If the men died, women's problems could be permanent. But there was also the effect on women in general. Before the war, their position had started to change with new opportunities to be educated, to enter paid employment, to take part in public life, to have an alternative to marriage. What effect would the war have on this?

Almost all Australians approved when the country entered the war, and many men enlisted. Lillian Paton's boyfriend Rob was among the first to join the Light Horse, and came to say goodbye with a chaste, formal kiss. Mary Jane's husband also joined the army. Over the four years of the war, 400,000 men enlisted to fight in Europe and the Middle East, out of a population of under five million. The government arranged for about half their pay to go to their families, but quite apart from missing their husbands, many women were still faced with problems. Their share of soldiers' pay was not large; many, like Mary Jane, gave birth while their husbands were away; women had to run families and often family businesses.

There was the ever-present fear that their menfolk would be killed, and many women lost fathers, husbands, brothers, sons, fiancés or friends. Jemima Erskine, her husband and seven children lived on a selection at Penrose, eating rabbits and wallabies, and using possum skins for blankets. Life was challenging but satisfying until Jemima was devastated by a series of deaths. Her husband died, then a son was killed when a motor bike ran into his sulky. Her remaining four sons enlisted. Fred was killed in France in 1916, and Jack was badly gassed. Arthur won the DCM, but he too died, on Anzac Day 1918. When the war ended the family was delighted to welcome home Phil and Jack, and Jack

The First World War

was able to hide his serious illness from his mother until her death. He died soon afterwards. Few women lost so many men to the war, but it did leave a trail of bereavement through the country.

With Germany the enemy, those with German connections also suffered. In 1907 Mary Campbell of Brisbane, a factory machinist, married Otto Dabelstein, who had been born in Brisbane of German parents. When war broke out, because of his German origin he was sacked from his job. He tried to find work, becoming a carrier and working on the roads, but when people heard his name he was dismissed. Finally he got a job at a country sawmill, and told Mary to sell their house and furniture (which broke her heart) and join him with their four children. She hated country life until the day she died, wrote their daughter Thelma: there were ticks, snakes, itinerant men looking for work, and the worry of illness – when Thelma caught pneumonia Mary had to take her to hospital in Brisbane, a long and worrying trip. They moved from job to job, sometimes living in tents, a hard existence.

Many women supported Australia's part in the war by helping the war effort. The Red Cross organisation, which aimed to help victims of war, had already been established. As the war progressed, thousands of women joined. When the wounded started to return from Gallipoli, Red Cross became vital. Volunteers met ships, transferred soldiers to convalescent homes and nursed them, provided soldiers with meals and helped discharged servicemen. Overall, 82,000 women were involved. Red Cross was excellent at fundraising, and formed a strong, vibrant group of professionally organised women who provided a substantial service.

The army provided no comforts for soldiers, and in the bitter winter of 1916 troops in the trenches in France ran out of socks. General Birdwood, in charge of the Australian troops, asked for help, and in a huge effort women provided 80,000 pairs. They continued to knit for the rest of the war, producing 1,354,324 pairs of socks alone. 'Everybody knitted socks & balaclavas for the soldiers as it was so cold in France in the trenches & that is where

I learnt to knit', wrote Mildred Jackson, a maid in Gawler. In Towrang, dances and concerts were held in Lillian's mother's tearooms to farewell soldiers and raise funds. When war broke out few women could knit, Lillian commented, but everyone learned, and made socks, scarves and gloves for soldiers. As postmistress, her mother had the sad job of delivering messages of soldiers' deaths to their families. It was even worse when the boys' letters arrived after news of their deaths.

All over Australia, many women did their bit. Violet Wurfel lived in the hamlet of Brim in Victoria. She wrote to all thirteen local boys who went to the war, sending news of home to cheer them. Narrogin, Western Australia, was one of many towns whose women filled boxes for soldiers with 'comforts' – knitted items, condensed milk, dried fruit, chocolate and sweets. Girls often added their name and address. For Christmas 1916 Western Australia had a quota of 14,000 boxes, of which Narrogin sent 397, a huge effort for a small community. Overall, it was claimed that Australians were the best supported of all troops on the Western Front, and that comforts from home were a significant factor in their high morale, 'the envy of the other troops', according to Birdwood.

The many women's groups formed before the war proliferated,

A mother finds the Army heartless

Mary Drummond's son by her first marriage, Victor Farr, took part in the Gallipoli landing in April 1915, and in June the army authorities informed Mary that he was wounded. In July, August, September and October she wrote asking for more news, and in December she was informed that Victor was missing. In January 1916 a Court of Enquiry decided he had been killed. Two years later Mary received his effects, and in 1920 the army wrote asking if Victor had any nearer kin than herself, such as his father. Her reply is not recorded. A year later the army asked where Victor was buried. 'I only wish I could tell you I knew he was buried my sorrow would not be so great', answered Mary. The army sent her a pamphlet entitled 'Where the Australians rest'.

The First World War

with societies formed to provide items ranging from Babies' Kits to Tobacco for Troops. Each member of the One Woman, One Recruit League tried to persuade, cajole or even bully a man into enlisting. One woman's victim was her baker. After 'two years of unremitting effort' she succeeded, the baker rushing back from his rounds to tell her he had enlisted. 'Cheer-Up' groups helped soldiers before they went overseas, providing meals (ten thousand a month in Adelaide), entertainment and public farewells. Later they welcomed returning soldiers. South Australian groups were organised by Mrs Seager, who chose 'reliable' young girls as helpers and felt they had a marked moral effect. Many a soldier, she reported, said the girls helped them 'go straight'. As casualty lists lengthened, Cheer-Up groups remained steadfastly cheerful, with Mrs Seager carrying on even when her own son was killed.

Hundreds of thousands of Australian women helped the war effort in these ways, but some wanted to do more. A few aimed at a military role, but the authorities said war was not for women. In 1917 two hundred girls in a Melbourne clothing factory agreed to spend one night a week making shirts and underclothes for the war effort. They went on to form the Khaki Girls, where squads of girls in khaki uniforms raised money by displays of drill and physical culture, and bugle music. This was fine, but when they offered themselves for active service, the Defence Department refused. It did allow the formation of a Women's Auxiliary Army Corps, but members only helped with recruiting and caring for soldiers' children.

An example of an individual who threw her whole life into helping the war effort was Annie Wheeler. Nicknamed 'The General' by her family, she grew up on a station near Rockhampton, did some nursing training, and married one of her patients, a grazier. After his death, Annie took their daughter Portia to England for her education, and they were in London when war broke out.

Annie was keen to play her part and joined the Australian War Contingent Association, but, frustrated by its lack of organisation, resigned to devote herself to helping soldiers from central Queensland. She and Portia visited them in hospital, and found many with no money or news from home. So she wrote to their families, and answered queries from Australia. Word spread. Annie was far more efficient than the Army postal service, and soon she was receiving so many letters and parcels that the post office provided her with her own van. She had 2,300 troops on her books, and also handled money cabled by families, welcomed soldiers on leave, and sent newsletters to prisoners of war and newspapers back home. Nothing was too much trouble for 'her boys'. London policemen knew to direct any soldier with a slouch hat to her home, and she was called 'Mother of the Anzacs'.

In 1919 the Australian government paid Annie and Portia's passages home, and when they arrived in Rockhampton, returned soldiers dragged her car to her hotel through cheering crowds. She was given civic receptions and a furnished house, and was one of the first Australian women to receive the OBE.

The one area of active service where women were welcomed was nursing. Women had nursed soldiers in the Boer War, with hundreds volunteering and about sixty going to South Africa. 'My God, Australian Sisters, what shall we do?' groaned one medical officer when a group arrived at a hospital. They proved so competent, however, that prejudice against them started to break down. In the First World War it was taken for granted that women would nurse the troops, and 2,139 served overseas.

In 1913 Sister Nellie Pike volunteered for the Australian Army Nursing Service. Born in 1889 in Wellington, she was the second of twelve children, and became a nurse because she did not want to spend her life caring for her younger siblings. She was tiny, under five feet, but strong physically, and also mentally. This was just as well. Nellie was sent first to Egypt, then to the island of Lemnos, where an Australian hospital had been set up to care for men wounded at Gallipoli. At first there had been no equipment or even water, and patients lay on the ground. Nurses tore up their own clothes for dressings, but felt they could do little. 'Could only wish all I know to be killed outright', wrote Matron Grace Wilson.

By the time Nellie arrived, so had equipment, and she worked in a tent. 'I could imagine no greater joy than to be working under

The First World War

canvas so close to the gallant men of Anzac', she wrote. 'They were grim and tragic but somehow inspiring days.' Some men had been treated on hospital ships, others came straight from the trenches, filthy, bloodstained and sobbing from pain. Often lack of treatment had caused gangrene to set in. 'We could do little for some soldiers, except to help them die decently.' Some had typhoid, dysentery, jaundice or trench feet, a very painful disease in which feet rotted from standing in water.

Conditions were poor for men at Gallipoli, but not much better for nurses. No sheets, rough mattresses, long hours and poor food, mainly corned beef and biscuit, for there was no bread. Fortunately Red Cross sent parcels, which, said Nellie, kept patients and nurses alive. There was another source of bounty. Nellie's senior orderly once beckoned her outside the tent and cautiously passed her a soiled parcel of sacking with blood seeping from it. It contained a large chunk of steak, which the orderly had purloined from a ship anchored in the bay, where British staff officers lived in luxury. When blankets were in short supply for patients, orderlies produced some from the same source.

After the withdrawal from Gallipoli, Australian soldiers and nurses moved to the Western Front in France, and nurses worked in hospitals just behind the line, dealing with the aftermath of battle. 'When our backs refused to hold us up any longer, we sat on the floor and cut the boots and socks off the stone cold and swollen feet, wrapping them in cotton wool and bandages.' 'The depression which settled on one watching these men die in spite of all you did for them was awful.' 'A nightmare, blood, blood, blood everywhere, and suffering, God forgot us, I am certain.'

Nellie Pike and the other nurses saw the other effects of war: men drinking themselves insensible, wounding themselves or feigning illness to escape the horrors of war, shooting bullying officers, catching venereal disease from prostitutes. Nellie knew fifty ways the men used to bring on a high temperature. To the men, nurses were angels, and several later told Nellie's son how 'Little Sister', as they called her, brought them back from the dead, or saved them from having feet amputated – 'she told the sawbones that she could pull me through and by God, she did!' Nellie herself was appalled by the waste in human life. 'Don't talk to me about the glory of war!' she told her son. 'It was a wicked waste of good men!' She was awarded three medals for her war service, one bearing the inscription 'The Great War for Civilisation'. '*What* civilisation?' Nellie demanded.

For Nellie personally, the war had a happy outcome. While she was working in France she fell in love with an Australian lieutenant, and they married in 1917. Nellie was discharged from the army, and nursed privately in England until the war ended. The army refused to repatriate her and her husband had to pay her fare – and then they were not allowed to travel on the same ship. Their son John was brought up on the stories of diggers, trenches and nursing, but he felt that army nurses did not receive the honour they deserved. In school, teachers often said to the class, 'Hands up those children whose father went to the war'. Once John said that his mother had gone as well. 'That's absurd', said the teacher, Miss Cross. 'Women didn't go to the war!' John tried to explain, but Miss Cross was only convinced when a classmate corroborated his story by saying he had seen John's mum wearing her medals.

Back in Australia, with so many men away there were a few more jobs for women. They moved into clerical positions in particular, in banks and the public service, but their expansion was limited by prejudice (one bank only employed them after direct orders arrived from London), by businesses, particularly farms, absorbing the loss of labour themselves, and because as many jobs as possible were given to returned soldiers.

Women continued to be vocal about a number of issues, such as urging the appointment of women in responsible positions. During the war several became jail matrons and magistrates, and Kate Cocks, a member of the Woman's Christian Temperance Union, became South Australia's first policewoman, with Annie Ross employed soon afterwards. They investigated complaints about ill-treatment of women and assisted when women were charged with offences, ranging from procuring abortions to fortune-telling. They earned respect for both mental and physical courage – during a strike Annie overpowered a burly wharfie who tried to intimidate her. Another victory of the Woman's Christian Temperance Union was six o'clock closing of hotels. To persuade the government to instigate it, women gave public addresses, wrote to newspapers, distributed pamphlets and put up posters 'which cost much brain fag and large sums of money', and when early closing was put to referendums, the vote was overwhelmingly in favour.

Women also took to the streets on matters concerning the war. Some women's groups supported government recruiting drives, while others fought for peace. The Women's Peace Army toured Australia advocating peace, and its song 'I didn't raise my son to be a soldier' was judged so dangerous that it was banned. At a meeting in Brisbane, the organisers were notified that anyone who sang the song would be arrested, but the audience stood as one and sang it.

Feelings became even more inflamed in 1916 and 1917 when the government held referendums over whether to introduce conscription. Women campaigned for both sides, and both sides appealed to women, mainly as mothers. Anti-conscriptionists argued: war is male aggression, women naturally love peace, don't give up your sons to slaughter; their opponents argued: give up your sons to support the men already at the Front and see the crisis through. Bitter battles, passionately fought, polarised the nation, and women both committed and suffered violence. Conscription was narrowly defeated both times. But despite the considerable activity by women, their publicly acknowledged position was as mothers or as passive supporters, keeping the home fires burning.

This was true in that most women lived a domestic life at home, as depicted in the diary of Inez Weatherhead of Tynong North, Victoria. In 1918 Inez was twenty-six, and she and her husband Arthur, a sawyer, had two small sons. Her brother and two of Arthur's brothers were fighting in the war, but Inez' diary is mainly concerned with her work: cleaning, washing (on washing days she rose at 5.00 am), baking, making jam and sewing clothes; growing vegetables and fruit; caring for her eight goats; helping Arthur clear a block of land; setting rabbit traps; lining the bedroom walls with hessian; coping with family colds and the baby's teething. For occasional recreation she visited her or Arthur's parents, played the piano or listened to the phonograph, and when there was a local dance she wished she could go. 'I was once the Belle of the Ball, but must stay home with my children now.' Finally, on 11 November 1918, Inez wrote: 'Peace declared. Germany surrenders. Great Joy. Fun in Tynong, too windy to go'.

When the cheering died down, Australia's women realised that the end of the war left many with problems. Some never had a chance to marry, as fiancés or friends were among the 65,000 Australian men who died. Others had lost husbands, fathers, brothers or sons. Widows were paid a small pension, but often found life hard, as Ann Vaubell pointed out to the army when they sent her the war medals awarded to her dead son. 'I am very sorry that those who have the spending of money do not know better how to spend it – it is a poor way to remember the dead by robbing the living', replied Ann. 'There are many poor soldiers who have wives and children have not enough to keep out hunger and cold who could be helped with the money spent on useless Medals.'

Those whose men did return often faced other difficulties. Many ex-soldiers were handicapped by the loss of a limb or continuing ill-health, and even among the apparently healthy, the appalling conditions of war had left their mark, so that depression, alcoholism and aggressive behaviour were common. Some brought back venereal disease which spread through the community – in 1927 it was claimed that 7.5 per cent of the entire population of Australia was affected. The divorce rate doubled in the decade after the war.

Lillian Paton went to Sydney to meet Rob's ship, wondering what he would be like after four years away. When he came near, she could not move her legs to walk towards him. But they got to know each other again, and travelled back to Towrang together. At the railway station, people had put detonators on the line, which exploded to welcome the soldiers home, and there was a public welcome that night. When Rob turned twenty-one, he asked Lillian to marry him. 'What Joy. I thought no one could be happier than I.'

The First World War

Women cope without men

Elizabeth and George Fay lived on their farm property near Euroa, and when war broke out, George was nearing middle age. He went to Melbourne to train young soldiers, but finding it hard to watch inexperienced boys sail away, eventually left with them for the Middle East. Elizabeth was left with the farm to run, and took over the local post office. She had six children to rear, the youngest newly born. Always close to her husband, she was sustained by his letters, and knew instinctively, without any doubt, the day he died at the El Burg Hills in Egypt in 1917. Her belief was later confirmed, when the sad news reached her.

Jessie Menzies' husband John also enlisted, leaving her with three children and one on the way. He was reported missing in action, but she could not draw a widow's pension until his death was ascertained, several decades later. So she had to go out to work to keep her children, and since there were no child-minding facilities in Sydney, her seven-year-old daughter Flora had to take the baby to school with her. With the help of a compassionate woman teacher, Flora fed and changed the baby between lessons.

Cara Poole was teaching in the country town of Nannup in Western Australia, where she met an engineer surveying routes for the railway. In 1911 Cara and Louis married, and they lived in tents in construction camps with their two sons. As a married man Louis did not enlist straight away, but perhaps felt the influence of recruiting drives, and in 1917 joined up. Cara took the children to her parents, and remained there after Louis was killed in action. For the rest of her life, her bedroom was filled with photos of Louis and other keepsakes, to keep his memory near, 'though in her heart she did not need them'.

But some women's boyfriends had married other women in Britain. The deserted women were often furious, in-laws frequently did not welcome the English brides, and the brides themselves had to cope with this hostility as well as having to fit into a new country. Edith Kenchington grew up in a village on the

A Wealth of Women

> ### A legacy of the war: Anzac Biscuits
>
> *Part of the ration to the ANZAC soldiers were jaw-breaking Anzac wafers made with oatmeal. At home this more palatable version became popular – easy to make, nutritious and delicious.*
>
> *1 cup rolled oats 2 tablespoons boiling water*
> *¾ cup coconut 1 cup sugar*
> *1 cup flour ½ cup butter*
> *1 teaspoon bicarbonate of soda 1 tablespoon golden syrup*
>
> *Mix oats, flour, sugar and coconut together.*
> *Melt syrup and butter together.*
> *Mix soda with boiling water and add to the melted butter and syrup. Add this to the dry ingredients.*
> *Place on a greased tray in tablespoons.*
> *Bake in a slow oven 20 minutes.*

Salisbury Plain, near a large army camp. She fell in love with a 'cheeky, handsome Australian soldier', Tom Tomkins, and they married in 1917. After the war Tom returned home with the troops, and Edith came later with their baby, travelling to an unknown land on the other side of the world. In Australia, Edith found a laid-back way of life different from the English decorum she was used to. Her mother-in-law never accepted her, and she never felt Australian. She had to care for Tom, who had been gassed and wounded, and their five children, and felt that her life would have been much easier if she had stayed in England; but 'she did a fantastic job of raising her family under sometimes daunting conditions'.

Marjorie Bunker experienced a less happy outcome. She worked in the office of a hardware store in Taralga, and became engaged to the owner's son, Eric. He enlisted, was wounded, and returned home in 1919. Meanwhile Marjorie had fallen in love with someone else, but he was a cousin so her family did not think the relationship was suitable, and she felt committed to Eric because of his war experiences. They were married in 1920 – not very happily.

The First World War could have been positive in enhancing

women's position and public role. Nurses had been heroines, some women moved into responsible jobs, others publicly promoted causes, and women played a huge role in supporting the war effort. But women continued to be perceived in their traditional passive roles of mother and home-maker, suffering but keeping home going, while men were the heroes who had shown the world what the new nation of Australia could do. In theory this meant that the war was a backward step for women. In practice, however, so many women had been so active in the war that the changes which started in the pre-war period were not obliterated. They were set to continue when the war was over.

Snapshot

HEALTH

1789	smallpox outbreak in Sydney causes many deaths, of Aborigines in particular
1847	ether first used to provide a painless operation, Launceston
1850s	new diseases appear: measles (1850), diphtheria (1858)
1860	first Australia-wide influenza epidemic
1867	antiseptics first used, by Dr Pringle of Parramatta
1868	first trained nurses, Sydney
1880s	fertility decline starts, lowering average children per white mother from seven in 1880 to four by 1911
-	aseptic midwifery appears, and lowers maternal mortality
-	some contraceptives are sold, but they are few and hard to obtain. Most women rely on withdrawal, abstinence, douching and abortion
1895	antitoxin available to fight diphtheria
1896	Queen Victoria Hospital opens in Melbourne, staffed by women for women
c. 1900	better sanitation and water supplies, cleaner milk, control of food sellers cut rates of disease; infant mortality starts to fall
1909	Bush nursing scheme brings professional nursing to country people, Victoria
1910	first ante-natal clinic in the world, Adelaide

Snapshot

1912	Maternity Allowance for all white mothers, of £5 per baby
-	Australian Inland Mission started by the Rev. J Flynn to assist isolated patients
1915	Aspro is first made in Melbourne, as aspirin supplies from Germany are cut off by war
1919	Spanish Influenza epidemic kills 12,500 people in Australia
1920s	maternity hospitals and baby health centres become widespread
1930s	polio epidemics. Sister Kenny opens her first polio clinic, in Townsville
1937	antibiotics begin to lower maternal mortality significantly
1950s	ante-natal care becomes universal
-	relaxation techniques appear to ease childbirth
1957	Salk vaccine is used against polio; Sabin vaccine appears in 1967
1961	contraceptive pill is available, and by the end of the 1960s Australian women are the world's highest users
1975	Medicare provides universal, compulsory health insurance
1980	first 'test-tube' baby born, Melbourne, after in vitro fertilisation

chapter five

Beginning the Struggle

by Prue Torney-Parlicki

For Indigenous women the Victorian period meant only a continuation of the severe hardships they had endured since the beginning of European settlement. By the end of the nineteenth century, few Aboriginal people had not experienced disruption to their traditional lifestyle; most had been dispossessed and were living in camps on the outskirts of white society or on reserves and missions. To write about the lives of these women presents challenges for a white historian. Aboriginal people have always had a rich oral tradition, and much of this material is now being recorded and transcribed. This has enabled Indigenous men and women to present some of their more recent history in their own voices and to counteract the dominant European versions of their past. Writing about the colonial period, however, necessarily relies on European accounts.

The task of documenting the lives of Aboriginal women before contact with whites is even more problematic, for there are no available accounts of Australian life before literate people produced them. We are thus reliant upon the impressions of early white observers – usually men – which reflect the assumptions and preoccupations of European society at the time, and in which Aboriginal women are often barely visible. Furthermore, those who produced these accounts were seldom the first whites to encounter Aboriginal peoples; they were thus describing societies already altered to some extent by European invasion. Observations about the lives of Aboriginal women before the arrival of whites, therefore, can be no more than generalisations.

The relationship between men and women in traditional Aboriginal society was essentially a partnership; each regarded the other as inter-dependent. Women usually went out daily with other women and children to hunt small animals and fish, and to gather wild honey, yams, lilies, seeds, raw materials for baskets and other utensils, medicinal herbs and ochre, while men were responsible for large-scale hunting and fishing. Women thus assumed the main burden of providing the daily food supply, as well as cooking the food, making the camp for the night, and procuring firewood and water; but both men and women produced trade items and were thus economically dependent on each other.

Women controlled the important functions of childbirth and rearing, and were responsible for teaching their young about the land, and how to survive in the bush. In the rituals and ceremonies which formed an important part of Aboriginal life, women generally played a different but complementary role from that of Aboriginal men. They were directly involved in death and mourning rituals and responsible for the care of bones of the deceased. Some observers also recorded dances from which men were excluded, and noted the significant contribution of women to male initiation ceremonies.

Marriage arrangements were generally made by senior males, although there is evidence that women wielded influence in some communities. A complex kinship system determined who one could and could not marry. Young males and females had little say in their choice of partner, and were heavily penalised if they eloped. Often marriages were arranged through a 'promise' system whereby it was agreed, sometimes even before the conception or birth of the child concerned, that he or she would marry a particular woman or man. This practice continued well after European settlement in areas where traditional life remained relatively undisturbed. Ethel Hassell, the wife of a pastoralist living at remote Jarramungup in Western Australia in the 1880s, was

Beginning the Struggle

surprised to find a young Aboriginal mother discussing her baby daughter's matrimonial arrangements with female relatives just hours after giving birth. She was told that it was the custom to betroth an infant girl to a man or youth who had to provide some food for her. If the parents died, or if the mother was captured by another tribe, he had to support the child. In such circumstances, she would be taken care of by his female relatives until old enough to be his wife. However, he would not be expected to remain single during this period, and had often fathered other children by the time the marriage took place.

The land held, and continues to hold, deep spiritual significance for all Aboriginal people. During the creation period the ancestral heroes, who were simultaneously human, animal and bird, had moved across the tribal territory, and these beings still lived in the local country, generating life. Each tribal group followed the boundaries set by these ancestors in their Dreaming stories, and each Aboriginal person was part of a totem that derived from the ancestral beings and was determined by the place where his or her mother conceived. If a woman became aware that she was pregnant when near a goanna Dreaming site, for example, her child would have an intimate connection to the goanna and would be associated with the goanna totem.

The European invasion brought violence and massive destruction to traditional communities, but it met strong resistance. Some women took an active role in resisting the invaders. Jandamurra, the Bunaba man who resisted European invaders for three years in the Kimberley region, has long been of interest to writers and historians, but Bunaba people have begun to reveal how women contributed to the campaign, loading the guns while Jandamurra shot at police from caves and hilltops. A little more is known about Walyer (or Tarereenore), a Tasmanian woman who was abducted in her teens by sealers in the Bass Strait Islands. Escaping from the sealers, she eventually returned to her people, the Plairherehillerplue, of Emu Bay, and led them in resisting the officials and servants of the Van Diemen's Land Company. She was again captured by sealers, but refused to work for them. As punishment for her lack of co-operation she was sent to Penguin

Island but on the way she attempted to kill her captors. Finally she was sent to George Augustus Robinson's mission on Swan Island, where she was kept isolated from other Aborigines because of fears that she would incite revolt. This did not prevent her, however, from boasting to other inmates about her knowledge of firearms and claiming that she had killed many white people and robbed their huts. Walyer died on Swan Island in May 1831.

After the arrival of Europeans, the scarcity of white women on the frontier created a demand for the sexual and domestic services of Aboriginal women, and in many cases women were taken by force and subjected to violence and rape. Referred to sexually by the slang term 'black velvet', Aboriginal women were frequently abused, beaten, infected with venereal disease, and then abandoned; it was alleged that some European men believed that by transmitting the disease to an Aboriginal woman they would rid themselves of the infection. Yet not all women were passive victims of this violence. Some offered themselves, or were offered by their husbands, to the Europeans in exchange for food, tobacco, alcohol and other goods. Rather than viewing their behaviour as prostitution, they believed that by performing such acts they were

A little princess

Mathinna, who was also known as Mary, was born in 1835 on Flinders Island, of Toogee descent. When she was six, the beautiful Mathinna was taken into the home of Lady Jane Franklin, the wife of the governor, who taught her to regard herself as a princess. However, this illusion was suddenly terminated two years later when the Franklins left Tasmania. Mathinna was placed in the Queen's orphan school where she learned that she was just another black child. She returned to Flinders Island in 1844, and remained there for three years, but was sent back to the orphanage where she stayed until she was sixteen. Mathinna was then reunited with her people at Oyster Cove, where she died in 1856.

establishing reciprocal ties in a traditional way. Many attempted to make their relationships permanent or semi-permanent in order to obtain rations and better treatment for their extended family, and others welcomed the opportunity to gain access to European goods and shelter. But often conflicts arose when Europeans did not reciprocate in the manner desired by a woman's Aboriginal kin.

For the large number of Aboriginal people who worked on cattle stations in Australia's north, the frontier experience was one of survival and accommodation rather than total submission. As Ann McGrath has shown in her study of Aborigines in the cattle industry, Aboriginal workers had much to teach whites, and their work allowed them to preserve their self-esteem and parts of their culture in an otherwise racist environment. Women played a central role in this survival, providing a link between the homestead and the camp as well as negotiating with Europeans. White authorities conceded that Aboriginal women were indispensable to the development of the pastoral industry. In 1928, JW Bleakley, Queensland's chief protector of Aborigines, concluded in a report on Northern Territory conditions that the white man could not have carried on without the assistance of Aboriginal women, even in areas where white women had ventured.

Many Aboriginal women on stations worked in jobs traditionally performed by white men, including droving, buffalo shooting, road and fence building, slaughtering and skinning. One white observer, writing about stations in northern Queensland in 1883, was struck by the appearance of pipe-smoking female stockworkers wearing moleskins and flannel shirts; another drover estimated that women made up 50 per cent of all stockriders in the Kimberley in the 1910s. Women who performed these tasks such as Amy Laurie, May Yunduin and Maudie Moore challenged the masculine image of the cattle industry. Laurie, whose mother was a Djaru woman and father an Aranda, was born around 1913 at Kincimbie station, and raised by a white drover who leased the station. As a teenager she performed stockwork with Aboriginal men, and went droving with her first husband, Alec Smith, until the birth of her first child. Yunduin also accompanied her husband in droving work in the Northern Territory and Kimberley. Maudie Moore, of Dunham River station, was an excellent stockworker, proficient in mustering and chasing cattle and throwing bullocks; she eventually became a head stockworker at the station. Women were proud of their achievements as stockriders, and at first Aboriginal men did not object to their involvement, some even taking orders from female riders.

However, women's participation in this work gradually became less common. Assisted by the development of government policies regarding suitable work for men and women, stockwork came to be seen as a 'male-only' role. Most Aboriginal women on cattle stations earned a living by working as domestic servants or by providing casual or semi-permanent sexual services for white men. The managers of many pastoral properties were single men, who wanted black women to perform basic domestic and sexual duties. On those stations where white women were present, Aboriginal women were required to provide more domestic labour and their sexual role was reduced.

Most Aboriginal women on stations, like their male counterparts, were not paid. Often they were 'adopted' in exchange for payment in kind. Daisy Djunduin, a Gadjerong woman who was born at Bullo River, lived in the bush with her grandmother until Billy Weaber came and took her to work on Ningbing station; for Daisy's services, Weaber 'paid' her grandmother, father and stepfather some flour, sugar, clothes and blankets. The Aborigines who co-operated in this 'bartering' system realised that whites who needed labour would take their child regardless of whether or not they consented. They were also realistic about the difficulties of competing with whites for their land. Co-operation afforded those who lived in station camps a measure of protection and security, and their children were given the chance to learn how to survive in the dominant white society.

Young girls were gradually introduced to their work by the station manager or his wife. Helen Sullivan, whose mother was Aboriginal and father Chinese, began at about the age of seven by cleaning the yard and collecting eggs. As she grew older, she would round up the cows for milking and bring them in, and then help in the house. She would set the table, prepare the kitchen, light the wood stove, and bring the cows in again. Winnie Chapman's job as an eight-year-old was to pick up and burn any litter around the homestead and kitchen. Later she was taught to wash and iron clothes, and later still, to cook and make bread. She was also required to clean the kitchen, a big job that entailed cleaning its entire contents as well as sweeping and washing the floor. Inevitably, many girls made errors during this training period. One 'missus', Helen Skardon, complained that it 'took three lessons a day for weeks before Sarah was able to set the table, and then she invariably left the jam-spoons off or put the knives on the left side'.

The workload of adult women was onerous. Winnie Chapman would rise at dawn, milk the goats and prepare the kitchen before carting water from the bore to clean the kitchen. She then prepared the food for the workers' lunch. After breakfast she would work either in the homestead kitchen or the manager's house, carry water, and then rest. After lunch she watered the garden, collected eggs, and cleaned the kitchen again. When the housework was finished, she tended the goats, collected rubbish, and performed other odd jobs. She then prepared supper, washed the dishes, carried water away, and swept the floor. Housework on most stations followed a weekly routine, with certain days allocated to washing and baking; domestic servants were usually permitted a Sunday 'walkabout' during which they collected bush foods.

On isolated stations, Aboriginal servants were indispensable during white women's pregnancies and labour; they delivered babies and nursed their mothers, using traditional skills and herbal remedies. When the children were born, Aboriginal 'nursegirls' assumed much of the burden of looking after them while the 'missus' followed other pursuits. Yet white employers often complained that their Aboriginal servants needed constant supervision, and could not be left in charge of the house or children. The author of *We of the Never-Never*, Mrs Aeneas Gunn, was typical in portraying her female staff as unreliable and disorganised. Yet many older Aboriginal women on stations taught and supervised young girls, and took much responsibility; even Gunn noted her appreciation of one servant who 'rounded up' other women when they shirked their duties. Some women were reluctant to assert their authority in front of their white employers, and so their leadership went unnoticed.

Despite its shortcomings, station life provided a measure of security and stability for some Aboriginal women that was denied to others. Many families eked out an existence in camps, or were forced by governments and church authorities onto reserves and missions. Reserves had been established from the early nineteenth century, ostensibly for the care and protection of Aboriginal people who had been dispossessed of their land and uprooted from their traditional lifestyle. The remnants of tribal groups were forcibly removed, placed under the control of either colonial governments or missionary organisations, and encouraged to abandon their traditional beliefs, customs and ceremonies. Later, the ideal of 'protecting' Aborigines was enshrined in a series of parliamentary Acts: the Aboriginal Acts of Victoria (1886), Queensland (1897), Western Australia (1905), New South Wales (1909), Northern Territory (1911), and South Australia (1911). The Queensland Act of 1897, which provided the model for much subsequent policy in all states except New South Wales and Victoria, brought all Aboriginal people, unless they were exempted, under the control of 'protection boards'. Indigenous people were denied freedom of movement, association and marriage, the right to control their money and property, and other civil rights including the right to vote, drink and own dogs.

Torres Strait Islanders, who have a distinctive ethnic identity and culture, initially avoided inclusion under the 1897 Queensland Act by arguing that their skills and settled lifestyle demonstrated that they were more developed on the evolutionary scale than mainland Aborigines. The Islands' labour-intensive pearling industry had much to gain by exemption from the Act which included restrictions on employment. Nevertheless, the Islands gradually came under the Queensland administration, and from 1930 they became government reserves. Their inhabitants needed permits to move between the islands, and a curfew on Thursday Island prevented Torres Strait Islanders from seeking employment there. In 1936, however, a strike by pearl luggers over control of their wages resulted in more autonomy for island councils, and the abolition of the permit system for travel between the islands.

The 'protective' legislation of the early twentieth century was presented in humanitarian terms, but was motivated by a range of eugenic and moral imperatives in which the protection of whites was the overriding concern. At this time there were fears of white blood becoming 'contaminated' by blood from what was regarded as an inferior race. Eugenic theory, which remained influential until the 1940s, saw a potential crisis arising from the failure of the 'racially fit' to reproduce themselves at the same rate as the 'racially unfit', and eugenists supported segregation policies which reduced opportunities for the reproduction of the 'inferior' group. From this followed the assumption that such races in Australia and elsewhere would eventually die out. The climax of control over Aboriginal peoples was reached in the 1930s in a series of legislative amendments; these included the extension of laws governing permission to marry and miscegenation (sexual relations beween the races). Permission might be obtained for a lighter-skinned Aboriginal woman to marry a white man because it was believed that would lead to 'breeding out of colour', but marriage between a woman of full Aboriginal descent and a white man was considered undesirable.

Aboriginal people were rounded up and taken to settlements such as Moore River in Western Australia or Barambah (later renamed Cherbourg) and Palm Island in Queensland. The conditions on Palm Island, off the coast of Townsville, have been vividly evoked by Marnie Kennedy, an Aboriginal woman of mixed descent who was taken there as a child with her mother, a Kalkadoon woman, and baby brother. The older girls at the settlement slept in bug-ridden beds, while the younger ones slept on the floor – one blanket beneath and one over them, summer and winter. While there was some organised entertainment, their lives were austere. Driven out of bed before dawn, the girls were required to clean and scrub the dormitory five days a week, sweep the yard every day, and go into the bush each day to collect grass to make brooms. Their activities were run by a bell: 'bell to start work, bell to stop, two bells at night', and they were made to attend church three times on Sunday. Discipline was harsh and relentless. On one occasion Marnie was thrown in jail overnight for singing a song, and she endured many beatings for minor misdemeanours. During the Depression years the children were often hungry, resorting to green fruits, roots, frogs, and even the slops buckets to supplement their meagre diet.

Marnie left school at thirteen and started working, first in the nurses' quarters on the island, and later as a domestic servant on the mainland. Signed on under 'the Act' (the 1897 *Aborigines Protection and Restriction of the Sale of Opium Act*), Marnie could not leave her employer unless she obtained exemption, but her employer wanted to release her head stockworker from the Act, so she suggested that Marnie marry him and they would both be free. Marnie agreed, and in 1936, aged seventeen, she married; the couple's exemption came through a year later. Theoretically, they were now free: they could handle their own finances, and leave any job they did not like. But they were unprepared for the discrimination and racial insults they received. The marriage was failing, so Marnie left with her year-old baby and worked in various jobs until she was warned by police to return to her husband or be sent back to Palm Island. She returned to him shortly before the outbreak of the Second World War.

Sandra Hardy also remembered Palm Island, where some of her cousins were sent, as 'a terrible, terrible place'. Her family had to apply for permission to visit the island, and could not speak privately with their relatives when they saw them. They found the residents separated from their parents and siblings in long dormitories, women walking about wearing dresses cut out of flour bags as a form of punishment, and a tiny jail where one could be sent for 'almost anything'. Sandra believed her immediate family escaped being sent there because they were quiet, kept to themselves, and their father had regular employment as a fettler on the railways. She recalls her childhood in the Tully-Ingham area

Beginning the Struggle

> ### An audacious woman
>
> Louisa Briggs was born in 1836 on Preservation Island, Bass Strait, of Woiworung descent. Around 1853, Louisa and her white husband John went to the Victorian goldfields. Later they worked as shepherds in the Beaufort district until 1871 when they were admitted destitute to Coranderrk Aboriginal Station. Coranderrk was now under the control of the Protection Board and producing hops. At the settlement, Louisa worked as a nurse and midwife, and in 1876 she was appointed matron, the first Aboriginal woman to achieve that status. She became spokesperson for the residents, and was instrumental in securing the reappointment of the station's popular first manager.
>
> Louisa opposed the Board's plans to sell Coranderrk and transfer residents to other reserves, and she gave evidence to the 1876 inquiry. Shortly after, however, she was forced off the reserve and moved to Ebenezer station. She was now a widow. After another inquiry in 1881, she moved back to Coranderrk where she was reappointed matron. Under the 1886 Victorian Aborigines Protection Act, 'half-castes' under thirty-five years of age were expelled from reserves. Louisa's sons were forced off Coranderrk and she followed, moving first to Muloga mission, and subsequently to Cummeragunja, Barmah, and back to Cummeragunja where she died in 1925.

between Townsville and Cairns as carefree, even idyllic; but racial discrimination was a constant feature of their environment.

From the early twentieth century, children of mixed descent were viewed as the group most likely to be 'uplifted' from their circumstances; one report in 1926 expressed the view that the separation of children from camp life would eventually solve the 'Aboriginal problem'. Children were removed from their families – usually by force – and taken to institutions such as Cootamundra and Kinchela in New South Wales, or Kahlin Compound in Darwin. In all of these homes children suffered deprivation and hardship. In some, conditions were unfit for human habitation. A report on the 'Half-Caste' home in Kahlin

Compound in 1927, for example, revealed that the building was too small and in disrepair: the floor was rotten, the shower out of order, the stove unfit for use, and the sink and table had collapsed, causing slops to fall on the floor. Above all, it was overcrowded: more than seventy babies, children and adults were living in a small cottage suitable for one family. At another institution in the Northern Territory known as the Bungalow, conditions were worse. A visitor in 1929 reported that a rough framework of wood had been erected, and sheets of corrugated iron roughly thrown over it; children slept on the floor, and were malnourished.

In the 1930s, Iris Clayton was taken with five of her siblings to the Cootamundra Girls Home. Her mother tried to pacify them before they left: 'It'll only be for a little while and we'll all be back together'. From Cootamundra, two of Iris' brothers were sent to Kinchela; she did not see them again until she was in her late teens. Life in the home was harsh and designed to suppress the girls' Aboriginality. If they spoke in their own language they were punished. 'There was a family there who had a real Aboriginal accent and Matron often checked them – you know, "I'll have none of that black talk here".' This was a shame, because 'they were lovely girls and they had a true, natural sort of real lovely, flowing Aboriginal accent and it was just taught out of them'.

Numerous stories would emerge of mothers attempting to hide their 'half-caste' children from white authorities, often by rubbing their bodies with fat and charred wood to darken their skins. Mona Tur's story is typical. In the 1930s Mona was living in a camp near Oodnadatta, South Australia. Whenever police were in the vicinity, her mother would take her out into the bush; sometimes they would remain there for two or three weeks. Her father, a ganger on the railways, and uncle, a tracker with the police, would have warning of the policemen's approach, and would tell Mona and her mother when they had gone. On one occasion, however, these 'communications' failed. It was a very hot day, and the family was sitting in the shade of their humpy when the police approached. Mona's mother dug a hole inside the humpy, buried Mona until only her head was showing, and cautioned her not to sneeze or cough. The camp dogs were shooed

Beginning the Struggle

inside, and Mona was covered with a blanket; it was so hot she thought she would die. She heard the policeman ask if there were any 'half-caste kids' in the camp, followed by her uncle's interpretation, and her mother's denial.

Other children such as Ethel Buckle and Myrtle Campbell could not hide. Ethel was born in 1919 at Maranboy in the Northern Territory. Her mother worked as a shepherd for the police and usually took Ethel with her, but one day when Ethel was about seven, she told her to stay at home because 'Missus' was making her a new dress. That afternoon the police arrived, put Ethel in the new dress, and took her to Pine Creek where she was kept in police cells overnight. Next morning she was put on the train, but jumped off after it started moving; she was put back on by a police tracker, and taken to Kahlin Compound. There the authorities changed her Christian name Daisy to Ethel (because there were 'too many Daisys'), as well as her surname. Myrtle was also taken to Kahlin, along with her three sisters and a friend, from her home at Halls Creek. Her father, a stockworker, was away in Queensland at the time, and her mother mounted little resistance because she realised 'there was nothing that she could do'.

Illness, impoverishment, and an overwhelming conviction that the authorities would remove their children regardless of their consent led some women to relinquish their children voluntarily. In 1922, when she was eight, Victoria Archibald was handed over to the New South Wales Protection Board by her mother: 'she sort of handed me over ... because she had no home'. Her mother, a domestic servant, had been in and out of hospital for some time with a lung complaint. Victoria was the youngest of a large family, the rest of whom had left. Her father's whereabouts were unknown, and she and her mother would go from one relative's house to another. One day, after another bout of illness, her mother took her into Sydney, and asked the Board if they would put her in a home. The following day, Victoria was taken by train to Cootamundra. 'It was frightening ... I knew my mother was sick all the time and there was no one else really to look after me so I just better take it that way ...'

While the 1930s witnessed the climax of state control over

Aboriginal people, it also saw the beginnings of a new consciousness about their affairs. With the growth of anthropology as an academic discipline and its increasing influence on policy, the doctrine of segregation began to lose favour. Anthropologists such as A P Elkin argued that given better material conditions, Aboriginal people were capable of rising above their impoverished circumstances and assimilating with white Australians. At the same time, protests by various humanitarian organisations against frontier violence gained publicity, and Aboriginal protest movements began to gather momentum. In 1932 William Cooper established the Australian Aborigines' League; he also organised a petition to the King for better living conditions and Aboriginal representation in parliament. In 1938, during the celebrations to mark the 150th anniversary of European settlement, Aboriginal people declared a Day of Mourning and staged a protest in Sydney. The following year, about one hundred people walked off the Cumeroogunga reserve in protest against their conditions.

Pearl Gibbs, also known as Gambanyi, played a prominent role in the protest movements of the 1930s. Born in 1901, Gibbs grew up around Yass in New South Wales, and attended schools in the area. The family avoided control by the Protection Board, and lived only briefly on a mission. In the early 1920s, Gibbs worked in various domestic jobs; during this period her marriage failed, leaving her to raise three children. She became politically active in the late 1920s, assisting Aboriginal girls indentured by the Protection Board, and organising strikes among Aboriginal pea pickers at Nowra. Her activism increased from 1937, as Aboriginal protest re-established itself after the early years of the Depression. An early member of the Aborigines' Progressive Association, she spoke at meetings in Sydney's Domain, drawing crowds with her eloquent and passionate demands for full citizen rights and an end to the Protection Board. She was particularly concerned with women's issues such as domestic 'apprenticeships', health, and school and hospital segregation, and formed ties with white feminist and other political organisations. Gibbs helped to organise the Day of Mourning on Australia Day, 1938,

Beginning the Struggle

and played a prominent part in the subsequent deputation to Prime Minister J A Lyons.

A policy of absorbing Aboriginal people into the white population was agreed to at a meeting of federal and state representatives in 1937, but it was not until after the war that the goal of assimilation was formally adopted. Some policy changes were made, however, in the intervening years. In 1941 child endowment was made available to Indigenous people who were not nomadic or welfare-dependent; and in the following year Aborigines who were outside the control of the Aboriginal Acts became entitled to invalid and old-age pensions. In the 1940s, those Aborigines who met certain conditions were entitled to apply for certificates granting them rights of citizenship. However, these conditions – which included the requirement that applicants dissolve all 'tribal and native' associations except with regard to immediate family – were offensive to Aboriginal people, and the citizenship offer was derided as a 'dog licence'.

Nevertheless, the Second World War accelerated attempts to incorporate Indigenous people into white society. Around 3,000 Aborigines and Torres Strait Islanders contributed to Australia's war effort, either as servicemen and women or as labourers; and stories attest to a greater degree of cohesion between black and white Australians during that period. Oodgeroo Noonuccal (Kath Walker), who served as a signaller in the Australian Women's Army Service (AWAS), maintained that the army considered colour irrelevant: 'There was a job to be done ... and all of a sudden the colour line disappeared'. Yet in other ways wartime conditions led to greater discrimination. In the Northern Territory, the authorities tried to segregate Aboriginal and part-Aboriginal girls from white troops, fearing that the soldiers would contract venereal disease; in 1941, Territory legislation was tightened and curfews were imposed.

Authorities were also concerned that Aboriginal people would betray Australia to the Japanese, yet Aborigines in remote areas provided the first warning of the Japanese attacks on Darwin. The fear of a Japanese invasion that engulfed white Australians in early 1942 was just as real for many Aboriginal people. Sandra

Hardy remembered being very worried about the possibility of invasion because she had heard that the Japanese would come down through Queensland, torturing and killing along the way. She asked her father whether the 'Japs' would kill them. When he replied that the Japanese would only kill whites she was comforted, for her fear of whites – particularly the Protection Board and the threat of being sent to Palm Island – was greater than her fear of a Japanese invasion.

The war years saw the agitation for Aboriginal rights pushed further to the background of the political arena, although this activity did not cease altogether. In 1942, for example, Pearl Gibbs was writing articles for the press, supporting Northern Territory Aborigines in their battles with the justice system and calling for Aboriginal representation on the New South Wales Welfare Board. The gains made by the protest movements of the 1930s had set the stage for more intense struggles in the postwar period.

Indigenous women had seen no substantial change to their oppressed situation since the beginning of European settlement, but the activists working on their behalf looked to the new era with hope and unwavering determination.

chapter six

The 1920s

Recently our local historical society held a costume parade of pre-1914 women's clothes, using either original garments or exact copies. The models, history students, looked wonderful, but they were horrified at how constricting the clothes were, even though they were the right size. Even getting dressed was complicated with many layers and intricate small clasps, and once the dress was on, your arms were 'clamped into place' and you could not reach to do up buttons. Help was essential; the models could not get dressed by themselves.

When you were dressed, the clothes were so tight in some places – arms, wrists, neck, waist – that it was difficult to move your head and shoulders, lift your arms, bend, go up stairs, sit down or even walk, as you could only take mincing little steps. Sprawling was impossible. Hats were hard to balance, boots were hot and heavy. 'There wasn't a lot of freedom to do anything except sit round and look pretty.'

And this was without authentic underwear. The girl who wore a corset – again, help was necessary to put it on and pull it tight – found she could not laugh or yawn, as she could not take a deep breath, and she wasn't able to slouch, as the corset made her sit bolt upright. 'It was completely restricting – imagine if you had to live your life in one of those!'

A Wealth of Women

White women's clothes had been like this since they arrived in Australia. Fashions changed, but all included long skirts, long sleeves, plenty of material and layers of underwear, with petticoats, chemises and a corset. Of course, women of the time were used to these clothes, but they must still have been uncomfortable, hot, and hampering to activity. Major change came after the First World War, when clothes became much simpler, skirts shorter, and everything far more practical and less constricting. Some daring women even left off their corsets, and the brassiere or bra appeared.

In the early 1920s, the freedom of the new fashions extended into many areas of life, with women breaking away from the old Victorian shackles. The epitome of the new woman was the flapper, typically a young, single girl earning an independent living, often in an office or factory, and looking forward to a bright, carefree future. She cut her hair short, wore makeup, short skirts or even trousers, drank alcohol and smoked, danced the Charleston all night unchaperoned, rode motor bikes and even discussed sex. The world was her oyster as she went her blithe, twentieth-century way, wrote Dulcie Deamer, herself a flapper and pioneering journalist. 'She can do as she likes; and she has been doing so ever since she was able to sit up in her bassinet, point her finger at

The 1919 influenza epidemic

In 1919 the war was over and lives began to return to normal, as the soldiers came home and were demobilised. But they brought an unwelcome visitor – the influenza epidemic, which had already killed millions in war-weakened Europe.

Charlotte Chance was a nurse, living in Fitzroy, and cared for many people who had influenza. She and her husband, a blacksmith, had eleven children, and when she returned home she would head straight for a shed where she took off all her clothes and put on clean ones. She would then dig fresh onions from her garden for lunch, as she believed they protected her family – and none of them caught flu. They were fortunate, for tens of thousands did, and 12,000 Australians died.

what she wanted – and howl.' She was smart, well fed and complacent unless, said Dulcie, Reginald phoned to say that he had flu and couldn't take her to that studio party where there would be wine cocktails and a jazz saxophonist.

Flappers copied their style from American films, though locals added enthusiasm for sport to the world-wide flapper image. Australia had few fully-fledged flappers, but many women were influenced by the new ideas, and everywhere, it was reported, the burning question was how short to wear your hair and skirt. When even Brownie, the old housekeeper in Mary Grant Bruce's much loved (and conservative) *Billabong* series, admitted that life was much easier with a shorter skirt, it was clear that new ideas had come to stay.

Dulcie Deamer was an extreme example of a flapper. Born in New Zealand in 1890, she was the daughter of a doctor, and her sister became a nun. Not Dulcie: she went on the stage and married the manager, and while her mother looked after her four children, Dulcie toured the world and wrote popular novels. None of this made much money, her marriage failed, and in 1922 she found herself penniless in Sydney, her husband having run off to Melbourne with a blonde. She took a room in King's Cross (her mother still had the children) and earned a precarious living by investigative journalism, including dressing as a man to report on an abattoir.

But Dulcie's real interest was her social life. With the war over, she wrote, the Golden Decade started. Australians had 'our share of the lovely, irrational, general conviction that everything was now going to be good-oh', and everyone was 'subconsciously vibrating with a fun-and-games impulse'. From her breathless memoirs, there was not much subconscious about it. Dulcie found her spiritual home in Sydney's fast set, and became famous for wearing a leopard skin and not much else to the Artists' Ball in 1923. She and her friends held wonderful parties, drank, smoked and enjoyed 'community kissing' and witty conversation, while 'things grew pretty willing' in dark corners. They loved fancy dress, with men dressing as women and women as men, and at a Roman Night one girl wore nothing but Moreton Bay fig leaves stitched together. At one party Dulcie was crowned Queen of Bohemia, with 'holy oil' (wine, needlessly to say) sprinkled over a pasteboard crown. Then there was 'fun with a capital F', with everyone drinking claret punch from a washing-up basin and dancing wildly with 'spontaneous and hilarious enthusiasm'. In her autobiography Dulcie insisted that all these activities were innocent – and she had worn an undergarment beneath the leopard skin, which made everything all right.

There was a shadier side to Sydney's nightlife. Tilly Devine was one English war-bride the authorities could have done without. She married an Aussie digger, Jim Devine, and arrived in Sydney in 1920. With Jim's protection, she started working as a prostitute, and despite being prosecuted about once a fortnight, her prices were so high that she was soon able to buy an expensive Cadillac. Jim drove it while she solicited, and often actually worked, from the back seat. Jim was also involved in robbery, receiving stolen goods and illegal betting, though he often gave his occupation as 'fruiterer' – and Tilly did buy him a shop.

Despite more prosecutions Tilly flourished, and in 1925 opened her first brothel. She was tough and protected her girls firmly, once walking into a barber's shop, saying, 'This is from Mary B' and slashing a man in the face with a razor. She was imprisoned for two years, and by the time she was released Kate Leigh had taken her place as queen of the underworld. Hailing from Dubbo and known as the 'Snow Queen', Kate dealt in cocaine. Gang warfare with shootouts and slashings erupted as each tried to break the other's power. Both had powerful protectors, Tilly in the Labor Party and Kate in the police, but new laws in the late 1920s meant both went to jail, and their power waned, though they were still in evidence in the 1940s.

Before the 1920s some women had lived like Dulcie, Tilly and Kate, but their lives were not public knowledge: now their doings were reported in the press. None of them appeared ashamed of anything they did. This was the way they wanted to live, so they did. Strict standards were, however, still maintained by most of the population.

Other women moved into more respectable new areas. Some

By the early twentieth century, schools taught practical subjects and girls were given lessons in homemaking, as this class in 'washing' illustrates

Alison Ashby being instructed by her Aunt Meta on the verandah of her home, 'Wittunga' at Blackwood, SA, 1906

Lady students at the university': attractive young women become less so the longer they study. A grumpy male is included. This is from The Australian Sketcher, 1880.

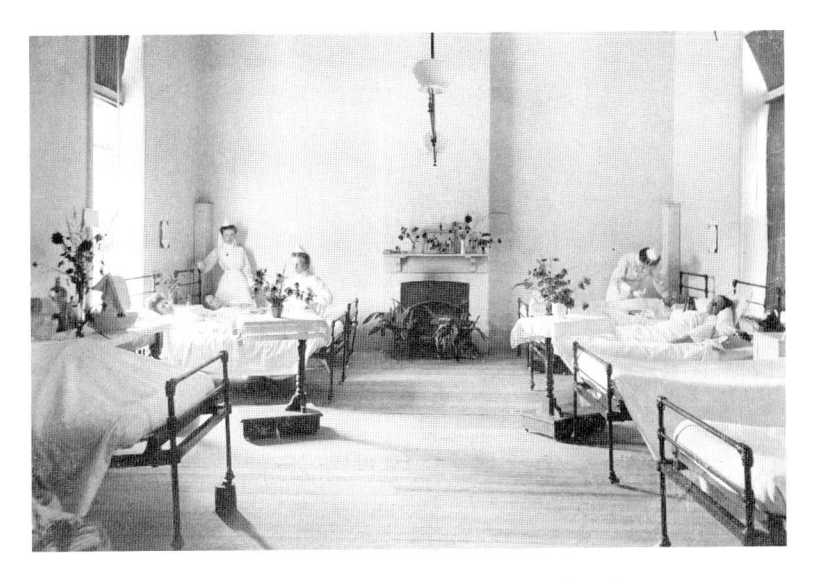

Ward at the Kapunda Hospital, South Australia, about 1910

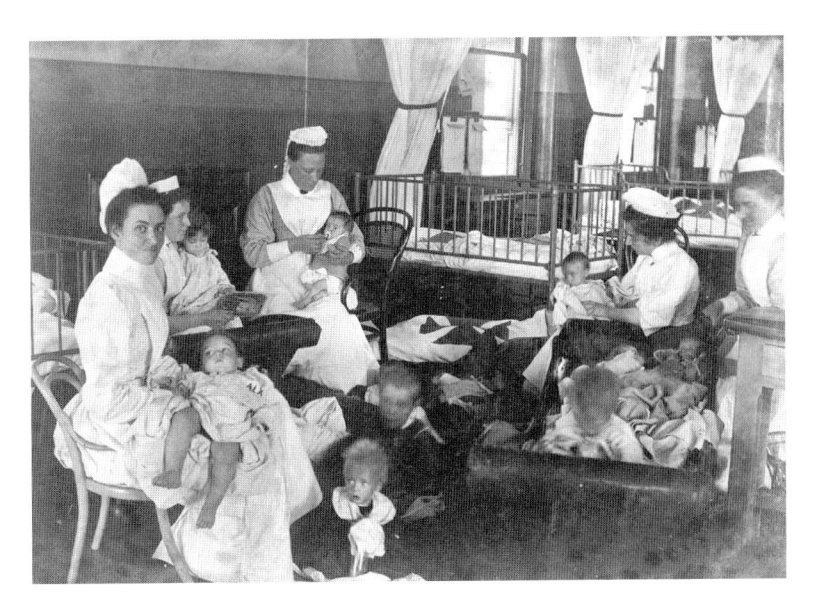

Children's ward in an unknown hospital, about 1900

Enfranchised!
A cartoon by Herbert Cotton, 1902

*Women might not have played an active part in union organisation,
but they could become active supporters.
Here they assault a non-unionist, Broken Hill, 1892*

*No details are known about this photo,
but the women certainly look daring and happy*

*Despite the rain, women continue to play on
Ladies' Bowling Day, the Esplanade, Perth, 1905*

'Young Boulder toilers',
children collecting firewood at Boulder, about 1900

Gertrude McKern and Maude Bate stirring the
washing over a fire in the backyard, about 1890

A family on the south coast of New South Wales: ten girls and two boys. Imagine washing, starching and ironing those white dresses.

Advertisement for contraceptives at the turn of the century: pessaries, condoms, a syringe to clean 'the most remote portions of the Vagina', and a 'Female Sheath'

The 1920s

stood for parliament, though only a few were elected. Edith Cowan became the first female in parliament in Western Australia in 1921, and three others were elected round the country during the decade. As one female in a parliament of men, each could achieve comparatively little, though Edith Cowan, a long-time campaigner for women's rights, introduced a bill which allowed women to become lawyers and argued in favour of sex education in schools, migrant welfare and infant health centres. In the interests of recognising women's work she once proposed, tongue in cheek, that wives become employees of their husbands, with set hours and wages. She said she had never heard anything funnier than the outrage and heckling which greeted this suggestion, or the premier's comment: 'I do not suppose there are many of us who are not controlled by our wives'.

One political leader was Lena Lee of Darwin. Educated at Hong Kong university and a devoted follower of the Chinese nationalist leader Sun Yat Sen, Lena became head of the Darwin branch of his party, the Kuo Min Tang. She represented the Northern Territory at the party's national convention, and instructed local Chinese in Sun's doctrines. In 1926 newspapers debated whether these activities were suitable for a woman, and a few months later Lena committed suicide, leaving a letter which said that recent disputes were to blame.

Some women had dynamic new careers. Daphne Mayo of Brisbane studied sculpture in London, and returned home in 1925. She was most successful, receiving several large commissions, such as one suggested by the Brisbane Women's Club for a sculpture to commemorate the war dead. Money was raised by forty-one women's clubs – religious, political, military, sporting, professional, intellectual and charitable – ranging from the Queensland Women's Hockey Association to the Council of Jewish Women and the Christmas Treat for Widows and Orphans of Fallen Sailors and Soldiers Society. The sandstone sculpture depicting soldiers pulling a gun carriage stands on the wall of Anzac Park below the Eternal Flame, with the wording, 'Erected by the women of Queensland – in memory of all who lost their lives through the Great War'.

Another area where a few women could shine was singing. Born in Orange about 1888, Ethel Walker learnt singing in the local convent, and as a teenager joined the back row of a chorus in Sydney. Nellie Melba heard her sing, and organised a scholarship at the Sydney Conservatorium. Later, Ethel joined J C Williamson's group and toured in Australia and overseas, often singing lead roles in Gilbert and Sullivan and other operettas. In New York she fell in love with a marquis who had been aide-de-camp to the Tsar's nephew, and at one stage gave birth to a daughter – a far cry from the Orange convent.

Films provided exciting new careers. Louise Carbasse was born in Sydney in 1895, the illegitimate daughter of a Swiss actress. Louise became a child actor, and starred in several local films. She married another actor, Wilton Welch, and in 1914 they tried their luck in Hollywood, where Universal Studios dyed Louise's hair blonde and renamed her. Raya Sunshine was one suggestion which haunted her for years, but eventually as Louise Lovely she starred in nearly fifty films, Australia's best-known star of the period. She also produced three films herself.

Wilton resented her success and their marriage became strained, so she joined him in a novelty performance which

Sexual liberation

English-born Molly Claux believed in vegetarianism, 'wise' nudity and physical beauty – 'I simply must have beautiful people round me'. After a failed marriage, in 1929 she emigrated to Australia with 'husband-like' Ray, their baby son and several like-minded people, and they started an alternative-lifestyle farming community near Cooktown, agreeably warm for nudists. But there were problems. Molly thought several commune members ate badly and were unsuitable aesthetically and underdeveloped sexually. She dumped two men as partners but decided to keep Ray, for though he too sinned about diet he was almost physically perfect. Not surprisingly, she complained that the locals were inquisitive. She failed to convert them to nudism.

The 1920s

Respectability starts to founder

For some, the Twenties meant a laxer moral code, especially sexually. Betty Roland, born in 1903, began her memoirs by saying that her previously published total of sixty-four lovers was wrong, as she had forgotten one. She accumulated this number despite her mother, who told Betty that her wedding night had put her off sex for good. Her husband used to slap her across the face with his penis when he became angry; once she tried to bite it, and he hit her on the head, this time with his fist.

By the time she was seventeen, Betty had lost her virginity to one of her many admirers. She became engaged to a handsome soldier settler, but he broke off the engagement when he thought she was having an affair. She had another affair with 'complete abandon', then found work at a fashion designers in Melbourne. In 1923 she married, entirely for security: she and her mother had no money, and she needed treatment for tuberculosis. Her husband, Ellis Davies, was divorced but wealthy, and paid for treatment which cured Betty. She bore a son, who was cared for by servants as she was too busy having affairs, with her lovers ranging from her doctor to a man who came to fix an electrical fault. She felt justified, for her son was not developing normally because Ellis had venereal disease.

Not surprisingly, their marriage floundered. The little boy died, and in 1932 Betty left Ellis and went to England with a dashing communist, who had deserted both his wife and a girl who had borne his child. Her autobiography shows that at least a few Australian women did not feel bound by strict standards, acknowledged sex as a pleasure, and thought there was nothing wrong with casual sex outside marriage.

showed audiences how films were produced. They brought it to Australia, and while performing in Hobart, Louise was approached by Marie Bjelke Petersen (aunt of the Queensland premier), who, despite a marked absence of male romance in her own life, had made an international reputation as a writer of romantic novels of the most throbbing, pulsating kind. 'In that long motionless kiss it seemed as if the burning deeps in him had found the tortured deeps in her, and as they came together they gloriously united, bringing the man and woman who caressed a delirious satisfaction.' Marie suggested that Louise film her most recent novel, *Jewelled Nights*. Set in the wild west coast of Tasmania, it told the story of a girl fleeing from persecution in Melbourne, dressing as a boy and falling in love with an osmiridium miner.

Louise was taken with the idea, and she and Wilton set up a film company. Louise said she raised the finance, wrote the scenario, found the cast, edited, co-produced and starred in *Jewelled Nights*, though Wilton also claimed some of these activities. Raising money was difficult, but Louise was inventive. She persuaded a number of Melbourne society people to invest in the film on the understanding that they appeared in it, so at one stroke she obtained funding and free extras, who provided their own expensive clothing. Filming took place with a great deal of publicity and extravagance, and the film opened to rave reviews, but it was not a financial success.

Louise and Wilton separated and she returned to the stage and remarried, while Marie Bjelke Petersen continued her highly successful career. She advocated less soul-destroying housework for women, and was herself independent of men, treating them as her equals. 'I was thinking what a rotten world this is for women: everything in it favours men – all our social laws and conventions – everything!' says one of her female characters. People might be polite to a woman, 'handing her muffins and tea; but in all things that really matter man has the advantage on his side'.

Daphne Mayo, Louise Lovely and Marie Bjelke Petersen were exciting and dynamic, but extremely unusual. Most women did not have the ability, the drive or the opportunity to undertake such careers. Elaine Lambert, for example, followed a more typical path. She grew up in the Sydney suburb of Kogarah, entered the domestic science stream at her local high school, completed a business course, then in 1923, aged fifteen, looked for a job. 'There were plenty available', and she started as a junior in a confectionery manufacturer's office, stamping letters, filing order

The 1920s

forms and keeping the stationery cupboard tidy. She rose to be assistant to the accountant, keeping the bank account, working out wages and making out cheques – 'interesting work'. During these years, she was attracted by a new member of the church choir; after going steady for four years, they were engaged when Elaine turned twenty-one. They did not marry until she was twenty-six because although her fiancé had qualified as an accountant, he felt called into the Christian ministry, which entailed four more years of study. Elaine was promoted, and kept a secure job during the Depression.

Teaching careers often started early as well. Winifred Buckley, born in 1910 in South Australia, wanted from her earliest childhood to be a teacher. When eighty children became too much for the local teacher, thirteen-year-old Win started to teach as a

An internationalist

Eleanor Mackinnon was a leader in many social, political and charitable causes. One newspaper obituarist summed her up: 'I cannot find fancy phrases for that lady. I only know that she was dinkum'. Educated at Sydney Girls' High, the wife of a doctor, she studied painting and wrote verse, but her main activity was in Red Cross. She became secretary to the New South Wales division in 1914 and conceived the idea of Junior Red Cross, of which she was world founder. By 1918 the movement was established in fifty-two countries. She founded and edited the magazine Red Cross Record, and compiled Red Cross cookery and knitting books. Eleanor was awarded the OBE in 1918.

An eloquent and forceful speaker, after the war she rallied women to support the Peace Loan; helped organise emergency hospitals during the flu epidemic; and toured the country to form new Red Cross branches and divert the organisation to peacetime activities. Her stature was shown when she was selected as an Australian delegate to the Sixth Assembly of the League of Nations in Geneva in 1925. It is not surprising that when portraits were being considered for the new dollar bank notes, Eleanor Mackinnon's name was on the list.

monitor. This was too young for payment, so she worked for nothing until she turned fourteen. At night she studied for the Intermediate exam and passed it subject by subject, and at home she had to help her mother. At seventeen, she had a year's training at Teachers' College, then was appointed to her own school, eleven children at Woorongboolong, a desolate coastal outpost. When the bus stopped there, Win recalled, another teacher said, 'If I get a school like this, I'm going home straight away!' 'But I thought it was a great adventure', said Win. After teaching for five years, she married a local man, 'and of course, had to stop teaching then'.

Both Elaine and Win worked for about ten years before marrying, a usual pattern for girls: 'as each child left school they went out to work to earn money'. The ratio of men to women was about even, and with increasing employment prospects and a higher standard of living, girls worked (and saved) for longer before marriage, at an average age of twenty-four. Though the great majority, 83 per cent, married, single women could gain respect, particularly those with high status jobs like headmistresses or doctors.

Not only new ideas and careers but inventions changed life for women. Disposable sanitary pads were available, but they were expensive and little used. More important were innovations in the home: tinned food, electric light, stoves, running hot water, and some appliances. Only the wealthy could afford many of these, but they did make housework easier, and the demand for domestic servants fell away.

The modern life was promoted by radio, film and magazines. Cinemas opened around Australia, and by 1927, a third of the population went to the pictures once a week. By 1929 there were radio licences in 300,000 homes. The popular press included women's magazines, cheap enough to have a wide audience, full of articles giving advice and explaining new ideas. All spread the message of modernity, fashion, glamour, romance and conspicuous consumption. They provided relaxation for women, but at the same time set a standard often hard to maintain – in looks and glamour, and in housekeeping. Men too were urged to con-

The 1920s

sider modern ideas, and there was cultural pressure on them to become companionable husbands, considerate lovers and responsible fathers.

In the cities particularly, people lived in an atmosphere of change. Mavis Bradbury, born in 1918, grew up in South Melbourne. Her family was working class, and their home had no carpets or running hot water, but Mavis remembered 'exciting things happening all the time': her father bringing home a new sweet called P.K. chewing gum; going to watch silent films, then a film which was half silent and half talkie; the family's first wireless, a crystal set with earphones which people took turns to use; an aeroplane flying overhead, writing the word HELLO in smoke; flappers with short skirts, close-fitting hats with kiss curls peeping out, and cupid bow lips; an electric advertising sign with letters lighting up one at a time to spell ASPRO; having her hair so short that a passer-by asked her if she was a girl or a boy; then finally electricity being connected. 'It was like magic, to just flick a switch and have instant light.'

At the same time, bath night was still only once a week, as hot water had to be carried in buckets from the wash-house in the back yard; an aunt died in childbirth; and there was a hanging at Melbourne jail, so life had not completely changed. And innovations were not always reliable. Elsie Plant always remembered the day that her sister Dot lost her knickers in Swanston Street, Melbourne. Dot was crossing the street with Elsie, when the elastic in her knickers broke. Elsie managed to get her across the street and behind the glass display cases in Ezy Walkin shoe shop so she could slip them off her feet, and she went to Coles to buy her some new ones. 'Terrible for poor Dot', said Elsie, decades later still laughing so much that she had to wipe away the tears.

But there were limits to how much women could take part in the new world. Every woman mentioned so far lived in a capital city, and rural women had far less chance of enjoying modernity and gaining an exciting job. Moreover, most of the successful women carved out careers for themselves. It was far harder when they tried to enter an employment area already dominated by men, as Ruby Davy's life shows. Born in Salisbury, South Australia

An irreplaceable woman

Freda Johnson was born in 1904, to a farming family in Kempton, Tasmania. A bright girl, she did well at primary school and won a bursary to the high school in Hobart. Determined to establish a career, she attended business college, then, aged seventeen, applied for a job in the office at the recently established, ultra-modern Electrolytic Zinc Works. While she was being interviewed, her grandmother rang the boss's secretary to find out whether it was suitable work. This created a good impression, as did Freda's qualifications, and she got the job. She was well treated, driven home each day in the director's car.

Freda was extremely competent, and when her boss was made head of the federal government's Migration Commission in 1926, he insisted on taking her with him. In the head office in Melbourne, she set up a huge filing system and earned a good salary. Questions were asked in parliament as to why a woman was holding this job when there were so many men with families to support, but an inspection decided that she was irreplaceable. Shortly after this, Freda married. Even though she was 'irreplaceable', the public service would not employ married women, so she kept this secret so she could retain her job.

in 1883, Ruby was an only child in a musical family. She was improvising tunes on the piano at five, and composed music at nine. She taught pupils with her mother, gave public performances, and studied privately to matriculate in music. When she formed a romantic attachment, her mother said she must choose between marriage and a career in music: Ruby chose music. At the Adelaide conservatorium, she gained first a degree then a doctorate, becoming Australia's first female Doctor of Music. A male would probably have been offered a post at the conservatorium – the only previous doctor was now its head, a senior male staff member had lesser qualifications – but there was no such offer for Ruby. At this time and for decades afterwards, universities were reluctant to give women supervisory roles.

So Ruby established her own career, setting up Dr Ruby Davy's

The 1920s

School of Music with her parents' help. It was extremely successful, and she became Adelaide's leading music teacher, as well as being a highly praised performer. This career came to a halt in 1929 when both parents died. Ruby was devastated and did not touch a piano for years, until an evangelist of the Apostolic Church persuaded her to take an interest in music again. In 1935 she established a second successful music school in Melbourne, though she was criticised by the conservatorium traditionalists. Four years later she set off on an overseas tour, but when war broke out she returned home. Still Australia's only female doctor of music, she took up teaching again and died in Melbourne in 1949. Because she was a woman, because she did not gain overseas experience, because she had to teach instead of being able to concentrate on performing, perhaps because of a rather autocratic personality, she never received the recognition her musical talent deserved. This was a typical experience of women who tried to broach male-dominated areas of employment.

Meanwhile, some women continued to work in what had always been the major area of employment for women, domestic service. It was still the main work available for country girls. Most hated it, but Win Bates left a positive description of her life as a laundress for the wealthy Austin family, at the Mt Widderin homestead near Skipton. Win arrived in 1921, aged seventeen, and 'the years I spent there were most happy'.

The work sounds constant and heavy, but Win described it as 'my pride and joy'. She boiled linen in the copper then put it through the mangle, dried it, then ironed it with one of twelve flat irons. 'The table cloths and napkins were my delight and surely repaid me for my work when finished.' She also cleaned, swept and dusted; there were no vacuum cleaners, so the maids tore up wet paper and sprinkled it over the carpets, then swept with a straw broom.

The Austins were most tolerant and kind, said Win. The three maids called Mrs Austin 'Madam' and Mr Austin 'Sir', though he was shy and avoided them. They wore uniform, and had an afternoon off each week. Boyfriends could visit twice a week, and the staff held dances in the laundry, with Win's sister Isabel playing the mouth organ. When the Austins were away the girls 'ran amok', trying on Mrs Austin's dresses and sleeping in the visitors' rooms. The job had many benefits, said Win: she learned social graces and appreciation of beautiful things, and read many books in the library, which was helpful as she had left school at twelve and her education was sketchy.

Life as a servant was far easier than her later life. In 1924, aged twenty, Win married forty-three-year-old Joe Baulch, and two years later, with their six-week-old daughter, they moved to a farm in the Mallee which he had taken up with his brother. It was a shock. The harsh country was isolated, extremely hot in summer, prone to dust storms, and short of water. The house was derelict, made of corrugated iron lined with hessian bags. But Win made a cupboard from an old piano case, and a sideboard from three kerosene boxes on top of each other, with a cretonne curtain in front. She made chairs by covering other boxes with chaff and tacking a cover on top. She painted with lime the fresh bags Joe hung in the bedroom. Kerosene tins and manure bags were their best friends, the tins used for basins, washing up dishes, cooking utensils, milk buckets, bread dishes, and bags for blinds, floor rugs, lining and blankets. Rabbits were plentiful and Win stewed, fried, roasted and curried them, but sometimes she had to make a meal with only gravy, potatoes, onions and other vegetables. Other problems were drought, difficult relations and a mouse plague, but 'it is marvellous what one can endure when one is young and in love', and somehow they carried on.

The hopes of the early 1920s that Australia would become a thriving Utopia through modern progress and development did not eventuate. Plans to put soldier settlers and British immigrants on the land, to start new industries, to revolutionise life with electricity and the other wonders of science, faded in the face of low prices for primary products, unsuccessful government schemes, unemployment and poverty, and dissent which divided political parties and the nation generally. There was a backlash against many modern ideas which seemed to be trying to bring too much change into life, and in the late 1920s this included feminism.

The 1920s

For many Australians, men and women, the developments before the war – women gaining the vote, some moving into new occupations and out of the home, the falling birthrate – had been quite enough. The changes after the war were too much. Dulcie Deamer demonstrated the changed atmosphere in her 1926 article, 'That Married Look'. The carefree flapper has left one novelty unsampled – marriage. So her mother orders a divine white frock, the bridegroom gives the sweetest platinum brooches to

Following wolfram and osmiridium

Brought up in an artistic London family, Lillian Gresson emigrated to Australia in 1911. A shipboard romance led to marriage, and she and her husband Arthur went to Tasmania to mine wolfram, which was in demand for war materials. They lived in a slab hut with a dirt floor, and Lillian did what she could to improve things, ordering a glass window and hanging up her brocade curtains from London. When Arthur needed to be protected from bees, she had to sacrifice her beautiful long pale blue chiffon veil covered with spangles.

In the 1920s Arthur joined the rush to mine osmiridium at Adamsfield in the south-west. Lillian joined him 'as I knew he would not trouble to feed himself properly'. Arthur met her and their son at the end of the road, and they set out on horseback. Though beautiful, it was a perilous trip. Snow was falling and the steep, narrow track was rough and slippery, with mud up to the horses' middles. Slithering and sliding, they finally managed to reach their tent.

Lillian helped Arthur – easy work, she said, just shovelling surface dirt into the sluice box and washing it, though it was hard to sell osmiridium and they never did prosper. To help out, Lillian cooked and sold mutton birds, barracouta, bread, cakes and scones. But they built 'quite a comfortable shack' for winter, and the men built a hall for concerts and dances. They also built a hospital and employed a bush nurse, a wonderful manager who soon turned the rough shed into a comfortable building with curtains. The one baby born in the hospital was called Osmua.

the bridesmaids, the bride's going-away dress is the duckiest ensemble you ever saw, and the couple wave goodbye, their faces aglow. A year later, the bride has 'that married look', the bitter disillusionment that comes from facing 'that old, old institution, the husband' with the inadequate weapons of alluring flesh-pink stockings and simple faith in a tin-opener. This is what happened to feminism generally when it tried to penetrate male enclaves in the Twenties. Though women continued to wear comfortable clothes and drink, smoke and dance unchaperoned, their public role could not broaden.

A major reason for the backlash was that the birthrate was still declining, from four children per white mother in 1911, to three in the 1920s. With fears of invasion, and fears that family life (and men's comfort) was threatened, this encouraged reaction to the independence of the flappers: women should stay at home as wives and mothers.

Pushing women back into the home was not entirely negative. This was the age of technological progress, and 'scientific motherhood' would ensure that all babies were born healthy and strong, leading to a stronger race. It enhanced the importance of motherhood and made women feel that they too were in the vanguard of progress. There had been some such activity before the war, but it was mainly the upper classes – professionals and volunteer women – trying to improve the standard of living of the working classes. In the 1920s the professionals tried to improve everyone.

A major protagonist was New Zealander Dr Frederic Truby King, who, while superintending a mental hospital, found that mortality in calves could be lessened by a rigid feeding formula. He and his wife were childless, and in their forties they adopted a baby girl. She did not thrive, so Mrs King asked Frederic to work out a better artificial food. Its success was the start of his complete system for mothers. To Truby King, there was one right way – his – which everyone must follow.

Contraceptives were 'against the law of God and nature ... their use invariably lowers both moral and physical health, leading to derangement of the nervous system'. So the wife became

The 1920s

Italians come to Australia

During the 1920s many Italians migrated to Australia. Giuiditta and Guerino Baltieri had arrived in 1912 and settled in Rutherglen, where Guerino worked as a miner and Giuiditta as a servant. Work failed, and Guerino went to Broken Hill. When he had a job he sent for Giuiditta and their two small sons. The train trip took four days and three nights via Melbourne and Adelaide, and Giuiditta could not buy any food as she could not speak English. She and the children almost perished, and she vowed to learn English as soon as possible.

Guerino's health was poor, so in 1919 they moved to Griffith where land was available. The day they arrived was extremely hot, the horse pulling the dray dropped dead from exhaustion, and they had to walk into town with their luggage and three children. They took up land in partnership with other Italians, and farmed with considerable difficulty. Because Giuiditta spoke English, she acted as midwife to the small Italian community.

In 1923 Guerino died, leaving Giuiditta a twenty-eight-year-old widow with four young children. Strong-willed and fiercely independent, she continued to run the farm despite the hardships involved. She could pick and pack grapes better than most men, and sometimes ploughed and pruned trees with her baby son strapped to her back in a hessian bag. Sometimes when she had no money, no food and no produce to sell, she pleaded with the bank manager, and he was so taken with her courage that he told her to go home and do her best. She could only afford one set of clothing for the children and would wash clothes overnight – sometimes they wore them to school still damp. She survived, brewing her own beer, smoking and chewing tobacco, speaking Australian slang with no hint of an Italian accent. Eventually she was able to buy the farm, and she worked there until her death in 1970, aged seventy-six.

pregnant, and her daily regime must include a cold shower every morning, a bath at night, plenty of rest, and a quick three-mile walk with a cheerful, kindly companion. She must scrub her nipples with a progressively harder brush, and her diet must include plenty of water, fruit and vegetables, very little tea or coffee, and no alcohol, cakes or biscuits. She could drink warm water flavoured with lemon juice. Father must help her, make sure she followed all instructions, be tactful if she was irritable – 'talk about the coming little one' – and practice self-control: no 'cohabiting' after conception. It sounds like a recipe for marital disaster.

Baby should be born in a hospital, and mother could go home after a fortnight, but do no hard work for a month. She must breastfeed the baby, strictly every four hours for nine months, with no night feeds, and no over-feeding as it caused gastric illness. If artificial feeding was unavoidable, baby should be fed 'humanised milk', made by adding exact amounts of water, sugar and fat to cow's milk. Baby must have sufficient sleep, fresh air and sunlight.

Baby had a strict timetable, of feeds, bath, sleeps, and a small amount of interaction with Mother, not too much as it led to 'spoiling'. Bowel training started at three days old, and nappies should be left off altogether at nine months. Babies should be taught to blow their noses, and thumb-sucking and the linked bad habit of masturbation should be stopped by giving baby something else to think about. And the result: a Truby King baby is healthy, happy, sleeps to order, 'a joy from morning till night'.

Any mother must blanch at this statement, knowing that no baby is perfect, but at the same time the Truby King system was implemented in New Zealand the infant mortality rate fell greatly, so many people were convinced that it could bring about a similar result in Australia. Governments set up welfare systems to convert all women to scientific motherhood and bring down infant mortality, maternal mortality and disease generally.

The Queensland government was particularly worried about its small white population and its vast underpopulated regions, and the strongly Catholic Labor Party was idealistic about the treatment of mothers and babies. In 1915 Queensland's first Labor government started to put these views into practice, making contraception and abortion more difficult, and using the profits of the Golden Casket Lottery to build free maternity

The 1920s

hospitals and baby clinics. By 1938 it had built 94 hospitals and 122 clinics and most women lived within reach of them. The government claimed its facilities provided the best service in the world.

Women welcomed hospitals in particular, as they provided anaesthetics to relieve pain – women's greatest fear in labour – and also the only rest many women ever had. The infant mortality rate continued to fall, though probably mainly for the same reasons as the earlier fall – better sewerage and drainage, and improved water and milk supplies. But maternal mortality did not fall, mainly due to medical incompetence and undue interference, 'meddlesome midwifery' as it was called, overuse of forceps, anaesthetics and, from 1930s, induced births, or slowing down or rushing labour for doctors' convenience. And the new hospitals did not cater for everyone, with Aboriginal and single white mothers not welcome. There was little criticism at the time, however. The new maternity hospitals, staffed by trained doctors and nurses, were part of the 'modern' way, which most embraced willingly.

Once the baby was born, the mother received advice in childcare from trained nurses in the new baby clinics. They disapproved strongly of the old ways, and told mothers to follow modern methods. Some mothers followed the nurses' advice to the letter, but others did not. They found it too impractical or too inflexible, listened to their own mothers, cuddled and kissed their babies, and fed them when they were hungry. They found modified milk unsuitable and used supplements such as Lactogen, which clinic sisters disliked. Generally, they only took the sisters' advice if it agreed with what they thought was sensible. Many thought it was ridiculous for the government to think that they needed expert assistance to rear their children. 'It was men that thought that, probably.' Overall, infant welfare clinics did not have the impact that maternity hospitals did.

Dolly Grebert's life shows the popularity of the new maternity hospitals, especially in the rural and remote areas of Queensland. In 1912 her father, Walter, and three brothers took up land on the Atherton Tableland, and her mother Annie and younger children moved there three years later, when Dolly was sixteen. Their new home was a two-roomed shack with a tin roof and dirt floor, an open fire to cook on, beds made of sacks and mattresses of straw. When Annie saw it, she sat down and cried. She decided that she had to make the best of it, however, so set about 'getting a bit of order into the place'.

Fortunately, nearby lived Joe Grebert, a young farmer and carpenter who had failed the army's medical test so had not enlisted. Annie asked him to build a new house, and while he was doing this he started courting Dolly. Annie approved, as Joe did not drink, smoke or gamble like Walter did, but Walter did not want to lose a good worker. When Joe and Dolly became engaged he made her break off the engagement, but eventually Annie managed to persuade him to agree to the wedding, which took place in 1918, when Dolly was nineteen.

She and Joe lived in his humpy by the creek, and Dolly helped

Flood, fire and unassisted childbirth

Nancy McPherson was only three in 1924 when her mother Doris gave birth to her second daughter, in their home on a twenty-acre fruit block in the Dandenongs. They had no telephone, the doctor and midwife had not yet arrived, and there was only Dad to help, reading from a book of instructions propped up on the mantelpiece. Fortunately all went well.

Though life was generally peaceful, there were other dramas. Doris had the terrifying experience of crossing a flooded river in a horse and buggy, across a single line railway bridge, clasping her baby daughter in one arm and holding on with the other as they bumped across the sleepers. Several years later she was alone with the little girls and her two young sisters, when fire in thick scrub surrounded the house on three sides. She put the children in the middle of a ploughed paddock, the baby strapped in her crib with her older sister to watch over her, and gathered buckets of water and wet bags round the house, then brought out the valuables. Many hours later the wind changed, and the house and family were safe.

The 1920s

him build a house, as well as making a garden, cooking, housekeeping and cutting wood for the fire. She soon became pregnant, but one day fell while she was walking to the creek to get water. That evening her labour started, months early. It was a three-day ride to the nearest hospital, and the only help was a local farmer, Alan Knudson, who had basic but capable first aid skills. Joe had to leave Dolly at home and rode to the Knudsons' for help, but his horse fell over a cow lying on the road, and he was thrown off and knocked unconscious. Four hours later he recovered and continued on foot. He woke the Knudsons, and they arrived back at the farm at daylight. Mr Knudson's idea was to keep Dolly walking round, and the baby arrived unexpectedly. He dropped head first on to the dirt floor, suffering a bruise to his head. The baby, Wally, was so small that he fitted into the palm of his father's hand. He could not suckle, so Dolly expressed milk and fed him with an eyedropper, and kept him in a shoebox, wrapped in cotton wool.

Nineteen months later, Dolly's second baby was delivered by Mrs Annie Knudson, who acted as midwife in the district. She did not want Joe hanging round, so hunted him off to cut scrub while the baby was born. For the third birth, Dolly rode the seven miles into Millaa Millaa then caught the new railmotor to the new maternity hospital in Atherton, while Joe minded the children at home. When it was time to return, Dolly caught the train back, then rode home with the new baby. Then 'it was a never ending job feeding the three children, washing clothes and drying them around the stove as well as help with the farmwork'. Joe built a new house to fit in all the family. He also built a cow yard and started dairy farming, and helping with the milking was another job for Dolly. A fall brought on a miscarriage, which filled Dolly's gumboots with blood. Once again Alan and Annie Knudson came to the rescue.

The government built a small maternity hospital in Millaa Millaa, staffed by a sister who also gave advice about any illness. It was in time for Dolly's fourth confinement, which was imminent when Wally decided to help her by cutting wood. The result was a big gash on the youngest child's head. Joe was building a house two miles away, so Dolly patched up the gash as best she

A CWA pioneer

Mary Warnes was born in Adelaide, and in 1900 married and moved to an isolated station east of Burra. For years the only woman she met was her sister, who lived on a neighbouring property. Then her sister died, and Mary would go on a trip to buy an unnecessary piece of material, just to speak to other women. She loved handcrafts, especially quilting and tatting.

In 1926 Mary was invited by the president of the National Council of Women to start a branch of the Country Women's Association in her district. She put an advertisement in the local paper, and in November the Burra branch was formed, the first in South Australia. Mary became president, and held this office for fifteen years. Other branches began, and in 1929 a state executive was formed, with Mary the president. That year she was also the first international delegate of the South Australian CWA, when she travelled to London to start the international body. A quiet woman who had the gift of never forgetting a face, she became the 'little mother' of the CWA in South Australia, and did a great deal to provide friendship and company for women in the country.

could, then piggybacked 'this big lump of a kid' up the road, with the two others straggling beside her. They took two hours to reach Joe, by which time Dolly was exhausted. Joe took the child to the hospital, and by the time he returned Dolly was in labour. He borrowed a horse and found someone to mind the children, then took Dolly to the hospital, where the sister feared complications she did not feel qualified to handle, so organised two fettlers to man a pumpcar (a railway trolley) to take her and Dolly to Atherton. By the time they reached Minbun, ten miles from Millaa Millaa, not only were the fettlers exhausted but Dolly was in distress with severe labour pains, and before they could get her to shelter the baby was born on the pumpcar, with the nurse's help.

There was even more hard work for Dolly, with four children at home. Going anywhere meant riding: Dolly would carry the baby and one child would sit behind her, and Joe had two chil-

The 1920s

dren sitting in front of him. When the annual show was on, they used a packhorse to take their exhibits there. For years they won prizes, Dolly for bread, fancy work and crochet work, and Joe for farm produce. As in many parts of Australia, conditions of life were improving. They put a concrete floor in the cow yard, a separator made dairy work faster, and a tank and guttering meant that water did not have to be carried from the creek.

Baby number five was born in the Atherton hospital, and baby six in the enlarged Millaa Millaa hospital, delivered by a midwife. When it was due, Joe took Dolly in and told her he would come to see her in a week. The baby was born half an hour later, and Dolly rested in hospital until Joe arrived, a week later as he had said.

By now the family was 'a bit more financial'. Joe built a new four-bedroomed house and bought a utility, a big boost to the family, especially when a gravelled road was built past their house. It was only a fifteen-minute car ride to the maternity hospital when babies seven, eight and nine were born. Then Dolly decided she was sick of sitting on boxes at the table. She wanted decent chairs and a built-in cupboard, so she went on strike. She refused to cook dinner, then tea, and next morning breakfast. Joe gave in, and took her to Innisfail to buy the furniture. 'She realised she should have been on strike years before.' She had two more children, born in the Atherton hospital and delivered by a doctor. Dolly had a hard time at these births, probably, said her daughter, because her body was wearing out: 'all she knew was hard work'. She and Joe reared their eleven children very successfully. Though their story illustrates the effect of the government's policy of building maternity hospitals, baby health centres do not feature. The first one in the district was not built until 1946 – but Dolly managed well without one.

Similar changes to those in Queensland occurred all over Australia, with the result that more babies were born in hospitals, and most mothers visited a clinic at least once. Infant mortality continued to decline but maternal mortality did not, and the birthrate continued to fall. Many women appreciated government efforts, but there were some less pleasant results of the new

Gristed wheat and rabbits

Isabella Irving was born in Fernihurst, Victoria in 1881. When she left school her parents forced her to become apprenticed to a tailor, but she detested sewing so much that she did not follow the trade. Instead she took a job helping a family on the boat trip to Western Australia, and worked in similar jobs for five years.

In 1908 Ella became pregnant. She could not provide for baby Bert, so left him in the Salvation Army home and found a job in a shop. The owner, Frank Evans, proposed marriage. She accepted, and they moved, with Bert, to a block of land Frank had been allocated at East Kondut. There the family, now numbering four, lived in a bough shelter, then a bark humpy with a dirt floor. Seven years later Frank built a conventional house. Ella had five more children, and for the second birth tried to travel to Perth, but the baby was born in a hotel on the way. The next two were born at home with the local midwife, the last two in the local hospital. Times were tough, and the family's diet was basic, mainly gristed wheat, rabbits, and home made bread and dripping, or molasses. As conditions improved cows, fowls and pigs provided milk, eggs and pork.

At first there was no school and Bert grew up illiterate, but later a school was built, though the children stayed at home to help at seeding, harvest and shearing. Ella was particular about washing, starching and ironing, and always sent them to school well turned out. When the telephone reached Kondut, the exchange was put in the Evans home. Ella was always on duty, for all the children had a speech impediment and could not answer the phone. In 1935 Ella decided she had suffered enough hardship and ill treatment from Frank, so she went to Perth with her eldest daughter and returned to domestic work.

One of Ella's employers was so impressed with her sponge cake that he entered it in the Narrogin Show, where it won first prize. Her granddaughter Tresna provided the recipe:

The 1920s

Ella's Sponge Cake
4 eggs at room temperature
1 cup of sugar (Tresna prefers only half a cup)
1 cup of flour
1 teaspoon of carb soda
$1/2$ teaspoon of cream of tartar
2 tablespoons of boiling water

Heat the oven to 200°.

Sift the flour, carb soda and cream of tartar together three times and put it back in the sifter.

Put the egg whites in a bowl and beat till stiff, slowly adding the sugar a little at a time, beating until the sugar is dissolved. Add the egg yolks one at a time until all are added and thoroughly mixed. Beat another couple of minutes until the mixture has greatly increased in volume. (Ella did this by hand, using a fork or a whisk.)

Gradually fold the sifted flour into the egg mixture, shaking the flour through the sifter a few shakes at a time until all is gently folded in. Then fold in the boiling water. Hand movements must be light and gentle.

Pour mixture into a cake tin, which has the bottom lined with greased paper and the sides greased.

Place in the centre of the oven. Leave the temperature at 200° for twenty minutes. Sponge is cooked when it springs back to the touch.

Ella did not allow anyone to open the kitchen door, and certainly not the oven door, until the cake was cooked, as this would cause the room and oven temperature to drop and ruin the sponge. Ella preferred to be in the kitchen alone while she was baking, and anyone who was there could not walk past the oven or clomp around the room.

system, and some trained nurses were unsympathetic. Violet Ellett married at twenty, and left Melbourne for a two-roomed farmhouse in the bush. When her first baby was due she rode along a bush track into the Koo Wee Rup hospital on the back of a farm wagon, beside a load of peas on the vine. She was put to bed with the task of hemming a hospital sheet, to take her mind off the pain of labour.

More generally, scientific motherhood was a grave responsibility. Any imperfection in the child was seen as the mother's fault, and since no child is ever perfect, the mother's task was impossible. Then as baby grew up, it was again the mother's responsibility to see to the child's psychological development, treating each child individually, showing understanding and creativity. No child was innately troublesome, said the experts: problems were due to upbringing. This could create dreadful guilt, and was a far cry from older ideas, where children fitted in and parents were only responsible for feeding and clothing them and telling them what was right and wrong. Added to women's other work – in the house, helping the family or employment – scientific childcare was a considerable burden.

As before, some women tried to combine motherhood and paid work, but in the 1920s the increasing demands of motherhood led to extra problems. Dr Vera Scantlebury worked in women and children's health, becoming Victoria's first Director of Infant Welfare in 1926. By this stage she had married, and as Dr Vera Scantlebury Brown she was asked to work half-time, since the public service could not employ married women full-time. She was most successful, developing a state-wide system of infant welfare clinics, said to be more caring than those elsewhere because of her warm personality. At the same time, she put motherhood into practice herself when she gave birth to a son in 1928. She employed a mothercraft nurse and housekeeper, but did much of the childcare herself. 'I had to make the Rice Jelly twice (it burnt the first time!) Mothercraft in earnest!' she wrote in her diary, and she was upset at work when the baby was fractious – 'I am ashamed to say how my stomach seems to turn upside down when he is not perfect'. Combining employment and childcare was exhausting, and at times she longed only to be Mrs Brown and Edward's mother; she once wrote that as usual she felt torn in all directions. She considered resigning, but did not, due to professional pride and worry about the effects of the Depression. With support from husband, family and friends she carried on, remaining in her post for twenty years, before dying of cancer aged fifty-six.

It was not just in mothering that experts urged change, but in all domestic areas. Home duties must be done by rational, modern and efficient methods. Family meals were to be tasty and nutritious, with the correct number of calories and vitamins, prepared hygienically and cooked to retain the maximum food value. The house must be spotlessly clean, and there were campaigns against flies. To assist the housewife there were new consumer goods like cleansers and fly sprays. Women were instructed in the new ways, mostly through girls being taught at school where they were a captive audience, but also through lectures, pamphlets, magazine articles and radio.

What influence did scientific womanhood have on women's lives? Newspapers embraced the new ideas, and many women did as well. As we have seen, many more gave birth in hospitals under the care of trained staff. Many mothers, particularly if they were young and inexperienced, took the advice of infant welfare sisters. Cleanliness did improve – the amount of soap used per head rose by 1.5 kilos in the 1920s – but girls at school generally preferred academic or business subjects to domestic science. Advice had less effect if it was expensive, hard to follow, received less publicity or seemed ridiculous, and even Vera Scantlebury Brown did not always follow the experts. Once she wrote of her baby son, 'he was rather overtired and beside himself so I fear I broke the rules and gave a little nurse and held his hand and he went off to sleep at once – dear wee pet'.

As they had done all through Australian history, women used self-help to better their lives. In 1922 a group of wealthy graziers' wives decided to improve conditions for rural women, and formed the Country Women's Association. It has been suggested that they tried to unite women under conservative leaders to stop communist and radical ideas, but even if this were true it did not succeed. The CWA took off immediately, with hundreds of branches joined by all types of women, first in New South Wales then other states. Branches were autonomous, which meant that local leaders – sometimes but not usually the socially eminent – could introduce their own ideas. Some branches discouraged Aboriginal members, but others permitted any woman 'of good character' to join, and many Aboriginal women did.

The CWA tried to improve women's conditions, pressing for maternity hospitals, child welfare centres, rest rooms for country women visiting towns, hostels near hospitals where expectant mothers could stay, and holiday homes so country families could visit the beach. They also supported community facilities like hospitals, schools and ambulances. Members raised money by stalls and raffles, and held meetings where speakers might demonstrate some new activity, while women met their friends

Group settlers

Born in England in 1890, at the age of eight Florence Taylor left home to train as a trapeze artist. In the war she worked as a book-keeper in an Air Force laundry, and met her husband when he came to complain about lost collars. Not a highly romantic way to meet, said Florence, but the start of a very romantic and happy marriage.

In 1923 they emigrated to Australia with their baby daughter, and were sent to a group settlement on the Margaret River. There were usually twenty couples per group, each with a block of land. Like many group settlements, this one eventually fell through, due to problems clearing land, unproductive soil, poor administration, bushfires and 'numerous other problems'. The Taylors were given a dilapidated tin hut with no bed, but their co-settlers made them one from corrugated iron laid on a jarrah frame, with blackboy leaves and sacks for a mattress.

'There were often some strange results from the early efforts of the new recruits', wrote Florence. When her bread dough failed to rise she buried it, but a mound of earth a foot high rose on the

for afternoon tea. Dances, card afternoons and concerts provided both social activity and a chance to raise more money. So the CWA brought improvements to country areas, as well as fellowship and a strong sense of community which offset the loneliness many women felt in the bush. In talks and demonstrations it spread some of the experts' new ideas, but tended to temper innovations with common sense.

Holiday homes were particularly appreciated. A boundary rider's wife and children from an isolated inland area were completely awestruck on their holiday at the beach. The children hid under the bed to escape from strangers, and the mother, who had not spoken to another woman for eighteen months, was tongue-tied. But other guests welcomed them, and two days later the children had joined the crowd splashing in the sea, while their mother chatted happily to the other adults.

Another strong women's lobby were Housewives' Associations,

---

site, making her failure clear for all to see. The settlers were plagued by bull ants and mosquitoes, burnt by the sun, afraid of snakes and exhausted by hard work, but at the end of two months, Florence wrote, they had come to like Australians and learned to laugh at trials and frustrations. Then tragedy struck, when their baby daughter contracted enteritis and died.

Florence and Charles moved to manage a boarding house at Marmalup Mill. They spent their first pay on a bed. Florence bore their second child, but at six months he too contracted enteritis. She took him to Perth, a nine-hour train journey. He was in hospital for three months but survived, and the Taylors moved to a block of land they bought at Belmont. Here life was tough, for water had to be carried a quarter of a mile, and there were no roads or electricity. They lived in a tent until they built a two-roomed house, and Charles obtained a job as a brickie's labourer at Fremantle. Another son was born, and though life was still hard, 'all the ingredients for a family life and home were complete'.

A Wealth of Women

first formed in 1915 to protest about rising prices. They were vigorous in all states, and though it is difficult to assess how successful they were in their stated aims, they certainly showed that women could assert their own views. Like the CWA, they aimed at attracting women of all classes, seeing women as having the same interests, united by their gender rather than divided by their backgrounds. At the same time, as seen above, the scientific motherhood movement also addressed all women, and there were fewer domestic servants. Class distinctions were waning as Australia became a more homogenous society. But despite the hospitals, clinics and women's associations, many women found life a battle in the twenties, mainly because of difficult economic circumstances.

One girl's life illustrates starkly the effects of poverty. When Trudy Scott was seven, in 1921, her family emigrated from Britain to Western Australia as part of the group settlement scheme. Their farm consisted of a leaky 'broken-down' house, a horse on its last legs, an old cow nearly dry of milk and uncleared bush. Trudy's father tried to plough, but the land was hard and gravelly, so the family moved into Bridgetown. Her father collected the 'night soil' for the local council, her mother took in washing, and the seven children went to the convent school.

Trudy hated it. The children called her 'stinky' and 'poohie' because of her father's job, and as she had no shoes they stamped on her toes. After a couple of years her father became a wood contractor, chopping and selling wood, and the nuns offered to teach her music in exchange for wood. 'I was in seventh heaven.' This did not last, for her father decided he could earn more by selling the wood. Then, when her parents went out, her older brother forced fourteen-year-old Trudy to have sex with him. 'The horror never left me for a long time.'

Trudy went to work in a boarding house, glad to get away from her brother. The work was hard and embarrassing, including emptying chamber pots from under the beds, but Trudy saved her pay and felt rich when she had accumulated five pounds. Then her mother asked for a loan, but Trudy never saw the money again, or even received a thank-you letter. From then on, she

The 1920s

Battling against the odds

Maisie Smith lived in country New South Wales, and in about 1920 met Ted Debenham, a six foot tall, blond, blue-eyed returned soldier. Romance flourished, then Maisie realised she was pregnant. She went to Sydney to have an abortion, but decided against this and spent the money on presents. She and her boyfriend kept the pregnancy secret because he did not want to upset his mother. When Maisie's pregnancy became obvious, she went again to Sydney and became a domestic at the Crown Street Women's Hospital – it was common for pregnant girls from the country to work at the hospital for their board. Joan was born in 1921.

A woman friend minded Joan until her father, a clerk in the public service, was transferred to Moree. Her parents married, and arrived in Moree with their two-year-old daughter as an established family. Another daughter was born, but sadly Maisie died at the age of twenty-seven, when Joan was five. Joan was told that her mother insisted on moving furniture when she was pregnant, which brought on a miscarriage and her death from septicemia; but Joan wondered if in fact she had died from the effect of an abortion, which would never be discussed.

Joan went to live with her mother's seventeen-year-old sister, who was married and pregnant. Joan was miserable, so she joined her sister with their grandmother and experienced a warm family life, though everyone was expected to help. Joan was sent to stay with an aunt who was suffering from post-natal depression, to make sure she did not damage the baby or herself, a tough assignment for an eight-year-old.

spent her money on herself. She went to work for the local milkman and his wife, helping with their two small children, and was happy – 'they treated me like a human being'. But her parents bought a boarding house, and took her to be an unpaid waitress. By now she was sixteen.

The boarding house was isolated, and one of the guests was a pest, saying suggestive things, until one day Trudy tipped his soup over him. Her father thrashed her with his razor strop until she was black and blue, and locked her in her room for four days. 'I can still hear myself screaming after all these years.'

Time passed uneventfully until a new guest arrived, Roy. He started courting her, taking her for walks in the bush, and she was happy as he was polite and 'never made any attempt to touch me or anything like that'. Her parents sold the boarding-house, and Roy asked her to go and stay with his family. They welcomed her and Roy found work, but times were poor, and he was put off because he was the last one employed. Trudy and Roy decided to get married. 'What a wedding day!' She wore an apricot silk dress and hat, and was disappointed that her parents did not bother to come, only a brother. The newlyweds booked into a hotel for the night, and Roy went to the bar and started drinking. Trudy's brother took her to the pictures and they had fish and chips for tea. When they returned 'my new husband was drunk and fast asleep!'

Snapshot

FASHION

1788	white women arrive, wearing British fashions, the full, long skirts of the day
1800s	empire line frocks, high-waisted, straight skirts
1830s	full skirts back, with huge sleeves, low, horizontal necklines, tiny waists and heavily trimmed bonnets
1858	the crinoline appears in Australia, only a few months later than Europe
1860s	treadle sewing machines appeared, which made sewing much faster
1880s	skirts become flat in front, full at the back, held out with a bustle
1890s	tailored fashions appear, called the first sensible fashion: long, straight serge skirt with jacket, worn with a blouse
1900s	the S-shape is fashionable: long skirt with train, slim waist, bust thrust forward, bouffant hair and huge picture hat
1902	emigrant Helena Rubinstein opens Australia's first beauty salon, in Melbourne, and sells her own face cream, made from a traditional family recipe – the start of her international business empire

Snapshot

1908	casual clothes appear, inspired by sport – loose wrappers to wear in motor cars, comfortable jackets for golf, one-piece bathing costume for swimming
1920s	clothes become simpler, with shorter hems, flat silhouettes, dropped waists, straight lines, cloche hats, short hair, sometimes even no corset. Makeup becomes acceptable and some women wear trousers in public
1926	Berlei conducts the first scientific study of women's bodies and revolutionises corsetry round the world
-	Bonds makes twenty different natural shades of artificial silk stockings
1928	Speedo produces knitted, navy cotton one-piece swimming costumes for men, women and children
1930s	the natural figure returns, with higher waist, longer, swirling skirts, moulded hiplines. Trousers become common, shorts appear
Wartime	Australian fashions are copied from America rather than Paris, due to the war. Clothing is rationed, and skimpier, simpler styles enforced. The square, plain look is in

Snapshot

1947	the New Look brings femininity back into women's clothes
1950s	emergence of the separate teenage market, with girls wearing pony tails, full skirts over rope petticoats, flat shoes, jeans, then tight stretch pants and stilettos. Fashionable women wear tailored suits with slim skirts and tight jackets. Synthetic fibres become popular
1960s	the beat look, with jumpers, pendants, black stockings, flat shoes, long hair
1965	Jean Shrimpton causes a stir by appearing at the Melbourne Cup in a miniskirt, and no hat, stockings or gloves. Australian women take up miniskirts enthusiastically, along with pantyhose (1966)
1971	women reluctantly abandon the mini and take to the hippie look, with long hair, long Indian dresses, beads, kaftans, no makeup, minimal underwear and psychedelic colours and patterns
1980s	new female executives bring in power dressing
1990s	grunge is fashionable, also the minimalist look
-	fashion becomes more varied with a multitude of styles

Source: Alexandra Joel,
Parade: the story of fashion in Australia, Sydney, 1998

chapter seven

Hard Times

'I only hope the youth of today never have to face a depression; it is the most soul destroying thing that can happen to anyone', wrote Win Baulch. 'Prices fell to bedrock.' At their farm on the Mallee, 'we women used to steep cocky chaff (which is straw with the grain removed) by boiling the copper and mixing the boiling water with molasses to try and keep the cows alive. They died, some in the mud of the empty dams. Clothes wore out. Shoes were reduced to sand shoes. Sheets wore out and we replaced the mattress with bags sewn together and filled with chaff and more bags sewn together for extra warmth. Thin old blankets for sheets.' Occasionally there was a dance in the local hall, and everybody went – 'everyone was shabby but we all enjoyed these little diversions'.

Win and her husband Joe were in partnership with Joe's brother, but there had always been quarrels, and now they worsened. 'Squabbles, unhappiness, poverty – what a combination!' Then Win received a message to say her mother had been hurt in an accident. She had no good clothes, decent shoes or shoe polish, but a neighbour lent her a dress and she rubbed her old shoes with grease and set off. When she arrived her mother had died, so Win buried her then headed back to 'hell'. Joe went to the Western District to try and find work, leaving Win alone with her dominating in-laws.

Her aunt helped, taking in Win's seven-year-old daughter Lorna so she was near a school, but the little girl contracted polio. When she heard the news, Win left even the washing on the line, and rushed to Lorna. She cared for her devotedly and refused to return to the Mallee, so she and Joe walked away from all their work. Both suffered nervous breakdowns, 'but at last the sun shone again and the skies were blue'. They regained their health, Lorna recovered after four years of treatment, and as the Depression eased, Joe found work as a shearer and at a flax mill.

The Depression was the first event in Australian history which affected almost every woman, to judge from autobiographies. Few mention public events in the nineteenth century; women could ignore self-government, the gold rush and economic ups and downs as they got on with their own lives. Many more mention the First World War, but even then, some women with neither relations fighting nor war work were not greatly concerned. But almost every autobiography talks about the Depression. Its effects ranged from upsetting – seeing so many people in want – to catastrophic. There had been other depressions, notably in the 1890s, but the early 1930s saw *the* Depression, the worst in Australian history.

Most women depended on a male breadwinner, but few men

Keeping up standards

During the Depression, Margaret Rickard's father, a former sergeant-major in the British army, felt lucky to get a job on the railways in Western Australia. In 1933 he was transferred to the tiny township of Karlgarin, on a branch railway line. It was an isolated place with no facilities, and though Margaret loved the life, her English mother, a city-bred former nurse, found it challenging, especially as she refused to lower her standards. The family dressed neatly for dinner, used starched damask dinner napkins and always said grace – even when living in a tent, waiting for their two-roomed house to be built. Margaret's mother ran a Sunday School for local children, and passed her high standards on to Margaret.

retained their previous income. Unemployment soared to 32 per cent; most of those who were employed had salary cuts; those running their own enterprises, like doctors and shopkeepers, found their takings falling; and those on the land suffered as prices for primary products crashed. Consumer prices fell too, but overall almost everyone was worse off, often far worse. Governments provided a meagre dole for men, but women were generally not eligible.

Even those with husbands in the professions could have problems. Kathleen Lenthall, whose husband's salary as a teacher at Sydney Grammar was reduced by two-thirds, had to supplement the family income by making and selling children's clothes. Dorothy Plummer's father was an industrial chemist in Melbourne – he experimented with her mother's scones and sponges to find the perfect ratio of additives in self-raising flour – but the family was very careful with money, and Dorothy's mother worked hard to make the most of it. Entertainment was mostly home-made, everything possible was made at home, clothes had to last as long as they could, and neighbours helped each other by handing down clothing. 'I think there would not be a family, who was unaffected by the Depression in some way', wrote Mavis Bradbury of South Melbourne. Her father's wages were reduced to the level of female pay, but though she herself was never hungry, 'FEAR was all around us. What if Dad lost his job?'

Former wealth was no safeguard. Maureen Greene's father made a fortune on the Western Australian goldfields, and Maureen, born in 1894, grew up in luxury in Toorak, in a large house with seven servants. Her life was 'just hell', however, as her mother disliked her. She escaped to Sydney and became a commercial artist, then married a wealthy pastoralist, George Greene, twenty years her senior. They had two children and prospered, but in the Depression the price of wool fell so low that they went bankrupt and had to walk off their property. George was sixty, lame and deaf, and Maureen realised that she would have to become the breadwinner. Her mother found her a small grocery shop to run in Sydney; this failed, so Maureen took more knowledgeable advice from a commercial traveller and moved to a better shop,

A Wealth of Women

which prospered. It was very hard, however; Maureen worked seventeen hours a day, six days a week, with George helping by measuring out sugar, flour and other products bought in bulk. A far cry from a pastoralist's life.

Those who lost their jobs were reduced to living on the meagre dole and what they could produce themselves. Edna Leach's experience was typical. Her husband Jim was a miner near Boolaroo. 'It was a bad time for everyone', wrote Edna. 'Our Men all were put off & on the dole. But they had to work on the roads & bridges to get their allowance. Jim always had a vegetable garden & we had Chooks & a Cow so we weathered the storm.'

Widows could have an even tougher job. Frances Allison's husband had a good job in a shale works at Latrobe, but when he died in 1930 Frances was left penniless with nine children to care for, one crippled by polio. A good musician, she earned a living by playing the piano at local dances and picture shows, cycling round the district in her evening clothes even on freezing cold winter nights. Like Edna, she kept cows, poultry and a vegetable garden, the children all helped, and though life was hard, 'we were always fed, so you can't complain'. Dorothy Bolton of far north Queensland also made the most of her abilities. Her family took what employment they could and ate anything they could lay their hands on. Dorothy, the eldest child, left school to go to work to help feed the family. She was in turn a farm hand, roo shooter, jillaroo and bullock team driver.

Many people who owned nothing and had nowhere to live took to the roads. In 1931 Flora and Jack Lyons married, but shortly afterwards Jack lost his job as a farm labourer, then their first child died aged two months. They spent the next few years travelling, camping in a tent, living on the dole, trapping rabbits, prospecting for gold or finding occasional seasonal work to support their growing family. Flora's health suffered, and she became very thin. She hated this nomadic life, but loyalty to Jack kept her with him.

As all through Australian history, many women showed their strength of character. Kate Englart's husband was a well-known Labor leader and communist in Brisbane, but Kate was the real

Hard Times

A woman gets things done

Violet Powell had grown up in comfort and security in a well-to-do family. In 1922 she married George Lambert, and they purchased a farm property at Lysterfield in the Ferntree Gully shire. A daughter was born, but in 1930 George died. Violet continued to work the property, and as she was appalled at the poor state of the local roads and wanted to obtain better amenities for women, in 1931 she stood for council. She unseated the sitting member in a landslide, one of the very few women elected to local government in that era.

The other councillors showed her courtesy and paternal interest, but not the municipal engineer, who tried to thwart her desire for more road maintenance. She defeated him, and got things done. An excellent organiser, with a will of iron, she was an able debater and delivered impressive speeches. The women of the shire were immensely proud of her, and supported the institutions she founded, including a Baby Health Centre and a branch of the Country Women's Association. She was also a magistrate in the Children's Court, and made her mark at council meetings, which continued all afternoon without a break. Violet missed her afternoon tea, so started taking scones and making a pot of tea in the kitchen. The men, delighted, joined her, and in gratitude presented her with a silver teapot and coffee pot.

There were limits, however. In 1936 it should have been the turn of Violet's section of the shire to provide the president, but the councillors could not cope with a female president and a man from another section was installed. It was not until after the war that this competent woman did become shire president, only the second woman in Victoria to do so.

strength of the family, said her granddaughter. After bearing seven children in eight years, she told the Catholic priest she had had enough of the church and its ban on contraception. She was even stronger when dealing with debt collectors, bailiffs and police who came to evict the family when they could not pay the rent, locking the doors and 'having a plentiful supply of boiling water to throw over those bastards who attack our fortress'.

Many women tried to find work, which was marginally easier for them than men. Industries which mainly employed women – food and drink, clothing, services – were not as badly affected as men's industries like heavy metals and construction, and women were paid much less so some employers preferred them. Even so, one servant's job attracted two hundred applicants. And there could be problems if the woman became the breadwinner, taking the man's traditional role. Many men did not cope well, which added to the stress; while society generally disapproved. Married women were dismissed from many jobs, unions were hostile to women, and there was a general atmosphere of condemnation. It all added to the difficulties of the time.

Couples tended to delay marriage, partly out of general caution, partly because so many women had to leave their jobs when they married, and their wage was vital. So they stayed on, or hid the fact that they were married. Fewer marriages, and the expense of bringing up children, meant that the birthrate fell even further. Contraception was not improved and many women knew nothing about what was available, and it seems that again, the main methods of population control were withdrawal, abstinence and abortion. And trying to avoid having children often meant more tensions in marriages already under strain.

Despite their own problems, many women were sorry for those worse off than themselves, and helped swaggies and others in trouble. Ruby McKinlay's husband Irvine was the owner of a sawmill near Flinton in Queensland. Ruby worked extremely hard to care for her family, chopping wood and carting endless buckets of water to her vegetable garden, but no swaggie passed her door without receiving a meal, and one day she fed thirty-two from the family's meagre supplies.

The difficult situation inspired some women to join left-wing political groups. In 1932 future author Kylie Tennant, then a student, visited her teacher friend Roddy in Coonabarabran, where he had been sent because of his communist leanings. 'It was, of course, obligatory among radicals to sleep with whomever you intended to marry so I slept with Roddy on the bank of the

Castlereagh in the moonlight. Very romantic, but by bad luck a moth got into my ear. It fluttered and whirred and took all my attention. I did not think it would be polite to say: "Could you stop seducing me because I have a moth in my ear?" so I carried on, doing my best.' The next morning she suggested marriage. 'Done', said Roddy.

In Coonabarabran Kylie met many women coping as best they could. One, whose husband was in jail, supported her children by rabbit trapping. Another, tired of an itinerant life, spread her five children on the steps of the police station, and told the policeman to put them in gaol so they would be fed. The houseproud sergeant did not want children in his neat gaol so the woman and children received the dole, though the husband was told to get back on the track.

Helped by the Country Women's Association, Kylie and the local Labor leader's wife begged food and provided every family with Christmas dinner and a hamper. Delivering the hampers, Kylie found families with children as shy as bush animals, living in humpies with mud floors and leaky iron roofs, never coming to town as they had no means of getting there. She joined the Communist Party, but became disillusioned. She thought its members were ineffectual, and they thought women's place was in the kitchen. Kylie decided communists would only split the working class, so she resigned.

Others felt the Party had a more positive message for women. In 1930 Peggy Hill organised International Women's Day celebrations in Brisbane, the first in Australia, and also a panel of doctors to advise women about birth control. She explained the injustices of the capitalist society to dole queues, handing out leaflets and taking part in demonstrations, where she was once attacked with batons by the police. When her husband was ill, she maintained her family, working as a cleaner in banks and offices.

Jean Ellis had quite a different way of helping women. A refined and dignified woman who never appeared in public without a hat and spotless white gloves, she had a forceful character and was an excellent organiser. She felt that women would benefit by gaining experience in public speaking and public life, and in

A Wealth of Women

1937 helped found the non-political Penguin Club, which encouraged women to speak in public and emphasised good speech and appearance. It became popular among women, giving them speaking skills and a sense of confidence as well as fellowship with other members.

Even more popular was Girl Guides, which by now had members all over Australia. Beth Chamberlain grew up on a soldier settler block in the Mallee and loved farm life, and going hunting, shooting and fishing with her father and brothers. Guides was a wonderful interest for a girl on a farm, and she has continued to feel that it is of tremendous value, with its message of doing one's best and being of service to the community.

Another keen Guide was Kathleen Barges. An orphan, she was sent from Britain to Australia by Barnado's Homes in 1929, aged fifteen, and had a series of jobs looking after children. It could have been lonely and difficult, but she too gained much enjoyment and stability from Guides. She particularly enjoyed Guide Week in Sydney in 1931, 'this wonderful week' where girls were taken to see the sights – Manly, the zoo and the Peters' ice-cream

Sexual harassment

In 1937 two women took their employers to court for sexual harassment, probably the first such cases in Australia. In Southern Cross in Western Australia, a woman complained that she had to leave her work because of her employer's familiarity, and was awarded the full amount of her claim. The Southern Cross News *showed its opinion of this by warning men against employing 'the too-pretty candidate. Ten to one she won't be able to cope with her work. Also she will give his wife ideas, take the male staff from its work and antagonise the female side'.*

Judith Lipman came from a well-to-do family in Sydney. She attended Meriden school then business college, and started to look for office jobs. In 1937, aged eighteen, she was engaged by August Romer for a day's typing. While showing her some papers, he put his arm round her. She walked away, and August followed her and kissed her on the lips. Her reaction led him to factory – then attended a rally with thousands of Guides in their navy blue, headed by the Chief Guide, Lady Baden-Powell, who told them she liked Guides better than 'big hefty Scouts'. Kathleen also enjoyed Guiding activities like camping, hiking, singing camp songs and passing tests, all of which gave her a sense of 'our pride and joy that we were Guides'.

Through all the difficulties of the Depression, many women continued with one of their traditional tasks, bringing culture to the community. There are many examples, all around the country. In Brisbane, Barbara Sisley taught drama and pioneered amateur theatre. She established the Brisbane Repertory Theatre in 1925, and continued to promote theatre for twenty years. In Goulburn, artist Annette McDonnell opened a library and art shop in 1931. There she held art exhibitions, where she often persuaded leading Sydney artists to exhibit, feeling that it was important that country people had access to good painting. She herself continued to paint, her children remembering that this was more important than meals, which were often late. Veronica Malone ran the Great Northern Hotel in Marree, in outback

---

apologise and say it would not happen again. 'Too right it won't!' she said, and rushed out into the street, where she told a policeman. He confronted August, who denied the charge, but the policeman pointed out that he had 'some pink substance like lipstick' on his top lip. 'I cannot see it', said August.

A police magistrate fined him £20. August appealed and his fine was halved, the judge observing that men were only fined £3 for assaulting policemen. Some newspapers made fun of the whole affair; others quoted an eminent lawyer: 'An employer, no matter how deeply solicitous for the comfort and welfare of his typist, commits assault if he touches her without her consent'. Judith obviously agreed, for among her papers is the notice of August Romer's death, nearly sixty years after his offence. Her later career was more enjoyable: she worked for a photographer and became a photographer herself, married, then ran a successful business organising weddings.

Sister Kenny and polio

The most controversial woman of the 1930s was Elizabeth Kenny. Born in 1880, she was independent, energetic and strong-willed. She received the usual limited country education and her nursing training is debated, but she nursed her neighbours at Nobby in the Darling Downs, and in 1911 opened a cottage hospital. There she used hot fomentations to help puzzling cases which were finally diagnosed as the frightening new disease of poliomyelitis or infantile paralysis, 'polio', which attacked children in particular and left them dead or crippled, and for which there was no cure. During the First World War Elizabeth nursed troops, and gained the title 'Sister'.

Using money from an innovative stretcher she designed and patented, Elizabeth developed her treatment for polio and in 1932 set up a clinic in Townsville. In the 1930s there were several terrifying epidemics of polio, and treatment was hotly debated. Elizabeth shunned orthodox methods involving immobilisation and callipers, using instead hot baths and massage, and encouraging active movement. She had excellent nursing skills and worked tirelessly and affectionately with her patients, who adored her. Doctors ridiculed her, but Elizabeth had no hesitation in standing up to doctors. Despite almost total medical opposition but with huge popular support, the government set up five Kenny clinics to treat polio. Elizabeth's methods were widely accepted in America, where she became a heroine. She died in 1952, a year before a polio vaccine became available.

South Australia. The dining room had starched white linen tablecloths and napkins; beautiful silver cutlery was kept spotless; outside was the first rose garden in the town. Veronica was a talented musician, and held concerts and annual Christmas parties for the whole town.

The response to women's encouragement of culture could be unenthusiastic. The Scott family lived near Boggabilla, and their children were taught by a fifteen-year-old governess. She had the tough task of teaching Gene and Jack to play the piano, as 'Mum seemed to think that a bit of art and culture would never go astray'. Gene said she and Jack hated it, and were both hopeless. When Jack played a wrong note the governess would belt him over the knuckles with a ruler, and when things got really bad she would box his ears. He sobbed and cried; 'I can still remember the big tears rolling down his freckled cheeks, and falling on the yellowed keys of the blasted piano, stained in one place where a possum had pissed on them ... sooner or later she was only too happy to dismiss us, and we would race outside, with a smirk on our face, minus any sign of tears, call the dogs and get on our horses, and gallop off into the timber'.

Indomitable Kate Bates typifies the spirit many women needed to get through these years. Widowed young in 1905, she brought up her four children on a small farm near Merredin, in a house made largely of corrugated iron and hessian bags. For her the Depression did not make a great deal of difference as times were always tough, but they became even tougher when in 1933 her daughter-in-law died, and Kate took over raising her three youngest grandchildren, Billy, Phyllis and Zelma.

'OH BOY, GRANNY', wrote Zelma. 'We soon learnt not to underestimate Granny because she was a survivor. Tough, you have never seen a tough lady until you had seen Granny. No one argued with Granny Bates.' She never minced her words or showed fear, and never complained. She never owed anyone a penny, and was extremely thrifty. She had to be: there were 'a lot more dinner times than dinners ... I really cannot ever remember going to bed not hungry'. Granny was determined to get her money's worth for every penny, challenging shopkeepers so fearlessly that the children fought to get out of taking her into Merredin for her monthly shopping expeditions. 'No worries about plaque building up on the teeth, because believe me, the teeth chattering would shake the plaque off just at the thought of the trip.'

Granny only gave in once. She sent the girls to collect the mail without the key to the postbox, and the irate postmaster told them they should remember it, not ask him every time. Granny

A Wealth of Women

wrote him a letter: 'Sir if you lazy mongrels don't get off your backsides and give my girls the mail, I will come in there and smash the bloody box down'. The postmaster read it aloud in front of all the customers, the girls refused to go to the post office, and Granny did give them the key.

At home, Granny never had any time to herself as she was always working, cutting posts, mending fences, chasing cattle or growing wheat. She taught the girls to plough by tying a piece of white rag to a tree and telling them to drive the horses straight for it. 'If the line was crooked, which it mostly always was, she would cuff us in the ear and say that we were useless dumb fools.' The children also killed chooks, sheep or rabbits – they became good shots, said Zelma, since it was often a case of no rabbit, no tea. They boiled clothes over a fire in buckets of water and caustic soda (often while standing in dishes of water to keep ants off their feet), and scrubbed clothes on a board with home-made soap, which contained carbolic acid and rubbed the skin off their hands.

Granny made clothes out of calico flour bags, mattresses from wheat bags and straw, soap, shampoo, ointments, brooms, rakes and a 'whole host of things': the Bates family did not pass much money over the counter. A teacher who did not like the girls used to check their hair for nits in front of the class, not realising that nothing had a hope of living in hair washed with Granny's disinfectant and carbolic shampoo. The girls made themselves a wogger or home-made doona, by unpicking two wheat bags, putting a thin layer of kapok in the centre and sewing them together. With the mattress, the wogger, a blanket, Phyl's cats and Zelma's dogs, they were extremely warm.

Granny was a strict disciplinarian, with every member of the farm. Billy had a pet hen which used to lay its eggs in the kitchen. Granny didn't mind, until one day she saw the hen pecking the butter. 'Granny grabbed it by the neck, whirled it around her head, rung its neck and hurled it out the door', wrote Zelma. 'Granny wasn't to be taken lightly.'

Granny had a cure for everything. Every hurt was doused with the disinfectant Phenyle – 'we wore Phenyle like film stars wear body lotion' – and when mosquitoes infested the girls' bedroom, Granny burnt a bucket of manure there, which drove out both mosquitoes and girls. But while other children were dying of diphtheria, meningitis and polio, said Zelma, the Bates children were healthy.

Zelma thought it must have been a huge burden for Granny to have the care of three lively children, without much help. When Granny wanted a bit of peace she would sit on the outside dunny for a while, and the kids also used the dunny as a refuge, when Granny was after them with her strap. They never had money for ice-creams or lollies, and all they received in their Christmas socks was a small packet of jelly beans, but they were happy. At night Granny would put her arms around them after tea in front of the fire, and 'that made up for everything we may have missed out on. Granny provided us with everything we needed. She attended to our needs come hell or high water'.

The *Australian Women's Weekly*

In 1933 a new magazine was published for women, the Australian Women's Weekly. At this time other women's magazines described only home activities like cooking and sewing, while the women's pages in newspapers concentrated on social activities and clothes: what actors and audience wore at a play, what clothes to wear when bushwalking.

Journalist Alice Jackson joined the Weekly *staff in 1933, and became effective editor the next year. She developed its highly successful mix of fiction, news and articles on a range of topics, from household interests like food, clothes and gardening, to childcare, films and books, and women's achievements – 'something for everyone'. Though there were paper patterns for the latest Paris fashions, overall there was a strong Australian emphasis. The* Weekly *had a social conscience, criticising an authority who would not let an Aboriginal woman marry the man of her choice, commenting on problems facing women in employment, not always treating marriage as wonderful. It quickly built up a huge circulation of half a million.*

A Wealth of Women

What was women's overall reaction to the Depression? Most struggled on as best they could, trying to feed their families, reusing tea leaves, buying scrap meat, using every penny to best advantage, working harder than ever. Some started small enterprises, such as selling home-made butter or eggs, making and selling boiled lollies or ginger beer, selling clothes door-to-door, taking in boarders, or doing sewing for neighbours. Many battled hard to provide for their children, not only shelter and food, but education. Then, and ever since, the Depression has been seen as the most difficult time for all white Australians.

In September 1939, Nola Fisher's family was surrounded by bushfires. News came that war had broken out, and Nola's grandmother, her face deathly white and speckled with ashes, cried 'War again!' Her son had fought in the First World War, and two nephews had died. Dorothy Godfrey's mother came into her bedroom to tell her the news. She was crying, and Dorothy's father looked stern and sad. 'Twice in our life time, God help us', he said. These were typical reactions to the grim news that Australia was once more at war with Germany.

Many men joined up, once more leaving women to run the family and often family businesses. Lillian Paton's husband Rob

Baked rabbit

For many women, cooking in the Depression was not so much a household art as trying to get enough food of any sort to feed the family. As seen in several stories in this chapter, a staple for many families was rabbit, often caught by family members. It could be baked, boiled, stewed, curried or fried, but this was an easy and cheap way to cook it.

Soak rabbit, cut it into joints and place in a pie dish. Add bacon, onion rings and pepper and salt. Make a thick brown gravy by mixing flour and water, pepper and salt, coloured a rich brown with Parisian essence. Pour over rabbit. Cover with bread crumbs. Cover dish and place in a fairly hot oven. Cook for two hours.

Hard Times

> ### Land Army experiences
>
> *Mary Laus was born in Korcula, and in 1934, aged nine, migrated with her mother to Fremantle on a British passport, to join her father. In 1943 Mary joined the Land Army in Queensland, working on six properties, including two dairy farms, where she started work before dawn and ended after dark. One tomato grower exploited her, but her other three employers were excellent. Sometimes she lived in, but she also stayed at Atherton camp with up to seventy other Land Army members, which she enjoyed. Due to Mary's foreign birth she was listed as an Alien, and had to report to the police before and after she moved jobs. A police sergeant was amazed at this situation.*

had fought in the First World War; now Rob and their four sons all joined the forces, and Lillian ran the family shop while they were away. For those whose menfolk had had no regular work for a decade, the war did at least provide jobs. Flora Lyons' family had suffered in the Depression, but after her husband joined up, for the first time in their lives the Lyons children had a 'real house' to live in and Flora did not have to worry about where the next meal was coming from.

Fighting was at first confined to Europe, with no immediate danger to Australia. Men enlisted in the armed forces, but the government said women were not needed except as nurses. Many women were keen to play an active part, however – 'women can fight just as well in tanks and armoured cars', said one – and many volunteer organisations sprang up, 102 in Sydney alone by June 1940. They often had their own uniforms, and ranged from voluntary nurses to paramilitary groups who practised shooting and drill.

As in the First World War, women took up support work with enthusiasm. Voluntary Aid Detachments were formed, their members mainly involved in nursing. Red Cross, the Country Women's Association and other groups were busy sending comforts to troops. Such work was not for the faint-hearted. An instruction booklet told knitters severely that 'believe it or not, socks are still being knitted imperfectly'. Wool must be preshrunk and never knotted – lumps could be painful even under puttees – and careless grafting caused ridges in the toe which might lame a soldier. Patterns were provided not just for the perfect sock, but for skull caps and balaclavas, spiral socks and sea boot stockings, knee caps and pullovers, as well as a 'muffler waistcoat'. Women also made camouflage nets for tanks and guns, half a million in 1943 alone.

By mid-1941 the war situation was grim, with troops and nurses in action in the Middle East. Two nurses, Sister Mollie Nalder and Sister Sylvia Duke, described their experiences in Greece as 'an awful nightmare'. Nurses realised 'we were in for it' as soon as they arrived. Continual air raids meant a stream of heartbreaking casualties, and since there were few dressings or drugs, nurses could do little. The sadness of watching these young men die remained with Mollie all her life. As the Germans pushed south, Mollie and Sylvia were among nurses and soldiers evacuated in a convoy of trucks. After a terrifying night drive without headlights, planes appeared at dawn, and the evacuees ran into a field of wheat. The planes machine-gunned the trucks, the noise was terrific, and it was dreadful lying flat expecting to be hit, 'wishing our tin hats were somewhat bigger to cover more of us'. When the planes left they moved to a cemetery, which gave more cover, fortunately, as there was raid-after-raid all day. They ate bully beef from tins with their fingers, and at one stage managed to light a fire and make tea.

When night fell they started south again, then walked two kilometres to a beach. Two ships were burning furiously, and a small boat took the nurses out to a destroyer. As they were hauled aboard Mollie heard a sailor say, 'Funniest b... soldiers I've ever seen', then, said Sylvia, 'the great discovery it was an Australian destroyer, the crew went mad ... When they discovered we were Australian girls they hugged us tight'. The crew could not do enough for the women, who were all utterly exhausted.

Meanwhile, back in Australia the armed forces were running short of telegraphists. In 1923, Florence Violet McKenzie had qualified as Australia's first female electrical engineer, and since

Islander women walking behind the plough, planting sugar cane – backbreaking work. Bingera, Queensland, about 1897

Granny Lum Loy, a Darwin identity

Aboriginal people with European settlers near the Clarence River, NSW

Black and white children, Alexandria, NT, 1917

Funeral of Queen Narelle, Wallaga Lake ca. 1895

Tiwi woman Rosemary Tipiloura receiving NT Chief Minister's Women's Achievement Award in 2001

Athlete Nova Peris

Women ready to go in a Red Cross kitchen, World War I

*Modernity comes to the Northern Territory:
women of the Studderd family in the outback*

Humour of the 1920s:
'Do you approve of clubs for women, uncle?'
'Yes – but only after every way of quietening them has failed!'

Dulcie in her leopard skin, Artists' Ball 1923.
It was quite acceptable, she wrote, as she wore an undergarment.

Hard Times

no firm would take a female apprentice, she started her own electrical supply business, specialising in radio. Foreseeing a need, when war was threatening she formed the Women's Emergency Signalling Corps, training volunteers as wireless and signal telegraphists. When the Navy's shortage of telegraphists became apparent, 'Mrs Mac' suggested her volunteer women. Traditionalists were appalled, but the shortage continued, and on Anzac Day 1941, the first female telegraphists were admitted to the Navy, and the Women's Royal Australian Naval Service came into being. Later that year the Women's Auxiliary Australian Air Force and the Australian Women's Army Service were also established, their aim being that members take over jobs and release men to fight. Thousands of women joined, receiving two-thirds of servicemen's pay and almost equal benefits, though these were often grudgingly conceded. When Clare Stevenson, head of the WAAAF, was asked how long she fought for better conditions, she answered, 'Four years, nine months', the period she held the position. She never succeeded in gaining equal pay.

Few female recruits were accepted until December 1941, when the Japanese entered the war. Australia was threatened, the whole nation became involved, and a week after Pearl Harbour, the prime minister announced the 'extensive employment of women' for the duration of the war.

War news worsened. The Japanese landed in Malaya and pushed south rapidly, and danger grew. Street names were removed, recalled Joy Woodley, a young teacher in Fremantle, and at night there was a blackout, with street and car lights almost extinguished and house lights hidden by heavy curtains. People dug trenches for protection from air raids, and schools held air raid drills. Some people suffered real raids, when the Japanese bombed towns in the north. Grace Moore of Mareeba was pregnant, and could not fit in the hole leading to the shelter, so she sat on the top stair. Japanese planes were flying overhead, but she was never hurt.

Invasion was a real fear, made worse when some towns were shelled. In Sydney, Nola Fisher's family were prepared, their shelter filled with homemade Anzac biscuits, boiled water, bandages and bush panaceas like Condy's Crystals. When the sirens began to wail the family blundered out of the house in the dark, as anti-aircraft guns boomed and searchlights raked the sky. They held hands and went down into the shelter, but Nola's grandmother refused to go, though her father spent the whole raid pleading with her. 'If I'm going to die, I'm going to die above ground', she said. Several hours later, when the all-clear sounded, the family found her standing in the doorway, wearing her best clothes, holding her umbrella in clenched and gloved fists, ready to do battle with the enemy.

Darwin was worst hit of any Australian city. As the Japanese pushed further south, in December 1941 two thousand women and children were evacuated. It was hard, especially for women with young children: evacuees were allowed to take only one suitcase, often with only an hour or two's notice, and ships were overcrowded. When evacuees arrived in the south they had to fend for themselves, and when they returned to Darwin their houses had often been looted.

At least they were safe. On 19 February 1942 Darwin was bombed. The post office received a direct hit and six women telegraphists were killed, part of the total of 243 who died that

A varied career

Born in 1921, Gwen Rowe caught polio at three and was crippled, but treatment by Sister Kenny's methods enabled her to walk again. In the Depression her family tried to earn a living, farming angora rabbits, growing mushrooms, raising guinea pigs then poultry: Gwen beheaded two thousand chooks a week. Then she did a secretarial course, and during the war she was sent to be a glass cutter, cutting lenses for gunsights and submarine periscopes. After being injured, she joined the Land Army, 'constant and varied hard work', though she enjoyed organising concerts and a quartet, the Overall Harmonists. At the end of the war, Land Army members were offered further training. Gwen was one of only 37 out of 6,000 eligible women to apply, and she went to university.

Hard Times

> ### An unusual WRAN
>
> *When war broke out, Ruby Boye and her husband were living on a tiny island in the Solomons, where he managed a timber company. The tele-radio which connected the island with the outside world was in their house, and when its operator enlisted, Ruby volunteered to take his place. As she was in a strategically useful position, the Navy appointed her a civilian coastwatcher, reporting enemy movements. She continued to send in her reports, even when the Japanese invaded the South Pacific.*
>
> *After the Japanese tortured and murdered a coastwatcher in New Guinea, all coastwatchers were commissioned in the armed forces, so Ruby joined the WRANS. The Japanese knew of her existence and broadcast a warning that her days were numbered, but she calmly prepared to retreat to the jungle if the enemy landed, but fortunately they never reached the island. Officials at a coastwatchers' headquarters paid her what they thought of as a compliment: Mrs Boye could use the Morse key as fast as almost any male operator.*

day. Gwenda Hansen, a secretary with Qantas, recalled that when the bombs started to fall the staff dashed outside and went to ground in the nearest gutter. During a lull they set out to see if they could help anyone, but the planes returned and they dived flat in the nearest paddock. The planes were so low they could see the Japanese symbols on the wings; 'as long as I live I shall never forget the awful rat-tat-tat of machine gun fire'. When the all-clear sounded they went to the wharf to help, and saw men wading ashore from ships which had been bombed. Gwenda assisted a man whose arm was almost severed at the shoulder. She tore up her underclothes to make a ligature to stop the bleeding, managed to get the man to a car and drove him to hospital, where the nurses were 'magnificent'.

Military intelligence kept a lookout for spies, and suspected a neighbour of Joy Woodley. This woman owned large tracts of land, and had visited Germany and met one of Hitler's ministers. There were tales of lights on the coast to guide Japanese submarines, and of a real landing at some point, but nothing could be pinned on the woman, who ended up suing the army for damage to her property. All round Australia, men and some women of Japanese, Italian and German origin were interned in camps.

From early 1942 many women joined the armed services, working in areas ranging from cooking to radar, intelligence and code-breaking. Overall, 176,071 women enlisted, including nurses. Women in the Australian Women's Army Service performed a variety of jobs, though they never fought. Some remember their work as boring, some as fulfilling. Amy Taylor joined AWAS as soon as she turned eighteen. She volunteered to go to New Guinea, in the first contingent of women to serve overseas. The group sailed to Lae, a frightening trip as the Japanese were still active. The Commanding Officer was embarrassed at having women on board, especially when a very green junior officer 'cast overboard our first collection of certain disposables, but neglected to distinguish between leeward and windward!'

In Lae the women were housed in barracks, with rats in the roof and the latrine only a hole in the ground. Many suffered from tropical diseases – Amy contracted malaria. They were only allowed out of the barracks in groups with a male escort. Still, 'we were sent there to do a job, and we took it all in our stride'. Amy worked in the quartermaster's store, where she met Japanese prisoners, when she issued them with tools and equipment. She felt that women in AWAS learnt independence, to share and to help each other, to do without and make do.

Daphne Caine volunteered with two hundred other women when an AWAS recruiting team came to her home town of Newcastle. She was proud to be one of twenty-six accepted, though shocked when she arrived at 'rookies course' and found no doors on the showers. Daphne became part of a trial group to see if women could do everything men could on the large anti-aircraft batteries. 'We did!' Guns, instruments, rifle shooting, unarmed combat, guard duty, all were mastered, and the women took over the guns and released men for active service. 'With all we had to learn, military discipline, new friends, homesickness etc made

Hard Times

better people of us all.' Later that year she became engaged to Sid, 'my AIF soldier boy', and two years later they married. Daphne did not have enough leave so went AWOL and lost her stripes, but it was worth it. Sid was posted to New Guinea and she did not see him again until after the war, when he was introduced to their six-month-old daughter.

Meanwhile, north of Australia, nurses were becoming even more heavily involved in the war. Six were working in the Rabaul hospital, and when Japanese invasion was imminent the medical officers fled, leaving the nurses and a padre in charge. They surrendered and the nurses were taken to Japan, where conditions were so appalling that they were reduced to eating the glue they used in their work of making envelopes.

Nurses in Malaya were evacuated in three ships. Two reached safety, but one was sunk off Sumatra. Twelve nurses died, and the rest reached land and surrendered. One group was ordered to march into the sea. 'They all knew what was going to happen to them, but no-one panicked: they just marched ahead with their chins up', said Sister Vivian Bullwinkel. The Japanese machine-gunned them, twenty-one died, and only Vivian survived to struggle ashore when the enemy had left. She later surrendered, joining the other thirty-one nurses in a series of prison camps, where they suffered from overcrowding, disease, inadequate food and water, few medicines, hard labour, and harsh regulations and punishments. The nurses formed a close-knit group among the hundreds of women, remaining as cheerful as possible, making do with what they could find and keeping each other going. But eight died, and the rest became very thin: by 1945 Sister Betty Jeffrey weighed thirty kilograms, about half her pre-war weight.

The worst occasion was when the Japanese ordered some nurses to attend an officers' club, 'and made it pretty obvious that they expected us to become prostitutes', said Sister Nesta James. The nurses went together, wearing red cross armbands and what was left of their uniform, looking as unattractive as possible. They refused to drink alcohol or co-operate, and were eventually allowed to return to camp unharmed. Others had similar problems: one nurse was ordered to go outside with an officer who put

> ### Coping with a husband's absence
>
> *Isetta Conte was born in Italy in 1902, and came to North Queensland as a newly-wed in 1929. With great determination, she set about doing what was expected of her as the wife of the ganger of a cane farm, preparing three large meals a day for the gang of up to seven men, and trying to make the cement-floored barracks cleaner and more home-like. She and her husband Pietro had three children.*
>
> *During the war Pietro was interned, and Isetta wondered how to care for the children with no breadwinner. The authorities would not help wives until their savings were spent, and the only way to survive was to work. Isetta formed her own gang of cane-cutters, all Italian women whose husbands had been interned. The farmer agreed to give them a go, and they set to work, leaving their elder children to care for the younger ones. The women had watched their husbands, and knew what to do. Not only did they cut the cane, but they had to load it on their shoulders as well. It was exhausting, but the women persevered until their husbands were released in 1943.*

his arms round her and said, 'I love 'oo', but she hit him on the jaw and pushed him into a ditch.

Back home, women were taking up new work. Huge quantities of munitions, food and clothing were needed, and labour became scarce. In February 1942 the government started to organise the whole population for work. Married women with young children were excepted, as were the very old and young, but all citizens had to fill out application forms for identity cards, including the question, 'What are you prepared to do in the event of an enemy attack?' One woman recalled her aged, frail mother answering that she would like to be a guerilla.

Women were sent to the forces, factories, or the Land Army as agricultural labour, but their employment caused disputes. Employers wanted to retain women's lower rates of pay, while unions wanted equal pay as they feared that women's employment would harm men's conditions. The Labor government compromised by paying women in men's jobs about 90 per cent of the male wage. Sally Bowen worked for Lysaght, making, then demonstrating, Owen guns. The factory was unionised – Sally became a shop steward – and the women were paid three-quarters of men's rates, a fantastic change from half, Sally commented. When several women refused to join the union, the workers found a 'women's solution': rather than stop vital work, they threatened to dump one woman in the oil pot. She gave in, and there were no more rebels. Sally said that the war gave her the chance to develop self-confidence and the ability to express herself.

But work in munitions factories especially was often dangerous. Merle Green mixed ingredients for explosives. She could do this for an hour, then 'You'd have to go out and be sick ... It was very nauseating, making them. I was glad when I got out of that one!' Women found new opportunities in other fields, and Minnie Purves became one of the first female tellers with Victoria's State Bank. Many other women took the opportunity to quit domestic service, and there were very few servants by the end of the war.

Although women could reach high positions in the women's services, few women rose to great heights in general employment, and men remained firmly ensconced in power. Many women's jobs were badly paid. Only a tenth of female employees received the higher pay scale, and the rest continued to earn low wages in poor conditions, even worse off than before as regulations did not allow them to leave for better-paid jobs. Many women did enjoy some aspects of employment, like companionship, or feeling they were helping the war effort, but others found conditions too hard and avoided employment, despite a huge propaganda campaign.

Conditions were also hard for women at home. Food and petrol were rationed, and though food was adequate, catering for a family could be challenging. There were shortages of housing and clothes, and with stockings unobtainable, women painted their legs with suntan dye and drew on a seam. With so many men in the forces, social life could be boring. Many women had a difficult time, worrying about the war and their menfolk, fearing invasion, coping with shortages, trying to keep the family going. Dawn Baker, a young single woman working with an insurance firm and trying 'to do our bit to help' by raising money for the 'Children of Britain' fund, summed it up: 'the dreadful war still went on and on'.

Others found life exciting, particularly those young women who could go out with soldiers, Australian or American. In 1942 thousands of American troops arrived in Australia. Compared with Australian soldiers they were better paid, more polite, with more glamorous uniforms, and they treated women well. Every Australian hostess knew that at a party 'men will listen perfunctorily to a charmer or two, and then collect together at the other end of the room', wrote one woman. 'But Americans are different. Major Maine showed no signs of wanting to leave us. Captain Susequhanna seemed delighted with our company.' For many Australian women it was a wonderful change. Americans had supplies of the new nylon stockings and cigarettes; they had fascinating accents, just like films; 'it was all so exciting'. Some Australian girls felt disloyal going out with Americans, but thousands loved it. One nineteen-year-old Melbourne girl wrote in her diary that she wanted a 'Yank boyfriend ... I felt I'd missed life, not having even met one'. She eventually did go out with one, who kissed her, so 'I can tell my Grandchildren at least that during those momentous days when Aust. was rapidly accumulating thousands upon thousands of Yanks, when Melb. Went bad, & every girl discussed her "pick-ups" I too had a little experience'. Many women went much further, and 11,000 married Americans.

Australian men resented this; 'overpaid, oversexed and over here' was how they described Americans. One married couple remembered watching the Walt Disney movie *Bambi* in Brisbane, with its moving scene where little Bambi was lost in the woods, crying, 'Mother, mother, where is my mother?' A digger's voice called, 'She's out with a bloody Yank'. Everyone in the audience burst out laughing.

Many women experienced 'the desperate need to hold on to the present in case there wasn't going to be a future, and the deep

Hard Times

> ## War Widows
>
> *Ten thousand women were widowed by the Second World War, and they received a small pension. After Josephine Johnson's husband was killed at Tobruk, she took their eight children from his parents' farm to Melbourne, so they could gain better education. 'She was a ferocious mother, defending her brood against the many vicissitudes of poverty', wrote her daughter. The children were always well fed and adequately dressed, no matter how much Josephine had to struggle to achieve it. Every fortnight she had to queue up for her small cheque, and once it was tiny, as a previous overpayment had been discovered. Josephine took her three youngest children to the Repatriation offices, put them screaming on the counter and said she would return with the other five after school. Repatriation allowed her to repay the money over a longer period.*
>
> *Jessie Vasey was a wealthy war widow who fought for better conditions for all. She formed the War Widows' Guild, and protested publicly not only about meagre pensions, but at the way they could be lost if officials thought women were leading immoral lives. Jessie pointed out that women who led 'irregular' lives could bring up excellent families. 'If a mother is fond of her children and brings them up right, then I don't care if she sleeps with ten men a night', she said. This gained wide publicity, and slowly, widows' conditions were improved.*

and intense feelings unequalled in peacetime', as Dorothy Godfrey wrote. For many young women, the thousands of young men, the powerful aphrodisiac of war and the unobtainable or uninspiring contraceptives of the time, had their inevitable sequel. There were rumours of many pregnancies, of mass abortions for women in the forces, though in fact their pregnancy rate was similar to the civilian rate, just harder to hide. Venereal disease and prostitution also increased.

This was a worry for feminists, along with low pay and other injustices. In 1943 well-known activist Jessie Street brought together over ninety women's groups to draw up the Australian

A Wealth of Women

Women's Charter, which urged equality for men and women, and set out a program for social change. This did not include sexuality, for these women, often older feminists, wanted men's sexuality controlled rather than women's liberated. Younger women who wanted sexual freedom like men became disillusioned with the feminist movement, and the women's groups themselves later split. The Charter had little immediate effect, though the war did bring benefits for women in new social welfare payments, widows' and deserted wives' pensions and child endowment.

Though women played some new roles in the war, their major contribution was seen as their traditional supporting role of nursing, providing comforts and stepping in to take men's place while they were away. An example was Matron Sadie Macdonald. Born in Rockhampton, she was one of seven sisters in a well-known Queensland family. Six became nurses, and Sadie had a distin-

A one-teacher school

During the war, teachers were in short supply. After Barbara Nuttall finished her secondary education, she was sent, aged seventeen, to a primary school in rural Victoria. She was shown the curriculum, introduced to the thirty-five pupils in grade three, told not to forget to mark the roll, and left to teach them. Fortunately they took to each other well. Barbara's salary was 35/- a week, her board was 30/-, and her parents had to provide her other needs.

The next year, after a fortnight's training, Barbara was given her own one-teacher school, with twelve pupils aged from five to fourteen. The older pupils knew the routine well and were very helpful, aiding the younger ones with spelling or tables. The children were a joy to teach, wrote Barbara, and discipline was never a problem. She was determined that they would not miss out on anything. They entered school sports, performed in concerts, and the parents were always ready to help. Barbara's war was 'extremely interesting. Sometimes funny, sometimes sad, always fulfilling my love of teaching'.

Hard Times

guished career in the First World War, nursing in Egypt and France. She was much decorated, the first Queenslander to receive the coveted Florence Nightingale Medal for her contribution to nursing. Between wars she was matron of Ardoyne Hospital for returned soldiers.

When war broke out, Sadie, at the age of nearly seventy, became matron of Chelmer Red Cross Convalescent Home, beside the river on the outskirts of Brisbane. It cared for a hundred soldier patients, sent from army hospitals while awaiting surgery, needing long convalescence, suffering shellshock, getting used to blindness or living with artificial limbs. Mary Brice was posted there for a month in 1940 from the 1st Toowoomba Voluntary Aid Detachment. When she arrived, Matron, 'Matie' as the men called her, was having a breakfast cup of tea, awe-inspiring in her immaculate, stiffly starched uniform and veil. Her black brows lifted as she inspected Mary, and her eyes twinkled. 'Can you make scones?' she asked.

'Little did I dream then that I would stay six years', wrote Mary. 'Neither did I dream I could work so hard, make so many scones, feel so tired at the end of a day!' She became Matron's secretary, answering phone calls, typing, dealing with ration cards, mail, admissions and discharges, and acting as Matron's scratching post. It was her fault if the Medical Officer was late, if the butcher brought scraggy chops, or Private J. had worn out the toes of his slippers again. 'Does he CHEW them, child? Please see that it doesn't happen again!' Mary was in strife if Matron could not read her own writing. 'Tell me what I've written in this report.' She was also to blame if Matron lost her glasses, which happened ten times a day. They were often found in the most unlikely places – her corsets, or a jar of apricot jam.

The hospital ran on strict lines, with long hours and hard work for the staff. Everyone had meals together, and staff had to stand if Matron left to take a phone call and when she returned – which might happen twenty times a meal. But she never forgot that Mary liked the outside of the meat and Jean liked the skin off the rice pudding. She knew all about their families, and if a husband, boyfriend or brother came home on leave, that staff member was given a day off, no matter how inconvenient it was.

Matron was one of those people who never grow old, said Mary. She was infinitely wise, with a superb understanding of human beings. To soldiers, arriving after battle with limbs blown off, shattered nerves, faces scarred beyond recognition, crippled, paralysed or blinded, Matron represented hope and sanity, an anchor in the rough years. She taught them to laugh again. 'Three weeks at Chelmer Red Cross Convalescent Home' was a coveted sentence from the Medical Officer.

This was not because Matron was gentle; she ran the patients as strictly as the staff. Rules were made to be obeyed. Almost every night she was on duty, sleeping in a bed behind a curtain at the end of one of the wards. When patients slipped up the ramp, boots in one hand and a bottle in the other, matron would be waiting to confront them and confiscate the bottles. 'Doesn't she EVER sleep?' the men sighed. She rarely did: she was devoted to her job, and always saw herself as on duty. Her only concession was to take a cat-nap in the afternoon, telling Mary, 'Only wake me if the sky falls!' Even when she was not on night duty, she waited every night until the last soldier was in bed, and she was on duty again at 6.00 am. If she tried to read the paper and sip a cup of tea, the phone would ring or she would be needed in a ward. She was never too busy to attend to any demand, large or small.

Unruffled, Matron could deal with any crisis – an unexpected visit from a VIP, a private's insistence that he must eat his dinner in the broom cupboard where he was safe from German bombs, or a call from the police to say some of her 'boys' were fighting with Americans. She would hop into her old car and go and rescue them, then set them to peel potatoes for a week. Mary remembered the day when a lady visitor fainted from shock after a sergeant's new leg came off and got left behind on the front steps; and the parrot which a corporal hid under his bed, and which called suddenly in the middle of the night in a piercing and lady-like tone, 'Kiss me, darling!'

All the patients were Matron's 'boys', there not only to be brought back to health, but to become part of her life. Her marmalade was famous, and many a soldier became her reluctant assistant. 'Come along, my little peach blossom!' she would say to some unsuspecting sergeant, just on his way to the pub, 'just stir this for me for five minutes'. Half an hour later he would still be stirring, while Matron watered the cabbage plants. Her favourite endearment was 'pet'. The soldiers loved it, and so did the Duke of Gloucester when he came on an official visit. He was departing with much pomp and ceremony, complete with guard of honour, when Matron remembered something. 'Pet!' she exclaimed, thumping him on the shoulder, 'you forgot to sign the Visitors' Book!' Obedient as any of her other boys, the Duke retraced his steps, and placed his signature on the page.

'Matie' not only commanded deep respect, but became friend, confidant and sympathiser. If a soldier had a sick wife or child, she would move everybody in every department to get him home leave. Her own pay packet was often depleted. 'Get three shillings from my purse for Private S. so he can go to the pictures with the

'Escape from Women's Industry'

This is the title Rosemary Archdeacon-Davies gave her brief autobiography. The eldest of eight children, she left school on her fourteenth birthday to earn money for the family in the Depression. She worked in a shoe factory, which closed down, then as a dressmaker. Dickensian conditions led her to appeal to her union, and she was sacked. During the war she was among the first women to work repairing aircraft for Australian National Airways at Sydney airport, where about a third of the women joined the Sheet Metal Workers Union.

In 1942 the women were awarded 90 per cent of male pay, and their employers tried to delay payment. Rosemary organised a stop work meeting, a difficult task as most women did not understand the Union's role, but they did stop work for two hours, and became furious when their boss said he would speak only to men. (While they were waiting, Rosemary was busy with her usual hobby, knitting socks for soldiers.) The employers eventually gave in, and paid the award wage.

others. He needs to get out.' Next day it would be a bus fare home, or a packet of tobacco. At the end of each year the Home held a Christmas party, and the boys brought her flowers and presents. She loved it all, even when they carried her shoulder high and teased her with, 'The old grey mare, she ain't what she used to be ...' They came like small boys, said Mary, to show her their brand new legs, arms, hands or even eyes. After they were demobilised they came to show off a new wife or baby, and there was always a warm welcome and an invitation to stay for tea.

On VP night, Victory in the Pacific, the end of the war, Matron received word that three patients were in the watch house, following unruly behaviour in the centre of Brisbane. Not even pausing to get dressed, she leapt into her car in her dressing gown, with her hair in two long silver braids. By the time she confronted the police her eyes were pure steel, her black eyebrows drawn and fierce. 'How dare they arrest them?' she asked. 'They are all 6th Divvy men – they have fought for nearly six years in every theatre of war – why shouldn't they get drunk tonight?' Cells were opened, and the sight of Matie in the familiar red dressing gown had a sobering effect. The men climbed happily into the old Ford, and the fried eggs and bacon Matie cooked for them at 4.00 am formed a meal to remember.

After the war, after Chelmer discharged its last patient, Sadie Macdonald went to manage a girls' hostel, once again making an institution a 'home'. She received more awards, including an MBE, retired when she was well over ninety, and lived to be a hundred.

Matron's boys were not the only ones celebrating on VP night – or VJ night, Victory over Japan. Nola Fisher was a WRAN nursing in Sydney. Somehow, after the news broke, she finished duty, and with the other staff and patients, some hobbling, caught a tram into Sydney. 'Such jubilation! Such uninhibited joy! Everyone went crazy. Snowed under mountains of ticker tape, tossed with abandonment from upstairs windows, we were enveloped in a seething mass of humanity, delirious with excitement. In Martin Place, we celebrated and danced – was it levitating? Singing, laughing, remembering, crying ... There never was a day like

Hard Times

Surviving parenthood over great odds

Marjorie Oates was born in Sydney in 1910. When she was eight her mother died, and she went to live with two elderly aunts in a silent, Victorian household. At eleven she caught polio. Hospital treatment consisted of massage, hot and cold packs, and immobilizing the affected leg, but she was determined to walk again and after some months was sent home with her back in a brace and her leg in callipers.

Polio did not stop Marjie from being a champion vigoro player, with another girl to do the running. She entered the adult world without callipers, and married at nineteen. Soon the Depression struck, and her life consisted of staying with whatever relatives had room, or living in a tent by the Murrumbidgee River, eating any vegetables washed downstream, mainly pumpkins. A city girl from a quiet, reserved household, Marjie had to learn new skills fast.

By the time war broke out, she and her husband had four children. He enlisted and sailed off in a troopship, leaving Marjie pregnant, with the children to manage as best she could. She became ill and the two older children went temporarily to a children's home, but her husband's relations took her under their wing and found her a home in Croydon. The neighbours and local shopkeepers were generous – extra milk from the milko, groceries delivered with lollies for the children. Life had certainly improved, but Marjie continued to work hard, making the children's clothes, repairing shoes, toasters or the iron. As the children grew up the family was always a complete happy unit.

Her husband did not return to the family after the war. 'Marjie saw to it that all her children became qualified trades people', wrote her daughter, 'but her main achievement was that, on her own, with no mentor or book of instructions she raised five Australians to responsible adulthood, therefore contributing to the future generations of Australia. Her main mission in life was caring for her family.'

VJ day'. Even Constance Hodge, dying of tuberculosis in hospital, wrote in her last letter to her daughter Dalace, 'Its just wonderful to know that the War is over isn't it, we had a very nice time here – music & singing lollies & drinks & a very nice dinner'.

In Sumatra, prisoners of war were released, though of the

War time cookery

These recipes, both from the 1945 Australian Women's Weekly, reflect the necessity for using substitutes instead of some scarce luxuries, and the American influence.

Mock Cream Filling

Two dessertspoons butter   2 dessertspoons milk
2 dessertspoons sugar   1 teaspoon gelatine
$1/4$ teaspoon vanilla $1/2$ cup boiling water
Few drops lemon juice

Cream butter and sugar, add vanilla, lemon juice and milk. Dissolve gelatine in boiling water, and add gradually to the mixture, using a rotary beater to mix. Use as a cake filling.

American Peanut Butter Bread

One cup scalded milk $2/3$ cup peanut butter
$3/4$ cup boiling water   about $1 1/2$ oz compressed yeast
$3/4$ tablespoons sugar $1/2$ cup lukewarm water
1 teaspoon salt   about $5 3/4$ cups sifted flour

Combine milk, hot water, sugar, salt, peanut butter. Cool to lukewarm. Stir in yeast softened in lukewarm water. Stir in the flour until stiff enough to knead. Knead on floured board until smooth and satiny, abut eight minutes. Shape into smooth ball. Place in a greased bowl, brush with salad oil, cover and stand to rise in a warm place until double its bulk – about $1 1/2$ hours. Knock down lightly and shape into 2 loaves, and place in 2 loaftins about 9 by 5 by 3 inches. Brush with salad oil, cover, stand to rise until bulk doubled. Bake in moderately hot oven (400°F) for 20 minutes and then reduce heat (350°F) and cook further 25 minutes. Cool out of tins.

sixty-five nurses on the *Vyner Brooke* when it sank in 1942, only twenty-four were still alive. They were taken from their camp to an aerodrome, where a plane landed from Australia, and two female figures walked towards them in grey trousers and safari jackets. The nurses recognised their matron-in-chief and another sister, but were dumbfounded at the sight. 'What on earth had happened to everything, fancy sisters in pants!'

Other women to come to Australia were war brides from Britain and Canada. In England Betty Chapman had met a dashing Australian sailor, 'a gorgeous blond twenty (just) year old junior officer', and they married in 1946, three weeks before he sailed for Australia. Later that year Betty, now pregnant, also left for Australia. After initial homesickness, she settled down happily in Melbourne: it was really just moving from middle-class life in one town across the world to another, she wrote. Other women coped with larger transformations. Problems ranged from the bride who found that the mansion fronting Bondi beach did not exist, to those who wondered why the backyards all contained sentry boxes, or why a husband laughed when presented with boiled mangoes as a vegetable, or why there was a deathly hush when she asked, 'Who is Donald Bradman?'

Even people brought up in Australia had problems adjusting once the war was over, for war had become the normal state of affairs. Dorothy Godfrey had grown up during the war; now, 'I felt lost in a world of unreality. I couldn't find anything solid on which to fix my life'. Fewer women were bereaved than in 1918, as only about half as many men died, but this statistic did not make life any easier for those who had lost menfolk, while when men did return there were further problems of adjustment. Wives had forgotten what husbands looked like, children did not recognise their fathers, and family life had to be built anew. Rationing was still in force, many items were in short supply, and many people had a difficult job adjusting to the post-war world.

What influence did the war have overall on women's lives? 'Never before have women experienced such opportunities for showing what they can do', wrote a journalist in 1945. Women could leave home, do men's jobs, find interesting and responsible employment. Young women enjoyed more independence, and people accepted even married women working outside the home. Many women thought the war brought people closer together. But not everyone had these opportunities, which in any case had often been understood to last only for the duration of the war. For many, the war brought not new opportunities but difficulties. Fundamentally, men's more powerful position was challenged and to some extent modified, but relations between men and women were not transformed.

chapter eight

The Boom Years

One sociologist has called the 1950s a constrained and prescriptive time for women. As girls they were expected to develop modesty, charm and grace, with their lives culminating in marriage, motherhood and homemaking, in suburban boredom. Women were tied to home and husband economically; they did not count for much in the hierarchy of values; any problems in marriage were explained as the woman's fault; there was little which prepared them for any public role. Women featured nowhere in the landscape of power.

Yet women at the time and since have commented that the war made a great difference to them; that the independence and employment opportunities of those years meant they had more status; that society recognised 'their entitlement to something other than full-time service to the other members of the family'. 'We thought we had a new world', as one woman put it. Young women did not want to be like their mothers, 'tied to the kitchen sink. It is a wonder we did not have actual leg ropes tying us there'. How can these two views be reconciled?

I believe that the sociologist is too gloomy, that women did have a higher status, and the 'domestic feminism' which the women's movement of the turn of the century had desired was finally achieved. Though women's primary role was still seen as being in the home, they had a more equal role in marriage and the family, and the local community. As well, they could combine some employment with home life. Such a situation would be intolerable to a modern academic, but it suited many women of the time.

Certainly women had a strong domestic role. After the war the marriage rate soared and 95 per cent of women married, the same as in the mid-nineteenth century; with an average of three children per family, the large number of marriages resulted in the 'baby boom'. Once more many people felt that single women had failed, had never really lived. Women's main interest was seen as the family, and there was a strong, separate culture for women, helping the nation's vital task of postwar reconstruction by bearing and raising children and managing the home with their

Clearly meant for greatness

Peggy O'Dea was born in 1918 at Katanning, and at fourteen was the thirteenth man on the local cricket team, as officially women were not allowed to play. She felt that she was the epitome of the New Australian Woman, not Irish like her grandmother, not colonial, 'but an Australian, and clearly meant for greatness'.

In the Depression her father lost his money, and at fifteen Peggy started to work as a housemaid. She married at nineteen, and five children in quick succession meant poverty. Once when her husband was away working in the bush, she lived off the quinces in the backyard to avoid starving, and when he had an affair with another woman the relationship was shattered. Peggy taught herself music and started to play for dances, her earnings making the difference between struggling financially and 'getting ahead' – the family could buy a stove, fridge and car. Peggy formed her own band and played for dances all round the district, while her husband cared for the children. But that year the marriage broke up. 'We were all relieved because the fighting between Peggy and Harry was typically dramatic and frightening at times for children', wrote her daughter. Independence had its price, however – Peggy could no longer travel to play in her band, so that year she took a job as a hotel cook.

The Boom Years

traditional competence and resourcefulness.

Memoirs of the period make it clear that this was what many women wanted. 'When the war ended many of us who had worked long hours under difficult conditions and restraints were very happy to give total commitment to hearth and home', wrote Marjorie Tipping, a university graduate who worked as an industrial welfare officer in Melbourne during the war. 'Deprivation of domestic life can be a nightmare, and postwar reconstruction, to many, meant the calm and peace of rebuilding their lives in the traditional manner.' Marjorie found the transition from career woman to housewife difficult because accommodation was scarce and her family had to live in a small flat, and also because she was economically dependent on her husband; but she and friends in similar situations planned the future and adored their babies together. They also worked voluntarily to provide more childcare, to help other mothers continue their careers.

Mavis Fogarty married in 1946, resigned from work when she became pregnant, and went to live in a new Melbourne suburb, Moorabbin. 'To have the house was heaven ... I was quite content to be a housewife and mother, with our relations and friends to keep us company', she wrote. Mollie Tomlin agreed. She worked in an office, married in 1942, and brought up seven children in a working-class suburb of Hobart. 'I looked forward to raising a family and I was quite happy. It was my life. I never thought of anything else, and I never missed work. We were poor, you'd make an old coat into clothes for the children, but I took great pride in my sewing. You looked forward to CWA meetings, you had friends, we did things together.' Many women found satisfaction in doing a valued job which they could perform well, keeping a comfortable home, being the family linchpin. Some families were still run on the old lines with the husband in charge, but more and more were partnerships, with the wife having real equality in making decisions. Many husbands handed over their pay packets as a matter of course.

This attitude continued in the 1950s. Beth McLeod worked as a high school teacher, married in 1955 and continued to teach until early in her first pregnancy, as was by now reasonably common. 'I didn't mind resigning in the least', she commented. 'I was delighted at having a family. I threw myself into new ideas of childbirth and childrearing. I used to meet up with friends and we'd have an informal playgroup, the children playing together while we talked, and discussed common tasks and issues. It was an enjoyable way to meet our needs and those of the children.' Like many women, Beth had several interests outside the home; she and her husband were members of a church group of young adults, and she joined a committee which raised funds for building a pre-school.

So the nuclear family dominated: mum, dad and the children. It had always been strong in Australia, where many people had migrated from Europe and left relatives behind; but in the nineteenth century there had been more variation. Households had included grandparents, servants or lodgers, lacked a husband through death, desertion or itinerant employment, or lacked a mother through death in childbirth. Subsequent marriages meant blended families. In the 1950s there were fewer early deaths, fewer itinerant workers and a low divorce rate, while with rising prosperity young couples could afford to establish their own homes. Immigration rates were high and as in the past, immigrants left extended family behind. The 1950s were the heyday of the nuclear family. Strong encouragement of these family values came from government, the press and churches, which were at the peak of their strength.

There are two views of how women fared when the nuclear family dominated. Was life in the suburbs stultifying, just housework and family care, isolated and alienated from the broader society? Or did women enjoy the friendships and communal activities of suburban life, and place high value on their work at home, preferring this to the often demeaning and boring paid work available to women? The answer must be that both pictures are true, that different women had different experiences of life at the hub of the nuclear family.

Increasingly, married women could take up paid work. It became acceptable to take a job once children were at school – to help the family finances, provide an interest, or keep up a career established before marriage. Women's employment continued to grow: in 1947, they formed 22 per cent of the workforce; in 1971, a third, of whom half were married. At first there was some community disapproval, but gradually this eased, though it could still be hard for married women to gain permanence, and some employers, notably the public service, refused for years to employ them. Many women found that part-time work suited them; they had the income and (hopefully) interest of a job, but avoided the 'double shift' of full-time employment and home-making.

Others found out the hard way the huge amount of work involved in the 'double shift'. Kathleen Lenthall returned to teaching when her children were at school, the first woman at the all-male Sydney Grammar School. She was nicknamed 'Sabrina' (after a film star of impressive physique), and was a competent,

Pioneers in the 1960s

Maureen Ree married a policeman in Brisbane in 1956. Four years later she and her husband Doug bought a run-down property near Musgrave, as Doug liked working out of doors. 'Nothing could prepare me for what was ahead', wrote Maureen.

The homestead was built from ti-tree rails, with a dusty ant bed floor and a leaky corrugated iron roof, no windows, no bathroom, no electricity, no means of communication with the outside, no vehicle and few fences. There was not even toilet paper, just newspapers torn in squares. The first priority was to build a fence so the two children would not wander into the bush, the second to build an airstrip so the mail could be delivered fortnightly. Doug felled the trees and Maureen burnt them, and the airstrip was ready five months after they arrived. Since they had no means of earning income, Doug went droving or crocodile shooting while Maureen 'kept the home fires burning'. She had to learn how to make soap and bread, milk cows, use the treadle sewing machine and teach the children by correspondence; she boiled clothes in the copper and ironed with flat irons. Gradually she and Doug built up their stock, and Maureen learned to draft cattle and repair fences.

popular and hard-working teacher. She managed her two roles by not worrying overmuch about housework: her daughter-in-law commented that she never saw Kathleen's house tidy, though the children were never neglected. Kit Lambert also returned to work, and became highly regarded for her nursing skill in the farming district of Scottsdale. Her work helped make ends meet at home, but 'as soon as Kit awoke in the morning she started running, and didn't stop until she climbed into bed at night'.

Most jobs were in the usual feminine workplaces of the school, hospital, office, shop or factory. Some women without qualifications did housework for those who worked full-time, the new version of domestic service. A few women had outstanding positions: Margaret Sutherland composed music, Gwen Meredith wrote the popular radio serial 'Blue Hills', and there were many eminent teachers and doctors, such as Dr Doris Officer in Melbourne, who was largely responsible for setting up the Queen Elizabeth Hospital for Mothers and Babies, and wrote popular articles on motherhood for the *Sun News Pictorial*. When she died from a heart attack in 1967, her last words were 'Bother, it's Health Week and I won't be there!'

As in the 1920s, however, it was difficult for women to rise to senior positions. Joy Bear, a relation of feminist Annette Bear, wanted to study science, but her family could not afford it, so in 1944 she took a position as junior laboratory assistant with the Council for Scientific and Industrial Research (later CSIRO) in Melbourne. While working she completed a diploma in chemistry, then she gained experience in Britain, but she could not obtain a research position with CSIRO. When female public servants married they had to resign, and because most did marry, furthering their careers was seen as a waste of time. Joy became a technical officer, and found her research work interesting but frustrating, as she was not free to follow up her own ideas. However, in the early 1960s she fortuitously discovered a number of new zirconium sulphate compounds, and elucidated the mechanism by which they are formed. This groundbreaking work enabled her to join the research staff, the first woman in the Division to do so. She went on to have an extremely successful career,

The Boom Years

leading research in many aspects of solid state and mineral chemistry.

Could women make their voices heard in the wider public sphere? It was difficult for individuals, for example in parliament, where the few women had difficulty making their voices heard. Women were valued in politics, however – as supporters. Robert Menzies, conservative prime minister from 1949 to 1966, courted women voters and promoted their interests as wives and mothers; for example, bowing to pressure from Enid Lyons MHR, he increased child endowment. Many women were ardent supporters of Menzies' new Liberal Party. In 1945 Eunice Jacobson had just left the WAAAF and told Mr Menzies himself that she did not want to join anything else, but after hearing him speak, she did so. This was the start of forty-five years of work supporting the Liberals, largely in the electorate of Denison. An extremely capable person, Eunice was involved in holding functions, providing food for election workers, collecting postal votes from old age homes, and all sorts of support work. She rose to direct candidates' campaigns, but, she said, the men did not want women to go further. 'We weren't taken a lot of notice of. It was mainly behind the scenes work.'

Women did similar work in the Labor Party and the Communist Party, which had women's equality as part of its platform. Betty Searle joined in 1936, aged nineteen, and devoted her life to 'the class struggle and a style of living certainly not condoned by society at large'. After Russia joined the Allies in 1942, she worked with Jessie Street helping organise comforts for Russia, and she was 'taken to heaven and beyond by a charismatic journalist, a Party leader whom she later married. After the war, Betty was involved in working for peace and campaigns to Ban the Bomb, but anti-communist feeling was increasing, and once canvassing door-to-door, she was hosed out of a driveway by a hostile resident. But she was dismayed to find that the Communist Party had no notion of what equality of the sexes, so espoused, really involved. She was treated as her husband's adjunct, and during his long absences cared for their children. When she wanted to leave the marriage, she found Party did not condone personal problems that might hinder the revolutionary struggle, and thought the welfare of the male comrade more important.

Women achieved more outside political parties, in their own societies, lobbying for change. As seen in earlier chapters, they had been active in public since women's clubs became popular in the 1890s. Many of these continued to flourish, as well as thousands of newer clubs, which provided companionship and social occasions, widened women's interests, supported community efforts and urged improvements for women's lives. There were about 140,000 Girl Guides and Brownies throughout Australia, enjoying camping and other outdoor activities, undertaking community service, helping in the Olympic Village for the 1956 Olympic Games in Melbourne, and gaining life skills and confidence which often assisted them in their future careers. The Country Women's Association was also extremely strong, with 2,700 branches and 117,000 members. It pressed not only for better amenities for country areas, but for more educational opportunities for girls, and a referendum among women to ascertain their views on abortion, before this was decided by an all-male parliament. Such women were certainly not afraid to make their views known.

Most of these groups lobbied politely for their causes, but a few were more outspoken. During the First World War, Housewives' Associations had formed to protest against rising prices. They ted to unite all women, but could never really succeed, particularly in the 1930s when working-class women wanted to support their husbands' battles for increased wages, while middle-class women were opposed to strikes and left-wing influence. However, Housewives' Associations flourished in the 1950s, reaching a peak of about 200,000 members in the early 1960s. They declined after that date as more married women joined the workforce.

In 1950 a New Housewives Association was formed, on the initiative of mainly communist women. Four years later they decided to change their name and broaden their role, resulting in the Union of Australian Women, which aimed to identify more closely with working-class women and include employed

The Boom Years

women's concerns, such as equal pay. Though the Union was not large, with about 2,000 members, it was active. Its main interests were peace, the status of women, the standard of living, Aboriginal rights and the rights of children. A few communists saw it as too conformist, calling it derisively 'the hat and glove brigade', while some conservative women's groups saw it as too closely linked with the Communist Party. Was it possible to combine militant action with respectable housewifely concerns? The Union certainly tried. It presented many petitions and ran Cost of Living and Equal Pay campaigns, and marked International Women's Day with concerts and large meetings.

A notable achievement was that of Roma Gilchrist, president of the Perth branch. Street demonstrations were banned all round Australia, but in 1957 Roma organised a novel protest of five women wearing aprons and scarves printed with slogans such as 'Nuclear tests menace children'. They walked through the streets of Perth, but were charged with parading with placards, convicted and fined. Churches, unions and many individuals supported them, and they appealed against the decision, saying scarves and aprons were normal women's wear. They won, and street marches were permitted.

Did the Union and the Housewives' Unions succeed? For a variety of reasons, living standards did rise in the 1950s, and what both groups also demonstrated, like so many other women's societies, was that women were capable of running national organisations and putting their views forward, and that they had a place in public life.

But not all women were happy. Some hated domesticity and felt frustrated in their family role. Suburban life could be friendly and pleasant, but it could also be bare, isolated and lonely, with little transport and few ways to escape the house, especially with small children. Amenities often took years to appear. Helen Harbour, for example, moved to a new Melbourne suburb with no roads, paths, drains, fences, or even water. Life meant a great deal of hard work and she hardly ever left home, but she and her husband helped form a progress association, and gradually amenities were provided.

> ### Nursing Mothers' Association
>
> *In the twentieth century the percentage of women who breastfed their babies gradually declined, from 92 per cent in 1928, to 84 per cent in 1941, then a more sudden fall to half in 1952, and a quarter in 1969, as mothers came to believe that artificial feeding was safe, nutritious and easy. In 1964 Mary Paton, a Melbourne physiotherapist, wanted to breastfeed her baby, but could find no information. She and a group of friends in the same situation formed the Nursing Mothers' Association of Australia, to obtain information, circulate it, and encourage breastfeeding as being best for babies. Nursing Mothers flourished, especially in the 1970s when more natural methods of childbirth and childrearing became popular. By the early 1980s there were 18,000 members in about 600 groups all round Australia, and in 2000 there were about 13,000 members. Nursing Mothers played an important role in encouraging breastfeeding: in 2000, 80 per cent of mothers breastfed their babies when they left hospital, and about half continued for six months.*

Another drawback was that women could only enjoy society's benefits if they conformed. Australia in the 1950s was a conservative society which liked to keep its faults hidden, and women in unhappy marriages, suffering domestic violence or abuse, were expected to keep quiet and put up with it. Women who bore children outside marriage were social outcasts, one reason for the marriage boom. In previous years there had been about the same number of births outside marriage as births within nine months of marriage, where presumably the couple had married once they realised a baby was on the way. In the conformist 1950s there were twice as many of these 'shotgun' weddings. There was little help for women with problems, another reason to conform: if you wanted to leave an unhappy marriage there was nowhere to go.

There are many examples of how difficult women's lives could be. Dulcie Skinner married in 1929 aged eighteen and had three children. Her husband was not a stable provider and loved gam-

The Boom Years

bling, racing and drinking. He lessened these activities when he joined the Commonwealth Military Forces in the war, but afterwards he reverted to drinking heavily. 'We were then back to uncertainty as Dad quickly started to drink the money away', wrote Dulcie's daughter. Dulcie worked part-time, struggling to provide food and clothing for her children 'as she battled to keep us going as a family unit'. Her husband died in 1949 with threepence in his pocket, and 'Mum was left, still struggling, with no money'. In 1955 she remarried; her second husband had a good income, but was a skinflint, who watched every penny she spent. She had an easier life, however, and loved seeing her children marry and produce grandchildren.

Anabel Macdonald, born in 1934, was a rebel from girlhood, when she was caught by the nuns at school smoking in the hockey stick cupboard. She became a kindergarten teacher and in the 1950s married a 'classic rogue journalist'. Anabel bore him four children – 'no pill yet, and anyway still rather Catholic about contraception'. Her married years were 'a rocky time of poverty, hunger, loneliness, pawned possessions, moonlight flits and eviction'. She left the journalist, and brought up the children on a Deserted Wives' pension. Soon she found a new partner whose marriage had also ended, but as divorce was only possible after five years' separation, they had to wait until they could marry. In the meantime they had a son, 'not by any means the "done thing" in those days'. But in 1968 they married and moved to his farm.

Slowly, ways opened up by which women could obtain help in situations like these. Minnie Purves, widowed in the war, ran a drapery shop to support her two children. She was already drinking heavily when she remarried in 1949. Her second husband was a violent man, and she brought a black eye home from her honeymoon. The drinking and violence escalated, until on one desperate night in 1952 Minnie sent a letter to Alcoholics Anonymous, which had been established in Australia seven years earlier. She attended all their meetings, and finally found her own sobriety. Meanwhile she tried to revive her marriage, but the violence continued and it ended in divorce. When the Alcoholism Clinic opened in Melbourne, Minnie was its receptionist, using

Early steps in multicultural cooking

A Dim Sim recipe from Zeehan, 1958
This recipe could well surprise a Chinese cook.

Pastry
4 oz plain flour	good pinch salt
2½ oz grated cheese	pinch cayenne
1½ oz butter	1 egg yolk
½ teaspoon lemon juice	water

Rub the butter and cheese into the flour and salt. Mix the yolk with lemon juice and water. Blend together and make a rather stiff pastry. Line small cake tins with pastry.

Filling
Grated cheese, minced bacon, a little grated onion blended with a small portion of tomato sauce and worcestershire sauce. Place a spoonful in each case and bake in a moderate oven until the pastry is cooked and the filling is set.

Chow Ming, otherwise known as Mock Chow Mein, Kai Ci Ming and probably other names as well
This easy, cheap, Asian-influenced dish was popular all round Australia in the 1960s.

In a large saucepan fry one brown onion finely chopped. Add 1 lb. of minced topside with a teaspoon of curry powder. Cook for five minutes. Add one diced carrot and two cups of water. When carrot is cooked add pack of chicken noodle soup and ¼ cabbage finely sliced. Cook for further seven minutes and thicken with cornflour if necessary.

---

her own knowledge with great success. She had an unerring instinct about how ill the clients were, and was respected by both nursing staff and doctors, so was able to use her own experience to help others.

As well as the growth of the nuclear family, another major development in Australian women's history started after the Second

The Boom Years

World War, when women from non-British backgrounds made an increasing impact. At first, all white inhabitants of Australia were immigrants, and immigrants continued to arrive, but until 1945 almost all of these were British. In 1861, 55 per cent of Australia's white population had been born in Britain, 37 per cent in Australia and only 8 per cent elsewhere, of which the largest groups were Chinese (almost all male) and German. The White Australia policy stopped Asian immigration, and from then onwards, migrants were almost all British, though some Italians and Germans arrived, and the 1930s saw some European refugees from the Nazis. Most newcomers were Australian babies, however, and in 1947, 90 per cent of the white population were born in Australia, the highest percentage before or since. The rest came mostly from Britain. The consequence was that Australians were overwhelmingly British in their customs and traditions.

During the war Australia appeared vulnerable to invasion, and afterwards the government made great efforts to increase the white population, aiming at 2 per cent growth each year. The baby boom was welcome, but babies could not start work immediately, so immigration was necessary. Britain had full employment and little shipping, so emigration was slow to start. The authorities turned to the rest of Europe.

The first migrants came from the Baltic states, Estonia, Latvia and Lithuania, fairly similar in customs and looks to British people. They had left their homelands to flee from Russian rule, and in exchange for passages to Australia, they signed an agreement to work for two years. Men predominated, and Viltis Kruzas was one of the few women in the first boatload in 1947. Her first sight of Australia was the empty, wild Western Australian coast, but she was reassured when she stepped ashore and a woman handed her a bag of cakes. Overall she found 'everything so bright compared with the bleakness of Europe'.

Migrants were taken to reception centres to be introduced to the Australian way of life and allocated to jobs. On the first night at Bonegilla camp, said Viltis, they were given steaks larger than they had ever seen before. When they cut into them they found blood, so they ate bread and jam instead. One group of women noted that Australians kept saying 'How do you do?' to them. A Lithuanian, supposed to know English, told them that this was a greeting and the response was 'I do as I like'. The women were puzzled by the hurt expressions this produced.

Immigrants were brought out to work as labourers, and women were given jobs in factories, or as cleaners or cooks. At least at first, they could not use any previous training. Mrs Augustauskas had been a pharmacist in Lithuania, but was given a job as a hospital cleaner in Hobart. Noticing she was capable, the matron moved her to the accounts section, and she was soon offered a job in the hospital pharmacy. Later she resat her examinations and became a qualified pharmacist. However, many migrant women remained in low-paying and low-status jobs.

Having fled their homes then spent years in camps in Europe, most migrants arrived with very little, and had to start from scratch. Most could not speak English, accommodation was in short supply, and the way of life was unfamiliar. Still, they generally found Australians welcoming, especially churches and groups such as the Good Neighbour Council.

Most women were married and migrated with their husbands. Those who found a job, to help family finances, usually learned English at work, though childcare could be a problem, and older children often minded younger ones. Women who stayed at home found it more difficult to learn English, which could make life challenging. Visiting doctors and having babies in hospital was daunting when you did not speak the language, as was shopping. When migrants asked for eggs, shopkeepers often thought they wanted axes; the request for 'Tuzen aks, plis' would be greeted with 'Why do you want so many?' Women often found themselves imitating hens, or in butcher's shops mooing or baahing to show what they wanted. Once children learned English at school, mothers often used them as translators.

But women found difficulties as their children grew up as Australians and felt torn between two cultures, especially as many Australians had little time for foreign customs. 'I was terribly ashamed when my parents spoke Estonian in public', wrote Anu Mihkelson. People would comment, 'Bloody New Australians!'

The Boom Years

'Why can't they learn to speak English?' 'After the first experience of shame, my mother and I whispered to each other in public but my father made me feel all knotted up when he spoke in his normal tone. He had exposed our disguise but I desperately wanted to fit in, to assimilate, to disappear.' Anu anglicised her name to Ann and said she came from Sweden, as people had never heard of Estonia.

Those Australians who developed links with Baltic communities found people 'charming, wonderful, kind', according to a woman who married one. But she found that Balts could be racist themselves, and their languages were difficult to learn, particularly surnames. Another Australian wife recalled that at dinner on the first night of her honeymoon, the hotel waitress asked her name. The bride started to say, 'Mr and Mrs ...' then had to turn to her husband and whisper, 'What's our surname?' She was sure the waitress thought they were not married.

Customs were also different. On the way to Australia Edith Pecl had a shipboard romance with a Czech migrant, Bert, but in camp near Maitland, single men and women were segregated. Bert suggested getting married, but Edith said they should first find out how it was done, so on their day off they went to Maitland to inquire. They were sent to the mayor, in Singleton. He asked for their papers, and after a long wait they were ushered into the courtroom, where the mayor asked Bert to repeat various phrases after him. Edith realised this was the marriage ceremony, but she was too surprised and embarrassed to say anything. The wedding went ahead, the mayor brushing over the fact that they did not have a ring. 'I think we need a drink', said Bert as they left, so they went to the pub and bought a bottle of champagne, left over from the American 'invasion'. In came the mayor; he introduced them to the bar, and everyone sang 'For they are jolly good fellows'.

For accommodation, couples often bought a block of land and lived in a shed there while they built a house. As all through Australian history, women helped their husbands. Ieva Andrikonis remembered hauling rocks up from a creek bed while her husband loaded them in the car, to become foundations for their house. Then Ieva helped her husband build it, nailing and painting the weatherboards.

Single women were in great demand as wives among their compatriots, though many married Australians. Many immigrant men married Australian women; like the Americans in the war, they were often dashing, and they knew how to treat a woman as someone special. Once they married into an Australian family, it was easier to assimilate. Assimilation was expected, but immigrants formed cultural associations, so their children would remember their origins. Most, however, put down roots in Australia, with houses, cars and Australian friends. As the years passed many found that Australia really was a land of opportunity and freedom, where they could be part of a new country but also could keep their own culture. They also contributed enormously to Australia, one of the first new settlers to make headlines being Ilsa Konrads, a champion swimmer.

Once the government had seen that Balts were accepted, they offered assisted passages to people from all over Europe. These migrants generally had similar experiences to the Balts. Some women found Australian society liberating, coming from countries where wives were expected to devote themselves entirely to their families and accept their husbands' rule. Others missed the culture of Europe, and found problems with their menial jobs, prejudice, racism and sexual harassment at work, and some migrants, about 17 per cent, returned to Europe. But most women looking back on this period tell positive stories of life in Australia – after all, these are the ones who stayed.

Hermine Rainow called herself 'Mrs Cosmopolitan'. Her father was Austrian, her mother was Hungarian, she was born in Romania and married a Bulgarian, and the family spoke German – Hermine herself spoke four languages fluently, though not English. In the war she worked as a translator and newsreader in Vienna. In 1952 she and her husband migrated to Australia, where her husband found a job at the steelworks in Wollongong. They bought land and lived there with their three children, in a small caravan. It was cold, it rained almost incessantly for two months, there was no electricity or running water except what fell from the sky, and they were short of money because the steelworkers were on strike. Worst of all was the feeling of utter isolation and numbing loneliness. Hermine, pregnant again, felt wretched and worn out.

One day, when they were 'at rock bottom of our misery', a neighbour, Betty, invited two of their children to play with her daughter. Betty became their guardian angel, taking them into her warm kitchen, providing scones and sausage rolls, teaching Hermine English, drying the baby's nappies round her stove, caring for the children while Hermine had the next baby. Gradually life improved. The Rainows extended the caravan with a tent, then built a small chalet; their English improved; the older

Teenagers and jeans

Extended secondary education and the influence of America meant that in the 1950s a new social group appeared: teenagers. They were a distinct group, with their own interests and activities. In 1953 Frances Costa was fifteen, living at Dapto with her mother, a railway gatekeeper, and her invalid father. Frances' mother was keen to help Frances take part in the teenage world, as she wrote to her sister. '[Les] gave Frances £2 to buy jeens (or jeans) she is a real teenager. I made her a pleated skirt out of her school tunic & she has made a red jumper & with a black plastic belt looks quite nice.'

Teenagers like Frances were one thing, widgies another. Bodgies (male) and widgies (female) were the rebellious youth of the 1950s. Widgies wore white blouses and thrust bras, flared skirts with petticoats, Toreador pants or jeans, high heels, and pony-tails. Bodgies and widgies congregated in milk bars, hamburger joints and roller skating rinks, and enjoyed rock'n'roll and dancing as well as less innocent activities like shop-lifting and vandalism. The conservative press was horrified, reporting 'gross initiation ceremonies' for widgies, who should be at home learning to sew, iron and wash, as the Brisbane Telegraph *put it, instead of 'painting themselves like Red Indians and gallivanting about the countryside rock'n'rolling'.*

children started at school; Hermine's husband went into business and she became secretary of the local Good Neighbour Council, then a journalist with her own 'migrant column' in the local paper, 'Our New Neighbours'. This was the first regular weekly migrant column in Australia, published in the *South Coast Times* then the *Illawarra Mercury*. Hermine believed strongly that migrants should not abandon their original identities in Australia, but keep up their languages and culture, and in 1974 she was the convenor of the Association for Culture Exchange, whose main activity was a language school. Three years later she was awarded the MBE for services to the community.

Born in 1940, Koula Aslanidis grew up in a small, poverty-stricken village in Greece, where there was no money for the education and books she wanted, and the activities of the other girls, doing needlework for their dowries, did not appeal. Several men from the village emigrated to Australia, and Koula's neighbour told her that one of them, Angelo, wanted a wife. Koula agreed to marry him, since she knew he was a good man. It was hard to leave her mother, her friends and her home at the age of nineteen, but she was attracted to the idea of doing things that were impossible at home, like studying.

Shortly after her arrival in Adelaide she was taken to a sale of secondhand clothing and books, and saw mountains of books at twopence each. 'What a rich country', she thought. She and Angelo had two children, and ran a delicatessen in Adelaide. While she worked, Koula learned to speak and read English, and in the 1960s she became strongly involved in the Greek community, interpreting, helping people with job applications and letters, explaining forms. She also became involved with Greek theatre and worked on Greek community radio.

At this period, Asian immigration was severely restricted, but some Anglo–Burmese arrived in Australia. Margherita Fencott had both Burmese and British antecedents. She had a happy childhood and a wonderful wedding, but never saw any of her wedding presents, for she and her husband Fred returned from their honeymoon to find the Japanese bombing their home. They had to leave everything and trek to India, then lost everything again after the war, when they had to flee to China, and for a third time in 1964, when after two coups d'état in Burma they migrated to Perth.

Here, Rita's daughter Fay found an office job. 'A lot of the girls had a very strong Australian accent and I had a terrible, terrible time tuning in', she recalled. 'What with the strong Australian accent and the Australian slang, I really didn't know what they were talking about … I used to think oh boy I speak English and I don't know what these people are saying.' The social scene was different too, going to dances to meet boys instead of the group dates she was used to. 'It was all very weird to us, just couldn't get used to it. We weren't used to all this hanky-panky on the first date either and the boys were told to mind their own business.' Then she met Herbert, who was 'smart enough to mind his manners', and they married. 'Definitely the best thing they could've done', wrote their daughter about her family's emigration.

By 1971, nearly three million migrants had come to Australia, from the Baltic states, Britain, Russia, Poland, Hungary and other Eastern European countries, Holland, Germany, Italy, Greece, Turkey and Yugoslavia. They brought a multicultural element to Australia, and changes started quite quickly; cappuccinos were all the rage with modern young people as early as 1953. On the whole, 'Old Australians' accepted the newcomers with less hostility than might have been expected from such an isolated and monocultural people. Australia of the 1950s seemed stable and secure, and as women sewed their clothes and made their jam, became engaged and married and were the centre of their families, it must have seemed as if the old ways were continuing, with a few modern frills. But new ideas starting to develop meant much greater change was on the horizon.

The dominance of the nuclear family and the arrival of immigrants were not the only two major changes in the postwar period. Increasing industrial expansion, high prices for industrial goods and primary products, a buoyant economy, almost full employment including plenty of jobs for women, abundant overtime, all led to increasing affluence, the 'long boom' of 1945 to 1973 – not only for the middle classes but, more gradually, for the working classes as well. Most Australians could join in a development which transformed people's lives: the technological revolution. It affected everyone in many ways, but particularly housewives.

When white women arrived in Australia in 1788, they had little technological assistance with their housework. Equipment was simple – an open fire, buckets and saucepans, knives and brooms. During the nineteenth century various hand-powered pieces of equipment appeared, making this work a little easier. Probably the most helpful was the treadle sewing machine, powered by the foot. But machines were expensive, and even if families could afford them, housework still involved a great deal of hard, time-consuming, exhausting work.

Many women continued to run their families with this type of

Just a plain housewife

In 1953 Jessie Hadgraft was the wife of a university lecturer, living in Brisbane with their two children. Excerpts from her diary show the ups and downs of domesticity.

Jan. 16: (Overheard) Woman to children: 'What does your daddy do?'

Judith: 'He's a lecturer.'

Woman: 'Oh, my goodness ... And your mother. Is she a lecturer, too?'

Peter: 'No, she's just a plain housewife.'

Jan. 24: All sat down to hearty home-cooked meal. Family v. appreciative of home-cooking [after a holiday].

Jan. 31: Talked to Pat. Don't mind hearing about her babies, she can turn a witty phrase and has a light touch.

Feb. 4: How much happier not to be single but with a family and 'settled'.

Feb. 6: Going to party at B's Friday. Up betimes thinking of things to say. No-one listens to a woman, however.

Feb. 26: Still hot so glad I am a housewife and can relax.

Apr. 15: Lovely morning. C. [her husband] gone off in huff because no clean socks.

The Boom Years

equipment until the 1950s, and Jane Chapman described washing day at Hales Siding, where her family lived and her father mined tin. Her mother used a copper (a large bowl on a stand over a fireplace), a bench, three tubs, a bar of soap and a washboard, a sheet of ribbed glass in a frame. She lit the fire under the copper, pumped water from the well and put it on to heat. Then she put whites and shaved soap into the copper to boil, and after soaking dirty clothes, scrubbed them on a washboard, then wrung them out. She filled all three tubs with clean water for rinsing, put the blue bag in one and made a bucket of starch by mixing dry starch to a paste with cold water and adding boiling water.

When the whites had boiled long enough, Jane's mother lifted them out with a long stick, drained off most of the water and with a swinging movement conveyed them to the first tub. She put the next load of clothes into the copper, wrung out the first load by hand, rinsed them, then rinsed them again in the 'blue' tub. She dipped doilies, tablecloths, shirts, some dresses and curtains in starch, then hung the clothes out on the clothesline, which was strung between two trees and held up with a prop. On windy days the prop might drop and the whole load fall in the dirt. 'Mum would be very cross.' Washing took all morning.

Jane's mother put the water on the garden, and at about four o'clock she took the washing off the line, folded it, made the dinner, and after dinner heated the flat irons by the stove, put the ironing blanket on the table and started to do the week's ironing. The children were excited on wash day as they played in the creek while their mother worked. 'Can't say if Mum was, but she certainly made the best of it.'

The first form of labour-saving energy was gas. From 1841 it provided some lighting, and in 1873 the first gas cooker appeared. This was wonderful. No longer did a fire have to be lit well before cooking, and kept going; no longer did the cook have to put up with the fire's heat. Clean, controllable heat appeared instantly. Gas cookers took some time to become widespread – they were expensive, and many people had no access to gas – but by 1911, a third of Sydney's new homes had them. Gas lighting and heating were not so popular, for they were stuffy, as gas consumed air.

Neither were kerosene appliances, as kero was smelly and temperamental. Kerosene refrigerators meant people in the bush could have a change from endless corned beef, but they had to be perfectly level, out of a draught, with the wick just right: too low and the machine was starved of fuel, too high and the house was filled with black smoke.

Gas' main rival was electricity, first used for lighting in the 1870s. Some appliances appeared at the end of the century, but they only really started to sell in the 1920s, and then only among the wealthy. Many urban homes were connected to the electricity supply, which was mainly used for lighting, a huge improvement on lamps as it was instant, bright, much easier and relatively cheap. Most people could not afford appliances and memoirs rarely mention them; wood ovens and even camp ovens, flat irons, coppers, treadle sewing machines and ice chests continued to be used, with their attendant problems: very hot kitchens in summer, burns from the iron, sore feet from the sewing machine, the week pretty well taken up with housework. 'You were perpetually tired, that dreadful feeling of tiredness', recalled Betty Pybus. 'It came as a terrible shock when you married, having to do this hard, hard work.'

In the 1950s a combination of the affluence of the long boom, the extension of electricity to country areas and the availability of appliances meant most Australians could start to buy them: stove, refrigerator, vacuum cleaner, heater, sewing machine, kettle, iron, toaster, frypan, mixmaster, blender, hair dryer, freezer – a never-ending stream of new, clever gadgets. For example, 73 per cent of metropolitan homes contained a refrigerator by 1955.

It is rare in history to find all contemporaries agreeing, but on the topic of the introduction of labour-saving devices, almost all women were united. 'Just revolutionary, marvellous!', 'Absolutely dramatic!' 'Helen took great pride in her home', wrote Helen Harbour's daughter of her mother in suburban Melbourne. 'Each new acquisition – the refrigerator, the washing machine, the sewing machine, the floor polisher and the Mixmaster – provoked in her the delight and excitement of a child at Christmas; each provided Helen with new challenges and imposed new routines, which were met with immense energy and enthusiasm.' 'The washing machine was just wonderful. I thought I was in heaven,' said Judy Cooper of Hobart. When Japanese invasion seemed imminent in 1942, many people fled coastal areas, but Edna Ryan would not move from Sydney. She and her husband had just bought a washing machine, and Edna refused to leave it. 'I'd sooner face the Japanese.' Only the occasional woman thought a washing machine did not get clothes clean, and continued to use her copper.

New materials also lessened women's labour. Plastic and laminex surfaces were easier to keep clean, especially with the new cleaning agents on the market. Modernity was fashionable. 'I did not have a special desire for old things, as I had grown up with the new,' wrote Anu Mihkelson. 'I concluded that much that was old wasn't really comfortable or practical. In the fifties and sixties so did a lot of other people.' Magazines urged women to keep up with modern trends, and people became more aware of new products and more able to afford them.

Some people argued that appliances have not helped women: any time saved is spent in other forms of housework like shopping; more appliances meant higher standards and more work; housewives became alienated and isolated. The woman-in-the-street generally disagreed, saying that machines took drudgery out of housework, that standards were not raised, that hours spent doing housework by hand was the really isolating activity.

Electrical appliances also provided entertainment. Radio became popular between the wars, and in 1956 television appeared. 'We flocked to Mum and Dad's place after many evening meals, to sit with goggle-eyes, in a neighbour-packed lounge room, viewing the first of many good, bad and indifferent television shows', wrote Nola Fisher. 'It wasn't long before the "bug" had bitten most viewers, and us.' 'It was wonderful having films to watch every night!' said Mavis Fogarty. 'We would run in to the lounge just to see the clock going around, on the T.V. It was such a comfort, not to have to travel on public transport in the cold weather, to go to the theatre. Marvellous when the last show was over, to be able to hop straight into bed.' Television became

> ### For love of dance
>
> *Louise Lightfoot was born in Victoria in 1902. One of the first women to study architecture at Melbourne University, she worked with Walter Burley Griffin, but gave this up for love of dance. Inspired by Pavlova, Louise danced, studied and taught dancing, and with her partner Mischa Burlakov staged the first Australian-produced ballet, Coppelia, in 1931. They co-founded and directed the First Australian Ballet in Sydney during the 1930s, with Louise the main force behind the choreography, production, costuming and publicity. In 1937 a brief stop in India began her love affair with Indian dance and culture. She spent the years of the Second World War there, studying classical dance.*
>
> *After the war she introduced Indian dance to white Australia, bringing a young dancer from Kerala. He received rave reviews, and together he and Louise, his manager, proved great ambassadors for Indian dance in many countries. After years of promoting dance in America and helping set up early yoga ashrams there, Louise retired to Australia in the late 1960s, continuing to support multicultural dance in Melbourne until her death in 1979.*

the dominant leisure activity in most homes. Telephones also helped to connect people at home with the outside world, and were useful to women in the traditional activity of caring for parents – it was easy to keep in touch. It can be argued that television and radio broke down closeness in communities and stopped people making their own entertainment, but they had strong advantages for women at home in particular, helping to entertain children and bringing the illusion of company and social outings. 'If you live in a lonely, isolated place ... dress up for your radio entertainment at home', suggested a magazine. A shower, a shake of talcum powder, clean undies and a nice frock would turn the family drudge into a dainty leisured lady. 'It may startle the family at first, but it acts as an example.'

A huge change came once the family could afford a car. No

The Boom Years

more struggling on public transport for women with bags, bundles and small children; the car brought into reach shops, recreation and leisure. Shopping was transformed. In the nineteenth century it was done at small specialist shops, then in the boom of the 1880s large department stores developed, selling a range of goods. Mass production in factories between the wars led to chain stores like Coles and Woolworths, but after the Second World War there were still plenty of corner shops, for it was difficult to carry things far. Many tradesmen called at the home – butchers, bakers, milkmen, grocers, greengrocers – which was convenient, but restricted choice and meant some women rarely left the house.

Once families owned cars, they could travel to shops, which grew into larger centres which could buy in bulk and give the customer more choice and cheaper prices, while the development of frozen food and home freezers and refrigerators meant people could buy more at one time. Supermarkets developed in the 1950s, and shopping centres in the 1960s, carefully designed to make shopping an outing. Some women saw it as drudgery, others as a pleasure, possibly including socialising with friends.

New synthetic fabrics like rayon and nylon also made life easier. They were cheaper and needed far less care than wool and cotton – easier to wash, dry, and iron. Fashions continued to become simpler, and mass production meant clothes cost less. With electric sewing machines it was faster and easier to make clothes at home, but during this period it became cheaper to buy some items. Mass production and cheaper clothes meant that women could look smart for little money, and helped in the process, gathering force since the 1920s, of making women more equal, united by being women rather than divided by background. Another revolution was that trousers, comfortable and practical, became acceptable wear.

The effect of many of these technological changes can be seen in the life of Mary Aldridge. She came from Melbourne, and married during the Second World War. After her soldier husband Arthur was sent to New Guinea, Mary worked as a clerk with the

Department of Aircraft Production, and wrote every night to Arthur.

After the war Arthur wanted to farm, and they accepted his uncle's request to help with his dairy farm and orchard. Conditions were primitive, with Mary washing in troughs and only able to cool jellies and custards by covering them with a wet towel in the shade. Through trial and error she became a reasonable cook, 'and could cook a sponge cake and crisp biscuits with the best of them'. Then Arthur bought his uncle's old car, which made them more mobile.

In 1948 Mary became pregnant. She knew nothing about childbirth and there were no books for expectant mothers, only older women saying things like, 'Oh, you poor thing, I had a terrible time with my sixth', and going into gory details. 'A bit frightening, but there was always the optimistic feeling that it couldn't be that bad or there wouldn't be so many happy mothers.' When Mary's labour began, Arthur drove her to the local hospital. A kind and supportive nurse and doctor saw Mary through 'the ordeal, and ordeal it was', and a daughter, Sue, was born. As was usual, Mary stayed in bed for ten days and was only allowed out of bed on the last day. After so long in bed, she was weak, which made it hard to cope at home. So did the nurse's strict instructions to feed the baby every four hours only, with strictly no feeding after 10.00 pm.

'I can still remember those first few weeks, being reduced to desperation when the baby began crying at 2 am and was still crying when her feed was due at 6 am.' wrote Mary. 'Trying to do the right thing, we put up with the screaming, red faced baby until in desperation, I thought, "Hang the rules, if a baby is hungry enough to cry for four hours and nearly destroys us, I'll see if a 2 am feed will help". And help it did.' Still, 'my first four months were sheer hell, tired all the time'. Fortunately, Sue thrived. Her sister Anne arrived four years later 'without too much fuss and bother, because I had learned a hard lesson with my first one and used plain old commonsense with the second'.

Arthur wanted a farm of his own, so suggested taking up a soldier settler's block near Numurkah. Mary was not keen, as she thought they were both city people, not 'the "stuff" pioneers were made of'. Nevertheless, she realised that this was Arthur's dream, and agreed. After the First World War, over 37,000 soldiers had been settled on farms, but many failed. Farms were often small, land was poor, farmers did not have enough knowledge or capital, and prices for farm produce were low and in the Depression even lower. The scheme was better run after the Second World War, with larger, more viable farms, more help and advice and more experienced men chosen. Prices for produce were also higher. Nevertheless, Mary was right in thinking there was hard work ahead.

Arthur was accepted as a 'blockie' and they moved to their farm. At first they lived in an old house on the block, with cheap lino on the walls and ceilings, an open fireplace, no electricity, no hot water, an outside toilet, and water tanks without taps. Mary 'set about making it into a home', but it was uphill work. Rats and mice spoiled the jams, pickles and sauces she had just learned to make. The family came down with stomach upsets, so they drained the tanks and to their horror found a layer of decaying possums, magpies and other wild life on the bottom. Once a week Mary and Arthur heated up water in kerosene tins and had a bath, and Mary boiled the nappies in kero tins over the fire.

But again, things improved. The health centre nurse was a great help to the district's new mothers. The scheme built them a fine house, with a large kitchen, three bedrooms, a lounge room, an inside laundry with a copper and troughs, and verandahs. They planted trees, the blockies worked together to plough, grade and sow their blocks, and the wives became acquainted when they went to town on Saturdays to shop. All in the same boat, they decided that the worst job was laying lino in the new houses. 'If you could lay lino with your husband without wanting to kill him, you had a pretty good marriage!'

Another job for wives was fencing, with Mary the 'stick holder'. Arthur would direct her to move the stick until the fence was in a straight line, not an easy job with Arthur fussy about getting the line perfectly straight and the baby in her pusher to be kept amused and comfortable. Then Mary unrolled the reel of barbed wire, 'wicked stuff', and tied the fence up.

In 1952 Mary and Arthur took possession of their cows, at much the same time as their new watering system. 'I always noticed that Arthur seemed to have important water to go round when milking time came. So I would strap my little one in the pusher for safety and the older child would play happily around while I struggled first to get the pesky things into the bails and then to milk them.' Mary had never seen a separator, but had to use one. 'Turning the handle took all the strength I had ... washing it was another nightmare, there were so many pieces and all had to be washed.' Arthur, meanwhile, had many problems with the watering system 'so he was forgiven'.

The new pastures were flourishing and Mary and Arthur brought in the hay themselves. 'I carted the baby's playground down to the paddocks under a big gum tree and placed it on a rug and, with toys to amuse her, she was happy enough while we worked.' Mary packed the hay on the trailer, then forked it up while Arthur built the haystack. There were still the cows to milk and the watering to check, 'so all in all there was a lot to be jammed into twenty four hours'. Arthur built a hay shed which had to be filled, and Mary was relieved when he and a neighbour bought a hay baler so that she did not have to carry heavy bales of hay. She was just left with the milking.

The scheme built them a dairy, with milking machines and an engine to drive the separator, 'heaven', and in 1953 the wonderful news came that electricity was on its way. 'The change in our home life was miraculous, light at the flick of a switch, an electric jug to make an instant cuppa and, best of all, at last a refrigerator which meant fresh meat and vegs, and a place to store the left overs for another meal and no more sour milk and melted butter ... Now we could have homemade icecream, cold drinks and cold sweets in the summer all from the refrigerator.' Then 'another marvellous thing happened ... We had the telephone installed! [It] opened up a wonderful world for we wives as we could have a chat anytime'.

The phone was also useful for calling the vet, and Mary often helped him with the cows when Arthur was away. Once she had

The Boom Years

> ### 'A strong woman in every sense of the word' – the Drover's Wife, 1962
>
> *Fresh from Melbourne, in 1962 Dennette and David Long and their two small children went to live on a station in south-west Queensland. One day the wife of one of their drovers arrived at the homestead with her young children. 'Gidday love, I've come for stores to take out to camp', she said. Dennette offered refreshments. 'Ta love, now you kids sit on the verandah and don't youse bloody well move. Mind if I use ya phone love, me stores haven't arrived yet and I'm gunna ring the bloody storekeeper and give him a piece of me mind.'*
>
> *'I was absolutely transfixed by this wonderful woman, she had so much strength of character and so many skills', wrote Dennette. 'She knew what was essential and what was irrelevant to be in harmony with her life.' After telling off the storekeeper and drinking a cup of tea, she chose items from the store – 'a bag of sugar, a box of tea' – and admired Dennette's house: 'Jesus Christ you got some beautiful things here love'. She then gave advice as to which local doctor to go to – the one who cured the 'pain in me guts'. Dennette did not want her to leave, but she was not one to waste time and mustered up her brood efficiently. 'I have never forgotten that brief encounter', wrote Dennette. 'I felt my own education in bush craft so lacking. I also felt insipid – my language was colourless, polite, restricted so greatly by my environment and my upbringing. Just one of those wonderful people who make the outback.'*

to act herself. A cow had torn her udder badly and milk and blood were pouring out, the vet could not be reached, so Mary went to her sewing box and took a large needle and her strongest cotton, normally used for crochet. She sewed up the teat, smeared penicillin ointment over the wound and hoped for the best. When the vet did arrive he was amused to see the teat sewed up with crochet cotton, but Mary's treatment was successful. She also did the farm books and finances, as Arthur disliked this.

A Wealth of Women

After five years of continuous work, Mary and Arthur's ambitions were flagging a little, but in 1956 they won the Royal Agricultural Society of Victoria's state championship for a dairy farm under irrigation. This, wrote Mary, made all the mud, hard work and misery well worthwhile. After spending all day milking, helping Arthur, feeding the family, doing housework and seeing to the children and their school work, she felt she needed a little time to herself, so after tea she would do a crossword. This switched her mind from the day's activities, and she did harder and harder puzzles, which gave her a greater understanding of the English language.

Though the farm was doing well, 'there always seemed to be something ready to happen just when everything seemed to be going alright', such as a plague of grasshoppers. But 'two big, beautiful things happened to us in 1959'. They bought their first new car, a Holden, and an electric stove, with a timer and an automatically controlled oven, 'a godsend. No more rushing up during the milking to see if the fire was still burning and the tea still cooking. Now at the turn of a switch there was all the heat and convenience needed'. When the men came to put it in, Mary had just taken a cake from the wood stove. One of the men said, 'What do you want with an electric stove when you can cook lovely cakes like that?' He did not realise that to cook the cake, wood had to be chopped and carted in, the fire lit, the oven heated to the exact temperature, 'a thing only known by much trial and error'. 'Typical man!'

Each year Mary and Arthur found themselves a little better off, and 'a few trappings of success' appeared: carpets, new furniture, holidays, a motor bike, a new dairy arrangement which made work much easier. Then they installed a septic tank instead of the outside toilet. The walk there in the dark had been a nightmare as spiders wove their webs across the path, which gave women mild attacks of hysterics, and insects flew inside the toilet itself. Each time she went to the inside toilet at night time Mary thanked her lucky stars.

The Boom Years

Another major part of most women's lives which became easier was preparing food. Since the day white people arrived in Australia, they had eaten traditional British food. In the nineteenth century the staple foods were damper or bread, meat, tea, sugar, fruit in season and whatever vegetables were grown. Settlers did not make much use of native foods except fish and shellfish, though some kangaroo was eaten and there were other attempts, like sassafras tea and beer, usually given up gratefully when commercial brands became available. Visitors noted that food was abundant and cheap, particularly meat, which women often cooked for their families three times a day.

For 150 years food remained basically the same, but its preparation became easier. From the 1870s commercially prepared food became available. Tinned food was cheap, easy and provided variety, and other convenient foods were Arnott's biscuits (1870), condensed milk (1882) and Rosella tomato sauce (1899). Margarine was a cheap alternative to butter, and commercial ice-cream was available from 1907.

Ice-cream, breakfast cereals, and other helpful products like gelatine, custard powder, jelly crystals and self-raising flour became popular in the inter-war years. Recipe books imply, however, that women continued to make at home items which were commercially available, such as anchovy paste (made with herrings), camp pie, Worcestershire sauce, Vegemite, condensed milk, bottled fruit, jams, cordials, confectionery, floor polish, fly spray, window cleaner, soap and medicines. But unless home-made was cheaper (using fruit from the garden, for example) or tasted better (home-made biscuits), women usually turned to commercial products with relief.

From the 1890s Australian recipe books had appeared, with their recipes overwhelmingly British in origin, though some included indigenous products. Hannah Maclurcan achieved a national reputation as a cookery writer. She managed a Townsville hotel for her father, a prominent hotelier, married another hotelier, and in 1898 wrote *Mrs. Maclurcan's Cookery Book*. Many recipes were her own invention and she specialised in 'delectable dishes' made from seafood. As well as hundreds of traditional recipes, she included others using local foods, such as wallaby, scrub turkey, wonga pigeon and prickly pear, though it does not appear that these became widely popular. Hannah moved to Sydney and ran the Wentworth Hotel, which became renowned for its fine cuisine.

Interest in healthy eating grew after vitamins were discovered in 1911. The main activity was adding more milk, fruit and vegetables to children's diets in particular, and many people saw any further interest as eccentric. Some expensive restaurants served European dishes and there were some Chinese restaurants, but these were virtually the only outside influences on Australian cuisine, and neither affected cooking in the home. The one foreign-inspired dish was the British form of curry, which spread from British India, and was particularly popular because it was a different way to use cold meat.

Australia made three original dietary contributions. Some

More floggings than feeds

Betty Carter was born in 1923 and had a tough childhood on a farm at Bellingen: she hated school, and her mother was very strict. After she left school she helped her father, then at twenty married a farmer. 'Marriage was my way of leaving home and yet once I was able to leave, home didn't seem such a bad place after all', she wrote. She bore nine children and also cared for her husband's orphan niece, and 'it was a hard life'. Her husband drank and gambled, and Betty reared the children virtually on her own. Then her husband went too far. 'For years he'd given me and me kids more floggings than feeds', and finally, after he had bashed a door down and bashed Betty, she rang the police. Her husband deserted the family, working under an assumed name to avoid paying maintenance. 'We were all of us glad when he left. Life was so peaceful without him', wrote Betty. She took in boarders to make a living. 'I'm happy living on me own, working in my garden every moment I can', she wrote at seventy-seven. 'There might be good men out there, but I never wanted to take a chance again.'

The Boom Years

anonymous person invented the lamington, called after Lord, or possibly Lady, Lamington, Queensland's vice-regal couple from 1896 to 1901. The recipe first appeared in 1902: a cake with a cream filling, cut into squares, iced on all sides with chocolate icing and rolled in coconut. Though they were fiddly to make, lamingtons became an Australian classic. So did the pavlova. This was invented by Bert Sachse, a former farmer who was taught to cook by his wife Mary, and rose to become chef of the grand Esplanade Hotel in Perth. In 1935 the licensee, Elizabeth Paxton, asked him to invent something special for afternoon tea, so by adding cornflour and vinegar to egg whites he made a meringue with a crunchy top and a marshmallow filling, and named it in honour of the ballerina Anna Pavlova, who had visited Perth. (Similar recipes had already appeared in New Zealand, but none included both vinegar and cornflour.)

Then there was Vegemite, made by a Melbourne firm in 1923 from the Carlton Breweries' leftover yeast, to compete with the British product Marmite. It did not sell well, so the firm tried to boost sales by renaming it Parwill, a truly dreadful pun ('Ma might'). Not surprisingly, this was also unsuccessful, and Vegemite really only became popular when it was included in soldiers' rations in the war, then advertised intensely after the American company Kraft bought it in 1950.

Despite these three inventions, none of which was exactly a staple food, at the time of the Second World War most Australians ate a solidly British diet, as shown in the recipes in the *Women's Weekly*, where rice is a major innovation, and in the 1943 edition of a recipe book, the *Commonsense Cookery Book*, by the Public School Cookery Teachers' Association of New South Wales. In over four hundred recipes, the only hints of foreign influence are Macaroni Cheese (macaroni in cheese sauce) and Cauliflower au Gratin (cauliflower in cheese sauce). Dishes are plain. Vegetables, including spinach, are to be boiled for from twenty to thirty minutes, there are many boiled meat dishes and boiled puddings, and the only real interest comes in the recipes for desserts, cakes and biscuits. Women learned cooking from their mothers or at school and reproduced these recipes, with little interest in novelty. This was due to conservatism, and a lack of money, knowledge, interest and probably also time to read recipes, buy ingredients and prepare new dishes.

All this started to change in the 1950s. Several books of European recipes were published in Australia, and in 1955 the *Women's Weekly* started to include them, bringing them in reach of many women. The effect is seen in a CWA cookery book of 1958. Its 600 recipes donated by members are mostly traditional, but twenty, 3 per cent, are foreign and sound reasonably authentic, such as Russian fish pie, 'Goulash (Austrian Dish)', Indian fritters, Danish bun pastries, Jewish cakes, and what was for a child the culinary highlight of the era, Bombe Alaska – cake, sometimes fruit, and ice-cream covered with meringue and browned in a very hot oven. It was presumed to come from America.

If Mrs F Narrison from the small, isolated town of Smithton in north-west Tasmania could provide a recipe for German Roast, one can conclude that many Australian women were beginning to cook non-traditional food. Why had this come about? One reason was the presence of so many European immigrants. As shops started to sell the goods they wanted to buy, other Australians realised how delicious were salami, rye bread and continental cakes. More (though still not many) Australians were travelling overseas and bringing back ideas, and magazines did a great deal to spread them. And many new cooking ideas fitted into the growing desire for healthier food containing vitamins, minerals, protein and fibre. It was all part of the general atmosphere of the 1950s, that everything modern was exciting and desirable, the way of the future, and old-fashioned ideas were outdated, not only in furniture, decor and clothes but food as well.

Not only were women cooking with recipes from countries other than Britain, but they were moving away from heavy, traditional meals to lighter, less stodgy ones, symbolised in the change from boiled puddings to the new mousses and fluffs, easily prepared with the mixmaster, electric beaters and refrigerator. At the same time women were making more complicated European recipes for festivities, they were also making simpler recipes for the family, using convenience foods like a packet of chicken noodle soup, a tin of Ideal milk or tuna, or, when frozen foods became popular in the 1960s, a packet of frozen peas. Frozen foods meant more convenience, with frozen chips, fish fingers, TV dinners and other innovations which made life easier for the cook.

At the same time as technology revolutionised housework, it also revolutionised another aspect of women's lives – reproduction. By the 1940s sulphonamides, penicillin and blood transfusions, as well as better anaesthesia and management, meant that almost no women died in childbirth. Mary Aldridge's description of childbirth shows the general situation in the 1940s. Women often married knowing little about sex and nothing about pregnancy or childbirth, and some were still completely anaesthetised during labour. Almost all births took place in hospitals, but not all nurses were as kind as Mary's. Mavis Fogarty in Melbourne resigned from her job when four months pregnant, and when labour started went to hospital. 'I was completely ignorant of the workings of the body, and kept thinking of all the "old wives" tales I had heard!' She was not given any instructions or allowed visitors, and the birth took three days. She was shown the baby for a few minutes, then did not see him for three days. Back in the ward, Mavis was not allowed to set foot out of bed for a week, and was given a bedpan every four hours. She needed it more often, but a nurse told her she had to wait or wet the bed, as it was easier to change the sheets than get a bedpan. 'Each day was sheer misery.'

From the 1950s, childbirth started to change. Ante-natal care became universal, pain relief replaced full anaesthesia, and women themselves became interested in new childbirth techniques. Beth McLeod, married in 1955, followed a British gynaecologist, Grantly Dick-Read, who recommended relaxation techniques during labour, helped by the husband. Beth went to relaxation classes, and when the baby was born, in 1956, her husband Lyndsay stayed with her during labour, timing contractions and helping her to relax. The hospital staff were amazed, but admitted that it did work, though they did not let Lyndsay stay for the actual birth. Very gradually, relaxation became widespread, though it took even longer for husbands to be accepted at the birth.

Once the new mother took the baby home, commercial baby formulae were better and safer than in the past, and the view that modern was best persuaded more and more women to feed their babies artificially. A further change came in the way baby was reared, for from the mid-1950s there was a new guru on child rearing, an American, Dr Spock. He advised a far more relaxed attitude. Children needed love and cuddling, not regulations. Babies should be fed when they were hungry, put to bed when they were sleepy, receive affection, and have more freedom. Dr Spock has been criticised for encouraging children to be undisciplined, but in the 1950s he advocated quite firm discipline; however, his ideas were so different from Truby King's that he was seen as excitingly radical.

Women accepted Dr Spock's views readily, though clinic sisters were often conservative, some recommending Truby King's methods into the 1960s. But Dr Spock's way of rearing children fitted in better with the relaxed Australian atmosphere and was also easier on the family, especially with feeding on demand and a less baby-centred routine.

Other helpful innovations were disposable products. Disposable sanitary pads, worn with a belt, were uncomfortable but did away with the distasteful task of washing soiled towelling pads. Tampons were even better, more pleasant to use and less restricting. Disposable nappies were expensive and not widely used at first, but they were handy when visiting or travelling. But the really revolutionary technological change of the era was the Pill.

A recurring note through women's history to this date was fear of pregnancy. Single women who bore children were social outcasts. Married women found that large families meant even more work and poverty. From the 1890s many women were controlling their fertility, but even in the 1940s and 1950s, this could be difficult, as many women knew nothing about contraception. Catholics in particular had problems as their church was strongly opposed. Even doctors were taught little in their training, some recommending abstinence, or placing a man's handkerchief soaked in oil in the vagina. A birth control clinic had opened in Sydney in 1933, but few more were established.

There were new birth control devices, such as diaphragms, cervical caps, stem pessaries and the Grafenberg ring, an intrauterine device, but they were expensive and not always available. In Melbourne in the late 1930s, only 12 per cent of those using

Dawn Fraser and the flag

The best known women of the 1950s were sportswomen, with Marjorie Jackson ('The Lithgow Flash'), Shirley Strickland and Betty Cuthbert winning gold medals for athletics, Margaret Court in women's tennis, and Dawn Fraser in swimming. Dawn was also known as a rebel.

The youngest of eight children of a Balmain family, she suffered from asthma, and learned to swim at five. She left school at thirteen and worked in a dress factory, and loved to skylark in the Balmain Baths. A coach persuaded her to join his squad, she started to win races, and finally won gold medals for the 100 metres freestyle at the 1956, 1960 and 1964 Olympics, a fantastic feat. In 1964 she carried the Australian flag at the closing ceremony.

But Dawn was often in strife. In Tokyo in 1964, she smuggled herself into the opening ceremony, though athletes competing early were banned; she refused to wear the regulation swimsuit for heats, saying it was uncomfortable; and after winning her race, she went on a flag-souveniring expedition with two Australian men. They were arrested by the Japanese police, though not charged.

Others misbehaved as well, and complaints led to four women being banned from competitive swimming, Dawn for ten years. The men were not punished. There was worldwide criticism of this harsh sentence, which ended Dawn's swimming career. However, attitudes changed. By the time the Olympic Games were held in Sydney in 2000, Dawn was widely admired all over Australia, and she played a leading role in the ceremonies.

contraception used new devices. This figure rose to 18 per cent a decade later, and 27 per cent in the late 1950s. Other people used condoms, withdrawal, abstinence and the only method allowed by the Catholic church, the rhythm method, where couples only had sex at 'safe' times in the menstrual cycle. None of these methods was entirely reliable, some were very unreliable, many were unpleasant to use, many needed manipulation just before inter-

A world first – the School of the Air

For years, isolated children had received education through Correspondence Schools, but these provided little beyond written lessons. In 1950 Adelaide Miethke initiated the School of the Air, where these children could have radio contact with their teachers and with each other. It operated from the Aerial Medical Service in Alice Springs, and was the first such enterprise in the world.

This was far from Adelaide Miethke's only achievement. Born in South Australia in 1881, she became a teacher, and was a forceful advocate of more opportunities and better salaries for women. In 1924 she became an inspector of schools, and promoted teaching domestic science, 'preparing girls for their ultimate career', as she wrote. During both world wars she mobilised schoolchildren to raise huge sums for the war effort, and in 1936 she headed the Women's Centenary Council which raised another huge sum to establish the Alice Springs base of the Royal Flying Doctor Service, and the Pioneer Women's Memorial Garden in Adelaide. She also organised and designed a grand pageant, where her voice was strong enough to rally 14,000 children who symbolised 'in rhythmic movement, colour and music the major expansions of our great Empire'. A leader in Girl Guides and the National Council of Women, active in many women's areas, 'Addie' was like a block of Victor Harbour granite, rather chunky but enduring, said a colleague admiringly. She had no guile and never said an unkind word about another person, but was 'as shrewd as a bag full of monkeys' – a 'practical visionary' and the greatest South Australian woman, according to a later president of the National Council of Women.

course so lessened enjoyment; overall, none was ideal.

For those women who knew nothing about contraception or whose method failed, abortion was possible – for those in the know. Abortions were widespread, with one estimate claiming 50,000 to 100,000 in 1962. They were illegal, but were performed for money or out of sympathy by doctors, nurses, unqualified 'backyard abortionists' or women themselves. A study of abortion in Adelaide showed that women who had them were often desperate, several single women believing suicide was the only alternative. Single women wanted to spare themselves and their families the shock and social disgrace, or feared they might lose their jobs; married women had enough children already, and some had drunken or violent husbands. The women had been using no contraception, or their contraception failed, and many found it just as difficult to find out about abortion as they had contraception. The main sources were doctors, most in Sydney and Melbourne, preferred by middle-class women, or female abortionists, cheaper and more widespread, and preferred by working-class women.

There are dreadful stories of women having abortions with no anaesthetic and being left to cope alone afterwards, but others of more sympathetic treatment. One woman in Adelaide was a nurse, a divorced mother of two daughters. After having an abortion herself in 1957, she realised she could perform them. She worked at clients' homes or an arranged place such as a hotel or the back seat of a car, each abortion taking about twenty minutes. Having opened the cervix with her fingers, she syringed in disinfectant (midwives' and nurses' usual method), and claimed she had no complications. Her motive was sympathy for the women, and she had no regrets. In 1962 she was charged, deregistered as a nurse and spent two years in gaol, but when she came out she had no trouble in being re-registered – though she performed no more abortions. By this stage momentum for change was growing, and in 1969 South Australia made abortion more accessible and a court ruling in Victoria paved the way for increased access to it.

In 1961 the Pill appeared, arguably the most helpful product for women in the history of Australia. It was reliable, easy, and provided women with full-time protection and entire control of contraception – no longer was co-operation necessary from the partner. And it could be easily discussed without embarrassment, a great advantage. The Pill gave women increased independence from men; sex could be thought of separately from marriage and pregnancy. It was not widely available for several years and some doctors would not prescribe it for single women, but it made contraception so much easier and more reliable that women's networks passed round the names of co-operative doctors. Practical Australian women took to the Pill with enthusiasm, and by the end of the decade two-thirds of women in the reproductive years were using it, the highest proportion in the world. At last women were freed from the dread of unwanted pregnancy. With such equipment as the Pill, a washing machine, frozen food and a copy of Dr Spock, a woman in the late 1960s could lead a physically easier life than her mother had.

Snapshot

EDUCATION

1789	first school established, in Sydney, with Isabella Rossin the teacher
1850	first university, in Sydney; then Melbourne (1853) and Adelaide (1874)
1850s	new independent colonial governments show interest in developing primary schools
1872	free, secular and independent primary education in Victoria; other states follow
1870s	Catholic church develops its own separate education system
1879	first state girls' high school, Advanced School for Girls in Adelaide
1880s	many private girls' high schools founded
1880	Adelaide and Sydney Universities allow female students, Melbourne follows (1881) and new universities admit women from the start: Tasmania (1890), Queensland (1909) and Western Australia (1910)

Snapshot

1901	first kindergarten, in Melbourne
c. 1900	the New Education means less rigid classes, teacher training, and more government high schools
1940s	government support begins for kindergartens and creches
1943	ABC begins 'Kindergarten of the Air'
1951	Commonwealth Scholarships to universities greatly increase number of students
1950s	new universities founded
1950s	secondary education develops, and schools are within reach of all children
1974	university fees abolished; university enrolments grow
1999	about 85 per cent of girls finish year 12, and there are more girls than boys at universities

chapter nine

The Women's Movement

Until the late 1960s, almost everyone in Australia – feminists, the woman-in-the-street, and all men – took it for granted that women should be wives and mothers. This was their natural role, and it was vital for the nation. Some did not fare too well, of course – widows, deserted wives, women who were beaten or raped, who bore numerous children, who lived in poverty – but they could be explained away as misfortune or even the woman's fault ('she asked for it') or helped by the improvements reformers worked for, like pensions and contraceptives. It was now acceptable for both single and married women to enter employment, but women's primary role remained the care of the family. Few people disagreed, at least publicly.

The 1960s brought immense change to many areas of life. An increasingly liberal atmosphere meant more criticism of society appeared. Australians started to recognise Aboriginal rights, and in 1967 Aboriginal Australians were given citizenship of their own country. The media began to report domestic violence and child abuse, housewives' boredom, the rising divorce rate and the rising number of 'unmarried mothers', showing that family life was not always ideal.

Julie Rigg was among the interested journalists, and when she criticised the lack of opportunities for women, the huge response convinced her that Australia had a 'woman problem'. In 1969 she edited a book, *In Her Own Right*, which painted a grim picture. Society prescribed a narrow role for women. Wives had to sacrifice themselves for husbands and children. Employed women struggled with unequal pay and inadequate childcare. Migrant women were lonely, isolated by language, doing menial jobs. Aboriginal women were discriminated against. Pensioners and lower income-earners lived in poverty. Housewives had to try to live up to the advertisers' ideal of womanhood – house-proud, glamorous – and many became alienated and addicted to prescription drugs. There were almost no women leaders in politics, business or trade unions. Education and the sexual revolution which followed the contraceptive pill resulted in the New Woman, liberated and articulate, but where was the New Man? Australian men were the world's worst lovers, wrote Julie, and despite the Pill, abortion was widespread. The only positive picture she gave was of young, single working women.

Overall, women were no worse off than they always had been, and in many ways better, but this sort of criticism reached a much more receptive audience than ever before. There was a general climate of concern about social justice, so that complaints which would once have been ignored as mere whingeing were now listened to. With secondary education universal and a huge increase in tertiary education, young women were better educated and more articulate than women had ever been. The technological revolution promised release from the hard toil of childbearing and endless housework. The buoyant economy meant full employment, and young people did not see the need for security at all costs, as their parents had, and hated what they saw as the boring conformity of their families' suburban life.

It was largely the women most affected by this situation – young, intelligent, well-educated, middle-class, urban – who led the revolt. Schools encouraged them to achieve equally with boys, university was available with scholarships, but after this liberating education, choices were limited. Olwyn Hanigan's grand ideas of being a mechanic, surveyor or radiographer were met by all-male

Lydia and Tom Pinington and their daughter Ada migrated from England in 1929, and Tom found a job working on the construction of the Lake Grace-Hyden railway. For three years they lived in a tent by the line, in harsh conditions. Lydia has kept her family extremely neat, despite the primitive conditions.

Eileen Fitzer winding up water, central Australia

Land Army member milking a cow, Western Australia

*New careers for women.
Back in Sydney after serving in the Army, Amy Taylor joined the police
force and became the first woman to perform traffic duty.*

Sister Michael with Third Class, West Heidelberg, 1954

*A modern kitchen, designed on the lines of the
'preparation cycle' in kitchen routine.
The housewife is using a new quick-boiling electric jug. 1950*

*Farmer's wives preparing a meal at a picnic race meeting
at Talbingo Station, 1956*

The great Australian invention of the 1950s: the Hills hoist. Note the assumption of how a housewife will want to use her spare time.

Women in new positions: Dame Roma Mitchell QC in action

Folk singer Margret Roadknight performing on International Women's Day in Brisbane

Concert group from the Older Women's Network entertaining members

Many families treasure items they have inherited from past generations. Here Beryl Pearson, her daughter and granddaughters Jessica and Kate and her family show the meat platter which Beryl's great-great-grandmother brought with her from Ireland in the 1830s. It has been used by seven generations of the family.

Jihad Hawar and family after a citizenship ceremony, 1988

The Women's Movement

interviewing panels with 'You will get dirty', or 'If a male applies, then he will get the job as women only have babies'. With a marriage rate running at about 95 per cent, these girls' fate seemed clear: becoming a housewife, like their mothers, while their brothers kept on enjoying the opportunities of the prosperous 1960s. These women took up the battle on behalf of all, and the climate of the early 1970s meant that media, governments and society generally paid attention.

For decades, some women had been trying to right one of their most bitterly-resented injustices – unequal pay. Early in the century their wage had been set at 54 per cent of men's, for man was seen as the breadwinner, and woman the dependant homemaker. Training and university degrees were no guarantee of reasonable wages. Beryl Lindsay, university-educated and in the 1930s president of the Victorian association of female teachers at private schools, was the highest-paid female teacher at Melbourne's Methodist Ladies' College, but earned less than the male gardener. During the war women's labour was vital, and their pay rate was raised to three-quarters of men's – an improvement, but still less. Protest continued but did not embrace a majority of women, since many accepted the argument that men had to support families and should earn more. But in the climate of the 1960s support for equal pay grew, especially as more and more women entered the labour market. In 1969 the issue came up before the Conciliation and Arbitration Commission.

Excellent publicity was provided by Zelda D'Aprano. Born in 1928 in Melbourne, Zelda worked in a number of factories, married and had a child, but did not want more children and suffered a series of painful abortions. She and her husband separated and she returned to employment, where she found women treated poorly, with few opportunities for promotion or even permanent work. She wanted to fight to improve conditions, but no one supported her: she wrote that men never listened to women, the Communist Party was snobbish because she was working class, the union movement was not interested in women's work, and her fellow female workers were unwilling to back her. In 1969 she decided that 'something more than just talking was needed'.

A Wealth of Women

Women held a meeting promoting equal pay, which the media ignored, then Zelda chained herself to the door of the Commonwealth Building while other women walked up and down with placards. Reporters arrived in droves. The Arbitration Commission granted equal pay to women who performed exactly the same work as men, 18 per cent of female employees. The tide was turning.

Zelda was by no means the only woman to make headlines, for in the 1960s women worldwide were protesting. In Australia most protests were against involvement in the Vietnam war and military conscription, introduced in 1964. First was the women's group, Save Our Sons, whose polite protest had as much immediate effect as polite protest usually did. Members of a delegation to Canberra found that politicians ignored them, or called them communist stooges and told them to take the first plane to Peking.

Later protest against the Vietnam War could not be ignored – huge demonstrations by thousands of people from 1968. But as in political parties, women found that men expected them to be supportive, distributing leaflets and making the tea. Many young women were no longer prepared to put up with this, demanding to be taken seriously. They did not join the established women's groups, which often had similar aims; even left-wing groups like the Union of Australian Women attracted older women and were respectable and moderate, exactly what young women were rebelling against.

Though the majority of women did not protest and only a small percentage actively demanded change, these women produced an astonishing result in a few years. Protest really started in 1970. Zelda D'Aprano and several friends, encouraged by their earlier success and realising that 'women would have to do their own fighting', formed a militant group, the Women's Action Committee. Its main demands were equal pay, employment and education opportunities, and access to childcare, abortion and contraception. Though never large the Committee was active, protesting against sexist advertisements and beauty contests, and holding protest tram rides where women paid only

The Women's Movement

three-quarters of the fare, since they were paid only three-quarters of men's wages.

Female university students, intelligent, articulate and energetic, were often at the forefront of those dissatisfied with women's lack of opportunities. Born in Adelaide in 1945, Anne Summers grew up in a stultifying environment, with an alcoholic father and expectations at home and at her convent school that girls should be well-behaved young ladies. Only three careers seemed possible: marrying and having children, becoming a nun or ending up an old spinster. Anne left school at sixteen and had a series of jobs, 'simply filling in time, waiting for the right man to come along', a challenging quest as most young men she met were mean and sexually predatory. Contraception was a problem: the Pill was hard for single women to obtain, condoms were embarrassing, and withdrawal, the main method used, was awkward and unreliable. Many girls became pregnant and 'had to get married'; one friend of Anne's was abandoned by her boyfriend at the church, and put in a psychiatric hospital by her family. When Anne herself became pregnant as a result of forced sex, she had an illegal abortion, with great difficulty, anguish, pain and expense.

Eventually Anne went to university, at last a place where women were treated equally. She married in 1967, but found the dependence of married life frustrating, and two years later left her husband. Increasingly she was drawn to the New Left, Marxist radicals, and to the ideas of the American women's liberation movement, which was redefining what being female was all about: women should not be confined to a domestic role and the stereotype of sex siren or mother, but have the same chances as men. They were entitled to independence, not dependence on father or husband. Late in 1969 Anne and several friends formed a women's liberation group in Adelaide, about the same time as groups were formed in Sydney and Melbourne. Their main demands were access to childcare, abortion and contraception, equal pay, equal job opportunities, and an end to sexist advertising and images of women in the media. More groups were formed round Australia, mostly connected with universities. In

Melbourne Zelda D'Aprano's Women's Action Committee members said that women's lib 'exploded our minds', and Zelda found, to her surprise, that 'these young women were no different from me. We all had the same problems'.

Women's Liberation published articles on previously-taboo subjects like contraception, tackled topics like rape and lesbianism, and became increasingly intolerant of patriarchal behaviour by men. Consciousness-raising groups talked their way through a range of subjects, drawing out ways in which individual problems were common to all. International Women's Day was celebrated

The women's movement round Australia

Many branches of women's lib and WEL were formed in towns round Australia. In Perth, recalled Joan Williams, the movement started in 1971, with consciousness raising, study groups, banners and T-shirts proclaiming 'Womanpower', a campaign against sexist language, and women standing for local government. While the sale of contraceptives was being discussed in parliament, women smuggled in a banner and hung it over the balcony. They were ordered out. The movement was determined not to have a traditional masculine hierarchy, but leaders emerged anyway, actually helped to power by the lack of structure. When Patricia Giles convened the more structured WEL, it was 'something of a relief' for the more moderate.

In Cairns, journalist Pat O'Hara was a founding member of WEL. After attending a meeting which described violence against women, she became 'fired up' and with a few friends established Ruth's Women's Shelter, one of the first in Queensland. She also set up a second-hand bookshop to help fund the shelter, and a women's information line where women could talk about their problems. 'We were very naive; we thought we were going to change the world', she commented. Later she fought to liberalise gay laws, and her contribution as a human rights campaigner was recognised when she was awarded the Order of Australia in 1997.

The Women's Movement

enthusiastically. National conferences were held. Sisterhood was born, exciting and exhilarating. Support came from many woman who read Australian feminist Germaine Greer's *The Female Eunuch*, the first bestselling argument for women to stop accepting male dominance and take responsibility for their own freedom.

Many women's groups started all round the country, trying to influence general attitudes and encouraging individual women to seize equality. They opposed women being exploited or presented as sex objects, in beauty contests and advertisements. They pointed out sexist language, and suggested improvements: 'person' instead of 'man', 'Ms' as a universal female title not based on marital status. They also argued that women were entitled to just as much pleasure from sex as men; that just as women shared in employment, so men should share in duties in the home; overall, that women should be treated equally.

More practically, women's groups tried to support those women in need, and in Sydney in 1974 started three particularly successful ventures: a rape crisis centre, the Leichhardt Women's Health Centre, and Elsie Women's Refuge, which Anne Summers and others began by squatting illegally in an empty house in inner-city Sydney. The response was overwhelming, as dozens of women and children arrived, usually traumatised by violence, which none of the organisers had experienced – they were learning as they went. Money was short, there was often not enough to eat, there were arguments and some class issues, but there was an infectious spirit of survival, wrote Anne. She found a source of funds by selling marijuana until government money came through in 1975, and meanwhile, as the residents started talking to each other, Elsie moved beyond the women who founded it to become 'the story of the women who sought refuge there and who together learned the strength to move on to new lives of independence and dignity'. Elsie inspired others, and by mid-1975 eleven refuges had been established round Australia, an astonishing achievement in one year.

A small number of more extreme feminists advocated abolishing the family and living in communes. Several separatist groups raised money to establish a self-sufficient women's farm in a remote and beautiful part of northern New South Wales. Communal living was part of the ethos, so the thirty or so permanent residents built a large living area and slept in caravans, huts or other shelters. Any woman, but no men, could live or visit, as 'a break from the struggle with male culture'.

Women's liberation generally made a great impact on cultural life, with women writers, actors, artists, musicians and filmmakers – a feminist renaissance from which all Australian culture benefited. Anne Summers noted that 'the sheer relief of having the world interpreted through women's eyes in writing, songs, paintings and films ... A mighty antidote to a lifetime of seeing almost everything through the male gaze'. She herself wrote one of the first books which gave Australian women a serious place in history, *Damned Whores and God's Police*. Why was the gulf between men and women so great? she asked. 'Within a supposedly free and independent Australia women are a colonized sex. They are denied freedom of movement, control of their bodies, economic independence and cultural potency. This oppressed state derives from the status of "the family".'

Some women who had been activists for years finally found that they were not alone. Edna Ryan, born in 1904, grew up in an outspoken, radical household, but even she wished she were a boy, for men were never at home except to be fed and looked after, by women. She won a bursary to high school and became an office worker. Always interested in politics, Edna joined the Communist Party and married another member, Jack Ryan, but they both left within a year. They had three children and ran a butcher's shop and a chicken farm, and Edna became involved with Labor politics, sitting on her local council and active in union affairs. When her daughters joined women's lib, Edna went to a meeting and found the experience 'all very heady', but many of the women 'a bit hardline'. She had become disillusioned, and told them that revolution would not bring emancipation – they had to plan practical achievements as well.

Edna was among those women immediately responsive when a less radical and more organised form of feminism appeared in

The Women's Movement

1972. Beatrice Faust, a political activist in Melbourne, read about an American feminist survey of political candidates, with the aim of finding their views on feminist topics. A federal election looked likely in Australia, and she approached a group of women who, like her, wanted change but preferred to work within the system, in a structured way (women's lib avoided masculine ideas of organisation). The Women's Electoral Lobby, WEL, was born. All over Australia, 'in country towns and far-flung suburbs, groups of women, surprising and even shocking husbands and children, decided to be part of the Women's Electoral Lobby'. They had much the same aims as women's lib, but saw these as achievable through parliamentary reform.

Many women felt WEL changed their lives. Joyce Nicholson of Melbourne was one of those who after the war plunged into domesticity, believing it would bring happiness. But she did not really enjoy mothering, though she tried to conform. In 1967 she took over the family publishing business and loved the work, but felt confused about her role as a woman. This was changed by reading *The Female Eunuch* and joining WEL: 'everyone late, everyone doing too much, everyone tired, everyone arguing, talking at once, but full of enthusiasm, determination, excitement. We were changing the world, and it is not easy, never will be easy, and why expect everyone to agree about methods ... Heady days'. Women stayed up all night, planning questionnaires, writing submissions, collating information. 'Those terrible WEL women' took part in demonstrations, attended political meetings and asked 'improper' questions about birth control and sex education.

A federal election was held later in 1972, and all over Australia WEL interviewed candidates and ranked them according to their attitude to reforms. They supported those who scored highly, mostly Labor candidates. It was a huge publicity success, for WEL knew how to deal with the media and received excellent coverage. Labor was elected, and acted on many women's issues, granting equal pay; establishing a national health insurance scheme under which abortions were cheap and legal; providing a supporting mother's benefit so single mothers could afford to keep their babies; introducing simpler, no-fault divorces which divided assets more equally between husband and wife; and granting equal custody rights to women.

The government appointed Elizabeth Reid as adviser on women's issues. She was deluged with thousands of letters, with women writing that at last there was someone to listen to them. Elizabeth encouraged the government to support women, particularly by increasing funding for childcare. The government also funded community services, which included many feminist activities which assisted women, such as refuges, rape crisis centres and health centres.

Government funding did bring problems to the women's movement. Moderate groups like WEL approved, but many radicals opposed involvement with the 'capitalist state'. It would lessen their independence, they argued, while places like Elsie Women's Refuge provided cheap labour for services which should be fully government funded. Overall, liberal feminists were happy with the progress made under the Whitlam government, but radicals felt Labor did not go far enough.

The United Nations pronounced 1975 International Women's Year, and the Australian government gave the huge sum of $2 million for projects. But the women's movement was divided: should the funds support all women or feminist ideals? Liberal feminists like WEL wanted to gain equality for women within existing society, radical feminists wanted a total assault on patriarchy. Lesbians accused even radical heterosexuals of assuming that women were all heterosexual, and trying to keep lesbians out of the movement in case they alienated others. Some heterosexuals felt that lesbians thought only they were real feminists. Outsiders felt that women's lib only welcomed educated, young, middle-class women.

However, by 1975 thousands of women supported the women's movement. They ranged from the relatively small number of ardent members of feminist groups to the much larger number of mainstream supporters, like Beryl Nothrop, a farmer's daughter from Yarrawonga who won a scholarship to university and became a teacher. She came from a conservative, stable fam-

The Women's Movement

ily and felt that she personally had not been discriminated against, but she was concerned about women's issues because she was keenly aware that many women were experiencing a range of barriers. Reflecting the idealism of youth, she felt that more important than equal pay and opportunity in employment was women's chance to contribute to society, to use their energy and insight and goodwill to make a positive difference.

Outside large cities, most of those involved in the women's movement were liberal feminists, like Pat Degens. Born in Canberra in 1931, she was educated at Canberra High School, where, she said, girls were tolerated in a boys' system. Her only career models were homemaker or spinster career woman, who was seen as a freak. Pat attended university and became a secondary school teacher; her first headmaster assumed that because she was female she was an infants' teacher. In 1961 she married Cornelis Degens, an engineer who had migrated eight years earlier. The Dutch community welcomed her with open arms, she and Cornelis had two sons, and she went back to work part-time when her younger son was two.

In 1972 the Degens family moved to the small country town of Coffs Harbour, where Pat was shocked to find women regarded as inferior and relegated to a purely domestic role. She and two other teachers set up a branch of WEL. Seventeen women came to the first meeting, and the level of anger was so high that everyone talked at once, telling stories of discrimination in the workplace and repressive sexist attitudes. Pat, the chairwoman, managed to get a program adopted of what the women wanted: childcare, preschool, family planning, equality in education, conservation, civil liberties, part-time work for women and an end to financial discrimination. Family planning was a delicate subject, for the Catholic Right to Life Movement was afraid that WEL would start an abortion clinic, and sent large numbers of women to meetings to block WEL members from speaking. But WEL managed to get a women's resource centre established, from which grew a family planning clinic and a women's health centre.

Pat and another teacher, Shirley Jones, got nowhere trying to broaden girls' choices at school and brought it up with the

Teachers' Federation, which resulted in the principal being ordered to allow girls to study all subjects. His reaction against Pat and Shirley was horrendous, with uncontrollable shouting and bellowing, but gradually the community came to support WEL's projects. Suggestions that a refuge was needed were met with cries of disbelief and rage, but by the time one was opened in 1978, it had popular support. Today it is nearly always filled to capacity.

Not surprisingly, there was opposition to the new, challenging feminist ideas, from men who hated the threat to male dominance, and women who enjoyed the feminine trappings which feminists attacked, or felt that feminism downgraded women's role in the home and only valued employed women. Older, happily married women in particular had doubts. 'Women's liberation never affected me. I was never bound up, I was always liberated', said Mollie Tomlin. 'I read *The Female Eunuch* at the time, and I thought, What a lot of garbage, what's the matter with the woman? I didn't understand half of what she was getting at.' Her friend Jean Bourne agreed. 'I was happy being at home. I didn't like being expected to go out to work. I went to work as a secretary when my daughter was three, and I hated it.'

The most controversial topic was abortion, to which Catholics in particular were opposed. Babette Francis was born in India, educated at a convent and university, then on her way to Britain met an Australian barrister. She married him and moved to Melbourne in 1954, finding that Australians welcomed an Indian; indeed, her mother-in-law Constance made newspaper headlines by supporting her. To recreate the large happy family of her youth, Babette had eight children. She strongly disagreed with the women's movement, feeling that it did not value children or women's nurturing capacity. Men and women were fundamentally different, and it was better for women to stand up for what they were, not slavishly try to imitate the 'rulers'. In 1979, with four other women, she founded Women Who Want to be Women, which strongly opposed abortion and aimed to improve homemakers' status and provide financial justice for motherhood so that pregnancy would be a joy.

The Women's Movement

Babette felt that after the first stage of feminism, emancipation at the turn of the century, and the second, liberation, which achieved equal pay and opportunity, it was time for realism, a recognition that women and men would make different choices, and that mothering and homemaking should have equal status with career jobs. Later, some men asked to join, so the name changed to Endeavour Forum. Babette has received several national and international awards for her achievements.

Lesbians were a group of women who became far more visible through the women's movement. Before the 1950s many people were not aware that women could be homosexual, and it was easier for women living together to pass unremarked. This gave homosexual women some freedom, but they did have to keep their homosexuality secret and had difficulty finding each other. They coped in different ways. Monte, born in 1882, lived for twelve years with her first love, and was heartbroken when she left. Homosexual men friends helped her, holding functions such as high camp mock weddings in the 1930s. Some women dressed as men, like Eugenia Falleni, who wore boy's clothes and ran away to sea from her home in New Zealand. In 1898 she arrived in Sydney pregnant, and after her daughter was born she dressed as a man and worked as a carter. She married a widow, Annie, who disappeared, then Eugenia married again, but she was convicted of murdering Annie. In 1938, seven years after her release from prison, she died in a car accident, and court reports of the woman in men's clothes aroused great interest. This was a sensational and most unusual case.

Homosexuality was accepted in theatrical circles, and in the 1940s Val worked as an extra at Melbourne's Tivoli theatre. She wore mannish suits and carried a silver-topped cane, though she never passed as a man. Her flat was forever full of people, so she opened a successful coffee lounge for homosexuals and theatrical people. In 1952 she moved to Cafe 31 in St Kilda, where the clientele were mostly homosexuals, prostitutes and criminals, 'all very well behaved and utterly delightful … The gay crowd has always been extremely loyal to me'. By this time more people were aware

A Wealth of Women

that lesbians existed, though this led to some opposition: some parents sent daughters to psychiatrists, the vice squad raided their clubs, and a lesbian discovered in the police force was reportedly turned into a zombie by electro-convulsive treatment. Nevertheless, some lesbians could live reasonably openly. Hearing there were lesbians in the army, Helen joined in the 1950s. She met plenty of lesbians and 'had a lot of fun'. The authorities found out and in 1963 stripped off her badges and buttons and drummed her out of the army in a humiliating parade. Her mother, appalled, tried to hide it from the neighbours, but her father supported her. It was hard to get a job, but finally Helen became a driver for the Blood Bank. At a family gathering, a great-aunt asked if Helen and her partner were married. 'No', said Helen. 'Well, she's a very nice girl', replied the great-aunt.

Some women kept lesbian desires hidden. At fifteen Jan was seduced by a thirteen-year-old girl. 'After that sex with men wasn't anything', but, worn down by family pressure, she married and had four children. She started getting crushes on baby health centre nurses, and her marriage broke up in the 1960s. Similarly, as a teenager Joan had a secret girlfriend, but she later married and had several children. Through her church she met Jean, with whom she had a clandestine affair for three years. But Joan had to have sex with her husband and became pregnant again, and Jean left her. Joan decided she could not desert her children, so stayed with her husband.

In the 1970s some working-class lesbians wanted nothing to do with the new middle-class women's movement, but overall lesbians benefited as they gained recognition, a public space, and more freedom to meet each other. Several of the women mentioned above enjoyed new opportunities. Monte 'came out', aged 104. Joan went to a coffee evening: 'That was really something – I was going to see some other lesbians! ... It was terribly nerve-wracking – to actually see them, other people like myself. Unbelievable!' She met a woman, left her husband, and they were companions for fifteen years. Helen became social organiser for the small-l liberal reform group Campaign Against Moral Persecution, running dances and a coffee shop.

The Women's Movement

Misogyny in Australia

The largely urban women's movement had enough to cope with in improving women's position, and did not take on directly a strand which was strong in rural areas – misogyny. This dated from Australia's earliest years of settlement, when the general misogyny of the time was strengthened by the shortage of women. It continued to be especially powerful in the outback, part of traditional mateship, which was for white males only.

Robyn Davidson noticed the 'aggressive masculine ethic', the 'cult of misogyny', when she moved from coastal Queensland to Alice Springs in the 1970s. She worked as a barmaid, and saw plenty of men like the typical misogynist she described, 'almost totally devoid of charm. He is biased, bigoted, boring, and, above all, brutal. His enjoyments in life are limited to fighting, shooting and drinking'. He would not accept as equal any woman, or any Aboriginal person or foreigner. One night one of the regulars in the pub told her that she should be careful, that she had been nominated by some of the men as the next rape case. Robyn was devastated, and frightened. Then one night, going to bed, she found a large lump of excrement on her pillow. She handed in her notice at once.

Overall, though lesbians' situation did not improve overnight, they were better accepted by 1975 than they had been. Because there had never been explicit legal sanctions against them, there was no need for campaigns of the kind which gay men started, but lesbians were active in women's lib, many becoming leaders. The first lesbian conference was held in 1973 and since then they have come and gone, a highlight in the early 1990s being a lesbian concert at the Sydney Opera House.

By 1975 the women's movement was both praised and criticised. Some felt left out: it was middle class, divided, and ignored migrants, the working class and Aboriginal women. Many men and more conservative women felt it was responsible for a more fractured society; as domesticity was criticised the divorce rate did rise, the birthrate fell and society was not as stable as in the halcyon days – for men – when they were supreme.

But a very short period had seen undeniable gains, in which most women could share: childcare; equal pay and anti-discrimination in employment; more welfare payments; easier divorce; access to contraception and abortion; health centres and refuges, and more equality in education. Gradually society did become less discriminatory, with less sexist language and less sexism in the media. In short, women were taken more seriously, and there were real choices besides wife and mother. As a symbol of change, when in 1974 the government adopted 'Advance Australia Fair' as the national anthem, without much debate the first line was changed from 'Australia's sons, let us rejoice' to 'Australians all, let us rejoice'.

chapter ten

The Struggle Continues

by Prue Torney-Parlicki

At the end of the Second World War, Aboriginal women remained deeply marginalised by white Australian society. The war years had witnessed a temporary reconciliation between Indigenous and non-Indigenous Australians, but discriminatory policies and practices remained firmly in place, despite the growing influence of assimilationist ideals. However, the wheels of change had been put in motion by the Aboriginal protest movements of the 1930s, and in the immediate postwar period Aboriginal people resumed their struggle against oppression. One of the most notable of these battles was the pastoral workers' strike for equal pay at Pilbara from 1946 to 1949.

Daisy Bindi was directly involved in the strike action. Born around 1900 near Jigalong, Western Australia, Daisy worked on Ethel Creek station as a child, performing household tasks as well as riding and managing horses. In 1945, on a visit to Marble Bar with her husband, she learned of the poor treatment, pay and conditions of Aboriginal station hands, and heard Don McLeod, a white man and former Communist Party member, urging the workers to strike for equal wages. Daisy decided to organise Aboriginal workers on stations near her, and called a meeting at 'Roy Hill' station. The manager contacted the police and welfare authorities, and threatened to have her removed from the area.

Under Western Australian law, it was an offence to entice 'natives' to leave their place of employment. Despite the threat of prosecution, the strike went ahead in May 1946. Daisy organised a truck from Port Hedland to pick up the strikers, and gathered more supporters on the way. Her actions helped to extend the strike to the Pilbara region, where it continued for another three years, supported by trades unions and church organisations.

The goal of assimilation, which had been gathering momentum since the 1930s, was formally adopted in 1951. The year before, Paul Hasluck, then a federal Liberal back-bencher, had called on the government to provide leadership to state authorities in charge of Aboriginal affairs to promote equality between black and white Australians. He also pointed to the inconsistencies between Australia's international defence of human rights and the degrading circumstances of Aboriginal people throughout the country. In 1951, following Hasluck's appointment as Minister for Territories, state authorities met at the Native Welfare Conference and adopted assimilation as official policy. Hasluck told federal parliament that over the course of time, all Aboriginal people of full and mixed descent would be expected to 'live like white Australians do'. He also explained that assimilation did not mean the suppression of Aboriginal culture; rather that 'cultural adjustment' would occur over the course of generations.

However, as historian Richard Broome observes, in practice the assimilation policy became a crude attempt to 'change Aborigines into Europeans with black skins'. The underlying goal of a homogeneous Australian society was encapsulated in government propaganda depicting freshly scrubbed Aboriginal children being trained in various tasks by white teachers. It was also made clear from the amended definition of assimilation, adopted at the 1961 Native Welfare Conference. All Aboriginal people of full and mixed descent were expected to 'attain the same manner of living as other Australians', and to observe 'the same customs' and be 'influenced by the same beliefs, hopes and loyalties' as white Australians. In 1965, however, the definition was again amended to include the element of choice for Aboriginal people. By this time, there was a movement towards greater racial tolerance, assisted by the arrival in Australia of large numbers of European immigrants, and by student protests against apartheid in South Africa, and the media's growing interest in Aboriginal affairs.

What effects did assimilation policies have on Aboriginal women? At first glance, the short-term effects seem to have been positive. The allocation of resources in areas such as health and housing led to improvements in diet, earlier menstruation, increased maternal fertility, and longer childbearing spans. The Aboriginal population grew dramatically from the 1950s; this was at least partly the result of better material conditions created after the war. But the growth in the birthrate may also have been related to a desire on the part of Aboriginal people to build up their communities to replace those taken by the state over previous decades. In Indigenous communities it was socially acceptable for women to have children fathered by more than one man, and many women had a series of male partners throughout their lives. Overall, the social and cultural upheaval associated with the movement of Aboriginal people from reserves to towns and cities created new pressures for Aboriginal women.

The move to towns brought women under increasing scrutiny from authorities who made regular inspections of their homes and assessed them according to white middle-class standards of housekeeping. The surveillance of personal and sexual relations, hygiene and childrearing became very intrusive, yet it did not take into account the lack of amenities in many areas. Aboriginal mothers were instructed on how to care for their babies using the 1950s model of strict routines and Western hygiene products, but in parts of the Northern Territory, for example, there was often no basic infrastructure such as running water to help them put the lesson into practice. There was greater pressure on Aboriginal women to conform to Western ideals of domesticity and parenting, yet they did not enjoy the same rights and freedoms as white women. Nor were their efforts rewarded. As one Aboriginal woman from the western New South Wales town of Bourke remarked in 1971: 'I bust my guts to make everything clean and the welfare come in and make me feel dirty'.

Kathy Northover suffered the consequences of failing to

conform to these ideals. Her husband left her with eight children, the youngest of whom was a baby. She coped for a limited time, living on child endowment and her father's invalid pension, until the authorities came and took her children to the Roelands mission in Western Australia. 'They took them all at once ... they said I had no visible means of support for me and my kids ...' It was not, she says, that she was a dirty woman: she always had a meal on the table for her children, and she kept the house as clean as possible. But she had few facilities and only odd items of furniture, including a table and stool, a cooler instead of a refrigerator, and a little Hoover washing machine: 'They didn't think that was good enough'. Kathy never really recovered from this separation from her children.

Jenny Grace's family also feared the welfare, and avoided it most of the time by staying on the move. As a child, Jenny travelled the Murray River between Renmark and Wellington in South Australia with her parents, Ngarrindjeri people, who trapped water rats for their skins and fished for Murray cod and other fish in season. The family lived in wurlies (makeshift shelters constructed of tree limbs and old wheat bags), and ate damper, ducks, swans, eggs and fish, and occasionally supplemented their diet with milk, cream or vegetables obtained from local farmers in exchange for fish or ducks. They kept a semi-permanent tin shack at Nildottie, to which they returned after each trip away trapping. Jenny attended several schools in the area, but she had no interest in her studies because they had no connection to her family's lifestyle. Above all, school reminded her that she was 'different'. If she had no money to buy her lunch, she would go without rather than bring food from home: she couldn't take damper or a piece of duck cooked in coals or anything similar because it was so different from other children's lunches. At recess and lunchtime she would stand around watching the other children play, and occasionally 'wagged' it: 'I only went to school because of threats of trouble from the welfare'.

One day, around 1960, the welfare did come, but Jenny 'took off' for the day. The authorities had established the family's whereabouts, and her father knew they were coming to talk, but,

The Struggle Continues

recalls Jenny, 'as soon as they mentioned welfare I was gone': 'We were happy living there, even though it was pretty basic. White people couldn't see it like that I don't think. They couldn't see how we could be happy like that'. The family did not live in a 'real' house until Jenny was about seventeen, when her father was offered a job at nearby Mannum making farm machinery.

Meanwhile, Indigenous women activists such as Pearl Gibbs and Faith Bandler were continuing the political struggle for Aboriginal rights. Pearl Gibbs had been a prominent figure in protest movements in New South Wales since the 1930s. In 1946, she and Bill Ferguson had established the Dubbo branch of the Australian Aborigines' League, the Melbourne-based organisation founded by William Cooper in 1933. In 1953 she became the organising secretary for a new body, the Council for Aboriginal Rights, and in the following year she was elected as the Aboriginal member of the Welfare Board, whose discriminatory attitudes she had previously attacked. Pearl remained on the Board for three years, but her ability to bring about significant change was limited by her exclusion from its real decision-making processes.

In 1956, Gibbs and Faith Bandler, the daughter of a South Sea Islander, established the Aboriginal Australian Fellowship. The Fellowship supported the campaign for civil rights, lobbied for the creation of scholarships, encouraged artists, and examined legislation and government agencies. As vice-president, Pearl Gibbs' organisational and communication skills helped to achieve a high Aboriginal attendance at the Sydney rally in 1957 which started the campaign to remove the discriminatory sections 51 and 127 of the Australian Constitution. Pearl's activism continued for another two decades. She established a hostel in Dubbo for Aboriginal hospital patients and their families in 1960, organised a Fellowship conference in 1965, attended other major conferences on Aboriginal issues until her health declined, and in the 1970s, lobbied the New South Wales government to enact land rights legislation.

The tenacity of Pearl Gibbs and other activists was vital, for in 1961 Aboriginal people were still subjected to restrictive legislation. In most states they were forbidden to drink alcohol, and in all except Victoria and New South Wales their freedom of movement, control of property, and freedom of association with Europeans were restricted. The Queensland and Western Australian governments still controlled Aboriginal marriages. In 1961, a Senate committee recommended that all Aboriginal people be given the vote in federal elections, and in the next few years new legislation removed most of the remaining restrictions on Indigenous people and granted them full citizenship rights. Aborigines living on reserves in the Northern Territory and Queensland, however, were still controlled by special Acts. In 1965, the 1897 Queensland Act was replaced with a new *Aborigines and Torres Strait Islander Act*, but it made little change to the lives of reserve dwellers whose movements, wages and property still remained under the control of reserve managers.

If Aboriginal people were still marginalised in domestic affairs, they were certainly expendable in international operations such as atomic bomb testing. Between 1952 and 1963, a series of British atomic tests were undertaken in the Monte Bello Islands, off the Western Australian coast, and Emu Field and Maralinga, both in the north-west of South Australia in traditional tribal lands. Aboriginal people were not consulted or informed about the use of their lands as a testing ground. Many of those living in the path of the radioactive clouds were barefooted, wore few or

Rainmaker

Alice Warrika Oldfield of the Kuyani people was born around 1885 on Callanna station, South Australia, and grew up on Millers Creek station where her parents worked. Alice married Sandy Dinta Oldfield, the last Ngamini rainmaker, and the couple lived and worked on stations on Strzelecki and the Birdsville Track. When Sandy died in 1964, Alice – a rainmaker in her own right – helped to keep the tradition alive. In the 1930s, she had organised the performance of the Wandji-Wandji corroboree at Stuart Creek, and she continued to make rain until she reached her mid-eighties, by which time she was almost totally blind.

The Struggle Continues

no clothes, and gathered their food and water in the open. A number of them suffered severe illness as a result of the radioactive fallout from the explosions. In 1985, a Royal Commission into the tests conceded that Aboriginal people in the Emu Field area had experienced the 'black mist' (fallout), and that it may have made some people 'temporarily ill', but it claimed to have received no evidence of any permanent illnesses or disfigurement among Aboriginal people. Part of the problem was a lack of medical records: a study commissioned in 1981 to examine, among other things, the long-term effects of bomb testing on Aboriginal cancer rates discovered that there were virtually no records for the north-west of South Australia for the period of the bomb trials. There were also problems relating to Aboriginal custom, including the practice of not mentioning the names of dead people.

Edie Milpuddie's story is perhaps the best documented example of the impact of the bomb trials on Aboriginal women. The Milpuddies were nomadic people, living in the north of South Australia near the Ernabella mission station. In May 1957, Charlie and Edie Milpuddie and their two small children travelled south, following the water holes towards Ooldea where they were to visit relatives. Their journey took them directly into the path of a crater at Marcoo, near Maralinga, where an atomic bomb had been exploded seven months earlier. They spent the night near the crater, lighting a fire and dining on a kangaroo that Charlie had killed. The next morning they were discovered by military officers who put them under showers to remove any contaminated material. This itself was a frightening experience: the Milpuddies had never seen a motor car, let alone a shower. The family was then loaded into a Land Rover with their dogs, and driven south to Yalata.

During the Royal Commission in 1985, Edie described through an interpreter the fate that befell her after the bomb trials. At the time the family was discovered at the Marcoo crater, she was pregnant. When the family was removed to Yalata, she gave birth out bush to a child who was dead. She was convinced that the death of her child was related to the 'poison' she was exposed to at Marcoo. Edie's next child, a boy named Allan who was born in 1961, died of a brain tumour when he was two, and a daughter, born after Allan, was very premature, weighing only one or two pounds at birth. Rosie, one of the two children who were with Edie at Marcoo, herself lost a child in 1973. Edie's husband, Charlie, died at Yalata the following year.

The anecdotal evidence of Lallie Lennon is also disquieting. At the time of the Emu Field tests, Lallie was married with three children, and living near Mabel Creek station where her husband Stan was doing fencing work. She was frightened to see the trucks carrying soldiers and equipment travelling through the area, and mystified by the huge mushroom cloud hovering over the area after the bomb was detonated, but her anxiety did not really start until about three weeks later. She was looking around for a tree containing sugar to suck, and found it covered in a fine black dust; when she was warned the substance could be poisonous, she became scared. Shortly after, she remembers, 'the kids started getting sick – you know vomiting and rash ... I sort of felt sickish you know and the kids were vomiting – all that'. Then the whole family developed dysentery and two of her daughters were having fits. Lallie's own symptoms persisted to some degree for decades afterwards.

One event that provided a powerful stimulus for change in the treatment of Indigenous people was the Freedom Ride of February 1965. A group of Sydney University students led by Charles Perkins and Jim Spigelman went on a bus tour through northern New South Wales to highlight the discrimination against Aborigines in that area. They encountered hostility from whites in the towns of Walgett and Moree, both of which had large Aboriginal populations. During a confrontation in Walgett, where the RSL club banned Aboriginal membership, a crowd of European residents scattered when an Aboriginal woman made an angry speech, identifying local white men who went regularly to the Aborigines' camp to have sex with young Aboriginal girls. In Moree, where Aboriginal children were denied entry to the swimming pool, the Freedom Riders confronted the management of the pool; after several hours of protesting, a group of Aboriginal children was allowed in. The students' actions – consciously modelled on features of the American civil rights movement – attracted national media attention, and led to some behavioural changes in the towns.

In May 1967, 90.77 per cent of Australians voted in favour of referendum proposals that Aboriginal people be included in the census count and that the Commonwealth government be given power to legislate on their behalf. This was an extraordinary result for a country with a tradition of rejecting referendum proposals, and it came to be seen as a high point in co-operation between Indigenous and non-Indigenous Australians. Faith Bandler, then a leading member of the Federal Council for the Advancement of Aborigines and Torres Strait Islanders (FCAATSI), an organisation formed in 1958 to fight for constitutional reform and equal citizenship rights, described the result as 'the greatest victory the Aborigines have had or ever will have'. Bandler believed it 'would solve many problems' because of the government funding that would flow from it. Pat O'Shane, Australia's first Aboriginal woman barrister and now a prominent New South Wales magistrate, recalled her feeling of exhilaration on hearing the result: 'I thought that it was really going to sweep away the past ... I think probably to one degree or another we all felt that'.

The symbolic importance attributed to the result by Bandler, O'Shane and many others was a natural response after years of struggle for civil rights. But as historians Bain Attwood and Andrew Markus have shown, the referendum has been widely misinterpreted, with many people wrongly assuming that it gave Aborigines the vote and citizenship rights (which they had been given earlier). It has been invested with a significance out of proportion to its original aim. The Holt government conceived the referendum as a means of demonstrating – to the outside world in particular – that Australia did not discriminate against Aboriginal people. Nevertheless, as Pat O'Shane pointed out, it made a significant psychological difference to the way Aboriginal people now operated. Despite the obstacles that remained, the referendum result gave them courage 'to fight other fights, wage other campaigns'.

A Wealth of Women

In practice, discrimination against Indigenous people in their daily lives remained undiminished. Lillian Holt recalled the 1960s as 'heady times', especially after the 1967 referendum. She was the first Aboriginal person to work at the ABC in Queensland, starting there in 1962 at the age of seventeen. She felt, on the one hand, that her opportunities were limitless. Yet it was during that decade that her awareness of her 'difference' began to develop. She was excluded from the 'surfie' scene because she did not fit the 'surfie girl' stereotype of blonde hair, blue eyes, and (suntanned) white skin, and remembers feeling like a stranger in her own land. For Evelyn Scott, who would later become chairperson of the Council for Aboriginal Reconciliation, the 1960s also marked her first conscious experience of blatant racism. In 1963, aged twenty-eight, she was prevented from trying on the wedding dress that she liked. 'In those days', she recalled, 'Aboriginal people weren't to be seen shopping in such places – the assumption being that we couldn't afford such dresses'. She ended up being married in a dress that she did not really like, and later cut it up for garments for her small daughters.

Glenyse Ward, a teenager in the mid-1960s, saw no evidence of attitudinal change in her situation. At the age of one, Glenyse was taken from her mother who was deemed unfit to care for her, and placed first in a Perth orphanage, and then, when she was three, in the St Francis Xavier Native Mission at Wandering Brook, eighty miles from Perth. She received an elementary education, and in 1965, aged sixteen, she was sent to work in the home of wealthy farmers, the Bigelows. Her first insight into the life of virtual slavery she was to lead came when her boss served tea into cups and saucers for the family, and then poured Glenyse's tea into an old tin mug. When Glenyse asked politely if she, too, could have a cup and saucer, her enraged mistress told her that she was her 'dark servant' and that she was to obey her orders. Later, Glenyse was taken to her 'bedroom', a room she had hoped would resemble some of the others in the beautiful house. It turned out to be a garage – feebly lit with a burner and furnished with an old wooden bed. Glenyse made the mistake of asking whether the dirty room was indeed for her, only to be told again

The Struggle Continues

that she was Mrs Bigelow's 'dark servant', and that this was to be her bedroom while she worked for her.

Discrimination also remained entrenched in schools. In the mid-1970s, Sheryl Rose was a sixteen-year-old schoolgirl attending Walgett High School. Walgett had achieved notoriety during the Freedom Ride of 1965, and a decade later racism was still prevalent among the town's white population. Sheryl noted the tendency for teachers to categorise Aboriginal pupils as 'slow learners' and to put less effort into helping them reach their potential than they did with white children. The aptitude of some Aboriginal children for drawing was given little recognition by white teachers because they assumed that it was a natural ability, only to be expected of Aboriginal people. Sheryl Rose hoped eventually to study law, to enable her to fight for her people 'with words'.

Jackie Huggins, now a prominent activist and historian, experienced similar discrimination at school. In Year 10, aged fifteen, she met the senior mistress at her Brisbane school to discuss future educational and vocational options. When she said she would like to complete Year 12, the teacher dismissed her intentions with a derogatory reference to her Aboriginality. Jackie had neither the words nor the courage to challenge her. She left school, and after a decade spent working first for the ABC and then the public service, she renewed her determination to study, and enrolled in an arts course at the University of Queensland. There she started to receive high distinctions, and realised that she was 'not dumb or biologically mentally inferior' to non-Aboriginal people. Jackie earned an honours degree in History and Women's Studies, and then went on to complete a Diploma of Education.

A major focus for Aboriginal protest from the 1960s was the movement for land rights. Primary industries such as wool, wheat and beef had long made demands upon the land, and discoveries of oil, iron ore, bauxite and uranium during the 1960s led to further exploitation which encroached on traditional Aboriginal communities. This was intolerable for Aboriginal people, not merely because they were prior owners of the land, but because the spiritual associations of the land made it essential for the preservation of their culture. In August 1963, the Yirrkala people from Arnhem Land presented a bark petition to the House of Representatives, opposing plans by the bauxite mining company, Nabalco, to use their traditional lands on the Gove Peninsula. Eight years later, the Northern Territory Supreme Court found that while the Yirrkala people had proven their spiritual relationship with the land, it could not provide the basis for compensation under Australian law.

In August 1966, the Gurindji people walked off Wave Hill pastoral station in the Northern Territory, demanding equal pay and better working conditions; Wave Hill was leased by the British company, the Vestey Corporation. Later, they sent a petition to the governor-general, asking for the land around Watties Creek. However, the government offered no excision; its only concession was to provide for a township in the Wave Hill area, but away from Wattie Creek. It would be another decade before the mechanism for granting land rights was established, and then only in the Northern Territory. The land rights issue held as much importance for Aboriginal women as for men, but later, the idea that it was 'men's business' began to prevail, largely as a result of the influence of white men in the Land Councils set up after 1976. However, in New South Wales, South Australia and Victoria, women played a significant role in negotiations at the grassroots level.

The frustration arising from the continuing denial of Aboriginal rights found expression in the erection of an Aboriginal tent embassy on the lawns outside Parliament House on Australia Day 1972. The action was prompted by Prime Minister William McMahon's announcement of a general purpose lease for Aboriginal people that denied them any form of land rights, but it was also the broader culmination of decades of struggle against discrimination and injustice. Several attempts throughout 1972 to pull the embassy down sparked violent clashes between police and Aboriginal supporters, and attracted embarassing publicity for the government. The leader of the federal opposition, Gough Whitlam, visited the embassy and made it clear that his party was sympathetic to Aboriginal claims regarding land rights and recognition of sacred sites, and pledged to restore self-determination to Aboriginal people.

Shirley Smith, also known as Mum Shirl, who earned recognition for her work among Aboriginal prisoners in institutions, remembers the erection of the tent embassy and its aftermath as a politicising event. Much of the political theory, she confesses, was 'beyond' her, but she was proud of the young activists – 'some of the best Black radical brains in the country' – who led the movement. When she heard that the embassy had been pulled down, and that young Aborigines were organising buses to go to Canberra to rebuild it, she gathered a group of children and went with them: 'I knew this would be a marvellous moment in history and I didn't want any Black kids to miss it'.

What she saw there, however, came as a shock. Hundreds of police wearing boots came running and began beating the black women who had joined hands and were standing in a big circle around the tent – punching them and knocking them to the ground. Shirley could hardly believe that such violence was taking place right outside Parliament House, 'that great white building where ... the country is governed', and in the presence of television cameras. Later she campaigned actively for the election of the Whitlam Labor government.

The years of the Whitlam government (1972–1975) saw massive spending on Aboriginal affairs. A Ministry of Aboriginal Affairs was established, a National Economic Strategy for Aborigines (NESA) introduced, and a range of financial and training programs devised to enable Aboriginal people to enter the paid workforce. Women's opportunities were greatly enhanced by programs such as the Aboriginal Health Worker Program which provided training through an apprenticeship system of teaching. Trainees received practical instruction working alongside nursing sisters, and attended short courses at training centres. As a result of this scheme, many Aboriginal women were trained successfully as health workers and some went on to establish their own health centres. The 1970s also witnessed a dramatic growth of Aboriginal organisations and pride in Aboriginal culture. Aboriginal literature, dance and theatre, distinguished by a militant rejection of European ways, flourished during this period; and a range of community welfare projects initiated by Aboriginal people were established in major cities and regional centres.

The reassertion of Aboriginal identity was reflected in the relationship between Aboriginal and non-Aboriginal women. By the mid-1970s, when the women's movement was in full swing, questions were starting to be asked about its relevance for Aboriginal women. In 1976, Pat O'Shane called on women involved in the movement to consider whether their aims were identical to those of black women. It seemed to her that for the majority of those women the fight was against sexism, whereas medical, housing, education, employment and legal statistics showed clearly that for Aboriginal women the major fight was against racism. 'Sexist attitudes did not wipe out tribes of our people, sexist attitudes are not slowly killing our people today – racism did, and continues to do so!' Moreover, some of the worst perpetrators of that racism were white women. As Indigenous historian Aileen Moreton-Robinson rightly points out: 'Acts of humiliation and cruelty by white women pervade Indigenous women's life writings'. These women seldom received an adequate diet, their partial wages were rarely paid, and they were beaten frequently by their white mistresses.

Agnes Williams observed of her life as a domestic servant in the 1930s: 'You know, the women were worse than the men in the way in which they treated you'. She recalled one occasion when her mistress 'scrubbed' her face with a steelo pad as punishment for not cleaning the silver properly, leaving her with a permanent scar. As Jackie Huggins wrote in 1990, white women played major roles in the implementation of oppressive policies in their capacities as welfare workers, institution staff, teachers and adoptive/foster mothers. Too often it had been white women 'responsible for taking Black children from their mothers' arms and placing them in the care of other white women who often abused them'. This issue is just as pertinent today. In the late 1990s, Jackie wrote of her feelings of marginality at women's

The Struggle Continues

A mother's pain

In the early 1960s, Olive Kennedy, a young Aboriginal woman of mixed descent, had recently married and was living in Melbourne. One day some parcels arrived, filled with dresses of the type worn by Aboriginal girls on missions. When she shook the dresses, five pound and ten pound notes dropped out. The parcels were addressed to Kathleen Kennedy, the name her mother had called her. Olive was puzzled. In 1947, aged three, she had been taken from her mother Maudie at the Phillip Creek mission north of Tennant Creek, along with seventeen other children. She was given the name Olive, and had always believed the story told her by the missionaries who raised her at the Retta Dixon home in Darwin: that her Aboriginal mother had abandoned her because she no longer wanted her.

She decided to look for her mother, but was advised against it by a welfare agent who told her she would find an old woman living in a squalid humpy with camp dogs. Undeterred, she made the trip to Warrabri, near Tennant Creek, where she was welcomed with immense joy and grief by her mother Maudie and a large extended family. Later, Olive took Lorna Cubillo, now well known as a member of the 'stolen generation', who had been taken from Phillip Creek on the same day, back to see her family. The two women were shocked and distressed to find mothers inflicting terrible wounds on their heads with shovels and other weapons to demonstrate their sorrow for what had happened.

studies conferences and feminist debates dominated by white women, and her yearning on those occasions for the 'solidarity and group nature of Aboriginal society and sisterhood'. The new direction taken by Aboriginal women, she wrote, would entail forming alliances with white women on some issues and acknowledging their differences on others.

One issue that was clearly of more concern to Aboriginal women than their white counterparts was the high incidence of Aboriginal deaths in custody. Women were not only at the forefront of the struggle to bring attention to the deaths in custody of their male relatives, but were themselves over-criminalised. In 1987 the Hawke government announced a Royal Commission headed by Justice James Muirhead to investigate the large number of Aboriginal deaths in custody since 1983. After inquiring into the circumstances of over one hundred deaths, Muirhead produced an interim report recommending changes to a range of sentencing, police and prison procedures. The final report into Aboriginal deaths in custody, completed in April 1991 and based on the case reports of ninety-nine deaths, found that the deaths were not the result of deliberate violence by police or prison officers, but that they stemmed from the disempowerment of Aboriginal people and the denial of their right to self-determination.

The effect on women of the deaths in custody of their male relatives attracted some publicity in 1992, when Alice Dixon, the mother of Kingsley Dixon who had died in an Adelaide jail, hanged herself as her son had done. Yet the related issue of Aboriginal women in custody remained largely unexamined. For decades women themselves had been imprisoned in disproportionate numbers for minor offences. Studies in the 1970s showed high numbers of Aboriginal women incarcerated for drunkenness and disorderly conduct, abusive language, vagrancy, and non-payment of fines; and prison census statistics for the years 1983–86 showed that the rate of imprisonment of Aboriginal women was constant over that period at sixteen times that of non-Aboriginal women.

Occasionally, efforts to improve the health and well-being of Aboriginal women were impeded by opposition within the Aboriginal community. Faith Thomas, an Indigenous woman who earned recognition as a cricketer for Australia, was also a trained nurse who worked among Aboriginal women in South Australia. She became convinced of the necessity for family planning when she observed the declining health of women who had had multiple pregnancies. She consulted experts at the family planning clinic at Adelaide hospital and managed to raise some money, but she remembers being criticised by those who saw such attempts

The Struggle Continues

to regulate women's reproduction as 'genocide'. Faith, however, was undeterred: 'It's racial genocide when a woman's pregnant every bloody year and she dies and what happens to her eight or nine kids?'

One contentious issue affecting all Aboriginal people, which developed in the 1980s and remains unresolved to date, was the call for a treaty between Aboriginal and non-Aboriginal Australians covering land rights, compensation, recognition of prior ownership, Aboriginal law, languages and sacred sites. First suggested in 1979, the matter was resurrected in 1987 by Charles Perkins, Galarrwuy Yunupingu (head of the Northern Land Council) and others. In June 1988, at the Barunga Festival in the Northern Territory, Yunupingu presented Prime Minister Bob Hawke with the Barunga Statement – a declaration of Aboriginal claims which sought to guide the government's thinking about a treaty. Hawke first promised a treaty by 1990; when that was not fulfilled, he named the centenary of Federation in 2001 as the likely occasion for a treaty.

The deaths in custody issue and the call for a treaty compounded the controversy surrounding the bicentenary of European settlement in 1988; inevitably the planned celebrations were seen by Indigenous people as insulting and divisive. The controversy reached a climax in January 1988. For months activists had planned a large protest rally in Sydney, and their plans attracted publicity when Oodgeroo Noonuccal (Kath Walker) returned her MBE in a personal protest. On 26 January in Sydney, up to 50,000 people rallied behind their banners bearing the slogan: 'White Australia has a Black History – Don't Celebrate 88'. Jackie Huggins recalled the day of the march as a 'magical highlight' of her life: 'I woke up with bursting emotions, as if I were standing on the shore the day Phillip and the "First Fleet" arrived …'

Alana Harris also remembered the march as a momentous event. She drove from Canberra to Sydney with her sister and cousin, and went first to La Perouse where thousands of protesters were converging. She found it gratifying to see non-Aboriginal people supporting the Aboriginal campers by supplying food, clothing and blankets. Some speakers persisted in referring to whites 'as if they were the enemy', but usually they were shouted down because the demonstrators appreciated the support they were receiving. On the morning of 26 January, the marchers gathered at Redfern Oval before moving on to Belmore Park in central Sydney; Harris was cheered to find a sea of Aboriginal faces, and the colours of red, black and yellow everywhere. Finally, they gathered in Hyde Park, where Galarrwuy delivered a poignant message: 'Australia's too old to celebrate birthdays'.

It was not until the 1990s, however, that the process of reconciling Indigenous and non-Indigenous Australians began to gather momentum. It began in 1991 with the establishment of the Council for Aboriginal Reconciliation, and received a major boost in June 1992 when the High Court recognised the rights of the Mer Islanders, including 'Eddie' Mabo, to native title, thereby overturning the concept of *terra nullius*. A few months later, Labor Prime Minister Paul Keating delivered a powerful manifesto during a speech in Sydney's Redfern Park: 'We took the children from their mothers. We practised discrimination and exclusion. It was our ignorance and our prejudice. And our failure to imagine these things being done to us'. The *Mabo* judgment, Keating argued, should be viewed as a starting point for reconciliation between Aboriginal and non-Aboriginal people. There was nothing to lose, and everything to gain, by recognising historical truth and extending social justice to Indigenous Australians. Keating concluded his speech by expressing confidence that reconciliation would be achieved in the 1990s.

However, Keating's prediction was not fulfilled. In 1996, the land rights issue was given further impetus by a High Court judgment which found that the native title to the Wik people's traditional land on Cape York peninsula had not been extinguished, despite the operation of pastoral leases in the area. But undoubtedly the most important event was the publication in 1997 of *Bringing Them Home*: the report by the Human Rights and Equal Opportunity Commission which documented the systematic removal from their families of thousands of Aboriginal children of mixed descent. As a result of its publication and the

The Struggle Continues

ensuing debate over its integrity, the issue of Aboriginal child removal has been brought to the foreground of public awareness. One of the most important recommendations of the report was that the Australian government offer a formal apology to the 'stolen generation' and their families.

In early 2001, there was still a huge groundswell of support in Australia for the reconciliation process. The need to maintain the momentum in order to bridge the gap between black and white Australians is compelling. In the words of Mary Darkie, a young Aboriginal woman who grew up in a remote community in the Great Sandy Desert in the Kimberley region of Western Australia: 'Reconciliation … means letting go of old ideas that all white-skinned people are the same or all black-skinned people are the same … [It] also means letting go of anger, hurt and blaming … We cannot forget the past but letting go of anger and hurt allows us to move forward'.

Snapshot

INVENTIONS

1832	rudimentary washing machines appear, agitating devices in a barrel or cradle
1841	the first gas lighting
1856	American enclosed cooking stoves appear
1860	kerosene lamps appear
1868	electric light demonstrated, Sydney; all cities have electric street lights by the 1880s
1873	first gas cooker in Australia
1887	gas is first used to heat bathwater
1911	a third of Sydney's new houses have gas cookers
1920s	many houses have electricity, used mainly for lighting, but appliances like irons and vacuum cleaners become popular with the well-to-do

Snapshot

1946 Hills Hoist clothes line

1950s electrical appliances become widespread: stoves, refrigerators, vacuum cleaners, heaters, sewing machines, kettles, irons, toasters and so on

- many families can afford a car

- synthetic fabrics are cheaper and easier to use

- disposable sanitary pads and tampons become popular

- disposable nappies appear

1970s dishwashers and microwave ovens appear

chapter eleven

Today

Since 1975, Australian women have continued to gain political and legal rights, as equal opportunity and affirmative action were legalised, and women in senior positions in the public service made headway in translating feminist ideas into policy. More women have entered employment and some have risen to senior positions: Australia has had female premiers, governors, political leaders, judges, business executives, and leaders in peace and environment movements. Women have had more importance in academia, both as lecturers and as subjects for study, and have contributed greatly to the arts. Welfare benefits, equal pay, assistance for victims, and legislation against violence, discrimination and sexual harassment have helped women suffering from the age-old problems of poverty and violence. Women have more independence and more options in their lives.

This is particularly noticeable in sport. All over the country, women play more sport, and women's teams have greater status than before with their victories celebrated – the Hockeyroos were acknowledged as the most successful team in Australian history. The opening event of the 2000 Olympic Games in Sydney particularly celebrated women's contribution to sport in Australia, probably the first such event in the country where white women and Aboriginal people had more prominence than white men. There were few complaints.

A new dimension has been added to Australian womanhood with the arrival of many immigrants from Asia and other non-European countries, and the acceptance of other cultures. Previously, newcomers were expected to assimilate into Australian society, but in the 1970s Australia adopted the policy of multiculturalism and the government outlawed racial discrimination. People's attitudes are not so easily changed, however, and many migrant women experienced racism and prejudice. Their own community leaders were predominantly men; and as migrant women had found in the 1950s and 1960s, employment was mainly confined to low-paying and low-status jobs, with evidence emerging in the 1980s about women from Asian backgrounds in particular working in appalling conditions.

Migrant women have been active in self-help organisations. As early as 1975, Koula Aslanidis and some friends began a women's radio program on Greek community radio in Adelaide. Some men objected and tried to stop them, which made Koula angry; she managed to keep the program going, and started to work voluntarily at three places, the women's information switchboard, health centre and community centre, where she initiated activities for women. Since then there have been many more such groups, such as the Vietnamese Women's Association in New South Wales. Women of ethnic origin have made their mark in other areas: for example, Franca Arena became the first female parliamentarian from a non-English speaking background.

In chapter two a typical Victorian woman's life was followed from birth to death. This was considerably simpler to reconstruct than it is for a contemporary Australian woman, for 150 years later there is much more variety. Going by statistics, our current typical Australian woman was born in this country, as are three-quarters of Australia's women, and called Jessica, the most popular name of the 1990s. She probably has British forebears, but she could belong to an Aboriginal, European, Asian, African or American family. Her parents are more likely to be married than not, but her mother may have no permanent partner. All these backgrounds are now more acceptable. Jessica probably has one or at most two siblings, and if she has a brother, she is treated reasonably equally with him. But she does far more to help

You don't have to be young to achieve

Venie Holmgren of Western Australia climbed her first mountain at fifty, and her last, Jingera Rock, at seventy. After her husband died, she spent three years wandering about Australia alone, then settled on the New South Wales coast, building a house herself. She started writing, and has published three volumes of poetry and a poetry CD. Venie has read her poems at peace and environment rallies, poetry festivals and in prisons. Twice she has been arrested for taking part in campaigns to save old growth forests, and she still has an unpaid fine from one arrest. Her latest achievement is to become 'modestly' computer literate.

Frances Donnelly had a successful career as housekeeper at Dubbo Base Hospital, then after retiring, volunteered to help at a hostel for disabled children. This developed into total care of the sixteen or so children, twenty-four hours a day – even when they were at school, Frances was making cakes, sewing clothes or preserving fruit for them. Determined to give the children all opportunities possible, she organised outings and birthday cakes, and provided endless care and love. She was loved and admired by the whole community, and when she finally retired – again – aged seventy-eight, she was awarded the British Empire Medal. She was particularly fond of one disabled boy, and as he was too old for the hostel she cared for him in her home until shortly before her death in 1986, aged eighty-eight.

For decades, Vida Humphries of South Australia helped her husband run a dairy and deliver milk. In old age she joined an Elderly Citizens Club; at ninety-six she won a trophy for indoor bowls, and at ninety-nine she could still recite word perfectly the poem The Wreck of the Hesperus *which she had learnt at school.*

around the home – though neither does much, and she is likely to be a messy teenager. (One Australian girl lost her bicycle, and found it three months later in her own bedroom.)

Jessica most likely lives with both parents until she is at least fifteen, along with three-quarters of Australia's children, though she could grow up in a single-parent household, usually headed by her mother. She probably lives in a town and attends a state co-educational school, though about 30 per cent of girls go to private schools. Whatever system she is part of, she can study any subject, with sexual education compulsory. It will not be surprising if she loses her virginity in her teens, and experiments with alcohol and drugs, probably marijuana rather than hard drugs. Serious dangers of teen years, such as suicide and anorexia, family crises or abuse which result in girls leaving home, can be disastrous but affect a minority only. Unlike her Victorian forebears, Jessica will have access to the world via television, films, magazines and the internet, and there will not be so much pressure to conform to some uniform feminine ideal.

In 1972 only a quarter of Australian girls finished Year 12, but this figure has soared to about 85 per cent, with girls now outscoring boys in leaving results. So Jessica finishes school, then has a wide choice of careers – theoretically little is barred to

Dinner with the Queen

All through her life Evelyn Macintyre was involved with the CWA, rising to become the Queensland state president. Her kindness and friendliness were greatly valued, as were her skills at smoothing over difficult situations. As president, she was asked to dine aboard the Britannia with the Queen and Prince Philip, and told her husband Kenneth that he must come too. He was not the type to enjoy such an occasion, and said he could not possibly go as he had no appropriate suit. Evie's neighbour told her there was a good three-piece dinner suit in the local St Vincent de Paul shop for $3, so Evie bought it, it fitted exactly, and off they drove to the wharf in Evie's little Mini to dine with the Queen.

women, though some careers are difficult to enter, partly at least due to stiff entrance requirements which affect both sexes. She could go to university or some other training institution: there are more female than male students at universities, and almost as many at TAFE colleges. Though some women enter careers their grandmothers never imagined, Jessica probably joins the vast majority of women who work in traditional female areas – nursing, teaching, office work, shop work, hospitality and manufacturing – which shows either that this is what women like doing, or that their choices and opportunities are still restricted in practice.

Women have had equal pay since 1975, but Jessica, as our average woman, faces earning about two-thirds of the average male wage, or 81 per cent if full-time workers only are compared. This is partly because of the type of job she is doing, and partly because she will probably not be promoted at the same rate as a man. Some women do not want promotion, finding satisfaction from other areas, for example starting their own small businesses or in family life. But those who do can still find it difficult: they are not encouraged; they feel they have to be twice as good as a man to get anywhere; their male colleagues sometimes bully them if they are promoted; and the 'glass ceiling' stops further promotion. Another problem is that, increasingly, women's jobs are casual or part-time, with disadvantages of less or no security, superannuation or holiday pay.

Though Jessica could be unemployed, probably, like the majority of young women, she does find a job, and enjoys a reasonable wage. She probably has a series of partners and lives away from home, though this is expensive and she might move back home for a while. She might remain single, like 23 per cent of Australian women, a great change from the 5 per cent of the 1960s. Single women are no longer looked down on, but are sometimes envied by their married colleagues, with their uninterrupted careers, independence and sole incomes.

Jessica could be lesbian, as is a small number of Australian women, but she is probably heterosexual, and is most likely to marry, along with most of her peer group – though not until she

A Wealth of Women

is in her late twenties. She might have a traditional white wedding in a church, or she might be married on top of a mountain, in a garden or on a beach – as in so many areas, there is a wide choice. She is unlikely to be a virgin when she marries, and her groom no longer expects this. There is a strong chance that she will continue to use her maiden name. She has high expectations of marriage; there is less tolerance of cruelty, neglect and lack of support than in previous years.

Unless she is unlucky, Jessica has reliable contraception, mostly the Pill, and can choose when and how many children to have. She probably does have children, one or perhaps two – the average is under two – though by the 1990s, 20 per cent of Australia's women have none. If Jessica becomes pregnant, good ante-natal care and childbirth classes are available, and though homebirths have become more popular, she probably gives birth in a hospital, with her partner present. Both she and her baby are almost certain to survive childbirth. Jessica is encouraged to get up within a few hours of the birth and breastfeed her baby on demand, and spends only a few days in hospital. She probably continues to breastfeed her baby for six months, like half Australia's mothers. Like her mother she can buy a book of advice on childrearing, possibly written by an Australian. Most such books are not nearly as prescriptive as earlier books, but help parents to make their own decisions about their babies, and accept that babies and parents are never perfect.

Jessica will have some maternity leave, probably unpaid. When this is over, she can resign and care for her child at home, or do a job part-time, or put the baby in childcare and continue her career. Whatever she does, there can be problems. If she resumes her career, childcare is costly, and the work load with a career, a home and children exhausting; if she stays at home she has no income, is looked down on by many as a 'housewife', and later finds it impossible or at best challenging to resume her interrupted career, losing seniority, experience and status.

Probably Jessica does go back to employment, as the majority of married women do, since to live comfortably, most families now need two incomes. Jessica might wait until her child or children are at school, but even so, returning to employment is likely to be hard, for neither governments nor the labour market has done much to encourage mothers, particularly in today's tough atmosphere of economic rationalism. There is a tendency to assume that employees are unattached single people, most places of employment are not child-friendly, and cuts to childcare subsidies have not helped.

There is more chance that Jessica will become divorced, with almost half of Australia's marriages ending this way. Most do so in the first few years, when children are less likely to be involved. This is not such a huge change as it appears, for in earlier days marriages were often broken by death, or by the husband deserting his wife or working away from home – in Western Australia, on the 1901 census night, 28 per cent of husbands were not living with their wives. At that time, just under half of Australia's married couples would still have been together after thirty years; in the 1990s the figure was not a great deal smaller.

Within marriage there can be problems. Though there is help for women suffering domestic violence, this still occurs. A far less serious but more common situation is the husband not helping with domestic chores. Like most Australians, Jessica and her partner say they believe that housework should be shared, but surveys in 1992 and 1997 showed this is not so, and Jessica does considerably more domestic work than her partner.

Girls living at home do an average of seven hours' domestic activity a week; when they move into a flat this rises to about twelve; when women marry, it zooms to twenty-four. The figures for males are: boys at home, two hours; in a flat, six to seven; married, fifteen. This work includes everything in, around and for the home: cooking, laundry, housework, shopping, gardening, car care and maintenance. It is still mainly divided by sex, with women doing the inside work like cooking, laundry and cleaning, and men the maintenance. Income, education and occupation have little influence on how much housework a person does. The main factors are gender, age and to some extent whether or not the person is employed: but when a married woman enters employment, her unpaid work does not drop much, while her husband's does not increase much at all.

When Jessica has a baby her domestic work soars again, to sixty hours a week, while her husband's share increases only slightly. Her domestic work will continue to be at least double his until the children leave home. The only time a man's domestic work increases dramatically is when he is widowed. Overall, domestic work is split between women and men in a ratio of 70:30. Women do less domestic work than they used to, but not to the extent the technological revolution of the postwar years seemed to promise. Machines have helped, but they can do only so much, and though women now spend less time on chores, they spend more time on childcare and shopping, especially associated driving. Some, 20 per cent, cope with the double burden of home and job by employing a cleaner. Overall, the amount of time men and women spend in all work – employment, domestic work, voluntary work – is about the same, an average of 428 minutes a day for men and 435 minutes a day for women, though the authority on these figures, Michael Bittman, points out that much of what is classed for women as 'leisure' includes work, such as taking children to a swimming pool or ironing while watching TV, and that the more paid employment women do, the higher their overall workload is.

Time spent in cooking has decreased from the 1970s due to two new appliances, dishwashers and microwave ovens, and to buying more convenience foods and takeaways. Indeed, some women never cook at all, but live on takeaways and eating out. But most women still do cook, and Jessica has increased her repertoire to include not just traditional British meals like roast dinners, but a range of meals like stir-fries, pasta with various sauces, curries and Asian dishes, using the huge variety of ingredients now grown in or imported to Australia. Her housework is far easier than it was a hundred years ago, and with today's good health care system, Jessica is not so responsible for family doctoring. But it is still mostly she who cares for the sick and elderly, and keeps up family connections and social mechanisms – still in a sense God's police, as Caroline Chisholm wrote 150 years ago.

Jessica has half an hour less recreation each day than her part-

Today

ner, but even so she has four hours, far more than her great-grandmother would have done. She spends this in watching TV, talking, reading and sport, as well as social and community activities like visiting people, attending church, watching sport and voluntary work. So, like almost all Australian women, Jessica works hard in her life. She leaves her job at about sixty, and let us hope that she enjoys her twenty years of retirement until her death in her early eighties, seven or eight years later than her male equivalent. She probably dies of cancer or heart disease.

Using statistics to describe the life of Australian women highlights their similarities but hides their differences. These are certainly present, as this series of vignettes of contemporary women shows. They are not intended to be exactly representative but to give an indication of the variety of lifestyles and activities among Australian women, ranging from the old to the young.

Many women embody the spirit of earlier generations. An example is Anna Pope, a freelance historian, writer, singer, wife, and busy mother of two toddlers. Anna owes much of what she is today to past influences, a crucial figure in her early childhood being her granny, Freya Booth. The daughter of painter Hans Heysen and his wife Sallie, Freya was born in Adelaide in 1908. As she grew up she contributed to the family's domestic arrangements and helped to teach her two younger brothers. After her marriage to Edward Booth, she devoted herself to caring for him, their two sons and their large house and garden, as well as working for community facilities including the kindergarten, childcare centre and hospital. She did not seek fame for herself, but instead had the gift of inspiring all she touched, and Anna remembers her as the embodiment of selfless love, a home creator who encouraged confident individuality in those around her.

Freya taught and encouraged Anna in many things: singing, reading, enjoying games and puzzles, appreciating art and music. There was a strong focus on the domestic arts, especially cooking which became enjoyable and creative; she and Anna made butter by hand and cakes from scratch, and preserved fruit for years to come. Even if Anna did not continue to use the recipes and techniques, her granny's lessons made her a confident cook who knows that creating with love and care achieves the best results. Freya did not expect Anna to learn everything she had to teach her, but allowed her to develop her own interests. 'She had the gift of making those around her stronger, and of allowing them to be themselves. She created security and a strong sense of place in her home. She left behind her a legacy of love which has inspired so many of my actions, and has encouraged me to strive to be a better person.' Anna herself expects compromise from her partner and will not restrict herself to domesticity, but she strives to continue her granny's spirit by instilling in her own family and friends a similar sense of love, security and self-worth.

Edith Gilmour is still demonstrating her own spirit and beliefs. She was born in 1894 in a co-operative village settlement in South Australia, which her parents established after asking for advice from all round the world, receiving among the replies a letter from Karl Marx. Economic reasons and drought forced the settlement to close after six years, and Edith's family farmed in western New South Wales. She hated war after the only eligible young man in the neighbourhood, who had been working on the farm, was killed at Gallipoli.

Edith went to high school and trained as a teacher in Sydney, where her progressive landlady took her to anti-conscription rallies and informed her about the Russian revolution and other world affairs. Edith joined the peace movement, but lost touch after she was sent to country schools. After the atom bomb was

The National Pioneer Women's Hall of Fame

This Hall of Fame was the brainchild of Molly Clark of Old Andado Station near Alice Springs, who wanted to make up for the absence of women in the Stockmen's Hall of Fame. Molly launched her project in 1993, leasing an old courthouse in Alice Springs. She has built up a collection of many books and artefacts, and shows permanent displays and occasional exhibitions. Finance comes from membership fees, 'Molly's Bash' held annually, raffles, donations and some grants.

Today

dropped on Hiroshima she again became strongly involved. She has continued this work ever since, joining Save Our Sons in the Vietnam War, and taking part in rallies, marches and protests against, for example, French tests in the Pacific, and American military bases in Australia. 'My work has been mainly only supportive of those with initiative, ability and drive', she wrote. However, in 1984 her grey hairs meant media interviews during rallies for peace, 'and once, to my dismay, a TV interview, which I couldn't wriggle out of because of the cause of nuclear disarmament, which I believe means life or death to our planet'. In 2001 Edith is not so active, but still follows world events and presses information about peace on any visitor.

Margaret House and her husband Ashley run a property, 'Fortuna', near Aramac in central Queensland, but the seven year drought of the 1990s brought problems. Ashley had to earn cash for their survival by driving trucks, and Margaret ran the property with her youngest daughter Nina, and supervised Nina's lessons on the School of the Air. As the drought worsened, the cattle could only be kept alive by droving them along the stockroutes to get enough grass and water, and in 1996 Margaret set off with nine hundred head of cattle, helped by various family members.

With a team of horses, and a truck covered with a tarpaulin which was the 'food wagon', Margaret and her assistants covered about five hundred kilometres. They experienced several cattle 'rushes' (stampedes) at night during wild storms, lost the spare horses on several occasions and spent many hours tracking them down (the horses proved more trouble than the nine hundred cattle), pulled bogged cattle out of muddy creeks, and delivered and nurtured baby calves. Once a month Margaret went home to the station to collect mail, for business still had to be attended to, and bills paid. The following day, back on the stockroute, she would take the bills, a cheque book and writing pad from her saddle bag at the midday rest, and attend to the paper work, using the shade of a big Gidyea tree as 'the office'. After three months she returned home, having lost only one cow.

The area round Fortuna is part of a largely 'forgotten region' known as the Desert Uplands, which was becoming fragile and degraded by the long years of drought. The Aramac Landcare Group, tired of the area being regarded as a backwater, approached other local Landcare groups and under the leadership of another farming wife, Lesley Marshall, galvanised the locals into action and formed the Desert Uplands Build Up and Development Committee. Canberra and Brisbane provided funding, which the Group uses for conservation work such as fencing off endangered ecosystems, making low-interest loans to allow farmers to become more viable through enlarging their properties and diversifying, and a variety of training sessions and workshops – altogether a most successful program.

Slavka Galea of Innisfail says her life revolves around three Fs, Faith, Family and Friends, 'and I'm fortunate to be blessed with an abundant supply of all three'. One of her favourite activities is taking the Host to elderly parishioners in their homes, doing odd jobs for them and getting help if they need it. Having been born in Innisfail, she has many lifelong friends, and her brothers, children and grandchildren also live nearby.

In 2000 Slavka took part in the Jubilee Pilgrimage from Cardwell to Innisfail for all local Christians, with themes of forgiveness and freedom. Walking and travelling by coach was interspersed with celebrations of Mass, communal meals, tree-planting, meditation and prayer services. Slavka found the pilgrimage inspiring, particularly the comradeship and interaction with other parishes; an early morning Mass where 'you were very much aware of God's presence as we watched the Sun weaving its way through the trees and over the glistening water'; and listening to an article by Miriam-Rose Ungunmerr of Daly River about *dadirri*, 'inner, deep listening and quiet, still awareness'.

Judy Freeman grew up in Hobart, attended Catholic schools and would have loved to become a doctor, but that could not be considered as it was too expensive. So she worked as a stenographer, and at nineteen married and had two sons. In the early 1970s when her younger son was two, she and her husband divorced, a dreadful experience as she had to prove his adultery in court. Supporting mother's benefits had just been introduced, so

Today

Judy provided for the boys from this, helped out by house cleaning rather than office work, as she thought the boys had been through enough, and wanted to be there when they came home from school.

After several years she met another man and although Judy did not want to do so, they married, as this made it easier to get a loan for a house. Her ex-husband applied for custody of her older son, but Judy won the 'terrible' court case. At fourteen, the boy went to live with his father, and Judy put her younger son through university with her cleaning. Later her second partner went bankrupt, and Judy feels that whereas the men in her life have generally managed to come out on top, she has suffered by their actions and is left with nothing. But she is determined not to feel resentful, to get on with her life: 'I've lost everything but I'm not going to lose myself'.

Geraldine Boylan has a rural background in the Eyre Peninsula, and was strongly shaped by seeing her parents help many people, using 'a fair, just and common sense approach'. She married at nineteen, and had seven children in a short period, a steep learning curve in which she became well acquainted with survival, hard work, routine, organisation, management and humour. She and her husband fostered children as well – 'what was one or two more!'

Always passionately committed to rural people, in the 1970s Geraldine trained in family planning, then in social work, family therapy and counselling, working for four years in a women's shelter, where she saw the impact of violence and abuse – 'another steep learning curve!' She moved into employment as care-worker with a family counselling service at Wudinna, helping families affected by the rural crisis of drought and recession. Her job was to try to combat the depression, fear, hopelessness and tension which rose from financial pressure, resulting in marital problems, domestic violence, family breakdowns, isolation and loss of self-esteem and confidence.

Geraldine's responsibilities increased as people appreciated her help. She listened to them and provided understanding and sympathy, genuinely concerned to help them. Often she could do a great deal just by talking over people's problems, and she pointed out options and tried to restore their pride and self-esteem. She collected data for government departments so that they could provide effective help. Geraldine's central interest is rural people, who taught her to appreciate their 'realness' and humour. 'I have many a moment of fun and many a memory of difficult times, however the overriding factor is about the richness of the rural communities.'

Clare Burton grew up in Canberra, in a family whose Methodist background encouraged a strong social conscience. After being immersed in domesticity with three small children, she returned to study and academia, becoming one of Australia's most prominent intellectuals and an international expert on gender and race bias, a passionate believer in the need for women's equality. Her research addressed the question of how to achieve equal status between men and women in employment: she argued that masculine cultures and practices in business posed barriers to women, and made women's place in the workplace marginal. She discussed what was meant by merit, and showed how gender bias entered many work areas. Her work was admired and respected by women's groups, the government and the public; she held senior government positions, and was the intellectual force behind employment equity programs of the 1980s and 1990s. She wanted to change the world, and she did.

Clare's two sisters have also been influential. Under both Labor and Liberal governments, Meredith Edwards was one of the most senior women in the public service, with a large input into federal policy affecting health, housing, education and family matters, and Pamela Burton, a barrister, previously headed her own legal firm and is at present involved in prison reform. In 1998 Clare Burton, aged only fifty-five, was diagnosed with cancer, and died twelve days later.

Pip Aisbett was born in 1952, and adopted into an academic family. She was close to her mother and older sister, but felt that she did not fit in and could not compete with her sister, so became rebellious. After leaving school she became a clerical assistant and in her search for security, at nineteen married a man

Today

> ### 'Starry eyed thoughts about being my own boss'
>
> *Elva Castino describes herself as an under-achiever at school who left at fifteen and couldn't spell to save her life, but she found an office position and learnt on the job. In 1989 she decided to set up her own secretarial business in Atherton. The bank refused her a loan, so she did everything herself, painting walls, building shelving, installing equipment, writing hundreds of letters. After three years, and a particularly painful session with her accountant, she realised the business was not profitable. Never one to give in easily, Elva decided she needed help, so enrolled in a business management course and engaged the help of a marketing consultant. Steadily she started to creep towards success.*
>
> *Employing staff was a challenge, but Elva applied her philosophy that if you treat people well and help them out when you can, you reap the rewards. Ten years down the track, she is still learning, but the 'ups' far outweigh the 'downs', and the bank even lent her money to buy a house. Sometimes, she writes, a tremendous sense of pride threatens to overwhelm her when she looks at the office and thinks, 'I dragged, pushed and wept over this and it's fine ... everything's just fine!'*

she did not love. She and her husband had three children, but they separated in 1978, when the youngest child was five months old.

Pip struggled to raise three children by herself, but her life turned round when she left Melbourne and moved to Adelaide, where in 1994 she was retrained in office work by a government-funded agency. She obtained a job with the Intellectual Disabilities Services Council, where her female boss saw her potential and offered her work as a Disabilities Services Officer. Pip enjoyed this challenge, and after in-house training has been promoted twice. 'It made me feel like a worthwhile person, independent, and I got back on my feet.' She also gains strength from membership of the Westside Christian Centre.

When Pip was thirty-two she sought out her biological family, meeting her mother and nine siblings and speaking to her father. Her mother had been single and very young when she became pregnant, so the adoption was understandable. The meeting was successful, helping fill a void in Pip's life. It was about this time, she said, that she 'woke up and smelt the coffee – I realised that it was no use feeling bitter about the past, that I had had a good home life and education, and that life moves on'.

Barbara Baird, born in 1958, was among the first generation of her family to go to university. After studying Arts at Flinders University and a stint in the public service, she did not feel driven to focus on a career. Instead, she spent much of her twenties creatively unemployed, 'having a great time' in a relaxed lifestyle with friends, living in collective households of women, and working paid and unpaid in public radio, women's rock bands and women's services, putting her ideals into practice by becoming involved in political activism, feminism and anti-racism. She completed a graduate diploma in women's studies, worked for several years in educating Australians about overseas aid and development issues, then late in the 1980s began a doctorate on the history of abortion. Adelaide has been a centre of women's studies, and Barbara enjoyed growing up academically among its supportive and inspiring feminist academics, especially her PhD supervisor Lyndall Ryan.

Living in women's households amid a feminist community and having lesbian friends meant that as her life unfolded Barbara realised undramatically that she was a lesbian. After an early alignment with lesbian feminism, in the early 1990s she became involved in lesbian and gay coalition politics, and worked with police to reduce homophobic violence and teach police new attitudes, with some success. She feels that since 1975 lesbians have enjoyed increased public space, with increasingly visible and diverse lesbian communities – though she notes that Australia has very few open lesbians in leading positions. Lesbians' acceptance depends on their family, workplace, neighbourhood and how 'out' they are, she commented; some are still very discreet. Barbara counts herself among those privileged lesbians – mostly those without children – not too severely affected by homophobia, though even they can never assume physical safety and freedom from harassment and discrimination.

After completing her doctorate Barbara decided on an academic career in women's studies. She worked in casual research and lecturing jobs in Adelaide, then in 1999 became co-ordinator of the women's studies program at the University of Tasmania. Although she is sceptical about university politics and resentful of heavy workloads, her skill and confidence, and supportive networks, are her mainstays, and she looks forward to making an intellectual and political contribution to university life.

Bait – her Philippine name, to keep her anonymity – is a teacher, who migrated to Perth in 1987, and began to advocate for Filipinas married to abusive Australians. She was also involved in the Ethnic Communities Council of Western Australia, interpreting and translating. In 1999 she became co-ordinator of a women's refuge in Perth, with support workers who are Fijian, Thai, Aboriginal and white Australian. Some refuges complain about local police, but Bait has worked to develop good relations with those in her area. The refuge can house up to five families, and the usual stay is about five weeks. Bait's clients come from all backgrounds, and she remembers them by the degree of physical abuse they have suffered.

Many of the women just want the bashing to stop. It usually takes them a long time to run away, as they want to keep their families together. Often they cannot serve restraining orders on their husbands as these have to be given in person, and the husbands go into hiding. On the whole there are more failures, but there are some successes – women who get a job, or who go back to school. Being co-ordinator of a refuge is a distressing and sometimes dangerous job: how does Bait cope? She is a strong woman in a stable and caring relationship herself. She likes the challenge of dealing with real life, the sense of achievement at the end of the day. But she is angry when women return to abusive relationships, as invariably they come back to the refuge again. One woman has been in refuges seventeen times in eleven years.

Kate Holz trained as an accountant, and has been working

A Wealth of Women

with computers since she finished high school in the late 1970s. In 1990 she set up her own Sydney company, an independent contracting business. She took on a partner and eventually eleven staff, and the company had great success in developing its Smart Systems business. In 2000 the third largest computer company in the world bought her out, appointing her general manager of Australia, New Zealand and the Pacific.

Kate's favourite recreation was sailing, but male yachties refused to take women as crew in major races. In 1989 she and a friend decided to enter the Sydney-Hobart race themselves, and WOW was born – Women on Water. After a great deal of hard work, they organised sponsorship, a boat, and a crew of eleven. They had to fight scepticism and vandalism – someone tried to cut their shrouds, someone else set the boat adrift in the middle of the night – but they set off successfully.

As crews were limited by numbers not overall weight, the women were disadvantaged and found the boat heavy to handle. They were inexperienced in the route, and one crew member received a serious head injury; but another crew member was a head injury nurse, the women worked well together, and they had a huge sense of achievement when they crossed the finishing line ninetieth in a field of 126, and twenty-third on divisional handicap.

WOW went from strength to strength, entering the Sydney-Hobart six times overall, rescuing another yacht in the dreadful conditions of the 1993 race, holding very successful women's regattas, and raising the standard and status of women's sailing – which culminated in Australian women winning a sailing gold medal in the 2000 Olympics.

Born in 1969, Natasha Stott-Despoja grew up in Adelaide and became a feminist at an early age, inspired by two strong women, her mother and her school principal. Her mother, journalist Shirley Stott, was a strong trade unionist and Labor supporter, but Labor introduced university fees as Natasha started university, so it was natural for her to join the Democrats. She learnt fast that a young woman can be seen as a threat in any organisation, but she won pre-selection, and after running a strong campaign, was elected to the Senate in 1995, the youngest-ever member of federal parliament.

In parliament, Natasha was disappointed at the sexism, the lack of solidarity among women and the relentless media scrutiny of what she was wearing; but she also found the opportunities and environment exciting. To many young women, Natasha Stott-Despoja, successful, articulate, with integrity, is the voice of the future. 'You despair about politics until you see someone like Natasha elected. She seems to represent me', as one put it. The Democrats agreed, and in 2001 elected Natasha the youngest-ever leader of a national political party.

Natasha herself is proud of Australian women's ability to juggle so many activities in their lives, and their enthusiasm about

Signs of the times

In 2000, Frances Ibbott of Hobart visited relations in the country, during one of the worst droughts for generations. Despite the gloomy situation there was a cheerful air about the family gathering, as people forgot their difficulties for a while. As usual, the men gathered at one end of the room in farming maleness, wrote Frances, leaving the women to their talk. 'Were they sharing recipes, comparing domestic products? No, the eavesdropper would have heard the ladies discussing the virtues or otherwise of their internet service providers.'

From the 1930s comes this household hint. 'The correct order in which to place the colours for a Rainbow Cake, counting from the bottom: dark cake, pink cake, white cake or light cake on top. Prizes in cooking competitions have been lost through having the colours reversed. Those who enter these competitions could have the best cake, and lose through wrong assembly.' Gail Thomas, the researcher who unearthed this, added, 'Struth, I'm glad we've come a bit further so that when we're having a bad day it's because the computer's not working, the price of our shares has fallen or the patient we were going to do brain surgery on has changed their mind – NOT because we got the colours wrong in our Rainbow Cake!'

new technology, particularly the internet, quoting with pleasure a survey which asked women whether they would rather do without their internet provider or their microwave. A huge majority would throw away the microwave. She greatly admires single mothers, and comments on 'the entrepreneurial nature of women, the strength of women, the fact that women are doing everything from raising families and working on many occasions, not getting adequate childcare, fighting for basic rights like never before. Yet this is not really noticed'.

International Women's Day in Bunbury

Around Australia, International Women's Day in March is celebrated with varying degrees of enthusiasm. One of the most exciting festivals happens in Bunbury, with fifty events held over a month. Not only does the festival create opportunities for women, but it raises the public profile of women's issues and is a great community event, 'a scene where women were encouraged to shine and the wider community to join in and have fun'. In 1999 the festival was a 'raging success', despite some obstruction from the local council.

One of the festival organisers, Julie Parsons, decided to make a banner out of bras. Women responded enthusiastically, donating piles of pre-loved underwear, and two workshops created huge banners which included bras and cheeky pictures of cherries, melons, milk jugs, knockers and cups. The public loved them. Other workshops in circus skills, drumming, belly dancing, and fire twirling with 'Soluna' the Goddess of Fire, meant that the final parade was a great success, despite threatening cyclones.

Other events ranged from singing, meditation, morning teas and lunches, to workshops on violence or using the internet, and a full moon gathering. Women's Night Out combined the old and the new – bring an act, such as songs, poetry, jokes, magic or dance, or a plate. 'The joy of creating opportunities for women to work their magic and perform is just delightful', wrote one of the organisers, Diedre Timms, about the whole festival.

Today

Zuleyka Zevallos is twenty-two, lives in Melbourne, and is about to begin a PhD in sociology. She came from Peru to Australia when she was eight, and quickly learned English and adjusted to the lifestyle, but 'I felt lonesome when it came to something my friends took for granted: the right to call myself and be accepted as an Australian'. Zuleyka's parents are proud to define themselves as Peruvian, but she thinks of herself as both Australian and Peruvian, which has caused immense friction. Her family mistook her actions, particularly speaking English at home instead of Spanish, as a renouncement of her ties to her background, but she feels that both cultures she lives in are pivotal to who she is and always will be.

As she grew up Zuleyka faced much racism and ignorance. People ridiculed her, finding it difficult to think of her as Australian because of her foreign-sounding name, the colour of her skin and the fact that she was not born here; but she felt that she fitted in well, and loved the way she grew up bilingual with two different cultures, so she could mix traditions in 'a hybrid of both Australian and Latin sensibilities'.

'We face the challenge of creating an environment where a person that affiliates themselves with another culture can also feel free to honestly call themselves Australian too', wrote Zuleyka. 'And this challenge for improvement and healing, to further understanding and knowledge about ourselves as a society, is what makes me proud to be an ethnic-Australian woman.'

Have the changes of the past decades been good or bad for women? Several women gave their views. Mary Brice regrets the loss of some aspects of the past, such as safety in the streets and, in a less material world, the pleasure which came from small things – 'the joy of choosing a pennyworth of lollies'. Janet Boddy, a Victorian artist, sees women as liberated from the confines of the morals of the past – and of the clothes of the past; life is easier with appliances and women have opportunities in many fields, from employment to sport. Many now exercise in the gym the muscles they used to use scrubbing floors, she comments. Anabel Macdonald sees a kinder society, in the treatment of women in childbirth and of people who do not belong to society's major groups. Relationships are more open and healthy, women more emancipated. But not all changes have been for the good, such as the double burden which comes from combining employment and running a family, and as Janet said, 'we still have far to go'. 'Women are still not really equal', said Maureen Holz; 'we've made wonderful gains, but there's still much more to be done, and we must maintain what we have', commented Audrey McDonald.

Many women gained enormously from the changes which have taken place since the 1970s – mostly middle-class women, who have the educational opportunities and finance to make the most of them. There is far more awareness of the inequalities women have been subjected to, but though much has been done to remedy this, awareness is still not entirely translated into action. Statistics show that many women still face problems. As always through Australian history, poverty affects many people, men and women, even more so in the 1990s when it has become a cliché that the rich are getting richer, and the poor, poorer – income inequality lessened from 1915, when records started, until about 1975, but has grown steadily since then. Those on welfare benefits, like single mothers, can find that benefits are not enough for comfortable living, the welfare system is increasingly unfriendly, and if they try to move off it and get a job there is not enough affordable support such as childcare. In fact most single mothers are employed, and they spend an average of only about four years on welfare, but at any one time there are about two hundred thousand single parents, overwhelmingly women, who live on benefits. Elderly people and others reliant on welfare, and people on low wages, also often find themselves with not enough money to allow a comfortable life.

Despite legal efforts to create equality for women in employment, attitudes are not so easily changed, and Jessica's 'story' shows the problems women can face with work, either in employment or in the home. No wonder many Australian women take anti-depressants, which doctors prescribe as they cannot provide real solutions: an adequate income, a satisfying job, a loving fam-

Today

Cookery in the 1990s

One of the best-selling authors of the 1990s is Stephanie Alexander, restaurateur and cookery writer, whose The Cook's Companion *has become a staple in many homes. The influence of Asian cooking on Australia, and increasing interest in vegetables, are shown in this recipe:*

Stir-fry of garlic chives and bean sprouts
vegetable oil
1 handful garlic chives, cut into 2.5 cm pieces
1 cup bean sprouts
1 tablespoon light soy sauce
few drops of sesame oil
2 tablespoons chicken stock
2 teaspoons cornflour
Heat a wok, then add a little vegetable oil and heat. Stir-fry chives and bean sprouts for 30 seconds. Add soy sauce and sesame oil. Mix stock and cornflour, then tip into wok and stir until slightly thickened. Serve with chicken dishes and rice.

ily, an end to loneliness. Violence is another problem which legislation can only do so much to conquer.

Despite the efforts of women's groups of all types, in Australia the man's experience is still the norm. A woman in a public role is less unusual than in the past, but they are still far fewer than the men who dominate Australian public life. In some areas, however, their numbers are growing considerably – such as in the Queensland parliament after the 2001 election. Opinions about the future vary, between those who feel that real equality is only a matter of time, and those who fear that in some areas, such as boardrooms, it will never really come. Feminism is less openly supported in some areas, seen by some as valuing only employed women. The research for this book has shown, however, that though women might not support feminism itself, they support ideas and schemes which assist women.

As this book progressed, two dominant features of Australian

A Wealth of Women

women emerged. One is how hard they have worked. Perhaps some researcher can find an example of an Australian woman who did not work in her life, but I cannot. All women I have found have worked, at home, in the family enterprise, in employment, in their own businesses, in voluntary work, in caring for the family, often in several ways simultaneously. Most have worked hard, often extremely hard.

The other aspect is the qualities which characterise Australian women. Many of the stories in this book came from the History Search held by the Office of the Status of Women in 2000, which asked the public to provide stories of women. Clearly, they are not representative of all Australian women; but the four hundred stories which arrived described women from all areas of Australia, all sections of the community, all backgrounds, and with a huge variety of achievements. The characteristics which kept on appearing in the stories were that women were capable, brave, strong, loving and cheerful – and a great inspiration to me in compiling the book. And despite complaints that the community is not what is used to be, that pioneer women had qualities which have disappeared in modern women, these characteristics can still be seen in the stories of contemporary women. These are the women whose lives have provided half our history. As Lesley Mansfield commented, writing her mother's biography for the History Search 'has made me realise how much the daily lives of the ordinary Australian citizen make up the strength and fabric of our nation'.

What a waste it is of Australia's women and their capabilities to undervalue women's work, and not use their abilities in public life. Much has been achieved, women are making a considerable contribution, but more can be done. If Australia really treated women equally and used their talents in building up the nation, where could we not go?

acknowledgments

Many people have helped in the preparation of this book, and I would like to thank the following for their assistance:

Prue Torney-Parlicki and the Aboriginal consultant, Suzi Hutchings, who were responsible for the two chapters of the book dealing with Aboriginal women.

The staff of the Office of the Status of Women, particularly the Head, Rosemary Calder, and the project officer, Liz Hickey; members of the Advisory Committee attached to the project, Pru Goward, Maggie Hamilton and Joan Rydon, and particularly the chair, Katharine Betts; and the publisher, Michael Duffy.

The editor, Sue Corrigan, for the sympathetic way she uses her skills, and the researchers for their enthusiasm and insight, and the excellent material they provided: Gail Thomas in Perth, Barbara James in Darwin, Julie Peterson in Adelaide, Deborah Jordan in Brisbane, Sue Georgevits in Sydney, Victoria Emery in Melbourne, and Emma Greenwood in Canberra. Sue was also illustration co-ordinator, and all the researchers not only provided information but were generous with advice on how to use it and general comments about the book, notably Deborah, Gail and Barbara. I would like to thank all these women very much indeed.

Contributors to the history search (names as they appeared in their letters):

Mrs Gillian Albers, Ms Sue Aldridge, Beth Allen, Fran Allison, Lyn Allison (Zonta Club of Bowen), Kate Alport, Betty Anderson, Helen Annand, Natalie Anuriw, Ms Judy Archer-Dawson, Mrs Margaret Arnel, Josie Arnold, Dawn Baker, Pamela Baker, Darryl Baltieri, Gillian Banks, Mrs Nerida Barges, Linda Barnes, Mrs Olwyn Barnes, Avis Barr, L Barry (South Australian Country Women's Association), John Bartlett, Michaell Bartlett, Irene Barwick, Mrs Eva Bass, Lucy Bates, Zelma Bates Claydon, Joy Bear,

A Wealth of Women

Jean Beasley, Frances Beatts, Peter Beaver, Margaret Beckett, Kaye Beckwith, Connie Bennett, Marie Bennett, Jill Berger, Mrs Jenny Bicanic, June Birkett, Nancy Blake, Marlies Blatz, Janet Boddy, Merrilee Boydell, Barbara Boxhall, Geraldine Boylan, Una Millicent Braby, Ivy Bradford, Margaret Bradford, Elaine Brain, Mary Brice, Tanya Britten, Margaret Broadby, Olwyn Broder, Lucy Brookes-Kenworthy, Barbara Brown Parker, Mrs R Bull (Ex-Wrans Association), Mrs R Bull (Greenacre), Stephanie Bull, Pamela Burton, Carol Byrne (Penguin Club of Australia);

Mrs D. Caine, Daphne Calder, Lois Calvert, Thelma Campbell, Mrs Eleanor Carney, Professor Emeritus Denis J. Carr, Pat Carroll, Mrs Mavis Carruthers, Ms Zoe Carter, Jess Castle, June Caunt, Lorraine Cazalar, Betty Chapman, E. Jane Chapman, Heather Chapple, Barry Cheales OAM, Lisa Christian, Muriel Clampett, Mary Clancy, Mrs Frances Clark, Mrs J D L Clark, Melva Clark, Leanne Clarke, Jennifer Cleveland, Pauline Cockrill Ross, Mrs Joan Cocks (Women's Christian Temperance Union of South Australia), Sally Colechin, Maire Cook, Frances Costa, Diana Coxhead, Geoff Coxon, Lyn Coy, Mary Coyne (Mothers' Union Australia), Sister Cheryl Cramp RSM, May Crane, Janet Crompton, Diane Cronin, Mrs Cecily Cross (Victorian Ladies Bowling Association), Una Cumberland-Day, Irma Dallwitz, Leila Daniell, Mrs Bonnie Davey, Penny Davie, Rhonda Dawson, Anny De Decker, Patricia Degens, Deb Delahunty, Stan Devlin, Mrs Glenda Dovile, Donelle Dowling, Mrs Joan Downward, Lindy Dudgeon, Samantha Duff, Nellie Dyne, Kevin Egan, Lorna Ellis, Margaret Escott, Dawn Evans; Tricia Fay, Beryl Finch, Sue Firth (War Widows' Guild of Australia, Tasmanian Branch), Nola Fisher, Mary Flanagan, Felicia Fletcher, Peter Fogarty, Terri Foley, John Forrest MP, Matthew Fowler, Susan Fox, Mrs Babette Francis, Elsie Francis, Mrs M Friederichs, Stuart Frost, Mrs Slavka Galea, Beryl Gamble, Glenda Gault, Daphne M Gaydon, Cate Gensky, Mrs Lina Gerbin, Lyn Giles (Queensland Ladies' Bowling Association), Marion and Paul Goard, Mrs Dorothy Godfrey, Elizabeth Godfrey, Marjorie Gough, Ray Goulter, Gwen Gower, Diane Graham, Rita Graham, Mrs Margaret Gray, E W Grebert, Doug Greypower, Val Guppy, Ms Colleen Hackman, Kathy

Acknowledgments

Hagon, Louise Hakendorf, Mrs E. Hanbury, Olwyn Hanigan, Audrey Harris, Mrs J K Haselton, Jill Heathcote, Gillian Heintze, Margaret Hemmings, Bronwyn Potts Hendy, Christine Heybroek, Joan Hilton, Colleen Hines, Kelly Hoare MP, Judi Hockey, Lois Hoeper (National Council of Women of South Australia), Wendy Hogan, Margaret Hollier, Hazel Hollingworth, Venie Holmgren, Mrs Maureen Holz, Isabelle Hooper, Alice Hungerford, Harold Hunt, Elizabeth Hutchins;

Mrs Mary Zenna Ireland, Mrs W B Ives, Margaret Jansen, Helen Jenkins, Margaret Jenner, Mrs Pamela Jensen, Di Jobbins, Katrina Jocumsen, Len Johnson, Brian Johnston, Megan Johnston, Janine Jones, Jean Kahan, Dawn Kassiotis, Mrs Julie Keating, Tony Keenan, Margaret Kelly, John Kerr, Pamela Kessell, Yvonne King, Val Kost, Dr John Laffin, Mrs E C V Lakeman (Overseas War Brides Club), Mrs Judith Lamb, Richard Lonsdale Lancaster, Maureen Lane, June Laszlo, Jeanette Laughton, Mrs Diane Laun, Isobel and Craig Learmont, Sandra Lee, Donna Lee Brien, C J Lenthall, Keera Le Lievre, Mary Lightfoot, Mrs B Lloyd, Carolyn Lillecrapp, Elizabeth Lonergan, Dennette Long, Constance Lowe, Heather Lyall (Women's Pioneer Society of Australasia), Mrs F M McCallum, Alice McCane, Rena McCawley, Gweneth McCusker, Anabel Macdonald, Audrey McDonald, Mrs Anna McEldowney, Lyn McEvoy, Mrs Fran McGrath, Mr Paul McGuire, Michelle McIntyre, Valerie McKenzie, Mrs Judith Mackintosh, Denise Kirby McLean, Ann McLeod, Phyl Macleod, Mary Macklin, Senator Jan McLucas, Carol McMaugh, Joan McPherson, Wendy Maddocks, Alberta Maggs, Margaret Magi, Joan Major, Mrs G P Makim-Willing, Robyn Mathison, Betty Mawdsley (Union of Australian Women, Newcastle Branch), Lesley Mansfield, Cree Marshall, Mrs G. May, Col Maybury, Penny Mercer, Eileen Micenko, Gail Miles, Jenny Mills (Guides Australia, Victoria), N D Millward, Merrilyn Minter, Sandra Minter Caldwell, Pat Moran, Ann Morgan, Ralph Morgan, Louise Morris, Maureen Moss, Margaret Muirhead, Rebecca Muldoon, Helen Mulligan, Margaret Murray, Betty M Murtagh, Amanda Myers;

Rosa Nastasi, Roslyn Navin, Rod Nazer, Mrs Jan Nelson, Bar-

A Wealth of Women

bara Newman, Jenny Nicol, Jennifer Nielsen, Mrs Mona Nolan, Thele Norris, Mrs Barbara Nuttall, Victoria O'Connor, Colin Officer, Margaret Oliphant, Judy Ormond, Mary Owen, Peg Parkin (City of Belmont Historical Society), Cathryn Parry, Linda Pascal, Mrs Barbara Payne, Beryl Pearson, Dr Dawn Peel, Eunice Petch (Victorian Ladies Bowls Association), Janet Grace Pine, Marg Pirie, Miss Barbara Pitt, Dorothy Plummer, Anna Pope, Gloria Primmer, Jennifer Rabach, Lucy Raig, Hermine Rainow, John Raymond, Joy Reeson, Jill Richards, Kevin (Ric) Richardson, Mrs Pamela Richardson, Margaret Rickard, Fay Riley, Sandy Rimington (Tuggeranong Women's Neighbourhood Group), Jane Nairn Roach, Dr Alan Roberts, Dr Jan Roberts, Daryl Roberson, Margaret Rogers, Tania Rogers, Mrs P B Ronald, Carol Rowe, Mrs Y Sanderson, Wendy Sansome, Glenys Savage, Muriel Scandrett, Peggy Schultze, Kathleen Scott, Betty Searle, Ms Cindy Seeberger, Denis Shaw, Colette Shelley, Joyce Shepherd, Lawrence Sherwin, Maryjane Sherwin, Tresna Shorter, Elva Shumack, June Skinner, Betty Smith, Louise Smith, Mrs Betty Snell, Mike Snoad, Mary Sommerville, Gwenda Spencer, Maureen Squire, Freda Stacey, Margaret Stafford, Gwenda Stanbridge, John Stanhope, Brenda Steven-Chambers, Pam Stoodley, Theodora Stoodley, Aileen Sullivan, Mrs Julia Sullivan, Yvonne Sullivan;

Tatura Business and Professional Women, Amy Taylor (Australian Women's Army Service Association), Patricia Thomas, Frances Thompson, Heather Thomson, Cheryl Timbury, Nona Toy, Elaine Tranter (Eacham Historical Society), Joan Trewern OAM (Women's Electoral Lobby, Cairns), Doreen Turner, E J Van Bowen, Lorese Vera, Mrs P W Verco (National Council of Women, South Australia Inc.), Vida Videon, Sue Volker, Gai Walker, Robert Walker, Iris Wallace, Janine Walmsley, Margaret Walsh, Tricia Walsh, Mavis Ward, Senator John Watson, Bruce Weatherhead, Pamela Wells, Philip Wheaton, Mrs Sylvia Whiley, Dawn White, Liz Wightwick, Yvonne Wildash, Dalace Williams, Dulcie Williams, Ms Kathryn Williams, Ken Williams, Patricia Williams, Maria Williamson, Mrs Enid Willis, Anne Wills, Mrs Shirley Wills, Marcia Wilson, Nell Wilson, Pam Wilson, Rita M Wilson, Gwyn Wiseman, Mrs B V Wolski, Jane Woodley,

Acknowledgments

Arthur Wright, Dianne Wright, G R Wright, Mrs Elma Wylie, Stephen Zivkovic.

A book of this type relies heavily on others' research, and I would like to thank especially those responsible for these books: *Gender Relations in Australia*, *Creating a Nation*, and the *Oxford Companion to Australian History*. Others to whom I am grateful are the helpful and competent staff at the University of Tasmania Library, particularly Jayne Clarke and Robyn Jones; the staff of the Department of Veterans' Affairs, Canberra, particularly Cathy Moore; the staff of the National Library; the owner of the excellent second-hand bookshop 'Book Lore' in Canberra, which specialises in women's history; and the staff of the Australian Bureau of Statistics, who provide such an excellent service over the phone.

I would also like to thank those who helped me by discussing aspects of the book and providing either professional or personal information and advice: Pip Aisbett, Janine Baxter, Michael Bittman, Mary Blackwood, Margaret Blow, Jean Bourne, Beryl Carmichael, Emma Cavell, Judy Cooper, Don Field, Pam Galloway, Frances Ibbott, Amanda Lohrey, Eunice Jacobson, Ruth Kerr, Beth and Lyndsay McLeod, Marian May, Wendy Newman, Edith Pecl, Catherine Prideaux, Betty Pybus, Megan Schaffner, Joscelynne Scutt, Wendy Selby, Dick Spencer, Natasha Stott-Despoja, Anne Summers, Ramunas Tarvydas, Mollie Tomlin, Jessie Wagner, Chris Wilson, Pam Young; and staff at the University of Tasmania: Barbara Baird, Michael Bennett, Megan Cassidy-Welch, Caroline Evans, Rhiannon Evans, Lucy Frost, Christine Goodacre, Margaret Lindley, Hamish Maxwell-Stewart, Jenna and Philip Mead, Stefan Petrow, Michael Roe and Elisabeth Wilson. I am particularly grateful to those who read all or some of the chapters: Barbara Baird, Mary Blackwood, Margaret Blow, Jenny Marshall, Pamela Pillinger, Megan Schaffner, Wendy Selby and Gail Thomas, and my daughters Judy and Cathy Alexander. My thanks to Les Murray for the title.

My family, especially the female members, have been an excellent sounding-board for ideas and have provided points of view from other generations, and I would like to thank my mother,

Pam Pillinger, my mother-in-law, Cynthia Alexander, and my daughters, Judy and Cathy. I have also been inspired by memories of my grandmother, an ardent champion of Australia and its women, and other female ancestors, ranging from a violent convict to the wives of a squatter, a stonemason and a soldier settler. Male family members were also helpful, and I would like to thank my son Ted and husband James for putting forward the masculine viewpoint and assisting with research.

notes

Main sources
Patricia Grimshaw, Marilyn Lake, Ann McGrath, Marian Quartly *Creating A Nation* Melbourne, 1994; Marilyn Lake *Getting Equal* Sydney, 1999; Kay Saunders and Raymond Evans *Gender Relations in Australia* Sydney, 1992; Graeme Davison, John Hirst, Stuart Macintyre *The Oxford Companion to Australian History* Melbourne, 1998
ADB = Australian Dictionary of Biography
When the information about a woman comes directly from her, this is not included in these notes.

1. Early Days
Betty King: Jonathan King *The First Fleet* Melbourne, 1982; John Cobley *The Crimes of the First Fleet Convicts* Sydney, 1970; Irene Schaffer & Thelma McKay *Exiled! Profiles of Norfolk Islanders to Van Diemen's Land* Hobart, 1992
Maria Lord: Alison Alexander *Obliged to Submit* Hobart, 1998
Ann Morgan: information from Isobel and Craig Learmont, Ralph Morgan, Paul Goard
Mary Wade: information from John Stanhope
Jane Hadden: Herbert Cullis *No Tears for Jane* Melbourne, 1982
Jemmy the Rover: Heather Radi *200 Australian Women* Sydney, n.d. pp. 9–10
Mary Smallshaw: information from Eleanor Carney, Lucy Brookes-Kenworthy
Life in the Rocks: Grace Karskens *The Rocks* Sydney, 1999
Jane Richardson: information from Barbara James
Clergyman's son's letter: Helen Heney *Dear Fanny: women's letters to and from New South Wales 1788–1857* Sydney, 1985 p. 220
Elizabeth Hawkins: George Mackaness (ed.) *Fourteen Journeys Over the Blue Mountains of New South Wales 1813–1841* Sydney, 1950; ADB 1/524–5
Charlotte Davis: information from Lyn Coy
Jessie Crozier: information from Keera Le Lievre
Anne Whatley : A. Burton 'Paper on diary of Anne Whatley', n.d., HS/300 & HS/613, Royal Western Australian Historical Society Research Library
Annie Caldwell: Susanna De Vries *Strength of Spirit Pioneering Women of Achievement from First Fleet to Federation* Sydney, 1995
Margaret Fulford: memoirs of Margaret Fulford, copy provided by N.D. Millward
Recipes: Edward Abbott *Cookery for the many ...* Hobart, 1864
Mary McConnel: The Wife of an Australian Pioneer *Memories of Days Long Gone By Queensland Reminiscences 1848–1870* Brisbane, 1905
Eliza Tuckwell: information from Barbara James

2. The Australian Woman
Margaret Grellier 'The Family: Some aspects of its demography and ideology in mid-nineteenth century Western Australia' in C.T. Stannage (ed.) *A New History of Western Australia* Perth, 1981
Caroline Chisholm: Patricia Grimshaw 'The moral reformer and the imperial major: Caroline and Archibald Chisholm' in Penny Russell (ed) *For Richer For Poorer Early Colonial Marriages* Melbourne, 1994

A Wealth of Women

Christiana Brooks: Patricia Clarke & Dale Spender *Life Lines Australian women's letters and diaries 1788 to 1840* Sydney, 1992 p. 100
Amelia White: information from Gweneth McCusker
Mary McConnel: Mary Macleod Banks *Memories of Pioneer Days in Queensland* London, 1931
Bishop's daughters: Norah Nixon (ed.) *The pioneer Bishop in Van Diemen's Land* ... [Hobart], [1953]
Mary Mowle: Patricia Clarke *A Colonial Woman The Life and Times of Mary Braidwood Mowle 1827–1857* Sydney, 1986
Australian Girl: Beverley Kingston *Glad, Confident Morning* Melbourne, 1988 p. 146; Ruth Teale *Colonial Eve* Melbourne, 1978 pp. 37–7
Governess: Patricia Clarke *The Governesses: Letters from the Colonies* Sydney, 1985 pp. 56, 84
Sarah Wentworth: Carol Liston *Sarah Wentworth Mistress of Vaucluse* Sydney, 1987 p. 25
Girl easily spared: Pam Young *Proud to be a Rebel The life and times of Emma Miller* Brisbane, 1991 p. 92
Margaret Fitzgerald: information from Margaret Oliphant
Mary Gilmore: Mary Gilmore *Old Days, Old Ways* this edition Sydney, 1963
Sarah Lawson: Heney p. 79
Josephine Bussell: Westralian History Group *On This Side: Themes and issues in Western Australian history*, Perth, 1985
Mrs Spencer: 'Mrs Spencer of Bunbury', file 8/1929, Royal Western Australian Historical Society Research Library
Mary Ann Scott: information from Pam Baker
Eliza Louden: Betty Roland *An Improbable Life* Sydney, 1989 pp. 4, 6–7
Louisa Clifton: Mrs E.D. Cowan 'Early Social Life and Fashions' in Western Australian Historical Society *Journal and Proceedings* vol. 1, part III, 1928 pp. 7–8; Lucy Frost *No Place for a Nervous Lady* Melbourne, 1984 p. 51
Childbirth: Margaret Anderson 'Marriage and children in Western Australia, 1842–1849' in Patricia Grimshaw, Chris McConville, Ellen McEwen (eds) *Families in Colonial Australia* Sydney, 1985 pp. 49–56
Mrs Gilbert: Heney pp. 169–70
Unsympathetic husband: Pamela Statham *The Tanner Letters* Perth, 1981 p. 128
Unsympathetic daughter: Diary of Joyce Sincock, MS 5320, Box 1811/4, La Trobe Library, July 1862
Ann Hordern, Sophy Dumaresq: Heney pp. 85, 97–8
Mary Ann Foote: information from Stephen Zivkovic
Rachel Henning: Teale p. 94
Food and cooking: Anne Gollan *The Tradition of Australian Cooking* Canberra, 1978, chapter 3
Sarah Nicolson: information from E.J. van Boven
Maria Windeyer: Heney pp. 162, 164
Emma Clark: Margaret James 'Not bread but a stone: women and divorce in colonial Victoria' in Grimshaw et al *Families* pp. 45–6
Mary Kennedy: Gollan p. 54
Edith Cowan: Mrs E.D. Cowan 'Early Social Life and Fashions' in Western Australian Historical Society *Journal and Proceedings* vol. 1, part III, 1928 pp. 1–17
Iley Hoddinott: information from Maureen Holz
Mary Jane Hunter: Society of Women Writers *Equal to the Occasion* Melbourne, 1986 p. 57
Mary Ann Merchant: information from Barbara Brown-Parker
Mrs Manning: Heney p. 116
Etiquette: People's Publishing Company *Australian Etiquette* Melbourne, 1885
Elsie Devlin: Stanley L. Devlin *Multiple Stains The Story of the Devlin and Associated Families in Australia* Canberra, 1999 pp. 315–317
Margaret Forrest: Janda Gooding *Margaret Forrest Wildflowers of Western Australia* Perth, 1984 pp. 2, 7–8

Notes

Jane Grant: Susan Hunt *Spinifex and Hessian Women's Lives in North-Western Australia 1860–1900* Perth, 1986 p. 48
Margaret Morrison: information from Pat Moran
Jane Yates: information from Val Guppy
Jeannie Young: copy from Margaret Muirhead
Anglican clergyman's wife: Mrs Millett *An Australian Parsonage ...* London, 1872 p. 337
Matilda Wallace: *Twelve Years' Life in Australia* n.p., n.d., in the possession of Dawn White
Mary Penfold and Mary Laurie: *Adelaide Review* September 1998
Isabella Marshall: information from Elizabeth Hutchins
Ann Crebbin: information from John Stanhope
Elizabeth McCallum: information from Ruth McCallum
Martha Turner: *The Woman Voter* 2 September 1915; Scott *The Halfway House* pp. 53–58
Jane Bardsley: John Atherton Young *Jane Bardsley's Outback Letterbook ...* Sydney, 1987 pp. 156–7
Bunker family: information from Ric Richardson, Margaret Broadby
Isabella Williams: information from Ken Williams
Baby's body: Teale p. 139
Dorothy Maguire: 'Memoirs of Dorothy Maguire', in possession of Ruth Bull
Emma Thomson: Diary of Emma Thomson, 24 April 1857
Annie Gold: information from Judy Archer-Dawson
Zenna Rintoull: information from Mary Zenna Ireland
Susanna Massey, Louisa Chard: information from Len Johnson, Dawn Peel, Dorothy Bench, Heather Lyall
Ursula Frayne: Patrick Francis Moran *History of the Catholic Church in Australia* Sydney, 1893 pp. 237–490, 960–76
Sarah Arbuckle: information from Alberta Maggs
Bridget Shepherd: information from Joyce Shepherd and Leanne Clarke
Granny Smith: information from Marion and Paul Goard
Recipes: The Public School Cookery Teachers' Association of New South Wales, *The Commonsense Cookery Book* Sydney, 1943 pp. 24, 101; Southern Regional Women's Committee *National Trust of Australia (Tasmania) Recipe Book* Hobart, 1969 p. 136, 'from a book dated 1883'

3. Building a Nation

Christina Houlahan: information from Margaret Bradford
Kate MacAllan: information from Cate Gengsky
Louise Mack: Louise Mack *Teens: A story of Australian schoolgirls* London, n.d.
Alice McKee: memoirs of Alice McKee from June Laszlo
Minnie Clarke: 'Girls' High School Magazine', October 1911, State Library of Tasmania
Barbara Mann: information from Barbara Payne
Lucy Osburn: Freda MacDonnell *Miss Nightingale's Young Ladies The Story of Lucy Osburn and Sydney Hospital* Sydney, 1970; Radi pp. 31–2; ADB 5/377–8
Sister Kate: Daphne Popham (ed) *Reflections Profiles of 150 Women who helped make Western Australia's History* Perth, 1978 pp. 66–7
Minnie Shoobridge: Walker Papers, 20 October 1889, University of Tasmania Archives
Anne Stafford Bird: Mrs A. Garnsey *Scarlet Pillows* this edition Malvern, 1980 pp. 16–21
Clara Saunders: Clara Paton *Notes from the memories of Clara Saunders, one of the pioneer women on the Coolgardie Goldfields* Perth, n.d. pp. 19, 22
Catherine Jackson: information from Deborah Delahunty
Victorian private school teachers: Kathleen Spence *The Only Abiding Solution A History of the teachers' (Girls' Schools) Award* Melbourne, 1997 pp. 1–8
Constance Stone: Radi pp. 63–4, ADB 12/98–100
Nita Kibble: Pauline Cockerill Ross *Ordinary Women, Extraordinary Lives* Alice Springs, 1997 p. 46

A Wealth of Women

Dorothy Izett: John Clark, 'The life of Sarah Ann (Dorothy) Izett 1844–1929 and her family', in possession of Mrs J.D.L. Clark

Dora Coghlan: information from Matthew Fowler

Harvester judgement: Michael Bittman & Jocelyn Pixley *The Double Life of the Family* Sydney, 1997 p. 218–9

Christina Gordon: information from Barbara James

Matchgirls: Jennifer Feeney 'Matchgirls: Strikers at Bryant and May' in Marilyn Lake and Farley Kelly (eds) *Double Time: women in Victoria, 150 years* Melbourne, 1985

Domestic service: Alison Alexander, 'The Public Role of Women in Tasmania, 1803–1914', unpublished PhD thesis, University of Tasmania, 1989 pp. 86–88

Johanna Stephan: information from Terri Foley

Emma Frey: information from Eileen Micenko

Ada Fletcher: Ada Fletcher 'Memories of a Nature Lover', OM67-2/3 pp. 9–10, Queensland Archives

Polly Payne: information from Hazel Hollingworth

Mildred Hood: Diary of Mildred Hood, Archives Office of Tasmania

WCTU, Elizabeth Nicholls, suffrage in SA: Isabel McCorkindale (ed.) *Torch-Bearers The Woman's Christian Temperance Union of South Australia, 1886–1948* Adelaide, 1948

Ann Hickey: letter provided by Mrs M. Friederichs

Federene Kirby: information from Denise McLean

Henrietta Dugdale: information from Doreen Turner; ADB 4/114-5; Radi pp. 25–6.

Maybanke Wolstenholme-Anderson: Jan Roberts *Maybanke Anderson Sex, Suffrage and Social Reform* Sydney, 1993

Alice Wickham: RD Smith (ed) *The Writings of Anna Wickham* London, 1984 pp. 92–113

Eva Andrew: information from Maureen, Valmai and Kevin Andrew and Wendy Sansome, including 'Eva's Story The life of Eva Hilda Andrew-Harris'

Flora Harris: information from Frances Clark

Girl Guides: information from Jenny Mills, Guides Victoria

Bowls: information from Eunice Petch, Victorian Ladies' Bowling Association

Fanny Durack, Annette Kellermann: ADB 8/385; Susanna De Vries *Strength of Purpose Australian Women of Achievement from Federation to the Mid-20th Century* Sydney, 1988 pp. 170–181; Harry Gordon *Australia and the Olympic Games* Brisbane, 1994

Annette Bear: information from Diane Wright; Radi pp. 59–60

Childbirth, contraception: Stefania Siedlecky & Diana Wyndham *Populate and Perish Australian Women's Fight for Birth Control* Sydney, 1990; Michael Gilding *Making and breaking ...*; John C. Caldwell 'The Delayed Western Fertility Decline: An Examination of English-Speaking Countries' in *Population and Development Review* 25 (3)

Janet Clarke: information from Hon. Michael Clarke; ADB 3/415

Marion Haynes: Society of Women Writers *Women By Themselves A scrapbook of writings by women in Australia ...* Melbourne, 1988 p. 101

Mary Dean: Donna Lee Brien 'True Crime Fiction as Criminal History: Illustrated with Selections from the Author's Manuscript "The Case of Mary Dean"' in *Australian Feminist Law Journal* September 1999

Ivy Cole: Society of Women Writers *Equal to the Occasion* p. 60

Hypatia Monk-Adams: Sydney *Daily Telegraph* 26 April 1957

Alice S–: Queensland State Archives, Police Dept 13585, COL 236

Northern Territory: Barbara James *Occupation: Citizen The Story of Northern Territory Women and the Vote (1894–1896)* Darwin, 1995

Ethel White: information from Mrs Colin Moodie, National Council of Women, South Australia

Margaret Golding: information from Thele Norris

Mary Pennefather: memoirs of Mary Pennefather, from Janine Warmsley

Sarah Thornbury: information from Irene Barwick

Notes

Emma Miller: Young *Proud to be a Rebel*; also assistance from Pam Young
Timmins girls: Gene Makim *The Tail Goes with the Hide* n.p., n.d. pp. 58–60, 73–4, 75–8
Mary Ann Dempsey: information from Aileen Sullivan
Caroline Hodgson: information from Geoff Coxon
Selma Stanitzki: information from Irma Dallwitz
Asian women: Hunt *Spinifex and Hessian* chapter 5; Barbara James *No Man's Land Women of the Northern Territory* Sydney, 1989, chapter 4
Pharmacists: Miriel Witt 'The genesis and achievements of two Victorian women pharmacists' associations', in possession of Pamela Wells
Melanesian women: Kaye Saunders 'Pacific Islander women in Queensland: 863–1907' in Margaret Bevege, Margaret James & Carmel Shute *Worth her salt Women at work in Australia* Sydney, 1892

4. The First World War

Mary Jane Miller: information from Rita Graham
Lillian Paton: Lillian Paton *Armchair Reflections*, in possession of Isabelle Hooper
Jemima Erskine: Connie Nazer *Jemima A completely factual story* [Canberra, 1982]
Mary Campbell: information from Thelma Campbell
Red Cross: Patsy Adam-Smith *Australian Women at War* Melbourne, 1984 pp. 37–42; Melanie Oppenheimer *Red Cross VAs: a history of the VAD movement in New South Wales* Sydney, 1999
Violet Wurfel: information from Gwenda Spencer
Narrogin: M. White *Memorial I: Narrogin and World War I* Perth, 1993 pp. 80–82
Khaki Girls: Jan Bassett 'Lyla Barnard: Khaki Girl' in Lake and Kelly
Mary Drummond: information from Col Maybury
Annie Wheeler: Douglas Fox 'Annie Margaret Wheeler, OBE "Mother of the Anzacs"', in the possession of Susan Fox
Nurses: Jan Bassett *Guns and Brooches Australian Army Nursing from the Boer War to the Gulf War* Melbourne, 1992; Richard Reid *Just wanted to be there Australian Service Nurses 1899–1999* Canberra, 1999
Nellie Pike: John Laffin *'Damn the Dardanelles!' The Agony of Gallipoli* Sydney, 1980 pp. 167–172; information from John Laffin, Patricia Williams
Policewomen: information from the Woman's Christian Temperance Union of South Australia; Tim Prenzler 'Women in Australian Policing: An Historical Overview' in *Journal of Australian Studies* vol. 42 pp. 79–80
Rally in Brisbane: Young p. 203
Inez Weatherhead: Muriel Clampett *Inez 1892–1952* Melbourne, 1999 pp. 45–51
Ann Vaubell: information from Dalace Williams
Elizabeth Fay: information from Tricia Fay
Jessie Menzies: information from Elizabeth Godfrey
Cara Poole: information from Julia Sullivan
Edith Tomkins: information from Peggy Schultze
Marjorie Bunker: information from Kathleen Scott
Anzac biscuits: Public Teachers *Commonsense Cookery Book* p. 167; *Oxford Companion to Australian History* p. 27

5. Beginning the Struggle

Problems of writing about pre-contact: Nancy M. Williams and Lesley Jolly, 'From Time Immemorial?' in Saunders and Evans (eds), *Gender Relations in Australia: Domination and Negotiation*, Harcourt Brace Jovanovich, Sydney, 1992, pp.9–14.
Sexual division of labour: Williams and Jolly, pp.14–15
Marriage: Williams and Jolly, pp.15–16; Ethel Hassell, *My Dusky Friends*, CW Hassell, Fremantle, 1975, p.90
Rituals: Williams and Jolly, pp.17–18.

A Wealth of Women

Spiritual significance of the land: Richard Broome, *Aboriginal Australians: Black Responses to White Dominance 1788–1994*, 2nd edition, Allen & Unwin, Sydney, 1994, pp.14–15.

Violence and sexual relations on frontier: Broome, *Aboriginal Australians*, pp.55–56.

Jandamurra and Bunaba women: Mary Anne Jebb and Anna Haebich, 'Across the Great Divide: Gender Relations on Australian Frontiers' in Saunders and Evans, *Gender Relations in Australia*, pp.39–40.

Walyer: Julia Clark in Heather Radi (ed.), *200 Australian Women: a Redress anthology*, Women's Redress Press, Sydney, 1988, pp.10–11; Jebb and Haebich, 'Across the Great Divide' in Saunders and Evans, *Gender Relations in Australia*, p.40.

Cattle stations: Ann McGrath, *Born in the Cattle*, Allen and Unwin, Sydney, 1987, pp.viii–ix, 49, 52; Jebb and Haebich, 'Across the Great Divide' in Saunders and Evans, *Gender Relations in Australia*, p.25

Pipe-smoking female stockworkers: Henry Reynolds, *With the White People*, Penguin, Ringwood, 1990, p.204

Percentage of women stockworkers in Kimberleys: Reynolds, *With the White People*, p.204.

Amy Laurie, Mary Yunduin and Maudie Moore: McGrath, *Born in the Cattle*, pp.51–2, 56

Increasingly a male-only role: McGrath, *Born in the Cattle*, pp.56–58.

Demand for sexual services: McGrath, *Born in the Cattle*, p.50.

Helen Sullivan: McGrath, *Born in the Cattle*, pp.59, 62

Winnie Chapman as child: McGrath, *Born in the Cattle*, p.62

Helen Skardon: quoted in McGrath, *Born in the Cattle*, p.62

Winnie Chapman as adult: McGrath, *Born in the Cattle*, p.65

Weekly routine: McGrath, *Born in the Cattle*, p.66.

Help to white women during pregnancy: Reynolds, *With the White People*, p.209–10; McGrath, *Born in the Cattle*, p.63

Needed supervision: McGrath, *Born in the Cattle*, pp.66–67.

Gunn: Mrs Aeneus Gunn, *We of the Never-Never*, abridged edition, Angus & Robertson, Sydney, 1982, pp.44–45.

Reserves and protection legislation: Bain Attwood, 'Aboriginal protection' in Graeme Davison, John Hirst & Stuart Macintyre (eds), *The Oxford Companion to Australian History*, Oxford University Press, Melbourne, 1998, p.10; Broome, *Aboriginal Australians*, pp.161–62.

Torres Strait Islanders: Regina Ganter, 'Torres Strait Islanders' in Davison et al, *Oxford Companion to Australian History*, pp.643–44.

Eugenic theory: Stephen Garton, 'Eugenics' in Davison et al, *Oxford Companion to Australian History*, pp.226–27.

Legislative amendments in 1930s: Broome, *Aboriginal Australians*, p.162.

Miscegenation and intermarriage: Patricia Grimshaw, Marilyn Lake, Ann McGrath and Marian Quartly (eds), *Creating a Nation*, PcPhee Gribble, Melbourne, 1994, pp.287–88.

Marnie Kennedy: Marnie Kennedy, *Born a Half-Caste*, Australian Institute of Aboriginal Studies, Canberra, 1985, pp.2–3, 7–9, 16–17, 19–21, 24–29

Sandra Hardy: Sandra Hardy, 'We didn't worry about the Japs …' in Jacqueline Kent (ed.), *In the Half Light: Reminiscences of growing up in Australia 1900–1970*, Doubleday, Moorbank, 1988, pp.185–86.

Removal of children of mixed descent: Grimshaw et al, *Creating a Nation*, p.290–91; Broome, *Aboriginal Australians*, p.162.

Conditions in Kahlin Compound and the Bungalow: Robert Manne, 'The Stolen Generations' in Michelle Grattan (ed.) *Reconciliation: Essays on Australian Reconciliation*, Black Inc, Melbourne, 2000, p.132.

Iris Clayton: Iris Clayton, 'Anybody Could Afford Us', in Ros Bowden and Bill Bunbury (eds), *Being Aboriginal: comments, observations and stories from Aboriginal Australians*, ABC, Sydney, 1990, pp.75–76.

Mona Tur: Mona Tur, *Word of Mouth*, quoted in Margaret Allen, Mary Hutchinson, Alison Mackinnon, *Fresh Evidence, New Witnesses: Finding Women's History*, South Australian Government, 1989, pp.47–50.

Notes

Ethel Buckle: Barbara Cummings, *Take This Child*, Aboriginal Studies Press, Canberra, 1990, pp.21–23.

Myrtle Campbell: Cummings, *Take This Child*, p.24

Victoria Archibald: Stuart Rintoul (ed.), *The Wailing: A National Black Oral History*, William Heinemann Australia, Melbourne, 1993, pp.153–54.

Anthropology and protest movements during 1930s: Broome, *Aboriginal Australians*, pp.163–68

Pearl Gibbs: Heather Radi (ed.), *200 Australian Women: a Redress anthology*, Women's Redress Press, Sydney, 1988, pp.211–12.

Child endowment, pensions, and 'dog licences': Broome, *Aboriginal Australians*, pp.170–71

Second World War/Oodgeroo Noonuccal: Grimshaw et al, *Creating a Nation*, pp.285, 289

Sandra Hardy: Hardy ' We didn't worry about the Japs ...'p.187

Pearl Gibbs during the war: David Horton (ed.), *Encyclopaedia of Aboriginal Australia*, vol.1, Aboriginal Studies Press, Canberra, 1994, p.412.

Mathinna: Horton, *Encyclopaedia of Aboriginal Australia*, vol.2, p.669.

Louisa Briggs: Horton, *Encyclopaedia of Aboriginal Australia*, vol.1, p.154; Radi, *200 Australian Women*, pp.34–35.

6. The 1920s

Costume parade: information from Emma Cavell, Rhiannon Evans, Catherine Alexander

Flappers: Barbara Cameron 'The flappers and the feminists: A study of women's emancipation in the 1920s' in Bevege *Worth Her Salt*; Deamer quoted in Beverley Kingston, *The world Moves Slowly* Sydney, 1977 pp. 43–4

Charlotte Chance: information from Carol Rowe

Dulcie Deamer: Dulcie Deamer *The Queen of Bohemia The Autobiography of Dulcie Deamer* Brisbane, 1988

Tilly Devine, Kate Leigh: Judith Allen *Sex and Secrets Crimes involving Australian women since 1880* Melbourne, 1990 pp. 168–173

Edith Cowan: Peter Cowan *A Unique Position: a biography of Edith Dircksey Cowan 1861–1932* Perth, 1978 pp. 190–196

Lena Lee: James *No Man's Land* chapter 6

Daphne Mayo: Radi pp. 191–2; information from Frances Clark

Molly Claux: Society of Women Writers *Equal to the Occasion* pp. 61–63

Ethel Walker: information from Glenda Gault

Louise Lovely, Marie Bjelke Petersen: Alison Alexander *A Mortal Flame Marie Bjelke Petersen* Hobart, 1994

Betty Roland: Betty Roland *An Improbable Life* Sydney, 1989

Elaine Lambert: information from Mary Coyne

Eleanor Mackinnon: information from Merrilee Boydell; ADB 10/315-6

Winifred Buckley: information from Bronwyn Potts Hendy

Mavis Bradbury: Mavis D. Fogarty 'I Like to Talk with People. An Autobiography', in possession of Peter AD Fogarty

Elsie Plant: information from Zoe Carter

Ruby Davy: Rita M. Wilson *Ruby Davy Academic and Artiste Australia's First Woman Doctor of Music* Salisbury, 1995

Freda Johnson: Edith Calvert & Lois Calvert *The Johnsons of Castle Hill* Sydney, 1997 pp. 173–5

Win Bates: 'Memories of Winifred Bates', 'True Life Experience', in possession of Lorna Ellis

'That Married Look': quoted in Kingston *The World Moves Slowly* pp. 43–4

Lillian Gresson: 'In the Path of the Pioneers', in possession of Janet Boddy

Scientific motherhood: Kerreen Reiger *The disenchantment of the home Modernizing the Australian family 1800–1940* Melbourne, 1985

Giuiditta Baltieri: information from Darryl Baltieri

Truby King: Mary Truby King *Mothercraft* Melbourne, [1943]; W.H. Oliver (ed.) *Dictionary of*

New Zealand Biography Wellington 1993 pp. 257–8
Queensland experience: Wendy Selby 'Motherhood in Labour's Queensland 1915–1957', unpublished PhD thesis, Griffith University, 1992
Dolly Grebert: information from Ted Grebert, Eva Bass
Doris McPherson: information provided by Nancy Blake
Mary Warnes: information from L. Barry, SA Country Women's Association
Isabella Irving: information from Tresna Shorter
Violet Ellett: information from Gillian Banks
Vera Scantlebury Brown: Kerreen Reiger 'Vera Scantlebury Brown: Professional Mother' in Lake and Kelly
Florence Taylor: information from Peg Parkin
Maisie Smith: Joan Hilton 'My Life', in possession of Joan Hilton
CWA: Helen Townsend *Serving the Country: The History of the Country Women's Association of NSW* Moorebank, 1988; Country Women's Association of NSW *The Golden Years: the story of fifty years of the Country Women's Association of New South Wales 1922–1972* Potts Point, 1972; Eliza Kenworthy Teather 'The Country Women's Association of NSW in the 1920s and 1930s as a Counter-revolutionary Organisation' in *Journal of Australian Studies* vol. 41 pp. 67–78
Trudy Scott: 'Autobiography of Trudy Scott', in possession of Jennifer Cleveland

7. Hard Times

Win Baulch: 'True Life Experience', 'Memories of Winifred Bates', in possession of Lorna Ellis
Margaret Read: information from Margaret Rickard
Kathleen Lenthall: information from C.J. Lenthall
Mavis Bradbury: Fogarty 'Autobiography'
Maureen Greene: Anthea Roberts 'A Life of Maureen Greene', in possession of Alan Roberts
Edna Leach: 'Autobiography of Edna Leach', in possession of Cathryn Parry
Frances Allison: information from Frances Allison
Flora Lyons: information from Elizabeth Godfrey
Kate Englart: Vince Englart 'Raised a radical – The Englarts in Brisbane 1920–1939', in possession of Tanya Britten
Violet Lambert: Heather B. Ronald *Farewell My Heart The Life of Violet Barry Lambert. O.B.E., J.P.* Melbourne, 1997 pp. 36–8, 42–50
Ruby McKinlay: information from Margaret Pirie
Kylie Tennant: Kylie Tennant *The Missing Heir The Autobiography of Kylie Tennant* Melbourne, 1986 pp. 7, 93–4, 100, 104
Peggy Hill: information from Betty Mawdsley, Union of Australian Women
Jean Ellis: information from Carol Byrne, Penguin Club
Beth Chamberlain: information from Gillian Albers
Southern Cross harassment: Lyall Hunt (ed) *Yilgarn: Good country for hard people* Yilgarn, 1988 p. 386
Judith Lipman: information from Victoria O'Connor
Kathleen Barges: 'Biography of Kathleen Elizabeth Barges', 'My Impression of Guide Week', in possession of Nerida Barges
Elizabeth Kenny: Selby 'Motherhood in Labour's Queensland' pp. 369–74; Radi *200 Women* pp. 123–5, ADB 9/570-571; *Oxford Companion* p. 363
Barbara Sisley: information from Judith Lamb
Annette McDonnell: information from Yvonne Wildash
Veronica Malone: Colleen Hines *Jim & Annie* Wallendbeen, 1999 pp. 66–7
Music lesson: Gene Makim *Stand up and be Counted* Wilberforce, 1996 p. 60
Kate Bates: Zelma Bates/Claydon *That's Not Rubbish That's Our Possessions* Merredin, 1995
Australian Women's Weekly: Radi *200 Women* pp. 158–9; Sue Bean, '*The Australian Women's Weekly*: an indicator of change in the lives of Australian women', unpublished Honours thesis, University of New South Wales 1981

Notes

Rabbit: Winifred Crisp (ed) *The 21st Birthday Cookery Book of the Country Women's Association in Tasmania* [Hobart], 1958 p. 59

Nola Fisher: Nola Fisher *'Part of a journey' An Australian Autobiography 1926–1946* Oyster Bay, 1996

Lillian Paton: Paton *Armchair Reflections*

Knitting: *What to Knit For Your Man At War* Orange, n.d., in possession of Sue Georgevits

Mollie Nalder: information from Judi Hockey

Sylvia Duke: letter in possession the Department of Veterans' Affairs, from Sister Duke, 12/5/1941

Mary Laus: information from Mary Macklin

Violet McKenzie: information from Mrs R. Bull, Ex-Wrans Association; Radi pp. 179–180

Joy Woodley: Joy Woodley's memoirs, in possession of Jane Martin

Grace Moore: Daphne M. Gaydon *The Life and Times of an Early Australian Pioneer Grace Isabella (Macgregor) Moore* Toowoomba, 1999 p. 27

Darwin: James *No Man's Land* chapter 7

Gwen Rowe: information from Ms Cree Marshall

Ruby Boye: information from Mrs B. Davey; Adam-Smith pp. 163–5

Nursing: Bassett *Guns and Brooches* pp. 133–149; Betty Jeffrey *White Coolies* Sydney, 1997; *Advertiser* 28 April 1997

Isetta Conte: information from Mrs D. Laun

Sally Bowen: Mavis Robertson 'Sally Bowen: Political and Social experiences of a Working-Class woman' in Elizabeth Windshuttle *Women, Class and History* Melbourne, 1980

Merle Green: Andrew Lindsay *Dancing in the Kitchen Portraits of Collingwood's older women* Melbourne, 1999 p. 75

Dawn Baker: 'Memories of My Early Years and life in the Bush', in possession of Dawn Baker, p. 3

'Every hostess ...': Molly Mann & Bethia Foott *We Drove the Americans* Sydney, 1944 p. 4

Girl's diary: Katie Holmes & Marilyn Lake (eds) *Freedom Bound II Documents on women in modern Australia* Sydney, 1995 pp. 85, 88

Bambi: information from Dorothy Godfrey

Josephine Johnson: information from Josie Arnold

Jessie Vasey: Mavis Thorpe Clark *No Mean Destiny: The Story of the War Widows' Guild ...* Melbourne, 1986

Sadie Macdonald: adapted from Mary Brice, 'Matie', in possession of Mary Brice

Rosemary Archdeacon-Davies: 'Escape from Women's Industry' in Union of Australian Women *Women and wages in the war years 1940–1945* Surry Hills, 2000

Marjorie Oates: information from Lesley Mansfield

Constance Vaubel's letter: in possession of Dalace Williams

War brides: Val Lakeman (ed.) *Overseas War Brides Memoirs* Sydney, 2000; information from Betty Chapman

8. The Boom Years

General: John Murphy & Judith Smart (eds) *The Forgotten Fifties Aspects of Australian Society and Culture in the 1950s* Melbourne, 1997; Gilding *Making and breaking ...*

Sociologist: Gisela Kaplan *The Meagre Harvest The Australian Women's Movement 1950s–1990s* Sydney, 1996 pp. 6–22

Marjorie Tipping: Marjorie Tipping 'On War and Reconstruction: A Memoir' in Lake and Kelly

Peggy O'Dea: information from Janet Grace Pine

Kathleen Lenthall: information from C.J. Lenthall

Kit Lambert: information from Audrey Harris

Maureen Ree: 'Memoirs of Kathleen Maureen Ree', in possession of Heather Thomson

Doris Officer: information from Colin Officer

Joy Bear: information from Diane Wright

A Wealth of Women

Girl Guides: information from Jenny Mills, Guides Victoria
CWA: Brenda Stevens-Chambers *The Many Hats of Country Women The Jubilee History of the Country Women's Association of Australia* Kyneton, 1997 pp. 32–3, 49
Union of Australian Women: Barbara Curthoys & Audrey McDonald *More Than a Hat and Glove Brigade The Story of the Union of Australian Women* Sydney, 1996
Helen Harbour: Pam Rehak 'Helen Harbour: Housewife of the 1950s' in Lake and Kelly
Dulcie Sims: information from June Skinner
Nursing Mothers' Association: information from Elisabeth Wilson, Nursing Mothers' Association of Australia
Multicultural cooking: Winifred Crisp (ed) *The 21st Birthday Cookery Book* ... p. 176
Minnie Purves: information from Helen Annand
Baltic immigrants: Ramunas Tarvydas *From Amber Coast to Apple Isle Fifty Years of Baltic Immigrants in Tasmania* Hobart, 1997
Anu Mihkelson: Ann Mihkelson *Three suitcases and a three-year-old* Sydney, 1999 p. 106
Widgies: Jon Stratton 'Bodgies and Widgies – Youth Cultures in the 1950s' in *Journal of Australian Studies* November 1984, pp. 10–24
Koula Aslanidis: Margaret Allen, Mary Hutchison, Alison Mackinnon *Fresh Evidence, New Witnesses* Adelaide, 1989 pp. 275–76
Margherita Fencott: information from Margherita Fencott, Fay Seeberger, Cindy Seeberger
Jessie Hadgraft: Stella Lees and June Senyard *The 1950s ... how Australia became a modern society* ... Melbourne, 1987 pp. 84–5
Appliances: Rosemary Broomham *First Light 150 years of Gas* Sydney, 1987; Kingston *My Wife, My Daughter* ... pp. 36, 41, 44; Penny Sparke *Electrical Appliances* London, 1987; Elva Shumack *Going Bush to Goolhi* Gunnedah, 1999 pp. 48, 86
Nola Fisher: Fisher *Journeying On* pp. 26–7
Louise Lightfoot: information from Mary Lightfoot
Shopping: Beverley Kingston *Basket, Bag and Trolley A history of shopping in Australia* Melbourne, 1994
Mary Aldridge: Mary Aldridge *A Blockie's Wife The Story of the Murray Valley Soldier Settlement* Numurkah, 1991
The Drover's Wife: information from Dennette Long
Food: Michael Symons *One Continuous Picnic A history of eating in Australia* Adelaide, 1982; Robin Walker, Dave Roberts *From scarcity to surfeit A history of food and nutrition in New South Wales* Sydney, 1988
Hannah Maclurcan: Susan Addison & Judith McKay *A Good Plain Cook An edible history of Queensland* Brisbane, n.d. pp. 4–5
Betty Carter: 'Betty Carter's Memories', in possession of Lindy Dudgeon
CWA Cookery Book: Crisp *The 21st Birthday Cookery Book* ...
Dawn Fraser: Gordon *Olympic Games* pp. 212–5, 253–5, 261–3
Handkerchief in oil: Zelda D'Aprano *Zelda the becoming of a woman* Melbourne, 1978 p. 22
Abortion: Barbara Baird *"I had one too ..." An Oral History of Abortion in South Australia before 1970* Adelaide 1990; *Gilding* pp. 78–9
Adelaide Miethke: ADB 10/497-8; information from National Council of Women (South Australia), especially Barbara Pitt, Paul McGuire

9. The Women's Movement

Julie Rigg: Julie Rigg (ed.) *In Her Own Right Women of Australia* Melbourne, [1969]
Beryl Lindsay: Spence *The Only Abiding Solution* p. 38
Zelda D'Aprano: D'Aprano pp. 118–120; Lake *Getting Equal* p. 217
Anne Summers: Anne Summers *An Autobiography 1945–1976 ducks on the pond* Sydney, 1999
Separatists: Judith Ion 'Degrees of separation: lesbian separatist communities in northern New South Wales, 1974–95' in Jill Julius Matthews *Sex in Public Australian Sexual Cultures* Sydney, 1997 pp. 97–113
Perth: Joan Williams 'Women carrying banners' in Joan Eveline & Lorraine Hayden (eds)

Notes

Carrying the Banner Women, Leadership and Activitsm in Australia Perth, 1999 pp. 15–31
Pat O'Hara: information from Joan Trewern
Edna Ryan: Susan Mitchell *The Matriarchs* Melbourne, 1986; information from Lyndall Ryan
Damned Whores and God's Police: Anne Summers *Damned Whores and God's Police The Colonization of Women in Australia* Melbourne, 1975 p. 29
Joyce Nicholson: Joyce Nicholson '"Sisterhood is Powerful": A Memoir' in Lake and Kelly
Pat Degens: Patricia Degens *From Canberra to Coffs Harbour* Coffs Harbour, 1999 pp. 134–8
Babette Francis: Babette Francis '"Equal but Different": A Memoir' in Lake and Kelly; information from Babette Francis
Lesbians: Ruth Ford, Lyned Isann & Rebecca Jones *Forbidden Love – Bold Passion Lesbian Stories 1900s–1990s* Exhibition Catalogue, North Fitzroy, 1996; Kaplan pp. 91–102; Sylvia Kinder *Herstory of Adelaide Women's Liberation 1969–74* Adelaide, 1980
Misogyny: Robyn Davidson *Tracks* London, 1980 pp. 23, 33–4, 35

10. The Struggle Continues

Daisy Bindi: Michal Bosworth in Heather Radi (ed.), *200 Australian Women: a Redress anthology*, Women's Redress Press, Sydney, 1988, p.223.
Hasluck and assimilation policy: Richard Broome, *Aboriginal Australians*, 2nd edition, Allen & Unwin, Sydney, 1994, pp.171–73.
Aborigines in towns under scrutiny: Patricia Grimshaw, Marilyn Lake, Ann McGrath and Marian Quartly (eds), *Creating a Nation*, McPhee Gribble, Melbourne, 1994, p.294–95; Ann McGrath (ed.), *Contested Ground: Australian Aborigines under the British Crown*, Allen & Unwin, Sydney, 1995, pp.41–42.
Growth in Aboriginal birthrate: Grimshaw et al, *Creating a Nation*, pp.295–96.
Woman from Bourke: quoted in Broome, *Aboriginal Australians*, p.153.
Kathy Northover: Stuart Rintoul (ed.), *The Wailing: A National Black Oral History*, William Heinemann Australia, Melbourne, 1993, pp.191–93.
Jenny Grace: 'Murray River Woman', in Adele Pring (ed.), *Women of the Centre*, Pascoe Publishing, Apollo Bay, 1990, pp.157–172.
Pearl Gibbs and Faith Bandler: Radi, *200 Australian Women*, pp.212–13.
Legislative changes in early 1960s: Broome, *Aboriginal Australians*, 177–79.
Atomic bomb testing in 1950s: Robert Milliken, *No Conceivable Injury*, Penguin, Ringwood, 1986, pp.130–135; *The Report of the Royal Commission into British nuclear tests in Australia*, vol.2, Canberra, 1985.
The Milpuddies: Milliken, *No Conceivable Injury*, pp.111–116.
Lallie Lennon: 'Maralinga Dust', in Pring (ed.) *Women of the Centre*, pp.89–98.
Freedom Ride: Broome, *Aboriginal Australians*, p.176.
1967 referendum: Bain Attwood and Andrew Markus, *The 1967 Referendum, or, When Aborigines didn't get the vote*, Aboriginal Studies Press, Canberra, 1997, p.66; Attwood and Markus, '(The) 1967 (referendum) and all that: narrative and myth, Aborigines and Australia', *Australian Historical Studies*, no.111, October 1998, pp.267–88; Paul Kelly, 'Unfinished Business', *Australian*, 14 March 2001, p.11.
Pat O'Shane on the referendum result: quoted in Rintoul, *The Wailing*, pp.49–50.
Lillian Holt: Lillian Holt, 'Reflections on Race and Reconciliation' in Michelle Grattan (ed.), *Essays on Australian Reconciliation*, Black Inc, Melbourne, 2000, pp.147–48.
Evelyn Scott: Evelyn Scott, 'A Personal Reconciliation Journey' in Grattan, *Essays on Australian Reconciliation*, p.21.
Glenyse Ward: Ward, *Wandering Girl*, Magabala Books, Broome, 1995, pp.11–14.
Sheryl Rose: quoted in Kevin Gilbert, *Living Black: Blacks talk to Kevin Gilbert*, Allen Lane, The Penguin Press, Melbourne, 1977, pp.253–54.
Jackie Huggins: Jackie Huggins, *Sister Girl*, University of Queensland Press, St Lucia, 1998, pp.51–52.
Yirrkala and Gurindji disputes: Grimshaw et al, *Creating a Nation*, pp.297–98; Kelly, 'Unfinished Business'.

A Wealth of Women

Aboriginal women and land rights: Grimshaw et al, *Creating a Nation*, p.307
Aboriginal tent embassy: Graeme Davison, John Hirst & Stuart Macintyre (eds), *Oxford Companion to Australian History*, Oxford University Press, Melbourne, 1998, p.637; Grimshaw et al, *Creating a Nation*, p.302.
Mum Shirl: Mum Shirl, 'The Tent Embassy' in *Voices of Aboriginal Australia: Past, Present, Future,* compiled by Irene Moores, Butterfly Books, Springwood, NSW, 1995, pp.117–21.
Whitlam years: Broome, *Aboriginal Australians*, p.181
Aboriginal Health Worker Program: Carol Bradley, 'A change in status for Aboriginal women? Aboriginal women in the Australian workforce', *Aboriginal History*, vol.11, no.2, 1987, p.147.
Revival of Aboriginal culture: Broome, *Aboriginal Australians*, pp.197–200.
O'Shane on the women's movement: Pat O'Shane, 'Is there any relevance in the women's movement for Aboriginal women?', *Refractory Girl*, September 1976, pp.31–34.
Moreton-Robinson on white women and racism: Aileen Moreton-Robinson, *Talkin' up to the White Woman: Indigenous Women and Feminism*, University of Queensland Press, St Lucia, 2000, p.28.
Agnes Williams: quoted in Huggins, *Sister Girl*, p.14.
The 'scrubbing' of Williams' face by her mistress: Jackie Huggins and Thom Blake, 'Protection or Persecution? Gender relations in the era of racial segregation' in Kay Saunders & Raymond Evans (eds), *Gender Relations in Australia: Domination and Negotiation*, Harcourt Brace Jovanovich, Sydney, 1992, p.55.
Huggins on the racism practised by white women: Huggins, *Sister Girl*, p.30.
Huggins on the women's movement: Huggins, *Sister Girl*, pp.56–57.
Aboriginal deaths in custody: Broome, *Aboriginal Australians*, pp.219–20, 223–26.
Aboriginal women in custody: Adrian Howe, 'Aboriginal Women in Custody: A footnote to the Royal Commission', *Aboriginal Law Bulletin*, no.30, February 1988, cited in *Aboriginal Deaths in Custody: a collection of articles and a detailed bibliography*, State Library of Victoria, 1994, pp.25–26.
Faith Thomas: 'From the Shoulder', in Pring (ed.), *Women of the Centre*, pp.41–2.
The call for a treaty: Broome, *Aboriginal Australians*, pp.220–22.
Bicentenary protest rallies: Broome, *Aboriginal Australians*, p.221.
Huggins on the bicentenary march: Huggins, *Sister Girl*, p.54.
Alana Harris: Alana Harris, 'The Big March' in *Voices of Aboriginal Australia*, pp.138–39.
Mabo case: Davison et al, *Oxford Companion to Australian History*, p.402.
Keating's Redfern speech: Paul Keating, 'The Redfern Park Speech' in Grattan (ed.) *Reconciliation*, pp.60–64.
Wik decision: Davison et al *Oxford Companion to Australian History*, pp.684–85
Bringing Them Home report: Manne, 'The Stolen Generation' in Grattan, *Reconciliation*, pp.130–31.
Mary Darkie: 'This is My Life', in Grattan, *Reconciliation*, p.115.
Alice Warrika Oldfield: David Horton (ed.), *Encyclopaedia of Aboriginal Australia*, vol.2, Aboriginal Studies Press, Canberra, 1994, p.822.
Olive Kennedy: Paul Toohey, 'Mothers of sorrow', *Weekend Australian*, 17–18 March 2001, p.24

11. Today

Unless otherwise stated, statistics come from W. McLennan *How Australians Use Their Time 1997* Canberra, 1998; and information from the Australian Bureau of Statistics
Koula Aslanidis: Allen *Fresh Evidence* 276–7
Single parent statistics: Bittman and Pixley p. 9; Kathleen Swinbourne, Kathy Esson & Eva Cox with Bronwyn Scouler *The Social Economy of Sole Parenting* Sydney, 2000 p. 19
Frances Donnelly: information from Jean Beasley
Vida Humphries: information from Vida Videon
Women not always wanting promotion: Victoria O'Connor 'Women and Men in Senior man-

Notes

agement – a "Different Needs" Hypothesis', *Women in Management Review* vol. 16, issue 7

Evelyn Macintyre: information from Michelle McIntyre

Year 12: Jennifer Buckingham 'The Trouble with Boys' in *Policy* Autumn 2000 pp. 9–15

Childbirth: information from Elisabeth Wilson, Nursing Mothers' Association of Australia

Domestic violence: Barbara Caine (ed.) *Australian Feminism a companion* Melbourne, 1998 pp. 337–344

Freya Booth: information from Anna Pope

Edith Gilmour: information from Edith Gilmour, Lucy Raig

Margaret House: information from Margaret House, Lynn McEvoy

Molly Clark: information from Colleen Hines

Clare, Meredith and Pamela Burton: information from Pamela Burton

Elva Castino: Eacham Historical Society *Voices Past & Present Stories of Women of the Atherton Tableland* Eacham, n.d. pp. 50–51; information from Elva Castino

Bait: Gail Thomas 'They Just Want the Bashing to Stop', in possession of Gail Thomas

Kate Holz: Anne Matthews with Kerry Goudge and Kate Holz, 'Women On Water The Story', in possession of Maureen Holz

Natasha Stott-Despoja: information from Natasha Stott-Despoja

International Women's Day: Diedre Timms & Judyth Salmon *Bunbury Regional International Women's Day Festival 2000 Evaluation and Report* Bunbury, 1999

Income inequality: Joshua S. Gans, Stephen P. King, N. Gregory Mankiw *Principles of Microeconomics* Sydney, 1999 p. 432

Recipe: Stephanie Alexander *The Cook's Companion* Melbourne, 1996 p. 221

picture credits

Picture credits – Abbreviations of library names are as follows: NLA = National Library of Australia; ML = Mitchell Library, NSW; SA = Mortlock Library, SA; JO = John Oxley Library, Qld. Where not otherwise specified pictures are from History Search. See the Introduction to this book for details of History Search.

Convict couple, 1793, Dixon Galleries, State Library of NSW. Off to the Diggings from the *Working Mens Educational Union 24 and 25*, London, NLA NK801/2. The squatter's first home, 1840s, AD Lang, NLA. A Holiday at Balmoral, *Illustrated Sydney News* 26/11/1881. Group at Piano, Australian Irrigation Colonies, London 1887, all from NLA. Vignette of mother and children, Mary Morton Allport, Tasmanian Museum & Art Gallery. Woman mourns dead child, 1870, SA. Grave stone in Hamilton cemetery TAS, author supplied. Another Danger: Snakes, ML. Domestic Science, washing, NLA. Alison Ashby and Aunt, State Library of South Australia. Women in Public Life, *Australian Sketcher* 24/4/1880. Kapunda Hospital, SA c.1910. Children's Ward, c.1900, all from NLA. Enfranchised 1902, HWE Cotton. Women assaulting non-unionist, Broken Hill NSW, *Illustrated Australian News* 1/9/1892. Social Life c 1900, all from NLA. Ladies' Bowling Day, Perth 1905, Battye Library, WA. Young Boulder toilers, Battye Library WA 3920B/86. Washing Day at Corkhill's Home 1890, WH Corkhill Tilba Tilba Collection, by permission of NLA. A family of ten girls and two boys, NLA. Advertisement for contraceptives at turn of the century, ML. Islander women behind the plough c.1897, JO neg no. 142351. Granny Lum Loy, photo by Clive Hyde, Barbara James personal collection. Bush settlement, ML. Black and White children, Alexandria NT 1917. Funeral of Queen Narelle, Wallaga Lake c.1895, WH Corkhill. Nova Peris 1998, L Seselja, all from NLA. Rosemary Tipiloura, Barbara James 2001. Kitchen no.1 Red Cross Rest Home from MS696 Novar Papers, NLA. Women of the Studderd family, Studderd collection PIC 056/025, Museum & Art Gallery of NT. Clubs for Women 1920s, *Australia's Yesterday* p151, NLA. Dulcie Deamer, Artists' Ball 1923, ML. Pinington family 1929, History Search. Eileen Fitzer, NT. Land Army member, courtesy of West Australian Newspapers, Battye Library WA. New careers for women, Sydney, History Search. Sister Michael with 3rd class, West Heidelberg 1954. Household appliance and equipment, modern kitchen, NLA. Farmers' wives preparing a meal, Talbingo Station NSW 1956, NLA. Great Australian invention – Hills Hoist, 1950s, author supplied. Dame Roma Mitchell QC, SA. Margret Roadknight performing, Brisbane, History Search. Older Women's Network, History Search. Beryl Pearson, daughter and granddaughters with heirloom from 1830s, History Search. Hawat family, 26/8/98.

Index

Aboriginal rights referendum viii, 259, 283
Aboriginal women chapters 5, 10; pp. viii, 8, 14–5, 19, 21–2, 53, 87, 163, 172, 193, 259, 260, 273, 308
Abortion 55, 100, 120, 162, 175, 186, 205, 222, 253, 260, 261, 262, 263, 267, 269, 270, 274
Advanced School for Girls 70, 256
Aisbett, Pip 310–2
Alcoholics Anonymous 225–6
Aldridge, Mary and family 239–44, 249
Alexander, Stephanie 319
Allison, Frances 84
American soldiers 204
Andrew, Eva and family 90
Andrikonis, Ieva 229–30
Ante-natal care 101, 160–2, 302
Arbuckle, Sarah 60
Archdeacon-Davies, Rosemary 209
Archibald, Victoria 141–2
Arena, Franca 298
Art 29, 45, 58, 149, 189, 317
Asia, emigrants from 111–2, 149, 227, 232–3, 298
Aslanidis, Koula 232, 298
Atomic tests 280–1
Attwood, Bain 283
Augustauskas, Mrs 228
'Australian girl' 27–8
Australian women, characteristics ix–xi, 8–9, 46, 320
Australian Women's Army Service 143, 197, 200–1
Australian Women's Charter 206
Australian Women's Weekly 193, 247, 248
'Baby farmers' 101–2
Baird, Barbara 312–3
'Bait' 313
Baker, Dawn 204
Baltic States, emigrants from 227–30, 233
Baltieri, Giuiditta and family 161
Bandler, Faith 279, 283
Bardsley, Jane and family 53, 108
Barges, Kathleen 188–9
Bates, Kate and family 191–3
Bates, Win 157–8, 181–2
Baulch, Win see Bates, Win

Bear, Annette 93
Bear, Joy 220–1
Bird, Anne Stafford 75
Bigelow, Mr and Mrs 284–5
Bignell, Margaret 91
Bindi, Daisy 275–6
Birthrate viii, 96–9, 100, 159, 160, 186, 216, 227, 277
Bittman, Michael 304
Bleakley, J W 133
Boddy, Janet 317, 318
Bolton, Dorothy 184
Booth, Freya and family 305–6
Bourne, Jean 270
Bowen, Sally 203
Boye, Ruby 199
Boylan, Geraldine 309–10
Bradbury, Mavis 155, 183, 217, 237, 249
Breastfeeding 10, 32, 96, 160, 224, 250, 302
Brice, Mary 207–10, 317
Brien, Donna Lee 99
Briggs, Louisa 139
Brockman, Mr and Mrs 31
Brooks, Christiana and family 27, 46
Broome, Richard 276
Brown-Parker, Barbara 40
Brownies 222
Bruce, Mary Grant 147
Buckel, Ethel 141
Buckley, Winifred 153–4
Bullwinkel, Vivian 201
Bunker, Hannah and family 52
Bunker, Marjorie 124
Burton, Clare 310
Burton, Pamela 310
Bussell, Bessie 44
Bussell, Josephine 29–30

Caine, Daphne 200–1
Caldwell, Annie and family 18–21

Campbell, Mary 115
Campbell, Myrtle 141
Carter, Betty 246
Castino, Elva 311
Chamberlain, Beth 188
Chance, Charlotte 146
Chapman, Betty 213
Chapman, Jane 235
Chapman, Winnie 135
Child welfare clinics, see Infant welfare clinics
Childbirth 9, 25, 31–2, 34, 80, 101, 130, 162–3, 165–7, 170, 217, 240, 249–50, 281, 302
Childcare 217, 262, 268, 269, 274, 303, 318
Childrearing 63, 96, 97, 130, 162–3, 170–1, 217, 240, 250, 277, 302
China, emigrants from 111–2, 149, 232–3
Chisholm, Caroline 25–6, 36, 66, 304
Christmas celebrations 42
Church, Mary Ann 40
'Civilising mission', women's 11, 25–6, 45, 61, 182, 189–90, 304
Clark, Molly 306
Clarke, Emma 37
Clarke, Janet Lady 96

Clarke, Minnie 71
Claux, Molly 150
Clayton, Iris 140
Clifton, Louisa 30–31
Clothing 30, 38–9, 86, 108, 145–6, 155, 178–80, 181, 213, 239, 284
Cocks, Kate 120
Coghlan, Dora 77–8
Cole, Ivy 100
Collins, Ann 2
Communist Party 187, 221–2, 223, 261, 266, 275
Conte, Isetta 202
Contraception
 before 1945 vii, 9, 32–3, 97–101, 126–7, 160, 163, 185, 186, 187
 after 1945 250–4, 260, 262, 263, 264, 269–70, 274, 302
Convict women vii, 1–11, 12, 16, 54
Cooking
 before 1920 19, 20, 35–7, 59, 62–3, 66–7, 104, 110–1, 124, 130
 after 1920 212, 219, 226, 235–6, 240, 245–8, 295–6, 304, 305, 315, 319
Cooper, Judy 237
Cooper, William 142, 279
Costa, Frances 231
Country Women's Association 166, 171–3, 174, 185, 187, 195, 217, 222, 248, 300
Cowan, Edith 38–9, 149
Crebbin, Ann 51–2
Crozier, Annie 27
Crozier, Jessie and family 14–15
Cubillo, Lorna 289

Dabelstein, Mary and family 115
Dance 238
D'Aprano, Zelda 261–2, 264
Darkie, Mary 293
Davidson, Robyn 273
Davis, Charlotte and family 13
Davy, Ruby 155–7
Dawbin, Annie Baxter 32

Deamer, Dulcie 146, 147–8, 159
Dean, Mary and George 99
Deaths in custody, Aboriginal 289–90, 291
Degens, Pat and family 269–70
Democrats, Australian 314–6
Dempsey, Mary Anne 108
Depression, the chapter 7 passim, p. vii
Devine, Tilly 148
Devlin, Elsie 43–4
Divorce 37, 47, 87, 122, 218, 268, 274, 303, 308, 311
Dixon, Alice and family 290
Djunduin, Daisy 134
Doctors, women 76, 170–1, 220
Donnelly, Frances 299
Dreaming stories 131
Drover's Wife 104–6, 243
Drummond, Mary and family 116
Dugdale, Henrietta 86
Duke, Sylvia 196
Dumaresq, Sophy and family 34
Durack, Fanny 92–6

Education vii, viii, 10, 28–9, 69–72, 82, 96, 97, 114, 256–7, 260, 262, 274, 300, 318
Edwards, Meredith 310
Electrical appliances 236–8, 242, 244, 294–5
Elizabeth, Queen 300
Elkin, A P 142
Ellett, Violet 170
Ellis, Jean 187–8
Elsie Women's Refuge 265, 268
Emigrants vii–viii, 46, 60, 81, 111–2, 195, 215, 226–30, 248, 260, 276, 277, 298, 317
Employment vii, 58–60, 72–81, 82, 96, 97, 114, 125, 152–8, 170–1, 186, 202–3, 209, 213, 216, 217, 218–21, 230, 259, 261, 262, 269, 274, 284, 285, 297, 301, 302–3, 305, 308
Englart, Kate 184–6
Erskine, Jemima 114–5

Index

Etiquette 43–4

Falleni, Euginia 271
Family, nuclear 218, 226, 233
Family planning, see Contraception
Farming, women and 1–2, 11, 18–21, 40, 47–50, 56–8, 106–7, 133–4, 158, 161, 172–3, 181–2, 184, 192, 219, 239–44, 307–8
Fashion, see Clothing
Faust, Beatrice 267
Fay, Elizabeth 123
Feminism, chapters 3, 9; pp. 143, 152, 158–9, 205–6, 259, 319
Feminism, first wave chapter 3; pp. vii, 114, 125
Feminism, second wave chapter 9; pp. viii, 288
Fencott, Margherita and family 232–3
Ferguson, Bill 279
Films, women in 94–5, 150–2, 266
Fisher, Nola 194, 197–8, 210–11, 237
Fitzgerald, Margaret and family 28
Flappers 146–7, 155, 159–60
Fletcher, Ada 81
Fogarty, Mavis, see Bradbury, Mavis
Foote, Mary Ann 33
Forrest, Margaret 45
Francis, Babette and family 270–1
Franklin, Jane 132
Franklin, Miles 26, 98
Fraser, Dawn xi, 251
Frayne, Ursula 61
Freedom Ride 282, 285
Freeman, Cathy viii, xi
Freeman, Judy 308–9
Frey, Emma 81
Fulford, Margaret and family 17

Galea, Slavka 308
Gas appliances 235–6, 294–5
Germany, emigrants from 110, 115, 227
Gibbs, Pearl 142–3, 144, 279
Gilbert family 31–2

Gilchrist, Roma 223
Giles, Patricia 264
Gilmore, Mary 29, 41, 42, 45
Gilmour, Edith 306–7
Girl Guides 91, 188–9, 222, 252
Godfrey, Dorothy 194, 205, 213
Gold, Annie 57
Golding, Margaret and family 104–6
Goldstein, Vida 98
Gordon, Christina 79
Government, women in 149, 185, 221, 297, 298, 314–6, 319
Grace, Jenny 278–9
Grant, Jane 45
Grebert, Dolly and family 163–7
Greece, emigrants from 232, 298
Green, Merle 203
Greene, Maureen 183–4
Greer, Germaine 265, 267, 270
Gresson, Lillian 159
Gunn, Jeannie 50, 136

Hadden, Jane and family 6, 7
Hadgraft, Jessie 234
Hanigan, Olwyn 260–1
Hansen, Gwenda 199
Harbour, Helen 223, 236
Hardy, Sandra 138–9, 144
Harris, Alana 291–2
Harris, Flora 89–90
Hasluck, Paul 276
Hassell, Edith 131
Hawke, Bob 291
Hawkins, Elizabeth and family 12–16
Haynes, Marion 98
Health Centres 265, 268, 269, 274, 287, 298
Helen 272
Henderson, Sara xi
Henning, Rachel 35
Hickey, Ann 83
Hill, Peggy 187
Hockeyroos 297
Hoddinott, Iley 39
Hodge, Constance 212
Hodgson, Caroline 109

347

A Wealth of Women

Hoe, Die 111
Holmgren, Venie 299
Holt, Lillian 284
Holz, Kate 313–4
Holz, Maureen 318
Hood, Mildred 82
Hordern, Ann 34, 39
Hospitals, maternity 162–3, 165–6, 167, 171, 172
Hotelkeeping ix, 7, 13, 28, 40, 59, 79, 108, 189, 245, 247
Houlahan, Christina 69
House, Margaret and family 307–8
Housework 3, 29, 35, 38, 63, 103, 152, 155, 171, 234–7, 239, 277, 299–300, 303–4
Housewives' Associations 173–4, 222–3
Huggins, Jackie 285, 288, 291
Humphries, Vida 299
Hunter, Mary Jane 40

Ibbott, Frances 315
Illa, Madame 77
Illegitimate births 11, 26, 27, 53–4, 90, 101–2, 109–10, 163, 168, 175, 205, 224, 225, 259, 268, 298–9
Illness 31, 52–3, 55, 57, 146, 173, 182, 211, 305
Industrial action 79–80, 275–6
Industry, work in 78, 79–80, 202–3, 209
Infanticide 55
Infant welfare clinics 149, 163, 167, 171, 172, 185, 241, 250
International Women's Day 187, 223, 264, 316
Irving, Isabella 168–9
Italy, emigrants from 161, 200, 202, 227
Itinerant life 104–6, 184
Izett, Dorothy 77

Jackson, Alice 193
Jackson, Catherine 75
Jackson, Mildred 115–6

Jacobson, Eunice 221
James, Nesta 201
Jan 272
Jandamurra 131
Japan, emigrants from 111–2, 200
Jeffrey, Betty 201
Jemmy the Rover 6
Joan 272
Johnson, Freda 156
Johnson, Josephine 205
Jones, Shirley 269–70
Joy, Rose and James 54–5

Kate, Sister 73
Keating, Paul 292
Kellermann, Annette 94–5
Kelly, Ned 45
Kennedy, Marnie 137–8
Kennedy, Mary 38
Kennedy, Olive 289
Kenny, Bridget 60
Kenny, Elizabeth 190, 198
Kerosene appliances 236, 294–5
Kibble, Nita 77
King, Anna and family 11
King, Betty and family 1–2
King, Joy 67
Kirby, Federene 85
Knitting 46, 116, 195–6
Knudson, Annie and Alan 165
Konrads, Ilsa 230
Kruzas, Viltis 227–8

Labor Party 107, 162, 221, 266, 267, 268, 292, 314
Laffin, John 120
Lambert, Elaine 152–3, 154
Lambert, Kit 220
Land Army 195, 198, 202
Land Rights 285–6, 291, 292
Landcare 308
Larra, Phoebe and James 9
Laurie, Amy 133–4
Laurie, Mary and Buxton 48
Laus, Mary 195
Lawson, Louisa 98

Index

Lawson, Sarah 29
Leach, Edna 184
Leake, Sarah 58
Lee, Bessie 98
Lee, Lena 149
Leichhardt Women's Health Centre 265
Leigh, Kate 148
Lennon, Lallie 282
Lenthall, Kathleen 183, 219–20
Lesbians 268, 271–3, 301, 312–3
Liberal Party 221, 312–3
Life expectancy 10, 46, 305
Lightfoot, Louise 238
Lindsay, Beryl 261
Lipman, Judith 188–9
Literature, women in 26, 29, 77, 147, 151–2, 220, 265, 266, 299
Long, Dennette 243
Lord, Maria and family 3–6, 7, 11
Louden, Eliza 30
Lovely, Louise 150–2
Lyons, Enid 221
Lyons, Flora and family 123, 184, 195

Mabo, 'Eddie' 292
MacAllan, Kate 69–70
McCallum, Elizabeth and family 52–3
McConnel, Mary and family 21–2, 23, 27, 42
Macdonald, Anabel 225, 317–8
McDonald, Audrey 318
Macdonald, Sadie 206–10
McDonnell, Annette 189
McGrath, Ann 133
Macintyre, Evelyn 300
Mack, Louise 70
McKee, Alice 70
Mackellar, Dorothea 77
McKenzie, Florence Violet 196–7
McKinlay, Ruby 186
Mackinnon, Eleanor 153
McLean, Denise 85
McLeod, Beth and family 217–8, 249–50
McLeod, Don 276

Maclurcan, Hannah 66, 245–6
McMahon, William 286
McPherson, Nancy 164
Maguire, Dorothy and family 56–8
Malone, Veronica 189–90
Mann, Barbara 71–2
Manning, Mrs 41–2
Mansfield, Lesley 320
Markus, Andrew 283
Marriage
  before 1920 3, 9, 25, 29–30, 33–5, 47, 63, 82, 86, 96, 103, 114, 122
  after 1920 154, 159–60, 186, 215–7, 261, 280, 301–2, 303
Marshall, Isabella and family 45
Marshall, Lesley 308
Massey, Susanna and family 59–60
Mathinna 132
Mayo, Daphne 149, 152
Medical activity ix, 19, 39–41, 53, 55, 63, 105, 126–7, 192–3, 197, 243, 304 and see Nursing
Melanesia, emigrants from 112
Melba, Nellie 77, 150
Menzies, Jessie 123
Menzies, Robert 221
Merchant, Mary Ann and family 40
Meredith, Gwen 220
Merrin, Louisa and family 60–1
Midwives 13, 22, 31, 59, 102, 126, 135, 165, 167, 168, 171
Miethke, Adelaide 252
Mikhelson, Anu 228–9, 237
Miller, Emma 107
Miller, Mary Jane 113, 114
Milpuddie, Edie and family 281–2
Minogue, Kylie viii, xi
Misogyny 273
Mitchell, Roma xi
Monk-Adams, Hypatia 100
Monte 271, 272
Moore, Grace 197
Moore, Maudie 133, 134
Moreton-Robinson, Aileen 288
Morrison, Margaret 45

349

Mortality
  infant 4, 9, 32, 50, 101, 102–3, 126–7, 162–3, 167, 302
  maternal 32, 34, 60, 98, 162, 167, 249, 302
Motherhood 103, 160–3, 170–1, 174, 259, 277
Mothers' Union, Church of England 89
Mowle, Mary and family 27, 32, 35, 38, 41, 42
Muirhead, James 290
Multiculturalism 298
Music 29, 41, 45, 58, 90, 150, 156–7, 158, 190–1, 220, 266

Nalder, Mollie 196
Narrison, Mrs F 248
National Council of Women 89
National Pioneer Women's Hall of Fame 252
Needlework, see Sewing
Nicholls, Elizabeth 84, 87
Nicholson, Joyce 267
Nicolson, Sarah and family 34
Nightingale, Florence 64, 72, 74, 91
Noonuccal, Oodgeroo (Kath Walker) 143, 291
Northover, Kathy 277–8
Nothrop, Beryl 268–9
Nuclear family 218, 226, 233
Nuns 61, 69–70, 73, 250, 174, 225
Nursing 22, 72–6, 82, 117, 118–20, 125, 126, 146, 163, 165–6, 170, 171, 190, 195–96, 201–2, 206–10, 213, 220, 301
Nursing Mothers' Association 224
Nuttall, Barbara 206

Oates, Marjorie 211
O'Dea, Peggy 216
Office work 77–8, 151–2, 156, 188–9, 301, 311
Officer, Doris 220
O'Hara, Pat 264

Oldfield, Alice Warrika 280
Olympic Games 94–6, 222, 251, 297, 314
Osburn, Lucy 72–5
O'Shane, Pat 283, 288

Parliament, see Government
Parsons, Julie 316
Paterson, Eliza 2
Paton, Lillian 113–4, 116, 122, 194–5
Paton, Mary 224
Pavlova 67, 247
Paxton, Elizabeth 247
Pay, women's 76, 78–80, 134, 197, 202–3, 209, 223, 261–3, 267, 269, 274, 297, 301
Payne, Polly and family 81–2
Peace movement 121, 306–7
Pecl, Edith 229
Penfold, Mary and Christopher 48
Penguin Club 187–8
Pennefather, Mary and family 106–7
Perkins, Charles 282, 291
Petersen, Marie Bjelke 151–2
Pett, Catherine 101
Pharmacists, women 91
Philanthropic activity 11, 15, 22, 44, 89, 90, 96, 115–8, 185, 186–7, 195–6, 305, 320
Pike, Nellie 118–20
Pioneer women vii, 11–23, 219
Plant, Elsie and Dot 155
Plummer, Dorothy 183
Policewomen 120
Poole, Cara 123
Pope, Anna and family 305–6
Powell, Violet 185
Pregnancy vii, 4, 101, 161–2, 249, 263
Prostitution 59, 109, 111, 148, 201, 205
Purves, Minnie 203, 225–6
Pybus, Betty 236

Rainow, Hermine 230–2
Rape crisis centres 265, 268

Index

Recipes
   American Peanut Butter Bread 212
   Anzac biscuits   124
   Boils, cure for   62
   Chow Ming   226
   Dim Sims   226
   Fritters, custard   63
   Kangaroo steamer   20
   Ketchup, walnut   63
   Lamingtons   66, 247
   Meat, to cure   20
   Mock Cream Filling   212
   Mutton, boiled   62
   Rabbit, baked   194
   Rice pudding   62
   Slippery Bob   20
   Soap   62
   Sponge cake   169
   Stir-fry of garlic chives and bean sprouts   319
Reconciliation   284, 292–3
Recreation   41–2, 70, 154, 237–8, 244
Red Cross   115–6, 119, 153, 195, 207
Ree, Maureen   219
Refuges, women's   264, 265, 268, 274, 309, 313
Reid, Elizabeth   268
Religious activity   22, 44–5, 51, 61, 84, 105, 106, 110, 112, 305, 308, 311
   and see Nuns
Removal of children from families   44, 139–41, 288, 292–3
Richardson, Jane and family   10
Rickard, Margaret and family   182
Rigg, Julie   259–60
Right to Life   269
Rintoull, Zenna   59
Rogers, Elizabeth   78
Roland, Betty   151
Rose, Sheryl   285
Ross, Annie   120–1
Rossin, Isabella   256
Rowan, Ellis   45
Rowe, Gwen   198

Rubinstein, Helena   178
Ruth's Women's Shelter   264
Ryan, Edna   237, 266–7
Ryan, Ellen   40
Ryan, Lyndall   312
Ryland, Eliza   101

Sachse, Bert and Mary   67, 247
Saunders, Clara   76
Save Our Sons   262, 307
Scantlebury Brown, Vera   170–1
Scarlett, Margaret and family   32
Scientists   77, 103, 220–1
Scott, Evelyn   284
Scott, Gene and family   190–1
Scott, Mary Ann   31
Scott, Rose   93, 94, 95
Scott, Trudy   174–6
Seager, Mrs   117
Searle, Betty   221–2
Separatist feminists   265–6
Service, domestic   2, 3, 35, 53, 54, 58, 78, 80–1, 101, 132, 134–6, 138, 157–8, 175, 186, 203, 275, 284–5, 288
Seven Little Australians   62, 77
Sewing   29, 38, 41, 46, 59, 104, 107–8, 234, 239
Sexual abuse   2, 51, 53, 132, 174, 224, 259, 282, 309, 313
Sexual activity   1, 2, 3, 9, 25, 31, 72, 98, 132–3, 134, 148, 150, 151, 186–7, 205–6, 260, 302
Sexual harassment   188–9, 230, 247
Sherwood, Enid   2
Shoobridge, Minnie   75
Shopkeeping   ix, 3–4, 39, 81–2, 183–4, 225
Shotgun weddings   224, 263
Shrimpton, Jean   180
Single mothers   267, 316, 318 and see Illegitimate births
Sisley, Barbara   189
Skardon, Helen   135
Skinner, Dulcie   224–5
Smallshaw, Mary and family   8

Smith, Maisie 175
Smith, Maria 'Granny' 61–3, 66
Smith, Shirley (Mum Shirl) 287
Smyth, Brettena 97–8
Social distinctions 44–5, 76
Societies, women's 34–92, 115–6, 119, 149, 153, 195, 197, 207, 262, 307
and see individual societies
Soldier settlers 158, 240
South America, emigrants from 317
Spence, Catherine 51
Spencer, Mrs 30
Spigelman, Jim 282
Spock, Dr 250, 254
Sport 41, 92–6, 230, 251, 290, 297, 314
Stanizki, Selma and family 110
Stephan, Johanna and family 80
Stevenson, Clare 197
Stone, Constance 76–7
Stott, Shirley 314
Stott-Despoja, Natasha viii, xi, 314–6
Street, Jessie 205–6, 221
Sullivan, Aileen 108
Sullivan, Helen 135
Summers, Anne 263, 265, 266
Sutherland, Joan xi
Sutherland, Margaret 220
Sydney Girls' High School 70, 153

Taylor, Amy 200
Taylor, Florence and family 172–3
Teaching 58–9, 61, 71, 76, 87, 120, 153–4, 206, 217–8, 219–20, 252, 269–70, 301, 307
Teague, Gertrude and family viii–ix
Technological advances vii, x, 36, 69, 103, 154–5, 160, 171, 234–9, 250, 260, 294–5, 304, 315, 316
Tennant, Kylie 186–7
Theatre, women in 59, 189, 266
Thomas, Faith 290–1
Thomas, Gail 315
Thomson, Emma 55
Thornbury, Sarah 107–8
Timmins girls 108–9

Timms, Diedre 316
Tipping, Marjorie 217
Tomkins, Edith 123–4
Tomlin, Mollie 217, 270
Torres Strait Islanders 136–7, 143
Trade unions 78, 79–80, 82, 107, 203, 260
Truby King, Frederic vii, 160–2, 250
Tuckwell, Eliza and family 22
Tur, Mona 140–1
Turner, Ethel 62, 77
Turner, Martha 51

Ungunmerr, Miriam-Rose 308
Union of Australian Women 222–3, 262
University education 72, 96, 256–7, 260, 263, 301, 310, 312–3, 314, 317

Val 271
van Boven, Bethe 34
Vasey, Jessie 205
Vaubell, Ann 122
Vegemite 67, 245, 247
Victorian Ladies' Bowling Association 92
Vietnam War 262, 306
Violence 2, 9, 37, 47, 50, 51, 83, 90, 131, 132, 224, 225, 246, 259, 297, 302, 303, 309, 313, 319
Vote, women's 47, 64, 83, 86–7, 92, 101, 159

Wade, Mary and family 7
Walker, Ethel 150
Wallace, Matilda and family 47–50
Walyer 131–2
War brides 124, 148, 213
War, First World chapter 4 passim, pp. 182, 194, 195, 222, 306
War, Second World 67, 143, 194–214, 215, 221, 239–40, 275
War Widows' Guild 205
Ward, Glenyse 284–5
Warnes, Mary 166

Index

Washing clothes 38, 104, 157, 235, 236–7, 294–5, 303
Weatherhead, Inez 121–2
Welfare benefits 101, 206, 274, 297, 308, 318
Wentworth, Sarah 28
Whatley, Anne and family 16–17
Wheeler, Annie 117–8
White, Amelia and family 26
White, Ethel and Samuel 103
Whitlam, Gough 268, 286–7
Wickham, Alice and family 88
Widgies 231
Williams, Agnes 288
Williams, Isabella and family 54–5
Williams, Jane 35
Williams, Joan 264
Windeyer, Maria 36
Wolstenholme-Anderson, Maybanke 87–8
Womanhood, Victorian ideal chap 2 passim, vii, 146
Woman's Christian Temperance Union 84–5, 86–7, 89, 120, 121
Women Who Want to be Women 270–1
Women's Action Committee 262, 264
Women's Auxiliary Australian Air Force 197, 221
Women's Electoral Lobby 264, 267–8, 269, 270
Women's Liberation 263–7
Women's Peace Army 121
Women's Royal Australian Naval Service 197, 199, 210
Woodley, Joy 197, 199–200
Wurfel, Violet 116
Wylie, Mina 94–5

Yates, Jane 46
Young, Jeannie 46
Yunduin, May 133
Yunupingu, Galarrwuy 291

Zevallos, Zuleyka 317

Also available from Duffy & Snellgrove

Slow Food
by David and Gerda Foster

For over twenty years, Australian novelist David Foster and his wife Gerda have lived a largely self-sufficient life in the Southern Highlands of NSW, growing and making much of their own food. The book follows a year in their garden, discussing the cycles of planting and harvesting, and providing a recipe each week which best complements the seasonal food in the garden.

While the focus here is always on the food and its ingredients, the book also shows what it's like to live close to the earth. It should appeal to everyone who ever dreamed of moving to the country, as well as those who have done so, or own hobby farms.

The book contains beautiful photographs by Peter Solness.

ISBN 1 876631 46 5

Also available from Duffy & Snellgrove

The Dressmaker
by Rosalie Ham

Tilly Dunnage was forced out of her small home town in Victoria after a horrific incident that occurred when she was a teenager. Ten years later, in the 1950s, she returns to look after her mad old mother, and to barter her dressmaking skills – acquired in the salons of Paris – for acceptance.

This unusual novel, with its bitter-sweet portrayal of small town life, will remind readers both of Barry Humphries' Sandy Stone monologues and of Dylan Thomas' *Under Milkwood*. Warm and at the same time nasty, it is a surreal and highly original piece of entertainment.

'A feral version of *Sea Change*'
                Sydney Morning Herald

ISBN 1 875989 70 6

Also available from Duffy & Snellgrove

The Trumpeting Angel
by Marshall Browne

A big novel about love, scandal and murder, set in Melbourne in 1899. Susan Fairfax is a successful businesswoman and leading suffragette. Although beautiful and in her early thirties, she has never married, and shares a house with a female artist. She finds herself attracted to John Deveraux, a wealthy politician, but discovers that his wife died in mysterious circumstances a year ago. She rejects Deveraux' offer of marriage and he takes his revenge by accusing her at the governor's dinner table of unnatural desires. She sues him for slander.

The resulting legal action becomes linked with efforts to prove that Deveraux was responsible for his wife's death. At the heart of this gripping story lies one of the most common illnesses of the nineteenth century, and the efforts of a powerful man to hide its devastating effects on himself and his family.

ISBN 1 875989 61 7